Athanasius' Use of the Gospel of John

Gorgias Studies in Early Christianity and Patristics

77

Gorgias Studies in Early Christianity and Patristics is designed to advance our understanding of various aspects of early Christianity. The scope of the series is broad, with volumes addressing the historical, cultural, literary, theological and philosophical contexts of the early Church. The series, reflecting the most current scholarship, is essential to advanced students and scholars of early Christianity. Gorgias welcomes proposals from senior scholars as well as younger scholars whose dissertations have made an important contribution to the field of early Christianity.

Athanasius' Use of the Gospel of John

A Rhetorical Analysis of Athanasius' Orations against the Arians

Wijnand Adrianus Boezelman

GORGIAS PRESS

2021

Gorgias Press LLC, 954 River Road, Piscataway, NJ, 08854, USA

www.gorgiaspress.com

2021

ISBN 978-1-4632-4257-2   **ISSN 1935-6870**

Library of Congress Cataloging-in-Publication Data

A Cataloging-in-Publication Record is available at the Library of Congress.

Printed in the United States of America

To Josja

TABLE OF CONTENTS

FOREWORD

Wijnand Boezelman's book *Athanasius' Use of the Gospel of John*
deals with an important theological subject and is a specimen of
excellent scholarship, which deserves the attention not only of
everyone who is interested in the history of history of Christian
thought, but also of systematic theologians.

Most Christians confess Jesus as the Son of God, and in the
official Confessions of the churches this is meant to imply that he
is the eternal Son of the eternal Father, the Second Person of the
Holy Trinity. It is, however, fair to say that many Christians show
little interest in and have little knowledge of this doctrine. This
may be part of the process of secularisation, in which more and
more members of the church distance themselves from articles of
the traditional faith which they no longer understand and even
do not want to understand. The next step may be that one leaves
the church.

One may ask: Athanasius is rightly regarded as the main ar-
chitect of the doctrine of the Trinity, certainly in the East, but is he
really a suitable guide to an understanding of this doctrine? To theologians in the East he certainly has an undiminished authority. I
remember Eastern orthodox theologians getting furious at a Patristic Conference, when Athanasius was criticised by one of the speak-
ers. On the other hand. I remember the well-known Plotinian
scholar A.H. Armstrong observing in a letter to me about a section
of Athanasius' *Third Oration against the Arians*: 'No serious journal
would accept a paper written in such a style!' Athanasius is still
regarded by many theologians as the 'father of orthodoxy', but also
loathed by many others as a highly unattractive polemical author,

who satisfies his lust for power by discrediting his opponents with all the tools of rhetoric.

Who can provide us with a picture of Athanasius which is historically reliable and at the same time relevant to all those who want to explain the doctrine of the Trinity to those Christians who have great difficulties in understanding it?

In his theological evaluation of the Arian controversy the famous historian of Christian dogma, the leading liberal theologian of his time, Adolf von Harnack, makes the profound and challenging statement that the very man in whose doctrine of Christ almost all traces of the historical Jesus have been deleted also saved Christianity as the religion of the living communion with God.[1] What does it mean that we believe that Jesus brought the communion with the living God, and at the same time have to admit that the Jesus of our faith has little to do with the Jesus of history?

If we want to get an answer to this question we can turn to Boezelman's book. The author displays excellent scholarship in his meticulous analysis of the sources and his broad knowledge and effective use of the secondary literature on the subject. Boezelman shows in his running commentary on the three Orations against the Arians that Athanasius, although he had no education in rhetoric, constantly uses rhetorical means to drive home his message, by showing his own reliability and by discrediting his opponents as liars and deceivers.

Boezelman demonstrates that Athanasius prefers, as far as Scripture is concerned, to corroborate his arguments with texts taken from the fourth gospel. But he is selective in his use of St. John. Boezelman points out that Athanasius ignores one important aspect of the Johannine message: the distinction between the Father and the Son, which implies a certain subordination of the Son to the Father. He focuses only on the texts which in his view confirm his doctrine of the ontological unity of Father and the Son. Boezelman realises that we are here confronted with a serious theological problem: does the evangelist himself envisage such an ontological unity? According to Boezelman, this remains

---

[1]Adolf von Harnack, *Lehrbuch der Dogmengeschchte II* (Tübingen: Mohr Siebeck, 1909), 223–224.

an open question. Athanasius gives an interpretation of the fourth gospel, and this is an interpretation of God's revelation in Christ. Athanasius stands in the long line of this interpretation, which began in the writings of the New Testament, and of which the fourth gospel is an important part. The significance of this observation can hardly be overestimated and it certainly helps us to overcome the crude alternative, of whether Athanasius' doctrine of the Trinity is right, in the sense of: in accordance with Scripture, or whether it is rather a clear misrepresentation of Jesus' own message of love. Throughout the ages many Christians have attempted such an interpretation, with the welcome help of others or in opposition to them. If we want to stand in this tradition and try to explain the substance of Christian faith to ourselves and our secularised contemporaries, then Athanasius could still be useful to us, if we follow Boezelman's example and try to read Athanasius as carefully as he does in this most welcome study.

Eginhard Meijering
Emeritus reader at the University of Leiden/the Netherlands

PREFACE

The academic discipline of theology and the position of churches in the Netherlands have changed dramatically over the last decades. The established and prominent position that churches in the Netherlands enjoyed for a long time has been marginalised. Both outside and inside the church, people sometimes question the relevance of doctrinal theology, especially those ideas and doctrines that cannot easily be grasped. The doctrine of the Trinity is one of those doctrines that is essential in virtually all Christian denominations and churches, but which is very hard to explain in detail. If one were to ask ordinary members or even pastors of whatever denomination about the significance of the doctrine of the Trinity in their lives, the most likely response would be silence and/or stammering. I recognised such an uneasiness myself, and for that reason, during my Master's studies at the VU University Amsterdam, I focused on the roots of Trinitarian theology. The present monograph is a reworking and adaption of my PhD thesis, defended at the Protestant Theological University in Groningen. It presents the continuation of my attempt to understand the doctrine of the Trinity. It is first and foremost a historical investigation into the patristic understanding of the Trinity and reception of the Scripture. Nonetheless, it is my desire that this study of the fourth-century bishop and theologian Athanasius of Alexandria will also contribute to the present-day proclamation of the gospel of Jesus Christ. Differences between the fourth and twenty-first century are numerous, but any account of Christianity should, I believe, relate to the confession of the one and only God and the Christian claim that God is revealed in Jesus Christ in a unique way. So I hope that this investigation into the sources of

Christianity will be made fruitful in the service of the present-day articulation and proclamation of Christian faith and the glory of God. All praise and thanks to Him.

While all that I have written is my responsibility, I am thankful for the help and support of others. First of all, I want to thank Prof. Riemer Roukema (PThU) and Prof. Dr. habil. Maarten Wisse (VU University Amsterdam) for guidance in completing this book.

I also want to thank the Protestant Theological University for offering me the possibility of doing the research necessary for this monograph from 2011 to 2014. The staff, fellow PhD students and not to forget librarians of the PThU provided a stimulating environment for working on this book. Other scholars that I want to thank are Dr. Eginhard Meijering and Prof. Paul van Geest. Dr. Jean Wagemans of the University of Amsterdam also took time to discuss at length with me the rhetorical dimension of my work, while Tertius Bolhuis, Jelmer de Jong, Efron Nitrauw, Anthony Runia, Prof. Kristof Vanhoutte and Daniel Worden helped me with writing and discussing about theological and/or practical matters regarding my research. I also want to thank the anonymous reviewer on behalf of Gorgias Press for their valuable suggestions for improvement.

In the process of working on my dissertation, I also enjoyed the generosity of scholars from abroad who were able to share some of their work with me. Dr. Kelley McCarthy Spoerl and Prof. Markus Vinzent allowed me to use their translation of the anti-Marcellan works of Eusebius of Caesarea, while Prof. Khaled Anatolios, Dr. Craig Blaising and Dr. David Gwynn allowed me to use materials that were not otherwise accessible to me as well. I further want to express my gratitude to the C.J. de Vogelstichting, Stichting voor Oudchristelijke Studiën and Vicariefonds RDO Balije van Utrecht for their contributions towards the publication of this monograph.

Finally, I want to thank my family and friends. I want to thank my parents and parents-in-law and the rest of my family for their love and care throughout my life. But most of all, I want to thank my wife Josja, who supported me throughout the writing process, and read parts of the original manuscript. But her support was much more than just that. Therefore, I want to dedicate this book to my wonderful wife Josja.

ABBREVIATIONS

Athanasius' works

Apol. c. Ar.	*Defence against the Arians (Apologia contra Arianos)*
Apol. ad Const	*Defence before Constantine (Apologia ad Constantium)*
CA	*Orations against the Arians (Orationes contra Arianos)*
CG	*Against the Pagans (Contra Gentes)*
Decr	*On the Council of Nicaea (De Decretis Nicaenae Synodi)*
DI	*On the Incarnation of the Word (De Incarnatione)*
EpAeg.Lib	*Letter to the Bishops of Egypt and Lybia (Epistula ad episcopos Aegypti et Libyae)*
EpAfr	*Letter to the Bishops of Africa (Epistula ad Afros)*
Fug	*On the Defence of his Flight (Apologia de Fuga sua)*
Ser	*Letters to Serapion on the Holy Spirit (Epistula ad Serapionem)*
Syn	*On the Synods of Ariminum and Seleucia (De Synodis)*
VA	*On the Life of Antony (Vita Antonii)*

Other primary sources

AH	Irenaeus, *Against the Heresies (Adversus Haereses)*
CM	Eusebius of Caesarea, *Against Marcellus (Contra Marcellum)*
Comm. Ioh.	Origen, *Commentary on John (Commentarus In Iohannem)*

Comm. Isa.	Eusebius of Caesarea, *Commentary on Isaiah* (*Commentarus in Isaiam*)
DE	Eusebius of Caesarea, *Proof of the Gospel* (*Demonstratio Evangelica*)
DP	Origen, *On First Principles* (*De Principiis*)
ET	Eusebius of Caesarea, *Ecclesiastical Theology* (*de ecclesiastica theologia*)
Inst.	Quintilian, *Institutes of Oratory* (*Institutio Oratoria*)
Praesc.	Tertullian, *On the Prescription of Heretics* (*De praescriptione haereticorum*)
Rhet.	Aristotle, *On Rhetoric* (*Ars Rhetorica*)

Modern Editions

AW	*Athanasius Werke*
ANF	Ante-Nicene Fathers
Dok.	Dokumente. See AW 3.1.3 (ed. Hanns Christof Brennecke et al.)
FC	Fontes Christiani
GCS	Die Griechischen Christlichen Schriftsteller
NPNF	Nicene and Post-Nicene Fathers
PG	Patrologia Graeca (ed. Jacques Paul Minge)
SC	*Sources Chrétiennes*
Urk.	Urkunden. See AW 3.1 (ed. Hans-Georg Opitz)

Journals and Series

ATLA	American Theological Library Association
BiAC	The Bible in Ancient Christianity
BZNW	Beihefte zur Zeitschrift für die neutestamentliche Wissenschaft
ETL	*Ephemerides Theologicae Lovanienses*
ESEC	Emory Studies in Early Christianity
FKDG	*Forschungen zur Kirchen- und Dogmengeschichte*
HBT	*Horizons in Biblical Theology*
JBL	*Journal of Biblical Literature*
JECS	*Journal of Early Christian Studies*
JEH	*Journal of Ecclesiastical History*
JSNT	*Journal for the Study of the New Testament*

JTI	*Journal of Theological Interpretation*
JTS	*Journal of Theological Studies*
MBTh	Münsterische Beiträge zur Theologie
NovTSup	Novum Testamentum Supplements
NTS	*New Testament Studies*
OCP	*Orientalia christiana periodica*
OECS	Oxford Early Christian Studies
PMS	Patristic Monograph Series
RCatT	*Revista catalana de teologia*
SBL	Society of Biblical Literature
SBLMS	Society of Biblical Literature Monograph Series
SBLSymS	Society of Biblical Literature Symposium Series
SBLNTGF	Society of Biblical Literature The New Testament in the Greek Fathers
SJT	*Scottish Journal of Theology*
StPatr	*Studia Patristica*
TS	*Theological Studies*
TRE	*Theologische Realenzyklopädie*
TynBul	*Tyndale Bulletin*
VC	*Vigiliae Christianae*
VCSup	Vigiliae Christianae Supplements
WUNT	Wissenschaftliche Untersuchungen zum Neuen Testament
ZAC	*Zeitschrift für Antikes Christentum/Journal of Ancient Christianity*
ZKG	*Zeitschrift für Kirchengeschichte*
ZNW	*Zeitschrift für die neutestamentliche Wissenschaft und die Kunde der älteren Kirche*

Other abbreviations

Fr.	Fragment
Frs.	Fragments
LXX	Septuagint
par	paragraph

CHAPTER ONE.
GENERAL INTRODUCTION

Athanasius, who was to become the greatest antagonist of the Arians and the stoutest defender of the church's faith, has grasped more firmly than his contemporaries the New Testament witness to the person and work of Christ, and is well armed for the battle.

T. E. Pollard, *Johannine Christology*, 1970, 137

The central purpose of this study is to use modern techniques of historical research to probe behind Athanasius' misrepresentations, many of which have held sway for sixteen centuries, in order to discover the true nature of the ecclesiastical history and the ecclesiastical politics of the fourth century.

T. D. Barnes, Athanasius and Constantius, 1993, ix

The two quotations given above assert Athanasius' influence in the history of Christianity in strikingly different ways. On the one hand, Athanasius is believed to have understood the New Testament better than his contemporaries, and on the other hand, Athanasius' misrepresentations are thought to 'have held sway for sixteen centuries'. The disagreement between the two scholars concerns the assessment of Athanasius' contribution to Christian faith and theology. For many centuries, Athanasius was undisputedly considered a great Church Father who was the great champion of Christian faith by safeguarding the divinity of the Son against the Arian heresy. Athanasius' own presentation of the problems in the Church resulting from Arianism was, by and

1

large, accepted up till the end of the 19th century. However, at that time, a drastically different perception of Athanasius emerged alongside the traditional picture. Since then, there is profound scholarly disagreement on how to characterise Athanasius. He has been presented as a theologian, Biblicist, politician, prime witness to the primacy of Rome,[1] ascetic with a political drive,[2] and even as a gangster.[3] Many of these contrasting evaluations can be traced back to Athanasius' position in relation to the Arian controversy.[4] Some of the descriptions above could, in theory, be complementary, but certainly not all of them. It is not easy to assess all the various aspects of Athanasius' life as it is clear that he functioned in several different roles that are often discussed in isolation from each other. David Gwynn has recently remarked that 'no easily accessible modern book in English ... draws together the different roles that he played', which is problematic, since the various elements in Athanasius' life are inseparable.[5] Such divergent opinions pose the question: What is the cause of these varying verdicts? This monograph will analyse an important work of this prominent fourth-century bishop, the *Orations against the Arians* to shed light on this question. I will first

---

[1] Vincent Twomey, *Apostolikos Thronos. The Primacy of Rome as Reflected in the Church History of Eusebius and the Historico-Apologetic Writings of Saint Athanasius the Great*, MBTh 49 (Münster: Aschendorff, 1982).

[2] David Brakke, *Athanasius and the Politics of Asceticism* (Oxford: Clarendon, 1995), 266.

[3] Timothy D. Barnes, *Constantine and Eusebius* (Cambridge, MA: Harvard University Press, 1981), 230.

[4] For some discussions on the various interpretations in the last centuries, see Nathan Kwok-kit Ng, *The Spirituality of Athanasius. A Key for Proper Understanding of This Important Church Father*, Europäische Hochschulschriften 23/733 (Bern: Peter Lang, 2001), 21–30; Johan Leemans, "Thirteen Years of Athanasius Research (1985–1998): A Survey of Bibliography," *Sacris Erudiri* 39 (2000): 107–29; Barnes, *Athanasius and Constantius*, 1–3; Charles Kannengiesser, "The Athanasian Decade 1974–84: A Bibliographical Report," *TS* 46 (1985): 524–41.

[5] David Morton Gwynn, *Athanasius of Alexandria. Bishop, Theologian, Ascetic, Father*, Christian Theology in Context (Oxford: Oxford University Press, 2012), x. See also 195–197.

sketch an outline of Athanasius' life and show how it was traditionally understood and then present the reasons for the strikingly
different line of interpretation that has subsequently emerged.

ATHANASIUS' EPISCOPATE

Athanasius lived from 295/298 to 373 and his life was far from
quiet and tranquil.[6] He became bishop of Alexandria in 328,
shortly after the Council of Nicaea (325). During his life, he was
exiled five times. The relation between Christianity and the state
changed tremendously during his life: Christianity was transformed from a marginalised, persecuted movement (303–311) to
the accepted religion of the emperor (313) and, finally, to the
religion of the Roman Empire (381), shortly after his death in
373. Since the years just before Athanasius' episcopate started in
328 heavily impacted is life, I will discuss some events in the period immediately before 328, and subsequently, Athanasius' position as bishop of Alexandria up to his second exile, (339–346).

Influences on Athanasius' Episcopate

The Council of Nicaea in 325 is the first of the great ecumenical
councils of the church. Two issues discussed at this Council are of
utmost importance to the life and ecclesiastical career of Athanasius: (1) the Melitian schism and (2) the dispute between Alexander of Alexandria and Arius.[7] The Melitian schism originated in
the aftermath of the Diocletian Persecution (303–311). The
Melitians, who called themselves the 'Church of the Martyrs', are

---

[6] Coptic sources suggest that Athanasius was born in 295. Nevertheless,
298 is more likely, because that would explain the confusion and turmoil
concerning his age when he became bishop in 328. On his life, see Timothy D. Barnes, *Athanasius and Constantius. Theology and Politics in the
Constantinian Empire* (Cambridge, MA: Harvard University Press, 1993);
Gwynn, *Athanasius of Alexandria*, 1–53; Khaled Anatolios, *Athanasius*,
The Early Church Fathers (London: Routledge, 2004), 1–39.

[7] See Barnes, *Athanasius and Constantius*, 19–55; Khaled Anatolios, *Athanasius: The Coherence of His Thought* (London: Routledge, 1998), 85–88.
A third issue at Nicaea, the Easter date, goes beyond the scope of this
investigation. For more information, see David Brakke, "Jewish Flesh and
Christian Spirit in Athanasius of Alexandria," *JECS* 9 (2001): 453–81.

named after Melitius of Lycopolis. They rejected the authority of
the archbishop of Alexandria, because of the bishop's lenient and
merciful stance towards lapsed Christians. They regarded themselves as more strict and rigid than the 'orthodox' Christians and
claimed to be true confessors of Christ. The Melitians seem to
have attracted a large number of Christians, which made them a
serious threat to the bishops of Alexandria. The Council of Nicaea
decided that ordinations performed by Melitius of Lycopolis had
to be confirmed by bishop Alexander of Alexandria. Melitius was
denied the right to ordain, or even to nominate someone for an
ecclesial office. These decisions were difficult to accept for the
Melitians and led to dissatisfaction on their part. This matter was
further complication by Alexander of Alexandria's unexpected
death in 328. To complete this process in an orderly manner, the
implementation of the decision needed to be carried out by a
strong and uncontested leader, but due to the death of the uncontested Alexander the tensions increased.[8] Athanasius was elected
as successor of Alexander, but his election was challenged from
the beginning. It was disputed on the ground that Athanasius had
not yet reached the required age of 30 to be ordained bishop.[9]
The Melitians, who according to the Council of Nicaea did not
have the right to participate in the election of new bishops, sensed
an opportunity to regain influence and they protested against the
procedures of the election. Therefore, Athanasius' episcopate

---

[8] Sara Parvis, *Marcellus of Ancyra and the Lost Years of the Arian Controversy, 325–345*, OECS (New York: Oxford University Press, 2006), 110–
11; see also Annick Martin, *Athanase d'Alexandrie et l'église d'Égypte au
IVe siècle (328–373)* (Rome: École française de Rome, 1996), 321–39.

[9] For the regulation, see Canon 11 of the Council of Neocaesarea (ca.
315). Cuthbert Hamilton Turner, ed., *Ecclesiae Occidentalis Monumenta
Iuris Antiquissima: Canonum et Conciliorum Graecorum Interpretationes Latinae*, 2 vols. (Oxford: Clarendon, 1899–1939), I:132–35; for a translation,
see James Stevenson and William Hugh Clifford Frend, eds, *A New Eusebius. Documents Illustrating the History of the Church to AD 337* (London:
SPCK, 1987), 293.

started turbulently and was dominated by several accusations of violence against the Melitians.[10]

Secondly, the theological dispute between Alexander of Alexandria and Arius, concerning the status of the Son of God, left a strong mark on Athanasius' life and ecclesiastical career. The dispute started locally but soon had a larger impact, because Arius appealed to the influential Eusebius of Nicomedia and Eusebius of Caesarea, and gained their support. Traditionally the conflict is thought to have started in 318 ce, but in the last few decades several proposals have been put forward arguing that the conflict ignited in 321 ce.[11] At any rate, the result of the Council of Nicaea in 325 ce is the most certain point of reference in the controversy and of most interest for the career of Athanasius.[12] At this council, the Nicene Creed was formulated and accepted by most of the participants, but not by Arius and some like-minded bishops. The aim of the Nicene creed was to formulate a declaration of Christian faith that satisfied the majority of bishops and to put an end to the theological discussions between Alexander and Arius. It is far from evident that Nicaea can be regarded as a victory of

---

[10] Martin, *Athanase*, 219–392; Barnes, *Athanasius and Constantius*, 17–33; Sir Harold Idris Bell, *Jews and Christians in Egypt: The Jewish Troubles in Alexandria and the Athanasian Controversy* (Westport, CT: Greenwood, 1972) contains a discussion of the Melitian schism, as well as some documents that contain the claims about violence by Melitians. See Duane Wade-Hampton Arnold, *The Early Episcopal Career of Athanasius of Alexandria*, Christianity and Judaism in Antiquity 6 (Notre Dame, IN: University of Notre Dame Press, 1991) for a more positive assessment of Athanasius' case.

[11] R. P. C. Hanson, *The Search for the Christian Doctrine of God. The Arian Controversy 318–381* (Edinburgh: T&T Clark, 1988), 129–38; Hanns Christof Brennecke et al., eds, *Athanasius Werke. Band III/Teil 1. Dokumente zur Geschichte des arianischen Streites. Lfg. 3. Bis zur Ekthesis Makrostichos* (Berlin: de Gruyter, 2007), xix–xxxvi.

[12] Although not undisputed, a good case can be made for Athanasius' involvement in the early phase, as he might be the author of Urk. 4b (= Dok. 2.2), known as *henos somatos*, traditionally attributed to Alexander of Alexandria. See Christopher Stead, "Athanasius' Earliest Written Work," *JTS* 39 (1988): 76–91.

Alexander of Alexandria and like-minded bishops. After Nicaea, Arius and some others were excommunicated because of their refusal to sign the creed. However, a few years later, Arius and other theologically suspected figures at Nicaea were rehabilitated by the emperor. Athanasius was immediately pressed by emperor Constantine to accept Arius into communion again.[13] Athanasius refused to do so, even when he became increasingly isolated because bishops of like mind were deposed or disappeared from the scene.[14]

Athanasius' position as bishop was very insecure, especially in the beginning, and this situation continued for several decades. From early on in his career, he was accused of violence, but he was able to defend himself several times before emperor Constantine against these charges brought forward by the Melitians. However, in 335 he was tried for the same charges at the Council of Tyre and was convicted. Athanasius left the council before the final verdict was pronounced, to appeal directly to the emperor in Constantinople in order to object to the biased procedure at Tyre. His main accusers also went to the emperor and, instead of repeating the charges of violence, accused Athanasius of delaying grain transports. Subsequently, Constantine exiled Athanasius to Trier without appointing an ecclesial replacement. Constantine had acted similarly in the case of Eustathius of Antioch. Therefore, it is likely that the emperor was not completely sure of Athanasius' guilt, but exiled the Alexandrian in order to have peace and quiet in his empire.[15] Athanasius later claimed that Constantine acted in this way to save Athanasius' life and to restore his ecclesial position when the situation was safe again, in his work *Defence against the Arians*, written around 357. Critics of

---

[13] See Timothy D. Barnes, "The Exile and Recalls of Arius," *JTS* 60 (2009): 109–29.

[14] Parvis, *Marcellus*, 96–133; Sara Parvis, "The Strange Disappearance of the Moderate Origenists: The Arian Controversy, 326–341," in *StPatr* 39, ed. F. Young, M. Edwards, and P. Parvis (Dudley, MA: Peeters, 2006), 97–102; Barnes, *Athanasius and Constantius*, 17–18.

[15] Barnes, *Athanasius and Constantius*, 19–24; cf. Arnold, *Episcopal Career*, 163–73.

Athanasius, like Timothy Barnes, doubt his claim because the emperor was dead at the time when Athanasius wrote this work. So,
Athanasius could have said this to clear himself of the charges,
even if he had been guilty.[16]

Constantine's three sons divided the Roman empire into
three parts and reigned as equals after the death of their father.
In the meantime, all exiled bishops were allowed to return to their
sees, including Athanasius. Undisturbed enjoyment of his see was
short-lived, because as early as 338 his position was once again
under attack from his old ecclesiastical opponents. They argued
that the charges of the Council of Tyre still applied, so that Athanasius did not have the right to remain archbishop of Alexandria.
Despite widespread support within Egypt, he went into his second
exile in 339, which lasted until 346. At that time, the difficulties
were not over and in the following decades he was exiled three
more times. Only after his final exile in 365 did his see in Alexandria remain unchallenged until his death in 373.

So far the basic facts of the situation that led to Athanasius'
ecclesiastical career. The diverging paths of understanding Athanasius flow from different interpretations concerning these
events. Traditionally, much weight and credence have been given
to Athanasius' self-testimony and the fifth-century orthodox
church historians who broadly accepted Athanasius' presentation
of the exiles.[17] In his writings, Athanasius juxtaposes his personal
troubles as bishop and the troubles of the Church at large. He
defines both types of turmoil as a continuing struggle between the
Church and Arianism. Athanasius' presentation of the Arian controversy remained virtually unchallenged until the late 19th century.[18] In this account, Athanasius is understood as a hero and

---

[16] See *Apol. c. Ar.* 9. Cf. Barnes, *Athanasius and Constantius*, 39, 173.

[17] See Mario Baghos, "The Traditional Portrayal of St Athanasius According to Rufinus, Socrates, Sozomen, and Theodoret," in *Alexandrian Legacy: A Critical Appraisal*, ed. Doru Costache, Philip Kariatlis, and Mario
Baghos (Newcastle upon Tyne: Cambridge Scholars, 2015), 139–71.

[18] Cf. Leslie W. Barnard, "Edward Gibbon on Athanasius," in *Arianism:
Historical and Theological Reassessments*, ed. Robert C. Gregg, PMS 11
(Cambridge, MA: Philadelphia Patristic Foundation, 1985), 361–70.

staunch defender of the faith. His *Orations against the Arians* is regarded as his most influential theological work, (adequately) refuting the Arians. In 1900, Gwatkin stated that Athanasius is influenced by 'the voice of Scripture only'.[19] Scholars up to this period were convinced that Athanasius' difficulties were solely the result of his uncompromising stance in theological matters. Generally speaking, scholars up to this time accepted Athanasius' concern for theology as genuine. Athanasius' opponents did everything in their power to negate the rightful Creed of Nicaea and proposed false doctrine to gain a foothold in the Church, but he remained faithful nonetheless. Athanasius' opponents invented false charges of misconduct against Athanasius.[20] Moreover, the different opponents of Athanasius, both the Arians and Melitians, used all their might and access to imperial power to suppress the theological truths that Athanasius defended. This is seen as the explanation for the highly turbulent ecclesiastical career of Athanasius, including the five exiles. Athanasius championed the right articulation of theology and devoted his whole life to this. He consequently encountered pressure and suffered exile. This line of research that primarily reads Athanasius' works through a theological lens is still current.[21] The most appreciated resource in such a reading of Athanasius are his *Orations against the Arians*, since they deal specifically with the divinity of the Son and the related Trinitarian question.

At the other of the spectrum, a highly critical approach to Athanasius is found among scholars that regard him as primarily driven by political ambitions and a desire for power. Since the end of the 19th century another line of research has discerned a hidden motive behind Athanasius' works. These scholars argue

---

[19] Henry Melvill Gwatkin, Studies of Arianism. Chiefly Referring to the Character and Chronology of the Reaction Which Followed the Council of Nicaea, 2nd ed. (Cambridge: Deigton Bell, 1900), 71.

[20] See Duane Wade-Hampton Arnold, *The Early Episcopal Career of Athanasius of Alexandria*, Christianity and Judaism in Antiquity 6 (Notre Dame, IN: University of Notre Dame Press, 1991).

[21] See for example Kevin Giles, *The Eternal Generation of the Son: Maintaining Orthodoxy in Trinitarian Theology* (Downers Grove: InterVarsity, 2012).

that Athanasius' difficulties were not the result of his courageous defence of Christian faith, but due to his use of violence against the Melitians.[22] They assume that Athanasius presents a distorted portrayal of the facts in his writings. The German scholars Otto Seeck and Eduard Schwartz rejected a 'theological' and hagiographical reading of Athanasius and asserted instead that Athanasius' difficulties were the result of his violent behaviour against the Melitians in the early period of his episcopate. According to Seeck and Schwartz, Athanasius' theological polemic against the Arians served as a smoke screen for hiding the violence he committed against the Melitians; Timothy Barnes argues along their line of thought as well.[23] More recently, the work of Karlheinz Deschner exemplifies this continuing critical reading of Athanasius' career mainly in terms of politics: 'Er wurde einer der zähesten und skrupellosesten geistlichen Verführer.'[24] In the same line, Hartmut Leppin, sensitive to both the theological and political dimension, judges the force of Athanasius' political power to be stronger than his argumentation: 'Unbeugsam verfocht Athanasius seine Sache. (…) Dabei wirkte er mehr durch die Macht seiner Persönlichkeit als durch die Kraft seiner Argumente.'[25] Leppin praises Athanasius' staunchness, but is critical of his use of

---

[22] '[E]ven the Nicene anathemas were not immune to Athanasian interpolation', according to David Morton Gwynn, *The Eusebians. The Polemic of Athanasius of Alexandria and the Construction of the "Arian Controversy"* (New York: Oxford University Press, 2007), 242. Athanasius' *History of the Arians* is 'a systematically deceptive work', Barnes, *Athanasius and Constantius*, 129.

[23] Barnes, *Athanasius and Constantius*, 1–3; Arnold strongly opposes this suggestion and discusses several scholars with this opinion Arnold, *Episcopal Career*, 11–23.

[24] Karlheinz Deschner, *Kriminalgeschichte des Christentums. Die Frühzeit. Von den Ursprüngen im Alten Testament bis zum Tod des hl. Augustinus (430)* (Reinbek bei Hamburg: Rowohlt, 1986), 431–63, here 452; cf. Deschner's section title: 'Nicht Kampf um den Glauben: um die Macht, um Alexandrien' (439–445).

[25] Hartmut Leppin, *Die Kirchenväter und ihre Zeit. Von Athanasius bis Gregor dem Großen* (München: C. H. Beck, 2000), 23.

violence at the same time.[26] Within the English-speaking world, Gwynn criticises Athanasius' 'polarized presentation' as 'a product of imposition upon' his opponents. He claims that Athanasius largely 'invented' his battle against Arianism.[27] Christopher Beeley's thought also deserves to be mentioned here. He asserts that 'Athanasius himself, more than any other church leader, (…) was responsible for the very polarization of theological parties that he laments in the twilight of his career, through a long and aggressive campaign to demonize all who did not strictly agree with his own position.'[28] The second line of scholarship reads Athanasius much more through a political lens and does not regard his five exiles as resulting from his faithfulness to Christ. Instead, they see him as an example of a bishop that became power hungry. In this context, Beeley speaks of the 'futility' of Athanasius' 'warmongering'.[29]

The tendency to read Athanasius' in a way that explains his polemic against 'Arianism' as a pretext for his misconduct has been opposed by several scholars. Duane Wade-Hampton Arnold asserts that Athanasius did not use any violence against the Melitians and he argues that the accusations against Athanasius 'must at least be considered unproved'.[30] However, a major weakness of Arnold's argument is that he criticises the Athanasian critics without offering a convincing alternative interpretation of the facts.[31] In contrast, Sara Parvis does not deny or excuse Athanasius' exercise of violence (as Arnold does), but she demonstrates the strong theological-political dimension of the Arian controversy (contra Seeck and others). The existence of political-

---

[26] Leppin, Kirchenväter, 26.

[27] Gwynn, Eusebians, 245–46; cf. Lewis Ayres, Nicaea and Its Legacy: An Approach to Fourth-Century Trinitarian Theology (Oxford: Oxford University Press, 2004), 100–10.

[28] Christopher A. Beeley, The Unity of Christ: Continuity and Conflict in Patristic Tradition (New Haven: Yale University, 2012), 126.

[29] Beeley, Unity of Christ, 125.

[30] Arnold, Episcopal Career, 186.

[31] Gerard H. Ettlinger, S.J., "Review of 'The Early Episcopal Career of Athanasius of Alexandria. By Duane Wade-Hampton Arnold," TS 53 (1992): 182.

ecclesiastical alliances is not the bishop's imaginative creation, but a reflection of the actual situation. She points to the representation of bishops at several councils in the period between 325 and 345 and the trial in Tyre, which she does not at all regard as objective and fair.[32]

Both types of readings of Athanasius' career and theology still coexist.[33] Although there is a clear difference in perspective between these two lines of scholarship, although these positions cannot be painted in black and white. But even if allowance is made for more nuanced positions in the middle, the lens through which Athanasius is understood has a huge impact on the outcome. The question to what extent Athanasius communicates what is really at stake, or his texts shape the discourse in which to understand his motives and behaviour, is clearly related to the rhetoric that is at play in Athanasius' work. I will therefore briefly discuss Athanasius' work and theology and then proceed to a discussion on the topic of rhetoric.

Athanasius' writings and theology

During his life, Athanasius wrote many works and letters, alongside performing his regular pastoral duties during the 45 years as a bishop and spiritual father to the Church of Alexandria and beyond.[34] His most famous works are his early apologetic treatises (*Against the Pagans* and *On the Incarnation*), a work refuting Arian theology (*Orations against the Arians*), and his biography of the monk Antony (*Life of Antony*). A majority of scholars favour Athanasian authorship of *Life of Antony*, although some have disputed

---

[32] See Parvis, *Marcellus*, 97–98, 123–27; Parvis, "Strange Disappearance"; David Gwynn has a more critical attitude towards Athanasius' polemic, see Gwynn, *Eusebians*; David Morton Gwynn, "Hoi Peri Eusebion: The Polemic of Athanasius and the Early 'Arian Controversy,'" in *StPatr* 39, ed. F. Young, M. Edwards, and P. Parvis (Dudley, MA: Peeters, 2006), 53–57.

[33] See Francesca Aran Murphy, George Hunsinger, and Bruce Marshall, "Book Forum: Khaled Anatolios, Retrieving Nicaea," *Theology Today* 71.4 (2015): 446–52.

[34] See Gwynn, *Athanasius*, 19–54, 131–58.

this understanding. However, the weightiest reasons speak in favour of Athanasian authorship.[35] *Henos somatos*, a letter featuring
in the Arian controversy and written in the name of Alexander of
Alexandria, is quite likely also by his hand.[36] Athanasius also
wrote historically-oriented works that broadcast his views on the
troubles of the Church due to Arianism.[37] This category includes
many documents and letters between the late 330s and 360s (*History of the Arians, Defence of the Flight*), works that comment on
synods that produced theological statements (*On the Council of
Nicaea, On the Synods of Seleucia and Arianism*) and many letters,
both annual circular letters concerning Easter sent to the Egyptian
church (*Festal Letters*) and letters sent to individuals.[38]

Even some proponents of a less favourable reading of Athanasius can engage with his theology, though the assessment can
be quite negative, as in the case of Beeley. He regards Athanasius'
Orations as a dogmatic work, but he laments the 'inflammatory
and vitriolic language' and its influence on patristic literature.[39]
On the assumption that it is worthwhile to assess Athanasius'
works and trace what he genuinely believed to be important,
scholars have struggled to define the relation between theological, biblical and logical aspects of Athanasius' works. I will now
outline very briefly the content of Athanasius' theology as

---

[35] Gwynn, *Athanasius*, 15; Peter Juriss, "In Defence of Athanasius, Patriarch of Alexandria as Author of the Life of Antony: A Discussion of Historical, Linguistic and Theological Considerations," *Phronema* 12 (1997):
24–43; T.D. Barnes argues against the Athanasian authorship. "Angel of
Light or Mystic Initiate: The Problem of the Life of Antony," *JTS* 37.2
(1986): 353–68.

[36] See Stead, *Athanasius' Earliest Written Work*, Parvis, *Marcellus*, 68–81.
Gwynn holds that the question of authorship must remain open. See *Eusebians*, 66.

[37] See Richard Flower, *Emperors and Bishops in Late Roman Invective* (Cambridge; New York: Cambridge University Press, 2013).

[38] More details, including editions and translations of Athanasius can be
found in Peter Gemeinhardt, ed., *Athanasius Handbuch* (Tübingen: Mohr
Siebeck, 2011); Charles Kannengiesser, *Handbook of Patristic Exegesis*, 2
vols., BiAC 1 (Leiden: Brill, 2004), II:708–21.

[39] Beeley, *Unity of Christ*, 146.

compared to that of other contemporary theological key players to position the question of these different aspects.

Athanasius' theology, as well as that of his predecessor Alexander, is characterised by a profound emphasis on the distinction between God and creation. He asserts that the Son of God must be unequivocally the eternal Son of God. Since the Godhead cannot be contaminated with creatureliness in any way, there is no intermediary category between Creator and creation. Athanasius' theological views were also closely linked (but not identical) to those of Eustathius of Antioch and Marcellus of Ancyra. In contrast, Arius confessed 'one God, the only unbegotten, the only eternal, the only one without cause or beginning, the only true, the only one possessed of immortality, the only wise, the only good, the only sovereign, ... the begetter of his only Son before endless ages,' while the Son is 'immutable and unchanging, the perfect creation of God'.[40] Arius' words illustrate his profound emphasis on the uniqueness of God the Father. The Son is higher than any creature, but nonetheless inferior to the Father. Arius' theological position shows much more affinity with that of Asterius, Eusebius of Nicomedia and Eusebius of Caesarea. Although Maurice Wiles points to the fact that Athanasius labelled his opponents as 'Arians' 'for a specific polemical purpose of defamation by association',[41] many scholars still consider it helpful to regard the positions of Athanasius, Eustathius and Marcellus on the one hand, and those of Arius, Asterius and the two Eusebii on the other, as opposite theological trajectories.[42] Both parties base their theological views on Scripture. Athanasius (and like-minded theologians) defend the eternity of the Son by pointing to the

---

[40] Urk. 6 (12,4–5. 7. 9); tr. Williams.

[41] Maurice F. Wiles, "Attitudes to Arius in the Arian Controversy," in *Arianism after Arius. Essays on the Development of the Fourth Century Trinitarian Conflicts*, ed. Michel R. Barnes and Daniel H. Williams (Edinburgh: T&T Clark, 1993), 42.

[42] Khaled Anatolios, *Retrieving Nicaea. The Development and Meaning of Trinitarian Doctrine* (Grand Rapids, MI: Baker Academic, 2011), 41–79; Parvis, *Marcellus*, 39–67; cf. Joseph T. Lienhard, S.J., *Contra Marcellum: Marcellus of Ancyra and Fourth-Century Theology* (Washington, DC: Catholic University of America Press, 1999), 28–46; Hanson, *Search*, 3–636.

reciprocal relation between Father and Son. However, the Eusebians claim to base their views on Scripture as well, and John in particular, so that John's Gospel cannot be understood as exclusively supporting one of both positions.[43]

This raises the question: how could someone say whether Athanasius' or Eusebius' theology is biblical? Some scholars frame the question in a different way. Rowan Williams understands the Arian controversy as the result of tensions between Catholic and academically-oriented dynamics. He posits the authority of the bishop and the Church as Catholic, which is 'allied with the idea of a monolithic social unit and the policy of religious coercion'.[44] But he also posits independent teachers, such as Christians interested in scholarship, ascetics or confessors as academics, since they possessed a status that could challenge the authority of the bishop. Alexander of Alexandria represents the Catholic tradition, which is more focused on controlling opinions and forming a unity,[45] whereas Arius exemplifies the academic model, resisting the authority of the bishop by an appeal to his position as *theodidaktos* (instructed by God). While Williams does not argue that the academic typology excludes the notion of spirituality, his framing suggests a tension between scriptural and logical or rational thought that was prevalent in the Arian controversy.[46]

Thomas E. Pollard uses the concepts of biblical and logical to understand the positions of Athanasius and Arius in his

---

[43] Hanson calls it 'the major battlefield in the New Testament during the Arian controversy', in Hanson, *Search*, 834; see further T. E. Pollard, *Johannine Christology and the Early Church*, Society for New Testament Studies Monograph Series 13 (New York: Cambridge University Press, 1970), 137, 184–245; Sara Parvis, "Christology in the Early Arian Controversy: The Exegetical War," in *Christology and Scripture*, ed. Andrew T. Lincoln and Angus Paddison (New York: T&T Clark, 2007), 121.

[44] Rowan Williams, *Arius. Heresy and Tradition*, 2nd ed. (London: SCM, 2001), 87.

[45] Williams, *Arius*, 88.

[46] Williams, *Arius*, 89.

Johannine Christology and the Early Church.[47] Pollard discusses the use of the Gospel of John in the first four centuries and concludes that Athanasius was able to defeat the Arians by making use of this Gospel especially. The Arians, on the contrary, are portrayed as rationalistic and unfaithful to the biblical message. To paraphrase Pollard's conclusion: Athanasius was faithful to the Bible (i.e. not rationalistic), while Arius was 'too logical', 'speculative and rationalistic' (i.e. unbiblical).[48] James D. Ernest states similarly about Athanasius: 'Die Sprache, die er fließend spricht und in der er am besten schreibt, ist nicht Griechisch, sondern »Biblisch«.'[49] Despite their nuances, the contrast between biblical and logical is present in both authors.

Other theologians are more cautious in applying the label 'biblical' to Athanasius and the Arian controversy at large. Already in 1968, Eginhard P. Meijering argued against a *communis opinio* that conceived Athanasius predominantly as a biblical and anti-philosophical theologian.[50] Similarly, R. P. C. Hanson acknowledged that Athanasius was interested in the Bible, but remarks that Athanasius sometimes needed 'extreme ingenuity'.[51] Although the extant sources of Arius do not contain many biblical references, this can hardly be an argument for seeing Arius as concerned with logical rather than biblical matters. On the contrary, Hanson asserts that exegetical questions were certainly

---

[47] Pollard, *Johannine Christology*, 137, 143; see also idem, "The Exegesis of Scripture and the Arian Controversy," *Bulletin of the John Rylands Library* 41 (1959): 414–29.

[48] Pollard, *Johannine Christology*, 143–44, cf. 137, 185, 245.

[49] James D. Ernest, "C.II.1 Die Heilige Schrift," in *Athanasius Handbuch*, ed. Peter Gemeinhardt, trans. Yorick Schulz–Wackerbarth (Tübingen: Mohr Siebeck, 2011), 282; see also James D. Ernest, *The Bible in Athanasius of Alexandria*, BiAC 2 (Boston: Brill, 2004); Gemeinhardt, in the same *Handbuch*, is more cautious in this respect Peter Gemeinhardt, "B.II.3 Theologie und Kirchenpolitik," in *Athanasius Handbuch*, ed. Peter Gemeinhardt (Tübingen: Mohr Siebeck, 2011), 96–97.

[50] E. P. Meijering, *Orthodoxy and Platonism in Athanasius: Synthesis or Antithesis?* (Leiden: Brill, 1968), 2.

[51] Hanson, *Search*, 834.

important in the movement of the 'Arians'.[52] Khaled Anatolios has clearly demonstrated that the contrastive labels of catholic/academic or biblical/logical are insufficient to describe the Arian controversy satisfactorily. He assumes that all participants (Arius, Athanasius, Asterius) in the 'Arian' controversy agreed upon (1) the scriptural canon and its divine authority, (2) the link between the bishop and the apostolic tradition, and (3) the primacy of faith and 'the necessity of applying reason to faith'.[53] According to Anatolios, many doctrinal elements were commonly affirmed by all participants, as well as the question which heresies were to be to avoided.[54] If this view is accepted, it raises the question of how references to the biblical texts and appeals to reason interact in the Arian controversy at large.

From all this, it is clear that theological and non-theological motives are difficult to separate in Athanasius' work. Such a division is too simplistic. Theology certainly develops at a certain time and place and not independently of a given political situation. However, theology cannot be reduced to politics or desire for power, for to deny the theological interest as a primary trigger is to miss one of the most vital concerns of the Arian controversy.[55] Neither is it possible to develop neat categories of biblical and logical, as pertaining to Athanasius versus the Arians.[56] It is true that Athanasius wanted to be biblical, but he did not give up the claim to be logical or reasonable as well. Likewise, the Arians intended to be biblical and reasonable at the same time. In the present monograph, it is assumed that theological and political motives are interrelated. The claims that scholars make

---

[52] See Hanson, *Search*, 824–49.

[53] Anatolios, *Retrieving Nicaea*, 36.

[54] Anatolios, *Retrieving Nicaea*, 36–38.

[55] Gwynn, *Athanasius*, 9.

[56] See Lewis Ayres, "Athanasius' Initial Defense of the Term Homoousios: Rereading the De Decretis," *JECS* 12 (2004): 339–41; Vincent Twomey, "St Athanasius: De Synodis and the Sense of Scripture," in *Scriptural Interpretation in the Fathers: Letter and Spirit*, ed. Thomas Finan and Vincent Twomey (Dublin: Four Courts Press, 1995), 85–118; Kevin Giles, *The Eternal Generation of the Son: Maintaining Orthodoxy in Trinitarian Theology* (Downers Grove: InterVarsity, 2012).

concerning Athanasius' motives as either theological or clearly non-theological presuppose a rhetorical dimension. This is both the case when he is presented as struggling for his theological case, and when he is considered to use theological arguments to cover up church-political issues that caused the problems throughout his episcopacy. While this rhetorical level remains implicit in many studies on Athanasius' career and theology, this monograph will explicitly address this rhetorical dimension. Such a rhetorical analysis of Athanasius' work is an excellent tool for achieving more clarity on the interrelation between Athanasius' theological and non-theological motifs and will provide a fresh perspective on the typologies that are prominent in scholarship on Athanasius. I will now proceed with exploring the field of classical rhetoric and *paideia* to be able to assess the rhetorical dimensions of Athanasius' *Orations*.

CLASSICAL RHETORIC AND *PAIDEIA*

When studying this field of classical rhetoric, it is quite crucial to take its educational system into consideration and here we soon run into the aim of *paideia*. In classical antiquity, over a long period of time, a whole system of rhetorical education was developed to prepare students for speaking in public. This system contained a large degree of consistency from classical antiquity to 500 ce; Henri Marrou claims that 'only one coherent and clearly defined educational system' existed within this time period.[57] He argues that classical *paideia* concerns more than just the system of classical or Hellenistic education. It is not just the outcome of educational efforts, but the realisation of the 'ideal of personal life' within the Hellenic culture.[58] *Paideia* – classical education – comprised a broad range of subjects. Besides reading, writing and pronouncing correctly, classical education consisted of subjects such as music, gymnastics and geometry. However, in this monograph, I will focus on the textual part of classical education.

---

[57] Henri Irénée Marrou, *A History of Education in Antiquity*, trans. George Lamb, 3rd ed., Wisconsin Studies in Classics (Madison, WI: University of Wisconsin Press, 1982), xiii.

[58] Marrou, *History of Education*, 137–44, here 143.

Education often took place in the setting of one teacher and a number of students. Classical education consisted of three steps. First, around the age of 7 years, students received instruction from a grammatist. After completing their basic studies, they went to the grammarian and finally received instruction from a rhetor. While studying under a grammatist, students had to learn to read, write and pronounce the letters of the alphabet, syllables and complete words. Once students were proficient in this, they would turn to reading sentences and larger sections of texts, as well as copying small sentences by writing them down. Reading and writing were intertwined in this process of education.[59]

At the second level, of the grammarian, the initial study of classical literature and its correct pronunciation took place. At this stage, students practised with several προγυμνάσματα – preliminary exercises. Students needed to master figures of speech, such as the fable (μῦθος), narration (διήγησις), anecdote (χρεία), maxim (γνώμη), refutation (ἀνασκευή), confirmation (κατασκευή), topic (τόπος) and several others. Some of these rhetorical handbooks with instructions have been preserved.[60] Pupils were expected to complete the basic exercises before they could be enrolled in a rhetorical school. These exercises consisted of a standard form to enhance the student's ability to respond to a variety of situations. The exercises gradually increased in difficulty. The more advanced exercises – comparison, *ethopoeia*, defending a thesis, and the discussion of law – could only be studied when students qualified for study under a rhetor. At this stage, students were expected to practice actual declamation as well.[61] Often, students rehearsed texts so frequently that they memorised them.[62] The grammarian also taught about the moral aspects of the poets; 'acquaintance with the poets was looked upon as one of the first attributes of an educated man, one of the highest cultural values.'[63]

---

[59] Marrou, *History of Education*, 210–22.
[60] See e.g. George A. Kennedy, *Progymnasmata: Greek Textbooks of Prose Composition and Rhetoric* (Leiden: Brill, 2003).
[61] Marrou, *History of Education*, 239.
[62] Marrou, *History of Education*, 228–31.
[63] Marrou, *History of Education*, 235.

Because rhetoric was such a central aspect of education – and prestige – in antiquity, it had a tremendous impact on all literary output in antiquity. For that reason, I will discuss some formal elements of the Greco-Roman rhetorical tradition, also known as classical rhetoric.

Key Concepts and Definitions in Classical Rhetoric

This section will deal with several topics within the Greco-Roman rhetorical tradition. It will start with two definitions of the subject, and will subsequently discuss various major topics of classical rhetorical theory.

Definitions of Greco-Roman Rhetorical Tradition

George A. Kennedy gives two definitions of classical rhetoric, a historical and a theoretical one. (1) Historically, classical rhetoric 'is the total record of Greek and Roman rhetorical teaching and practice'. It covers a large period, from Homer to the Sophists to the handbooks of composition at the time of the Roman Empire, and it covers a large variety of subjects and authors, such as poetry, sermons, speeches, orators, dramatists, poets and philosophers.[64] (2) Theoretically, classical rhetoric 'is a systematic and comprehensive body of knowledge primarily intended to teach public speaking, which was conceptualised between the fourth century BCE and the early Middle Ages'.[65] This section discusses several major elements of classical rhetoric in order to make an informed choice concerning the tools to be used in this monograph.

The Genres of Rhetoric

Greco-Roman rhetorical theory generally distinguishes between three genres of rhetoric. (1) The deliberative genre, that deals with future decisions in public or personal life, in which an orator can give advice that might influence decisions still to be made, for example political decisions. (2) The judicial (or forensic)

---

[64] George A. Kennedy, "Classical Rhetoric," ed. Thomas O. Sloane, *Encyclopedia of Rhetoric* (Oxford: Oxford University Press, 2001), 92–93.
[65] Kennedy, "Classical Rhetoric," 93.

genre, related to actions from the past, concerns speeches in courtrooms where judges must be persuaded. (3) The epideictic genre, concerning the present, is related to speeches of praise and blame. Many speeches are composed for a specific occasion, which generally lacks an incentive to take actions.

The deliberative genre was used often in the ancient *polis* system and in the Senate. On such occasions, all members present could speak up and influence decision making. However, with the rise of the Roman Empire and the increased power of the emperor, this form became less used on practical occasions. The judicial genre retained its function in the sphere of law and court. A development, mainly connected to the judicial genre, is Hermagoras' theory of stasis (1st century BCE).[66] According to stasis theory, an orator should first determine the basic proposition in a judicial case. A defendant can (a) deny a statement of fact (conjecture, στοχασμός), (b) admit to an action but argue that it is legal (definition, ὅρος), (c) admit the illegality of an act but find reasons why it was justified (quality, ποιότης), or (d) object to the competence or impartiality of the judges (transference, μετάληψις).[67] Thus Hermagoras defined the four issues as 'conjecture, definition, quality, and competence'.[68] The stasis theory was very important in the judicial discourse, to determine the content and wording of speeches in the courtroom.

The epideictic genre consists of speeches of praise or blame. This genre featured quite commonly during all kinds of ceremonial gatherings. It was an excellent way for rhetors to demonstrate

---

[66] George A. Kennedy, *Greek Rhetoric under Christian Emperors*, A History of Rhetoric 3 (Princeton, NJ: Princeton University Press, 1983), 73–86; cf. Heinrich Lausberg, *Handbook of Literary Rhetoric. A Foundation for Literary Study*, trans. Matthew T. Bliss and David E. Orton (Leiden: Brill, 1998), 63–96 (par 140–223); Josef Martin, *Antike Rhetorik: Technik und Methode*, Handbuch der Altertumswissenschaft 2/3 (München: Beck, 1974), 28–44.

[67] Cf. George A. Kennedy, *Classical Rhetoric & Its Christian and Secular Tradition from Ancient to Modern Times* (Chapel Hill: University of North Carolina Press, 1999), 99.

[68] Robert Dick Sider, *Ancient Rhetoric and the Art of Tertullian*, Oxford Theological Monographs (London: Oxford University Press, 1971), 16.

their rhetorical skills. A panegyric is a type of speech that contains high praise of a person or object. Originally, panegyrics were delivered in ancient Greece, but the panegyric also had a significant function during all kinds of ceremonies in the Roman Empire. Rhetorical handbooks, such as that of Menander Rhetor, Aelius Theon and others, gave ample attention to speeches of praise. The handbooks contained several rules and *topoi* for composing hymns and the praise of cities and countries, as well as the praise during ceremonies held in honour of important arriving notables or imperial officials.[69]

Rhetoric was an important and profitable art, due to its importance in all kinds of public settings, such as politics and the courtroom. Many 'sophists' travelled around to earn a living by training others to be persuasive. These 'sophists' often published their speeches, which were subsequently imitated by students for educational purposes. The title 'sophists' received both a neutral and negative connotation. Practitioners of the discipline of 'sophistic rhetoric', such as Gorgias and Isocrates, regarded style and eloquence as a goal in itself and were not critical (or at least less critical) of the sophistic practice that did not attempt to find truth but to win the argument by arousal of emotions. Practitioners of 'philosophical rhetoric', such as Socrates, Plato and Aristotle, were critics of the sophistic attitude that relativised the search for truth.[70] According to them, the sophists sought pretentious wisdom, while they themselves loved and searched for true wisdom. They did engage with rhetoric nonetheless, despite their criticism of the practice of the sophists. To preserve the genuine art of rhetoric, Aristotle wrote a handbook on rhetoric that distinguished between legitimate use of rhetoric and its misuse by sophists. He achieved this by separating his understanding of rhetoric from the practice of the sophists. In this way, he paved the way for rhetoric, eloquence and the preservation of the ideal of *paideia* that was quite mainstream for a long time. To what extent Plato shared Aristotle's view on this subject is a matter of some debate. Plato expressed great hesitance about the study of rhetoric in his

---

[69] Flower, *Late Roman Invective*, 43–46.
[70] Kennedy, *Christian and Secular Tradition*, 29–97.

Phaedrus. Modern commentators are divided as to whether he fully rejected it or not. While Kennedy holds that Plato left room for genuine philosophical rhetoric,[71] Brad McAdon contends that Plato denounced the art of rhetoric completely; ultimately, Plato does not believe in any form of philosophical rhetoric. McAdon argues that contemporary scholars holding Plato's dialectic to be the true, philosophical rhetoric base themselves on a modern understanding of rhetoric, rather than on an ancient one.[72] This very disagreement on what classical rhetoric actually is, shows the broadness of the concept of rhetoric.

Two Overarching Principles for Creating Speeches

Greco-Roman rhetorical handbooks are generally organised according to one of these two governing principles: the parts of the speech (*partes orationis*) or the duties of an orator (*officia oratoris*). These two governing principles show two different perceptions on rhetorical education. Organisation of the rhetorical handbooks according to the parts of the speech (school rhetoric) developed first and is a convenient way to instruct beginning students. Any speech consists of the introduction, main body and conclusion. Aristotle distinguished four elements: introduction (προοίμιον), statement of the facts (πρόθεσις), proof (πίστις) and conclusion (ἐπίλογος), while other rhetoricians added extra subdivisions.[73] The function of this categorisation is to instruct orators on what to say and when to say it during a speech. The introduction makes the audience attentive and well-disposed; the statement informs the audience of the occasion of the speech; the proof section provides arguments *pro* and *contra*; finally, the conclusion summarises what has been said before and urges the listeners to undertake the intended action. This system is easy because the basic steps of an orator to deliver a proper speech are immediately visible.

---

[71] Kennedy, *Christian and Secular Tradition*, 66–74.

[72] Brad McAdon, "Plato's Denunciation of Rhetoric in the 'Phaedrus.'" *Rhetoric Review* 23.1 (2004): 22.

[73] For an elaborate discussion of the parts of the speech, see Lausberg, *Handbook*, 112–208 (par 255–442).

The Means of Persuasion

The means of persuasion, or proofs (πίστεις), are crucial in the process of persuasion. These proofs are divided into 'non-artistic' proofs (πίστεις ἄτεχνοι), which are mostly useful in the courtroom, for example, laws and contracts,[74] and 'artistic' proofs (πίστεις ἔντεχνοι), which must be invented and applied by the orator or writer. Rhetorical handbooks, starting with Aristotle's, devoted most of their attention to the three artistic proofs: *ethos* (character, ἦθος), *logos* (logical proof, λόγος) and *pathos* (emotion, πάθος). These are related to the three parties involved in the process of persuasion.[75] *Ethos* is related to the orator, *logos* to the subject matter (content) and *pathos* to the audience.[76]

Although these three means of persuasion can be and often should be used throughout the text alternately, the introduction is primarily associated with *ethos*, the main body of the text with *logos*, and the conclusion with *pathos*.[77] Quintilian (c.35–c.96) remarks that if the appeal to *pathos* is only made in the conclusion without any attempts beforehand, the appeal will be too late.[78] The artistic proofs (*ethos*, *logos* and *pathos*) are related to the domain of invention, and should subsequently be arranged in the most effective order to enhance the process of persuasion. The third step, after the invention and arrangement of proofs, is choosing the appropriate tone and style. For that reason, the different means of persuasion are expected to appear intertwined throughout the speech – although *ethos* is often most prominent in the introduction, *logos* in the main body, and *pathos* in the

---

[74] Kennedy, *Christian and Secular Tradition*, 82.

[75] On the antecedents of Aristotle's three means of persuasion, see William W. Fortenbaugh, "Aristotle on Persuasion Through Character," *Rhetorica* 10 (1992): 211–20.

[76] Aristotle, *Rhet.* I.2.3

[77] This idea returns in the Roman rhetoricians, albeit less strictly formulated; see Manfred Kraus, "Ethos as a Technical Means of Persuasion in Ancient Rhetorical Theory," in *Rhetoric, Ethic, and Moral Persuasion in Biblical Discourse: Essays from the 2002 Heidelberg Conference*, ed. Thomas H. Olbricht and Anders Eriksson, ESEC 11 (New York: T&T Clark, 2005), 85.

[78] Quintilian, *Inst.* IV.2.115; cf. *Inst.* IV.1.23–32.

conclusion. This overview shows that classical rhetoric is a whole system of education in the art of persuasion, in which pupils were often trained from their youth. They were educated in a practical discipline, which would most likely be reflected in their writings on a both conscious and subconscious level, because of their frequent training in using rhetorical features. For that reason, it is possible to infer with some degree of certainty from an author's actual writings whether he has received a classical rhetorical education or not, even if there is no reliable information about an author's educational background.

The political dimension in the Greek and Roman civilisations is closely related to their structure of education. While a description of the system of rhetorical education might sound quite dry and technical, Peter Brown has firmly and convincingly located the usefulness of the art of rhetoric within the interplay of power and persuasion in the period 300–450.[79] Within the political realities of governing cities, rhetoric had an obvious function. The functioning of bureaucracy and civic life at the local level resulted in a requirement for many formal speeches to take place; for that reason, a rhetorical education was 'a saleable commodity'.[80] Demonstration of *paideia* was an essential way in which civic elites interacted with each other. In many cases, when bishops rose in prominence, they integrated into this system quite well – albeit with some modifications. In the Eastern part of the Roman Empire, the fourth century marked a significant shift of power from the local governments to the centralised government in Constantinople. This shift in power affected the autonomy of individual town councils to a significant extent. Nevertheless, local officials were still powerful, not so much as the independent elites of cities, but in the capacity of being necessary to execute imperial decrees.[81] Roman governors ran the risk of being isolated after any future changes in political realities. This situation resulted in

---

[79] Peter Brown, *Power and Persuasion in Late Antiquity. Towards a Christian Empire* (Madison, WI: University of Wisconsin Press, 1992), 3–34.

[80] Averil Cameron, *The Later Roman Empire, AD 284–430* (Cambridge, MA: Harvard University Press, 1993), 152.

[81] Brown, *Power and Persuasion*, 14–15, 19–25.

a 'strictly delimited, but constant, role for the use of a language of persuasion. (...) Rhetoric transposed the creaking of an unwieldy political organism into elevating, classical music.'[82] Most of all, rhetoric became a tool by which victorious factions celebrated their victories.

Peter Brown stresses the fact that there was hardly any protection from violence in late antiquity. Effective use of persuasion to appease other parties offered protection, albeit minimal, against violence. At least in theory, persuasion was emphasised as influencing people with words over against using violence to achieve the desired end. Thus, *paideia* was not just about persuasion, but also a 'school of courtesy'.[83] Robert Flower outlines the relevance of rhetoric and the epideictic genre for politics in the Roman Empire. While the panegyric might sound empty and could be considered at times a case of dishonest flattery, with the predefined *topoi* that a panegyric should address, Flower argues that the importance of panegyric 'stretched far beyond the individual words spoken'. In a society with regularly changing power dynamics, it enabled the elite 'to retain authority' even when linked to previous rulers that had fallen into disgrace. For that reason, panegyric, and rhetoric in general, preserved a 'political currency' over the course of several centuries.[84]

Access to literacy and rhetorical education was not available to the masses in antiquity; only the privileged elite was able to offer the training by grammarians and rhetors to their offspring.[85] This *paideia* was an important qualification to be able to claim leadership in cities. There are a few examples of lower-class, uneducated persons having successful careers, but these were exceptions. Social mobility for persons with a less privileged background was only possible with patronage from wealthy benefactors.[86] Access to governing positions in the fourth-century Roman administration was commonly closely connected to a classical

---

[82] Brown, *Power and Persuasion*, 30.
[83] Brown, *Power and Persuasion*, 45.
[84] Flower, *Late Roman Invective*, 39–40.
[85] Brown, *Power and Persuasion*, 37.
[86] Brown, *Power and Persuasion*, 39.

upbringing and good education. Education created an effective form of social distance and prevention of social mobility between the ruling elite and the less privileged masses; only those who could afford it were able to be educated in the traditional Greek way. This education generated a great deal of homogeneity and recurrent patterns of rhetoric among the ruling elite. By accommodating to conventional forms of classical education and using classical references that only other equally well-educated persons would recognise, the upper classes found an important practical tool in *paideia*.[87] *Paideia* had the potential to unite 'potentially conflicting segments of society'.[88] The educational system ensured that the representative of the Roman government could still identify with those from the local elite as equals, even though the role of the Roman government had shifted significantly. It also aided communication throughout the Roman empire and instilled a sense of local pride, as learned men could still imagine being heirs of a more glorious and autonomous past.[89] When Christian bishops entered the scene as important notables of the city, they did not, typically, break with tradition and the dynamics of *paideia*, although there were some significant modifications.

Use of Rhetoric in Biblical Studies and Patristics

This analysis of the function of rhetoric in the fourth century has significance for understanding the role of classical rhetoric in early Christianity. There is hardly any evidence that Christians aspired to replace classical education with a Christian education.[90] In fact, several church fathers are very well known in the history of rhetoric. Augustine, with his contribution in his *On Christian Doctrine*, as well as Gregory of Nazianzus and John Chrysostom with their eloquence (the art of speaking well), are among the most famous Christian rhetoricians.[91] More generally,

---

[87] Flower, *Late Roman Invective*, 35.

[88] Brown, *Power and Persuasion*, 38–39.

[89] Brown, *Power and Persuasion*, 40–41.

[90] Marrou, *History of Education*, 314–29.

[91] Kennedy, *New History*, 265–70; Kennedy, *Greek Rhetoric*, 215–55, esp. 255. See further Andreas Spira, "The Impact of Christianity on Ancient

bishops were often incorporated into the ruling elite of towns, thereby importantly adjusting the set of expectations as regards the ruling elite. Brown even claims that numerous 'Christian bishops owed their prestige in society at large to the fact that they once had been rhetors'.[92] For that reason, there is a large degree of continuity between pagan classical rhetoricians and Christian rhetors. At the same time, there are variations among fourth-century Christians in this regard. Flower balances these aspects in his judgment on Christian bishops. It is clear that, even when challenging aspects from 'pagan' *paideia,* 'they did so from within a shared late-antique culture where its value was widely recognised, rather than as inhabitants of a hermetically sealed 'Christian community' that did not engage with the traditions of education in the rest of the Roman world.'[93]

A great deal of continuity between classical *paideia* and Christian *paideia* is evident. However, this needs some qualification.[94] While it is obvious that Christians were not isolated from their surrounding society and its educational system, Henrik Rydell Johnsén has argued that not every school in antiquity pursued the same aim with *paideia.* While no one doubted the usefulness of studying under the grammatist and grammarian, Epicurean and Cynic philosophers highly prioritised studying morality at the expense of studying rhetoric. This hesitance to embrace rhetoric as the queen of subjects entailed a criticism of the ideal of *paideia.*[95]

Rhetoric," in *StPatr* 18,2, ed. Elizabeth A. Livingstone (Kalamazoo, MI: Cistercian, 1989), 137–53.

[92] Brown, *Power and Persuasion,* 75.

[93] Flower, *Late Roman Invective,* 16.

[94] Marrou, *History of Education,* xiii; Cf. Flower, *Late Roman Invective,* 67.

[95] Henrik Rydell Johnsén, "The Virtue of Being Uneducated: Attitudes towards Classical *Paideia* in Early Monasticism and Ancient Philosophy," in *Monastic Education in Late Antiquity: The Transformation of Classical Paideia,* ed. Lillian I. Larsen and Samuel Rubenson (Cambridge; New York: Cambridge University Press, 2018), 226–33; See also Marrou's criticism on learning simply for the sake of studying. Marrou, *History of Education,* 234.

A similar emphasis on the priority of virtue over eloquence as in Epicurean and Cynic circles also appeared during the rise of the monastic movement, a movement in which Athanasius was quite influential.[96] Brown recognises that the monks claimed to be heirs of true *paideia*, thus challenging the model of classical *paideia*.[97] While monks are generally portrayed as illiterate in ancient sources, we find numerous indications that there were many literate and well-educated monks.[98] The claim of illiteracy should therefore be seen in the light of a competing claim to true *paideia*, a reformation of the concept of *paideia* within Christianity, rather than a revolution in which illiteracy would be an end in itself.[99] While many highly rhetorically skilled Christians sympathised with monasticism and its emphasis on illiteracy, such as Augustine in his introduction to *On Christian Doctrine*, they continued to cherish and use their rhetorical skills as well.[100]

The study of classical rhetoric remained a topic of study for Christians for the largest part of Western history. It only fell into general disuse during the 19th century and the first half of the 20th century. The art of rhetoric was largely neglected in biblical and patristic studies, as it was in other disciplines in this period.[101]

---

[96] Rydell Johnsén, "The Virtue of Being Uneducated: Attitudes towards Classical *Paideia* in Early Monasticism and Ancient Philosophy," 226.

[97] Brown, *Power and Persuasion*, 71–73.

[98] Lillian I. Larsen and Samuel Rubenson, eds., *Monastic Education in Late Antiquity: The Transformation of Classical Paideia* (Cambridge; New York: Cambridge University Press, 2018).

[99] Lillian I. Larsen and Samuel Rubenson, eds., "Introduction," in *Monastic Education in Late Antiquity: The Transformation of Classical Paideia* (Cambridge; New York: Cambridge University Press, 2018), 4.

[100] Peter Gemeinhardt, "Translating *Paideia*: Education in the Greek and Latin Versions of the *Life of Antony*," in *Monastic Education in Late Antiquity: The Transformation of Classical Paideia*, ed. Lillian I. Larsen and Samuel Rubenson (Cambridge; New York: Cambridge University Press, 2018), 35–40; See also Brown, *Power and Persuasion*, 71–78.

[101] Burton Lee Mack, *Rhetoric and the New Testament*, Guides to Biblical Scholarship. New Testament series (Minneapolis, MN: Fortress Press, 1990), 12; R. Dean Anderson Jr., *Ancient Rhetorical Theory and Paul*, 2nd

The appearance of the English translation of Chaïm Perelman's and Lucie Olbrecht-Tyteca's *The New Rhetoric* in 1969 marked a significant change within the study of rhetoric. Through this work, many scholars rediscovered the importance of rhetoric in literary texts in general and biblical literature in particular.[102] This work broadened the understanding of argumentation. Argumentation can not only be found in logical treatises but occurs (in a less formal way) in any type of text. Besides that, Muilenburg's Presidential Address to the Society of Biblical Literature in 1968 is seen as a landmark in rhetorical analysis within biblical studies.[103] While Muilenburg related the nature of biblical rhetoric to the study of the Old Testament, others have extended his insights to the study of the New Testament.[104] Although the biblical writers were not motivated by 'distinctively literary considerations', linguistic patterns and precise formulations are meaningful and 'influenced by conventional rhetorical practices'.[105]

Both types within George Kennedy's definitions of classical rhetoric, the historical and the theoretical, have been used within biblical studies. In research with a historical understanding of rhetoric (also known as 'primary' or 'textual' rhetoric), an analysis shows a conscious attempt to relate the biblical texts to the procedures of the Greco-Roman rhetorical tradition. In this type of research, only those texts that were available for the biblical writer can be used in the interpretation of a biblical text. In research with a structural understanding of rhetoric, rhetoric is used as an analytical model that enhances the understanding of the biblical text. A historical relation between the biblical text and the Greco-Roman rhetorical tradition is not necessary in this

---

ed., Contributions to Biblical Exegesis and Theology 18 (Leuven: Peeters, 1999), 17–21.

[102] Chaïm Perelman and Lucie Olbrechts-Tyteca, *The New Rhetoric: A Treatise on Argumentation*, trans. J. Wilkinson and P. Weaver (Notre Dame, IN: University of Notre Dame Press, 1969) translation of *La nouvelle rhétorique: traité de l'argumentation*, published in 1958.

[103] James Muilenburg, "Form Criticism and Beyond," *JBL* 88 (1969): 1–18.

[104] See e.g. Mack, *Rhetoric*.

[105] Muilenburg, "Form Criticism," 7, 18.

type of research. The first type, textual rhetorical analysis, tries to determine the sources that a given author has used, or at least traces such conventions to elicit the understanding of an ancient text. By contrast, structural rhetoric aims to clarify the understanding of any text, whether ancient or modern.[106] Concerning this structural model, Joachim Classen argues that when elements described in rhetorical handbooks feature in a given text, it may originate 'from four sources: from rhetorical theory (and its deliberate application); from a successful imitation of written or spoken practice; from unconscious borrowing from the practice of others; or from a natural gift for effective speaking or writing'.[107] The latter three traces of rhetorical strategies that Classen enumerates are in his view appropriate for conducting a structural rhetorical analysis.

Within the discipline of rhetorical analysis of the New Testament, the Pauline letters have been subjected to both a textual and structural rhetorical analysis. Hans Dieter Betz assumes that Paul consciously appropriated Greco-Roman rhetorical theory, and holds that Paul might have chosen or omitted certain words on account of advice in rhetorical handbooks.[108] He notes several deviations and problems, but in general he maintains that the Pauline letters can be studied appropriately according to the rhetorical conventions, which are summarised conveniently in modern handbooks.[109] Betz's approach has been criticised for studying rhetoric in relation to Paul in a rather narrow way that does not take into account whether Paul received a rhetorical education, or in what way rhetorical handbooks could illuminate the study

---

[106] Kennedy, *Christian and Secular Tradition*, 2–3; George A. Kennedy, "Historical Survey of Rhetoric," in *Handbook of Classical Rhetoric in the Hellenistic Period, 330 BC-AD 400*, ed. Stanley E. Porter (Boston: Brill, 2001), 5–6; Anderson Jr., *Ancient Rhetorical Theory*, 28–33.

[107] C. Joachim Classen, "St. Paul's Epistles and Ancient Greek and Roman Rhetoric," *Rhetorica* 10 (1992): 323.

[108] See e.g. Hans Dieter Betz, "The Literary Composition and Function of Paul's Letter to the Galatians," *NTS* 21 (1975): 358, 362–64.

[109] Betz, "Literary Composition," 377–79, 356 n.2; the best-known of these handbooks is Lausberg, *Handbook*.

of Paul.[110] Other scholars have analysed the Pauline writings from a structural rhetorical perspective, with rather modest assumptions about Paul's or others' rhetorical education.[111] This has produced fruitful investigations into the function of one of the three means of persuasion in biblical writings. Three subsequent collections of essays concern the use of *ethos*,[112] *logos*[113] and *pathos*[114] in biblical texts. This shows that rhetorical analysis of ancient works is possible, even if it is uncertain to what extent ancient authors received a conscious rhetorical education. At the same time, since rhetoric was strongly tied up with *paideia*, it is equally clear that the writings of those trained in rhetoric would also show traces of such an education.

STUDIES ON ATHANASIUS' RELATION TO RHETORIC

Since we have established that rhetoric and education are closely related, it is vital to pose the question of Athanasius' relation to rhetoric and rhetorical education. This will decide whether a historical or structural rhetorical analysis is more suited to Athanasius' works.

Studies on Athanasius' Rhetorical Education

In the 19th century, several studies traced a significant impact of rhetorical education and classical rhetoric on Athanasius. In *Studies of Arianism*, Henry Melvill Gwatkin claims, with reference to

---

[110] Cf. Classen, "St. Paul's Epistles," 343.

[111] Cf. George A. Kennedy, *New Testament Interpretation through Rhetorical Criticism*, Studies in Religion (Chapel Hill: University of North Carolina Press, 1984), 9.

[112] Thomas H. Olbricht and Anders Eriksson, eds, *Rhetoric, Ethic, and Moral Persuasion in Biblical Discourse: Essays from the 2002 Heidelberg Conference*, ESEC 11 (New York: T&T Clark, 2005).

[113] Anders Eriksson, Thomas H. Olbricht, and Walter G. Übelacker, eds, *Rhetorical Argumentation in Biblical Texts. Essays from the Lund 2000 Conference*, ESEC 8 (Harrisburg, PA: Trinity Press International, 2002).

[114] Thomas H. Olbricht and Jerry L. Sumney, eds, *Paul and Pathos*, SBLSymS 16 (Atlanta, GA: SBL, 2001).

the works of Eugène Fialon[115] and John Henry Newman,[116] that Athanasius' works show references to Plato, Homer, Aristotle and Demosthenes.[117] Many of those traces of rhetorical education stem from *CA* IV, nowadays unanimously considered to be pseudonymously attributed to Athanasius.[118] With the acceptance of the pseudonimity of *CA* IV or because of the general tendency to neglect rhetorical studies, nothing had been published until the 1970s about Athanasius' use of and training in rhetoric.

Since that time, other scholars have again discussed Athanasius' possible rhetorical education. Some indications of rhetorical education are identified by Stead and Kennedy. Stead demonstrates the potential rhetorical influence in Athanasius' work by showing that all 28 topics in Aristotle's *Rhetoric* (2,23) can be found in Athanasius' works. For that reason, he asserts that Athanasius must have been aware of some general rhetorical theory.[119] Gemeinhardt concurs with Stead that the rhetorical theory of *stasis* of the Later Greek Period is visible in Athanasius' works, but he deems it unlikely that Athanasius used rhetorical theory consciously.[120] George A. Kennedy describes Athanasius in relation to dialectics, which is the discipline that enables one to arrive at the truth by the exchange of logical arguments. He accepts Gregory of Nazianzus' comment that Athanasius studied philosophy and

---

[115] Eugène Fialon, *Saint Athanase. Étude littéraire suivie de l'Apologie à l'empereur Constance et de l'Apologie de sa fuite traduites en français* (Paris: E. Thorin, 1877).

[116] Athanasius, *Select Treatises of S. Athanasius, in Controversy with the Arians*, trans. John Henry Newman (Oxford: J.H. Parker, 1844), 501.

[117] Gwatkin, *Studies of Arianism*, 72–73. For references to Demosthenes, Gwatkin refers to Fialon, *Saint Athanase*, 285. These parallels are traced in *Apol. ad Const.*

[118] Markus Vinzent, *Pseudo-Athanasius, Contra Arianos IV. Eine Schrift gegen Asterius von Kappadokien, Eusebius von Cäsarea, Markell von Ankyra und Photin von Sirmium*, VCSup 36 (Leiden: Brill, 1996).

[119] Christopher Stead, "Rhetorical Method in Athanasius," *VC* 30 (1976): 126–28.

[120] Peter Gemeinhardt, "B.II.1 Herkunft, Jugend und Bildung," in *Athanasius Handbuch*, ed. Peter Gemeinhardt (Tübingen: Mohr Siebeck, 2011), 80–81.

considers it likely that Athanasius studied rhetoric as well.[121] Kennedy describes him as 'the best example of a consistent attempt to apply dialectic to Christian disputation'.[122] However, Athanasius is also a 'skilled dialectician' who misrepresents his opponents and often argues in a technically invalid way. According to Kennedy, Athanasius often employs the plain style and common figures of speech in his writings. His work might further reflect influences of classical encomia, structural principles of panegyric, and 'some signs of familiarity with progymnasmatic forms, such as the chreia and the prosopopoeia'.[123] Nonetheless, Kennedy describes Athanasius as 'antirhetorical' and 'anti-intellectual' because of the portrayal of Antony as having 'little use of rhetoric'.[124] Kennedy is thus both critical and appreciative in his evaluation of Athanasius' use of classical rhetoric. He sees Athanasius as a contributor to the Christian adoption of classical 'techniques of invention, but not of arrangement and style'.[125] Along the same lines, P. F. Bouter affirms that Athanasius' works do not show many rhetorical elements; he argues that Athanasius focuses on the message and therefore did not make use of rhetorical elements.[126]

This last remark betrays a certain conception of rhetoric, with strong emphasis on the stylistic element of rhetoric. As demonstrated above, a major part of the discipline of rhetoric through the ages concerns the effective communication of the content of the message. Style is often seen as one of the means to accomplish that purpose. For this reason, the classical rhetorical

---

[121] Kennedy, *Greek Rhetoric*, 208.

[122] Kennedy, *Greek Rhetoric*, 208.

[123] Kennedy, *Greek Rhetoric*, 210.

[124] Kennedy, *Greek Rhetoric*, 211–12.

[125] Kennedy, *Greek Rhetoric*, 255.

[126] 'Het rethorische [sic!] element treedt bij Athanasius op de achtergrond; alles staat in dienst van het doorgeven van de boodschap.' [The rhetorical element stays in the background in Athanasius; everything serves the purpose of passing on the message.] P. F. Bouter, *Athanasius van Alexandrië en zijn uitleg van de Psalmen: een onderzoek naar de hermeneutiek en theologie van een psalmverklaring uit de vroege kerk* (Zoetermeer: Boekencentrum, 2001), 29.

tradition cannot be reduced to a concern for eloquence, separated from the aim to communicate effectively. Nevertheless, although some clues to Athanasius' possible rhetorical education might be discovered in his works, such an education was limited at best.

In 1974, Robert W. Smith published a work on the art of rhetoric in Alexandria, in which he discussed Athanasius' homilies. Smith characterised Athanasius mainly as someone who relies 'on philosophic and argumentative reasons' instead of stylistic devices, and whose sermons lack vivifying illustrations or images, and are quite ill-structured and weak in adjustment to an occasion or audience.[127] Thus, Athanasius' homilies are adjudged to be of low rhetorical quality. In line with Smith, Stead does not evaluate Athanasius' use of rhetoric favourably either: although Athanasius' theology 'may be correct' and the way he describes his theology 'is impressive', his method is 'indefensible' and contains invalid and 'Mosaic' arguments – 'Mosaic' in the sense that he attacks an isolated proposition of his opponents, instead of considering 'ones opponent's case as a whole'.[128] Kennedy agrees with this evaluation: he blames Athanasius for putting words in his opponent's mouth and presenting dilemmas of which neither alternative 'would be acceptable to an intelligent Arian'.[129] Moreover, he argues that Athanasius blames his opponents in any case: if the Arians appeal to Scripture, Athanasius accuses them of blasphemy; if they appeal to reason, he accuses them of being unscriptural.[130] Other critical evaluations have been offered by Barnes and Gemeinhardt. Barnes criticises Stead's analysis of the correspondence between Aristotle's rhetorical topics and Athanasius' work. Although Athanasius' works contain similarities to Aristotle's work, he most likely did not consciously use 'traditional rhetorical methods'. Barnes argues that a comparison between Athanasius' style (i.e. use of rhetorical devices) and that of

---

[127] Robert Smith, *The Art of Rhetoric in Alexandria: Its Theory and Practice in the Ancient World* (The Hague: Martinus Nijhoff, 1974), 101–5, here 101.

[128] Stead, "Rhetorical Method," 135.

[129] Kennedy, *Greek Rhetoric*, 210.

[130] Kennedy, *Greek Rhetoric*, 210.

contemporary Christians excludes the possibility of an upbringing in classical culture.[131] At this point it is important to distinguish between the two types of rhetoric, namely that of conscious imitation and that of structural rhetoric. Examples of similarity to classical rhetorical models are not found in the studies mentioned above, but the topic of possible hidden motives in Athanasius' works is hotly discussed by the same scholars.

While Athanasius' rhetorical education is doubted or considered limited, the importance of the Christian Scriptures for his work as a means of persuasion is commonly acknowledged. The influence of Scripture on Athanasius' work and Athanasius' effective persuasion through the use of common sense are affirmed by Barnes and Gemeinhardt. According to Barnes, Athanasius' style seems to be more influenced by the Scriptures than by the classical rhetorical tradition, and therefore he excludes conscious influence of Greek rhetorical culture on Athanasius' works: 'the matrix of Athanasius' mind was and remained biblical'.[132] Moreover, he estimates that Athanasius perceived himself as 'the product of a Christian, primarily biblical, education'.[133] Gemeinhardt also points to the relative absence of citations of classics and concludes that the impression of Athanasius' lack of orientation to classical works is confirmed by the style of *Apology before Constantius, Defence of his Flight* and *History of the Arians*. Following Barnes, he notes that Athanasius did not employ a deliberate and conscious art, but instead made use of native wit and argumentative models from Scripture.[134] While Gemeinhardt remarks that some more information about Athanasius' (pagan) rhetorical education might be deduced from his writings, the impression remains that the Bible is Athanasius' 'primärer Bildungsgegenstand und Fundament seiner Argumentation'.[135]

---

[131] Barnes, *Athanasius and Constantius*, 11–12 and n.13.
[132] Barnes, *Athanasius and Constantius*, 126, cf. 64.
[133] Barnes, *Athanasius and Constantius*, 11.
[134] B.II.1.3 Gemeinhardt, *Athanasius Handbuch*, 80; see Barnes, *Athanasius and Constantius*, 126.
[135] Gemeinhardt, *Athanasius Handbuch*, 81.

However, Gemeinhardt has more recently written an article that sheds more light on Athanasius' view on education as well. Although Athanasius presents Antony as illiterate, Gemeinhardt asserts that Athanasius does not promote the absence of education, but rather 'an elaborate concept of ascetic education that integrated not only the abilities of reading and writing but even some elements of Classical *paideia*'.[136] This throws a different light on the question of Athanasius' education. Undoubtedly, the *Life of Antony* was instrumental for the spread of monasticism and its radical challenge to the ideal of classical *paideia*, by promoting 'illiteracy'. The *Life of Antony* soon became immensely popular and was translated into multiple languages of Christian areas.[137] Furthermore, Athanasius – unknowingly – started a new literary genre of hagiography by authoring the *Life of Antony*.[138] For that reason, Athanasius seems most likely not extensively educated in rhetorical theory, but he was able to be persuasive nonetheless.

Robert Flower has a more optimistic outlook on the matter of Athanasius' education. In his study on Late Roman invective, he discusses Athanasius' *History of the Arians* at length, as well as works of Hilary of Poitiers and Lucifer. Flower argues that there are clear traces of rhetorical indebtedness in their works, including that of Athanasius, by stating that 'their methods of praise and blame were highly traditional, retaining recognisably classical categories of assessment and schoolroom rhetorical commonplaces. No one familiar with the conventions of panegyric or invective could fail to recognise that these were engagements with the late-antique language of imperial power.' However, he simultaneously claims that Athanasius replaced classical literature with content from the Christian Scriptures, which was a significant break with the custom of *paideia*.[139] All in all, this would leave

---

[136] Gemeinhardt, "Translating *Paideia*," 35.

[137] Gemeinhardt, "Translating *Paideia*," 34–35; For the critical edition of *Life of Antony*, see Athanasius, *Vie d'Antoine*, ed. G. J. M. Bartelink, SC 400 (Paris: Cerf, 1994).

[138] Paul van Geest, "'...seeing that for monks the life of Antony is a sufficient pattern of discipline.' Athanasius as Mystagogue in his Vita Antonii," *CHRC* 90.2–3 (2010): 200.

[139] Flower, *Late Roman Invective*, 18.

more room for the possibility of classical rhetorical training. Nevertheless, since classical literature is replaced with the language of Scripture, it is clear that Athanasius' works feature limited elements of appeal to a shared *paideia* with pagan contemporaries. Flower's contribution clarifies that traces of *paideia* in Athanasius' works are likely to be found modified. This might well have happened under the influence of the counterclaim to true *paideia* as found in monasticism, not only contemporary to Athanasius, but even actively promoted in his *Life of Antony*.

On the whole, it seems beyond doubt that Athanasius' style and argumentation are primarily influenced by the Scriptures, more than by classical *paideia*. The remarks by Stead and Barnes help us to expect less from Athanasius' arrangement and style, but Kennedy's and Flower's remarks leave an opening to investigate Athanasius' rhetorical method. Since recent studies on Athanasius regularly trace motives in his works that are different from the issues described by Athanasius himself, this would rather call for structural rhetorical analysis. While his works are not closely modelled after classical rhetoric, he was able to convey his message quite well. In this sense, his works contain a host of rhetorical strategies.

Rhetorical Strategies Traced in Athanasius' Work

So, while it is difficult to establish the extent of Athanasius' classical rhetorical education, several scholars have paid attention to the rhetorical strategies in Athanasius' work in order to assess the persuasiveness of his writings. Vladimir Kharlamov has published an article on the rhetorical application of deification (*theosis*) in Greek patristic theology.[140] He argues that Athanasius skilfully employed *theosis* language as a rhetorical tool, and he is generally appreciative of Athanasius' rhetorical style.[141] This style is not conscious conformity to classical rhetorical handbooks, but,

---

[140] Vladimir Kharlamov, "Rhetorical Application of Theosis in Greek Patristic Theology," in *Partakers of the Divine Nature*, ed. Michael J. Christensen and Jeffery A. Wittung (Grand Rapids, MI: Baker Academic, 2008), 115–31.

[141] Kharlamov, "Rhetorical Application," 119.

nonetheless, he regards Athanasius' work as persuasive 'because of his oratorical skills and rather unsophisticated but very reassuring and repetitive style, which would capture the imagination of a popular audience'.[142]

Khaled Anatolios has also paid attention to Athanasius' successful rhetorical strategy. In a paper published in 2006, he traces a 'coherent strategy' in Athanasius' *Orations*. He argues that Athanasius is not just caricaturing Arius' and Asterius' positions, but is also engaging with their theology. Although his opponents present their argument in a subtler way than Athanasius suggests, the Alexandrian bishop rightly attacks them for separating the divine Word and Wisdom from the Son.[143] Anatolios reiterates this conclusion in his 2011 monograph as he traces a 'rhetorical-exegetical strategy' in Athanasius' work.[144] He calls Athanasius 'prolix in his literary style', but also strategic in his silences and in his positioning in the ongoing fourth-century debate.[145] He further discerns in the *Orations* 'a certain logic' with a 'rhetorical force' albeit not 'a logic of pure objective reason but a scriptural logic'.[146] He unfolds the logical and polemical elements of Athanasius' work and is aware that such a description is not commonplace in research on Athanasius; to discover an 'inherent logic' in Athanasius' theology of divine names is 'something of a novelty'.[147] Anatolios sees in Athanasius' 'polemical deconstruction of his opponent's teaching' a serious encounter, in which Athanasius engages with fundamental issues between himself and his opponents.[148] Anatolios' judgment, therefore, deviates from Stead, who views Athanasius' arguments as artificial and highly selective, and says that they often misrepresent his opponents.[149] It is clear

---

[142] Kharlamov, "Rhetorical Application," 122.

[143] Khaled Anatolios, "'When Was God without Wisdom?' Trinitarian Hermeneutics and Rhetorical Strategy in Athanasius," in *StPatr* 41, ed. F. Young, M. Edwards, and P. Parvis (Leuven: Peeters, 2006), 123.

[144] Anatolios, *Retrieving Nicaea*, 84.

[145] Anatolios, *Retrieving Nicaea*, 100, 102, 109.

[146] Anatolios, *Retrieving Nicaea*, 111.

[147] Anatolios, *Retrieving Nicaea*, 110–111.

[148] Anatolios, *Retrieving Nicaea*, 116.

[149] Stead, "Rhetorical Method," 135–36.

that Anatolios sees problematic elements in Athanasius' reasoning, but at the same time he points to the inherent logic of Athanasius' argumentation.[150] He thus discerns rhetorical motives in Athanasius' style and content of argumentation. In a recent article, Anatolios has elaborated on the strategic nature of Athanasius' work by demonstrating the subtle nuances of Athanasius' attitude towards Arius, Asterius and Marcellus, and showing that he often implicitly borrows arguments from others or silently criticises a position that he could not attack openly. Athanasius positioned himself 'carefully in the complex debates of the early 340s, even while reducing this complexity to a simplicity more amenable to public consumption'.[151] Athanasius simplifies the theological debate out of a catechetical approach, but shows 'to his more knowledgeable readers that he is entirely *au courant* with the diversity and complexity of the current debates'.[152]

Altogether, it seems that Athanasius was not thoroughly trained in rhetorical education and did not consciously use classical rhetorical models. His works do not show clear and consistent traces of indebtedness to classical rhetorical models. Therefore, I propose to investigate Athanasius' works from a structural rhetorical point of view, rather than perform a historical rhetorical analysis.

FOCUS OF THIS RESEARCH

Up till now, Athanasius' rhetoric has been analysed mainly from a textual rhetorical perspective with relatively limited results. Previous investigations demonstrated that Athanasius received hardly any formal rhetorical education; conscious use and

---

[150] 'Athanasius moves quickly from a logical statement of his argument to its rhetorical dramatization in scriptural idiom.' Anatolios, *Retrieving Nicaea*, 120, cf. 84.

[151] Khaled Anatolios, "'Christ the Power and Wisdom of God': Biblical Exegesis and Polemical Intertextuality in Athanasius's *Orations against the Arians*," *JECS* 21 (2013): 533.

[152] Anatolios, "Power and Wisdom of God" 535; cf. E. P. Meijering, *Athanasius: Die dritte Rede gegen die Arianer. Einleitung, Übersetzung, Kommentar*, 3 vols. (Amsterdam: Gieben, 1996–1998), I:16–20.

imitation of rhetorical models are lacking in his works. Nevertheless, a structural analysis of his use of rhetoric remains promising for the present research. A structural rhetorical perspective on one or more of the Aristotelian means of persuasion, i.e. *ethos*, *logos* and *pathos*, has been performed to analyse biblical writings with promising results. These analyses were performed without the necessity of knowing the rhetorical education of any of these authors, just like it is the case with Athanasius. For that reason, this research will use two of Aristotle's means of persuasion to study Athanasius' works from a rhetorical perspective, *ethos* and *logos*. The third, *pathos*, will be excluded from the analysis, for reasons that will be outlined in the conceptual framework.

Given the host of different motives that are ascribed to Athanasius, either theological, political or both, this investigation aims to shed light on the crucial question in the research on Athanasius that awaits a satisfactory answer: how are theological and non-theological elements intertwined in Athanasius' work? Since the *Orations against the Arians* are clearly concerned with theology, but also regarded by more suspicious readers of Athanasius as a crucial document for his construction of Arianism, I will perform this rhetorical analysis on his *Orations against the Arians*. The *Orations* contain crucial elements of Athanasius' theology and were written at a politically crucial moment, during his second exile. They contain theological arguments, but also several literary devices used to attack his opponents. It is, therefore, a suitable work for a rhetorical analysis to shed light on the highly divergent opinions on the relation between the theological and political dimensions of his writings.

The fact that Athanasius shifted quite significantly from the more accepted classical language to a much more scriptural discourse has been noted before. This has led some scholars to frame the Arian controversy in biblical versus logical terms. There is one portion of Scripture that Athanasius cited very frequently. It has long been acknowledged that Athanasius has a special relation to the Gospel of John. T. E. Pollard opens his work on Johannine Christology in the following way:

> At the turn of this century, F. C. Conybeare, in a review of Alfred Loisy's *Le quatrième évangile*, wrote: 'If Athanasius had

not had the Fourth Gospel to draw texts from, Arius would never have been confuted.' That is however only part of the truth, for it would also be true to say that if Arius had not had the Fourth Gospel to draw texts from, he would not have needed confuting.[153]

I would say that both parts, especially the latter, must be qualified, but it shows that Athanasius and his opponents both had a special interest in this Gospel. The present rhetorical analysis will therefore focus on the position of the Gospel of John in Athanasius' *Orations*. James D. Ernest's research has confirmed the prominence of this Gospel in Athanasius' *Orations*. Ernest demonstrated that Athanasius refers more often to the Gospel of John than to any other biblical book in the *Orations against the Arians*.[154] He provided statistical data on Athanasius' use of Scripture in the *Orations*: Athanasius cites or quotes Scripture 1247 times; the Gospel of John accounts for 302 of those references, which is 24% of the total. The Psalms, Proverbs, Matthew and Hebrews follow, with 122, 115, 114 and 103 references respectively.[155] It is thus legitimate to say that the Gospel of John is the single most used book of Scripture within his *Orations*. Moreover, since Athanasius' use of the Gospel of John is noted by scholars who called Athanasius biblical, it seems most natural to spell out the relation between biblical and logical in his *Orations* by taking a closer look at his usage of John.

Research questions

This study aims to uncover Athanasius' use of the Gospel of John in the *Orations against the Arians*, in order to clarify the interrelation between the concepts of biblical/theological, logical and

---

[153] Pollard, *Johannine Christology*, 3. He refers to Conybeare in *Hibbert Journal* 7 (1903), 620.

[154] Ernest, *Bible*; James D. Ernest, "Athanasian Scripture Citations," in *StPatr* 36, ed. M. F. Wiles and E. J. Yarnold (Leuven: Peeters, 2001), 502–8. This conclusion only pertains to the *Orations against the Arians*, not to all his other works.

[155] I have combined the number of citations and quotations for these numbers. See Ernest, *Bible*, 116–17.

political, by means of a structural rhetorical analysis. To that end, appeals to his own character (*ethos*) and his opponents (negative *ethos*), as well as appeals to the subject matter (*logos*), are analysed. The main question of this research is, therefore: How does Athanasius use the Gospel of John as an ethical and logical means of persuasion in the *Orations against the Arians*?

This research will highlight the role of the Gospel of John in the interplay of ethical and logical means of persuasion and will subsequently discuss the *Orations* I, II and III. In order to discover the particular usage of the Gospel of John as an ethical and logical means of persuasion, this research will also include other relevant material in the *Orations* that contains ethical and logical rhetorical features.

OUTLINE OF THIS MONOGRAPH

This monograph reads Athanasius' use of the Gospel of John in the *Orations against the Arians* from a structural rhetorical perspective. It has been established that Athanasius' rhetorical education is limited at most, but a structural rhetorical perspective might, from another angle, shed light on the conformity of his works with rhetorical theory. The special role of Scripture, and particularly the Gospel of John in his *Orations*, has long been noted. The research question has been formulated to uncover the relationship between the Gospel of John and the means of persuasion in Athanasius' work.

To answer the research question, chapter 2 will present a conceptual framework. I will define and clarify the concepts of the means of persuasion, *ethos*, negative *ethos* and *logos*, as well as my understanding of the Christology of the Gospel of John. Some general remarks concerning method and procedure will follow. Chapter 3 will discuss various elements that illuminate the understanding of the context, setting and audience of Athanasius' *Orations* and his exegetical method. In chapters 4–6, *Orations* I through III are discussed respectively. The pervasive importance of the Gospel of John underlying his argument will become clear, as well as his polemical attacks on his opponents. The conclusion will answer the main question and synthesise the results from the previous chapters.

Chapter Two.
Conceptual Framework

This chapter discusses the conceptual framework and methodology of this study. I will deal with two main concepts that need clarification in order to analyse Athanasius' *Orations against the Arians*: (1) the means of persuasion within the system of rhetoric, and (2) the Christology of the Gospel of John within this research. I will conclude with some general methodological remarks.

The Means of Persuasion

First of all, I will clarify the role of the means of persuasion in this study. In the historical development of the means of persuasion, many different aspects can be outlined, but this section focuses solely on the structural elements that contribute to the analysis in the subsequent chapters.

As I mentioned in the previous chapter, rhetorical theory generally distinguishes three means of persuasion, *ethos*, *logos*, and *pathos*, corresponding to three main factors in a speech: orator, text and audience.[1] This inquiry will be restricted to two of the means of persuasion, *ethos* (related to the orator) and *logos* (related to the subject matter). It is often impossible to draw a clear-cut distinction between different means of persuasion, because of their complex interrelation in actual speeches and

---

[1] George A. Kennedy, "The Genres of Rhetoric," in *Handbook of Classical Rhetoric in the Hellenistic Period, 330 BC–AD 400*, ed. Stanley E. Porter (Boston: Brill, 2001), 43–50.

writings.[2] Nevertheless, they are valuable tools that contribute to the understanding of the *Orations against the Arians*. The means of persuasion *pathos* will be excluded in this study. The audience that Athanasius imagined when writing the *Orations* must be wholly inferred from the text. Ethical and logical persuasiveness can be gauged from the words of the text, but the effect of his words on the audience cannot. Furthermore, because Athanasius did not receive any thorough rhetorical education, it is more difficult to apply the classical rhetorical theory concerning *pathos* to his work.

Ethos

Ethos is related to the trustworthiness of the speaker. Aristotle argues that an orator should use *ethos* as a technical proof (ethical proof) to 'appear prudent and good', even in front of an unknown audience.[3] 'Ethical proof' is thus formed by *ethos* (character or personality) within the speech. It is the means of persuasion that establishes the trustworthiness of the orator within the speech or written text, and is not established by a preconceived reputation.[4] Persuasion through character occurs when the orator is able to present himself as trustworthy (ἀξιόπιστος) and fair-minded (ἐπιεικής), for such people are trusted to a greater extent; Aristotle

---

[2] James L. Kinneavy and Susan C. Warshauer, "From Aristotle to Madison Avenue: *Ethos* and the Ethics of Argument," in *Ethos: New Essays in Rhetorical and Critical Theory*, ed. James S. Baumlin and Tita French Baumlin, SMU Studies in Composition and Rhetoric (Dallas: Southern Methodist University Press, 1994), 179.

[3] *Rhet.* II.1.7; cf. *Rhet.* I.2.4 and the comments of Kennedy, *Aristotle. On Rhetoric. A Theory of Civic Discourse. Translated with Introduction, Notes and Appendices*, 2nd ed. (New York: Oxford University Press, 2007), 22, 148–49; on the difference between Aristotle and Isocrates, see James S. Baumlin, "Introduction: Positioning *Ethos* in Historical and Contemporary Theory," in *Ethos: New Essays in Rhetorical and Critical Theory*, ed. James S. Baumlin and Tita French Baumlin, SMU Studies in Composition and Rhetoric (Dallas: Southern Methodist University Press, 1994), xi–xvii; Kennedy, *Christian and Secular Tradition*, 82.

[4] Cf. Aristotle, *Rhet.* I.2.3 and Antoine C. Braet, "Ethos, Pathos and Logos in Aristotle's Rhetoric: A Re-Examination," *Argumentation* 6 (1992): 311.

calls persuasion through *ethos* 'almost ... the most authoritative form of persuasion'.[5] Since the first impression is crucial to winning trust, rhetorical handbooks emphasise the importance of an appeal to *ethos* in the introduction of a speech. Although Aristotle suggests using appeals to *ethos* throughout a speech, and not only in the introduction, he acknowledges that the introduction is a convenient place to make readers well disposed and benevolent towards an orator.[6]

Aristotle states that people become convinced by three elements in a speaker's character: good sense (φρόνησις), moral character (ἀρετή) and good will (εὔνοια).[7] James L. Kinneavy and Susan C. Warshauer interpret these Aristotelian concepts as follows. Good sense is the 'ability to make practical decisions', which is displayed by 'self-assurance and expertise of the speaker'.[8] A good orator shows these characteristics by understanding the subject matter, the interests of one's audience, and the situation at hand.[9]

Moral character is established when orators show 'that they are sincere and trustworthy' and that they possess virtues like justice and courage.[10] Demonstration of *paideia* – proper classical education – would be one aspect of showing moral character. References to a common education often functioned to establish links between those who shared membership of the educated elite.[11] Another crucial virtue to display in this respect is *parrēshia*, boldness to speak the truth. This virtue was associated with philosophers, who were able and willing to speak the truth, even when it meant confrontation with emperors or other powerful persons.[12] Speaking boldly could create the image of being in

---

[5] Aristotle, *Rhet.* I.2.4; tr. Kennedy.

[6] Cf. *Rhet.* III.14 and Kennedy, *Aristotle*, 234.

[7] Aristotle, *Rhet.* II.1.5–7.

[8] Kinneavy and Warshauer, "Aristotle," 178; cf. William W. Fortenbaugh, "Aristotle on Persuasion Through Character," *Rhetorica* 10 (1992): 224–25.

[9] Kinneavy and Warshauer, "Aristotle," 179.

[10] Kinneavy and Warshauer, "Aristotle," 174.

[11] Flower, *Late Roman Invective*, 34–35; Brown, *Power and Persuasion*, 39–40.

[12] Brown, *Power and Persuasion*, 65–70.

possession of *parrhésia* if directed against powerful persons. To speak boldly against 'authority was admired by both the fourth-century pagan elite and the emergent Christian hierarchy'.[13]

Within Christian discourse, knowledge of the proper application of Scripture can regarded as virtue as well. This indirect form of *ethos* can be established by using a certain type of style, the appearance of expertise and sensibility, or through the demonstration of a profound knowledge of Scripture or any other authoritative text.[14] Being in line with Scripture confirms one's trustworthiness and moral character. Ancient rhetoricians would often have considered an appeal to sources outside the realm of the artistic proof of *ethos*. However, within Christianity, it was possible to establish *ethos* on the basis of other parameters than in classical antiquity. This is the case because the mechanism behind those parameters remains the same. Just as references to classical works functioned in the speeches of classical rhetors as a way of presenting themselves as knowledgeable, references to the shared set of Christian Scriptures established a link between those who shared membership of the educated elite, in this case, those with knowledge of the Christian Scriptures.[15]

Good will, which is 'the speaker's display of good intentions toward his or her audience', overlaps slightly in meaning with moral character.[16] An orator should not only possess virtues, or appear to possess them, but he or she must also employ these virtues in the service of the audience. By showing good will (εὔνοια), an orator convinces an audience that the good sense (φρόνησις) and virtue or moral character (ἀρετή) will benefit them. William Fortenbaugh brings both concepts together by pointing out that 'virtue is being immune to all kinds of temptations, and goodwill is proper orientation: that is, wanting the best for the city and its citizens'.[17]

---

[13] Flower, *Late Roman Invective*, 25.

[14] Kinneavy and Warshauer, "Aristotle," 180.

[15] Flower, *Late Roman Invective*, 179–80.

[16] Kinneavy and Warshauer, "Aristotle," 176–78, here 176; Braet, "Ethos, Pathos and Logos," 311–14.

[17] Fortenbaugh, "Aristotle," 222.

Perelman and Olbrechts-Tyteca, the authors of the *New Rhetoric*, supplement Aristotle's category of good will with the concept of communion building. It can be effective for a speaker to refer to a common milieu, culture, tradition or past.[18] Whereas judicial and deliberative speeches 'make use of dispositions already present in the audience', in an epideictic speech 'the sharing of values is an end pursued independently of the precise circumstances in which this communion will be put to the test'.[19] In this case, an orator needs to have some authority already, because his words can be very effective in presenting and bringing into existence the communion, which has not yet been clearly articulated before. Via *ethos*, an orator can both appeal to common values and in a sense 'create' them. At this point, the concept of *ethos* comes close to *pathos*, which is focused on the audience as such, but I analyse it under the heading of *ethos* since it is Athanasius' attempt to connect to his audience.

Perelman and Olbrechts-Tyteca discuss several rhetorical figures: 'modes of expression which are different from ... ordinary' usage.[20] They focus primarily on the argumentative effects of these rhetorical figures, in contrast to authors that focus on the stylistic effects of rhetorical figures.[21] Modes of expression, also known as figures, are intended to induce feelings of choice, presence and communion with an orator. An author or orator often urges listeners to make a choice. The selection of data presented to an audience is crucial in argumentation, but also in winning the trust of listeners. This selection is crucial because it enables an orator to emphasise certain elements over others, thus bringing into presence the elements that he wishes to be highlighted. Perelman and Olbrechts-Tyteca state:

---

[18] Chaïm Perelman and Lucie Olbrechts-Tyteca, *The New Rhetoric: A Treatise on Argumentation*, trans. J. Wilkinson and P. Weaver (Notre Dame, IN: University of Notre Dame Press, 1969), 47–54, 163–79; cf. Richard Graff and Wendy Winn, "Presencing 'Communion' in Chaim Perelman's New Rhetoric," *Philosophy and Rhetoric* 39 (2006): 54–57.

[19] Perelman and Olbrechts-Tyteca, *New Rhetoric*, 53.

[20] Perelman and Olbrechts-Tyteca, *New Rhetoric*, 167.

[21] Perelman and Olbrechts-Tyteca, *New Rhetoric*, 172.

By the very fact of selecting certain elements and presenting
them to the audience, their importance and pertinency to the
discussions are implied. Indeed, such a choice endows these
elements with a presence, which is an essential factor in argumentation and one that is far too much neglected in rationalistic conceptions of reasoning.[22]

An orator's selection causes some elements to be brought into
presence, with the obvious result that other elements of argumentation might be forgotten by an audience or opponents. In communication with an audience, an author can effectively use maxims to move listeners to make a choice. A maxim is a brief expression that contains a general truth or principle. It may take different forms, such as a proverb or a slogan. A proverb is a short
maxim that 'expresses a particular occurrence and at the same
time suggests a standard'.[23] Both proverbs and slogans are designed to be easily remembered and help to secure the attention
of an audience.[24] Their role in persuading an audience is limited;
they are better able to compel attention to certain ideas and to
stimulate actions than to induce beliefs.[25] Maxims are distinguished either by a clearly prescribed structure, or by a use that
deviates from normal usage. Their deployment may follow both
rhetorical theory and the use of common sense; authors or orators
that do not consciously adhere to rhetorical theory employ maxims as well, often with a similar effect.

Figures that are likely to increase the feeling of presence are
repetition, synonymy and imaginary direct speech. These figures
have an emphatic effect. Repetition emphasises the importance of
statements, which strengthens the presence of the words repeated. Synonymy is a special variant of repetition, which contains a degree of stylisation. Imaginary direct speech can either
result in 'fictitious attribution of words to a person (*sermocinatio*)
or to a group of persons engaged in conversation'.[26] In this figure,

---

[22] Perelman and Olbrechts-Tyteca, *New Rhetoric*, 116.

[23] Perelman and Olbrechts-Tyteca, *New Rhetoric*, 166.

[24] Perelman and Olbrechts-Tyteca, *New Rhetoric*, 167.

[25] Perelman and Olbrechts-Tyteca, *New Rhetoric*, 167.

[26] Perelman and Olbrechts-Tyteca, *New Rhetoric*, 174–76, citation 176.

words or concepts are presented from a different angle, so that it can offer a distinctive perspective on a topic. Lausberg remarks that *sermocinatio* (also known as *ethopoeia*) is an emotive figure, which concerns 'the fabrication ... of statements, conversation, soliloquies or unexpressed mental reflections of the persons concerned'.[27] The primary requirement related to the figure of imaginary direct speech is to be in line with the character of the person assumed to be speaking.

Figures relating to communion can be referential in nature, such as allusions to and quotations (if not used to back up a statement) of commonly shared knowledge, such as well-known poets or a sacred text. In this case, the references must relate to something that the orator and audience have in common. If they are applied correctly, an orator wins the trust of an audience. Implicit references functioned both in classical and in Christian *paideia* as a means of connecting the author and the audience; it demarcated the difference between those who were able to grasp the reference and those who could not.[28] Other figures of communion are those that invite listeners to participate in an exposition. This includes the oratorical question, oratorical communication, and the '*enallage of person*'. This last figure consists of a switch between singular and plural, helping the listener to feel part of the exposition. The same effect is reached by a change from 'I' to 'we,' for example if a mother tells a child: 'We are going to bed.'[29] Although figures of choice, presence and communion have a subordinate role, they invite the audience to have confidence in the speaker, and should not be underestimated.[30] Through the speech, listeners must become convinced of the speaker's *ethos* or at least get the impression that he wants the best for them.

---

[27] Heinrich Lausberg, *Handbook of Literary Rhetoric. A Foundation for Literary Study*, trans. Matthew T. Bliss and David E. Orton (Leiden: Brill, 1998), 366–67 (par 820–21).

[28] Flower, *Late Roman Invective*, 16; See also Brown, *Power and Persuasion*, 118–26.

[29] Perelman and Olbrechts-Tyteca, *New Rhetoric*, 177–79, here 178.

[30] Graff and Winn, "Presencing 'Communion,'" 57–66.

In early Christianity, the concept of *ethos* functioned slightly differently compared to Greco-Roman classical rhetoric.[31] For Christians, trustworthiness is not located in an orator's character, but in the conformity between an orator's words and the divine revelation, i.e. Scripture. Many allusions to and quotations of Scripture functions therefore to enhance the credibility of the speaker indirectly.[32] As the *New Rhetoric* suggests, allusion and quotation often have the potential to build communion with an audience. Whenever an appeal to the authoritative Scriptures functions to make the orator trustworthy, it is analysed in ethical terms. Christof Rapp describes the effect of ethical persuasiveness: 'If the speaker appears to be credible, the audience will form the second-order judgment that propositions put forward by the credible speaker are true or acceptable.'[33] Within Christianity, a human orator is ultimately credible because Scripture, i.e. the divine author, guarantees that what is said is true. Indeed, Kennedy remarks that the status of authority within Christianity 'became a nonartistic analogy to ethos in classical rhetoric'.[34] The use of Scripture is therefore considered part of the character building (*ethos*) of an orator as long as it does not function in its role of backing up argumentation with authority.

Negative *Ethos*

Negative *ethos* is the negative counterpart of *ethos*, i.e. the undermining of the trustworthiness of an opponent. In the rhetorical handbooks the undermining of an opponent's trustworthiness is not often understood as an aim in itself. Aristotle is rather reticent on this subject in his *On Rhetoric*. Fortenbaugh gives three reasons why Aristotle did not discuss the attack of an opponent: (1) it

---

[31] Carol Poster, "Ethos, Authority, and the New Testament Canon," in *Rhetoric, Ethic, and Moral Persuasion in Biblical Discourse: Essays from the 2002 Heidelberg Conference*, ed. Thomas H. Olbricht and Anders Eriksson, ESEC 11 (New York: T&T Clark, 2005), 124.

[32] Flower, *Late Roman Invective*, 6.

[33] Christof Rapp, "Aristotle's Rhetoric," *The Stanford Encyclopedia of Philosophy* (Spring 2010 Edition).

[34] Kennedy, *Christian and Secular Tradition*, 138.

might be 'too common a phenomenon to be encouraged', (2) it might turn against the speaker, and (3) Aristotle might have considered *ethos* primarily with a view to the deliberative genre, and not to the judicial.[35] In *Rhet.* III.19.1, Aristotle may refer to the concept of negative *ethos*, when he argues that an epilogue should make a hearer favourably disposed toward the speaker and unfavourably toward the opponent. Although Fortenbaugh holds that this is not proper Aristotelian persuasion through character (*ethos*), Aristotle is aware of the importance of an attack on the opponent.[36]

In Aristotle's works that deal with dialectic, some clues might be found for a concept of negative *ethos*. Dialectic refers to the practice of an argumentative discourse between people that hold different opinions about a subject, with the aim of discovering truth. In Aristotle's time, a dialectical debate consisted of two parties, of which one has the role of questioner and one the role of answerer. In *Topics* VIII 10, Aristotle states that it is possible to prevent the completion of an argument by 'stating an objection to the questioner (for often he does succeed in solving it, but yet the questioner is not able to carry it forward any further)'.[37] In short, Aristotle acknowledges that debaters make use of negative *ethos* as an existing technique, but he considers it unsuitable for deepening one's understanding of truth. This technique is classified by Graciela Marta Chichi as an 'abusive' type of personal attack, which she calls *argumentum ad personam*.[38]

Chichi claims that Aristotle also distinguishes another type of personal attack. In contrast to the deceptive *argumentum ad personam*, aimed at attacking the person, and obstructing the discovery of truth, she asserts that Aristotle also described a form of personal attack that is directed against the coherence of an opponent's opinions. She considers this a non-abusive form of

---

[35] Fortenbaugh, "Aristotle," 230–31.

[36] Fortenbaugh, "Aristotle," 237.

[37] Aristotle, *Topica* VIII 10 (161a2–5); tr. Smith.

[38] Graciela Marta Chichi, "The Greek Roots of the Ad Hominem-Argument," *Argumentation* 16 (2002): 334–35. I would like to thank Dr. J. H. M. Wagemans for drawing my attention to this article.

argument, and considers it the legitimate form of an *argumentum ad hominem*.[39] This type of personal attack does not hinder the discovery of truth. In *On Sophistical Refutations* 15, Aristotle states:

> Moreover, as in rhetorical arguments, so likewise also in refutation, you ought to look for contradictions between the answerer's views and either his own statements or the views of those whose words and actions he admits to be right, or of those who are generally held to bear a like character and to resemble them, or of the majority, or all of mankind.[40]

This argument is directed against the person of the opponent, and as such, *ad hominem*. However, it is clearly distinct from the first attack, because it challenges the coherence of an opponent's viewpoints. According to her perspective on Aristotle, an *argumentum ad hominem* is a legitimate form of negative *ethos* either when it addresses two or more contradictory views of an opponent, or when it demonstrates a disagreement of the opponent with the opinion of someone whom the opponent values in this respect.

The Roman rhetoricians are well aware of the effectiveness of the negative counterpart of *ethos*, of both the *argumentum ad personam* and *argumentum ad hominem*. Cicero states in his mature work *De Oratore*: 'A potent factor in success, then, is for the characters, principles, conduct and course of life, both of those who are to plead cases and of their clients, to be approved, and conversely those of their opponents condemned.'[41] David Marsh attributes the idea of negative *ethos* to the practically orientated Roman rhetoricians. He states that attacks on personal character in '[c]lassical invective sought to denigrate an individual on the basis of birth, upbringing, 'mechanical' professions, moral defects, physical shortcomings, and so on. It was ... aimed at undermining the credibility.'[42] Marsh thus acknowledges that the discrediting of an

---

[39] Chichi, "Greek Roots," 340–42.

[40] Aristotle, *De Sophisticis Elenchis* 15 (174b19–23); tr. Foster.

[41] Cicero, *De Oratore* II. 182; tr. Sutton and Rackham.

[42] David Marsh in the introduction to Francesco Petrarca, *Invectives*, trans. David Marsh, The I Tatti Renaissance Library 11 (Cambridge, MA: Harvard University Press, 2003), xi.

opponent's *ethos* is often effective and is regularly practised. While Aristotle developed clear rules for defending rhetoric as an art (τέχνη), the Roman rhetoricians regarded the discipline as a practical tool to be used.[43] For that reason, notwithstanding the different opinions of rhetoricians on this subject, negative *ethos* is to be expected in texts. This research discusses appeals against the opponent as negative *ethos,* as long as the attack is directed against the character (or caricature) of an opponent. Apart from that, many of the rhetorical devices that contribute to the building of the *ethos* can also be used to construct an opponent's negative *ethos*. This holds true, for example, for the use of maxims: proverbs and slogans can be used for establishing the trustworthiness of an orator, but equally well for attacking the opponent's *ethos*.

Establishing negative *ethos* is closely related to the invective, the counterpart of the panegyric. According to Jacqueline Long, rhetors instructed invective to their students as an inverted form of panegyric, 'with the topics turned into vituperation instead of praise'.[44] However, the function was not exactly the same, because panegyric could be displayed at ceremonial occasions, while invective would not typically be allowed in such a setting. Since occasions for invectives were far more limited than for panegyrics, the number of invectives preserved is also much smaller. However, qua function, they have a clear rhetorical potential. Just as a panegyric is useful to construct authority, the invective is a powerful weapon to undermine it.[45] So, while the construction of negative *ethos* is much less discussed in handbooks than its positive counterpart, the fact that invectives were composed and preserved demonstrates that the force of creating a negative *ethos* of opponents cannot be underestimated.

---

[43] Fortenbaugh, "Aristotle," 236–44.

[44] Jacqueline Long, *Claudian's In Eutropium: Or, How, When, and Why to Slander a Eunuch* (Chapel Hill, NC: University of North Carolina, 1996), 78.

[45] Flower, *Late Roman Invective,* 58.

Negative Ethos *and heresy*

In patristic texts, the concept of negative *ethos* took a prominent shape in invectives to disqualify opponents as heretics. From early on, the need for distinguishing between sound and impious doctrine was felt. While many patristic authors mainly discussed the content of different teachings, there developed a body of polemic literature against the persons who espoused such heresies as well. Irenaeus of Lyon (c.140-c.202) is well-known work for his work *Against the Heresies*. In this work, Irenaeus attacked several heresies by outlining their deviation from the orthodox Christian faith. After him, Tertullian, in particular, established a tradition of polemical works against heretics.[46] Tertullian wrote several works against heretics (*Against Marcion, Against Praxeas, The Prescription Against Heretics*), and others like Hippolytus of Rome (*Refutation of All Heresies*) followed. In these anti-heretical writings, orthodox Christian faith was not only defended but in a sense also created by defining the boundaries of orthodoxy.[47] Most crucial to note at this point, however, is that these works against heretics initiated

---

[46] The word heresy (αἵρεσις) contains a neutral dimension (cf. Acts 24:5, 14), but in the history of Christianity it is mainly used pejoratively. For a recent overview of the history of heresy, see Robert M. Royalty, *The Origin of Heresy: A History of Discourse in Second Temple Judaism and Early Christianity*, Routledge Studies in Religion 18 (New York: Routledge, 2012); See also Alain Le Boulluec, *La notion d'hérésie dans la littérature grecque, IIe-IIIe siècles*, 2 vols., Études augustiniennes 110–11 (Paris: Études Augustiniennes, 1985); J. Rebecca Lyman, "A Topography of Heresy: Mapping the Rhetorical Creation of Arianism," in *Arianism after Arius. Essays on the Development of the Fourth Century Trinitarian Conflicts*, ed. Michel R. Barnes and Daniel H. Williams (Edinburgh: T&T Clark, 1993), 45–62.

[47] Catherine Osborne, "Literal or Metaphorical? Some Issues of Language in the Arian Controversy," in *Christian Faith and Greek Philosophy in Late Antiquity. Essays in Tribute to George Christopher Stead. In Celebration of His Eightieth Birthday 9th April 1993*, ed. Lionel R. Wickham, Caroline P. Hammond Bammel, and Erica C. D. Hunter, VCSup (Leiden: Brill, 1993), 148–50; see also Eduard Iricinschi and Holger M. Zellentin, eds, *Heresy and Identity in Late Antiquity*, Texte und Studien zum antiken Judentum (Tübingen: Mohr Siebeck, 2008).

a tradition of polemics and the creation of negative *ethos* between orthodox Christianity and heretics.[48] In heretical writings, it became commonplace to associate heretics with the devil, negative biblical characters and other types of negative associations.[49] This process did not just involve the labelling and association of heretics with biblical characters; it was a form of literary re-enactment as well. Flower argues that this technique of literary re-enactment goes well beyond labelling because it assumes that theological opponents are 'not only portrayed as harbouring the same beliefs as earlier anti-Christian villains, but also performing the same actions and uttering the same words as them'. In this way, they 'drew very close parallels between the authoritative past and the uncertain present'.[50]

In the fourth century, this polemical attitude does not remain limited to heretical sects; even living emperors that were in power came to be attacked in imperial invectives by several Christian authors. This was a serious break with the classical past, because in general, most invectives 'were composed and published when the political situation made it safe, or even advantageous, to air such opinions'.[51] This was not a general move, but certain Christian authors, including Athanasius, Hilary and Lucifer, deliberately chose to 'break with the classical past' in this respect; other Christians, like Gregory of Nazianzus, remained closer to the conventions of the rhetorical tradition.[52] In this way, Christian authors build a bridge between past and present, letting their own

---

[48] See Ilona Opelt, *Die Polemik in der christlichen lateinischen Literatur von Tertullian bis Augustin*, Bibliothek der klassischen Altertumswissenschaften 2/63 (Heidelberg: Winter, 1980); Ilona Opelt, "Formen Der Polemik Bei Lucifer von Calaris," *VC* 26.3 (1972): 200–226.

[49] Opelt, "Formen Der Polemik Bei Lucifer von Calaris," 205–16.

[50] Flower, *Late Roman Invective*, 181.

[51] Flower, *Late Roman Invective*, 17; See also Richard Flower, ed., *Imperial Invectives Against Constantius II: Athanasius of Alexandria, History of the Arians, Hilary of Poitiers, Against Constantius and Lucifer of Cagliari, The Necessity of Dying for the Son of God*, Translated Texts for Historians 67 (Liverpool: Liverpool University Press, 2016).

[52] Flower, *Late Roman Invective*, 17–19.

ethos shine all the brighter in contrast to the wickedness of the negative *ethos* of their opponents.[53]

Logos

Logos concerns proofs relating to the subject matter. According to Antoine Braet, Aristotle calls *logos* 'the means that exists "in the speech itself, in so far as it proves or seems to prove"'.[54] This means of persuasion involves the demonstration of arguments in a logical way. Aristotle's emphasis on the soundness of rhetorical proof and argumentation is exemplified in the opening words of his work *On Rhetoric*: 'Rhetoric is a counterpart of dialectic.'[55] An appeal to *logos* corresponds in this study with argumentation from logical proofs and appeals from Scripture that relate directly to the subject matter. It concerns both the confirmation of an orator's proposition and the refutation of that of opponents.[56] Within this monograph, *logos* is subdivided into two main categories: argumentation and Scripture.

Argumentation

The category of logic refers to two types of argumentation, which are analysed from a rhetorical point of view. *Logos* in this study thus entails a broader view of reasonableness than logic in the strict sense of the word; the focus of the analysis is on effectiveness instead of validity of argumentation. The two types of *logos* are examples and enthymemes. These are distinguished by their mode of reasoning: induction and deduction.[57] Examples provide proof inductively, i.e. reasoning moves from specific observations to a more general theory. The audience should be convinced of the plausibility of the specifics that lead to the generalised theory. In this mode of argumentation, everything depends on the

---

[53] See Flower, *Late Roman Invective*, 22.

[54] Braet, "Ethos, Pathos and Logos," 309. He refers to Aristotle *Rhet.* I.2.3.

[55] *Rhet.* I.1.1; cf. Christof Rapp, "Aristotle on the Moral Psychology of Persuasion," in *The Oxford Handbook of Aristotle*, ed. Christopher John Shields (New York: Oxford University Press, 2012), 589–611.

[56] Cf. Quintilian, *Inst.* IV.introduction.6.

[57] Cf. Aristotle, *Rhet.* II.18–26.

audience's acceptance of the soundness of the comparison. Examples are regularly used, but often supplemented by the other type of rhetorical argumentation.

Enthymemes offer proof deductively, i.e. reasoning moves from more general to more specific. The enthymeme is the rhetorical equivalent of a syllogism in dialectic. A syllogism offers generally valid proofs: ((1) All men are mortal. (2) Socrates is a man. Conclusion: Socrates is mortal). Enthymemes do not produce general validity, for one of the premises is omitted to leave something to the imagination of an audience, (Socrates is a man, therefore he is mortal).[58] An enthymeme shares with a syllogism that the conclusion is only accepted if the audience agrees with all the premises, but differs in that not all of the premises need to be present explicitly. Enthymemes can further be subdivided into signs and probabilities. Signs function as symbols; because x is present, y is the case. They can either be non-necessary, that is, refutable (there is water, so there must be a well), or necessary, that is, irrefutable (there is smoke, so there must be fire). In the first case, another possible explanation can be offered, in the second case, it is impossible. The other subtype of enthymemes, i.e. probabilities, features in cases when ultimate certainty cannot be gained. In life, there are of course many instances that cannot be demonstrated with absolute certainty, so this tool is often used in rhetoric, especially, but not exclusively, in the deliberative genre.

Scripture

When Christianity originated, it was influenced by the Greco-Roman culture. Some converts to Christianity had received a classical rhetorical education. This mutual interaction between Christianity and classical rhetoric resulted in a distinctive type of Christian rhetoric, in which Christianity's high esteem of the divine Scriptures became part of rhetoric.[59] Exegesis of the divinely revealed Scriptures became a means of logically persuading an

---

[58] Aristotle, *Rhet.* I.1; II.22.
[59] Kharlamov, "Rhetorical Application,", 116–17; Cf. Andreas Spira, "The Impact of Christianity on Ancient Rhetoric," in *StPatr* 18,2, ed. Elizabeth A. Livingstone (Kalamazoo, MI: Cistercian, 1989), 137–53.

audience. I discuss it under this heading, because Perelman and Olbrechts-Tyteca remark that Scripture and reason often coexist in argumentation. They state that in most cases 'the argument from authority will not constitute the only proof, but will round off well-developed argumentation'.[60] Allusions and quotations may strengthen the orator's *ethos* and his communion with an audience. More often, however, appeals to Scripture support argumentation in Christianity.

In this study, I focus on the Gospel of John as a subcategory of Scripture. Previous research has already demonstrated the relative prominence of the Gospel of John among the scriptural citations in Athanasius' *Orations*.[61] This monograph therefore examines the functioning of Scripture as a rhetorical process through the lens of the Gospel of John. The understanding of the means of persuasion presented here deviates somewhat from the Aristotelian view, which strongly distinguishes between artistic and non-artistic means of persuasion. Aristotle regards forms of authority, such as witnesses or documents, as non-artistic and strictly different from the artistic means of persuasion, *ethos*, *logos* and *pathos*. While Scripture might be considered a form of authority, the author's influence on the selection of scriptural passages in doctrinal debates of the fourth century should not be underestimated. With that qualification, I include the use of Scripture as an artistic means of persuasion.[62]

THE CHRISTOLOGY OF THE GOSPEL OF JOHN

The Gospel of John plays a prominent role within this study. In this section, I first delineate which questions I will and will not engage with in this research. After that, I will discuss the Christology of John's Gospel and then evaluate Athanasius' use of the Gospel.

---

[60] Perelman and Olbrechts-Tyteca, *New Rhetoric*, 307.

[61] See Ernest, *Bible*, 116–17.

[62] On this topic, see Perelman and Olbrechts-Tyteca, *New Rhetoric*, 305–10; cf. Kennedy, *Christian and Secular Tradition*, 138.

The Role of John's Gospel in this Monograph

While the Gospel of John is studied extensively as a New Testament document in its own right, the present investigation will be limited to questions relevant to its reception in Athanasius' *Orations*. Hence, I will ignore numerous historical-critical questions, such as the relation between the Synoptic Gospels and John, the authorship of the Gospel and the authenticity of Jesus' words in John's Gospel.[63] My own position on historical-critical matters comes close to that of Bauckham: the Gospel of John was written by John the Elder, an eyewitness of Jesus' ministry. The Gospel contains a plausible representation of the pre-Easter Jesus, with a subsequent theological reflection on the significance of Jesus' life, death and resurrection.[64] Nevertheless, I will not focus in any detail on this question, because neither Athanasius nor any of his opponents discussed these questions. References to the author of the Gospel of John in this study are used for convenience of reference, not with the aim of defending a specific theory on authorship. Furthermore, I will not discuss questions about redaction theories concerning the Gospel or questions concerning the either

---

[63] Some important contributions are Raymond E. Brown, ed., *The Gospel According to John*, 2 vols., Anchor Bible 29, 29A (Garden City: Doubleday, 1966–1970); Paul N. Anderson, Felix Just, and Tom Thatcher, eds, *John, Jesus, and History Volume 2. Aspects of Historicity in the Fourth Gospel*, vol. 2 of *SBLSymS* 44 (Atlanta, GA: SBL, 2009); John Ashton, *Understanding the Fourth Gospel*, 2nd ed. (Oxford: Oxford University Press, 2007); C. H. Dodd, *Historical Tradition in the Fourth Gospel* (Cambridge: Cambridge University Press, 1963). A standard work on our knowledge of Jesus is James D. G. Dunn, *Jesus Remembered*, Christianity in the Making 1 (Grand Rapids, MI: Eerdmans, 2003).

[64] Richard Bauckham, *The Testimony of the Beloved Disciple: Narrative, History, and Theology in the Gospel of John* (Grand Rapids, MI: Baker Academic, 2007), esp. 33–112; Richard Bauckham, *Jesus and the Eyewitnesses: The Gospels as Eyewitness Testimony* (Grand Rapids, MI: Eerdmans, 2006), 358–411; See for another stimulating contribution, C. Stephen Evans, "The Historical Reliability of John's Gospel: From What Perspective Should It Be Assessed?," in *The Gospel of John and Christian Theology*, ed. Richard Bauckham and Carl Mosser (Grand Rapids, MI: Eerdmans, 2008), 91–119.

Jewish or Gnostic roots of the Gospel, since these were not questions in the fourth century.[65] I will regard the Gospel of John as a
unity without considering the possibility of different editions or
sources underlying the Gospel and I will presuppose Jewish monotheistic roots of John's Gospel in my discussion on John's Christology.[66] I will focus on the question of John's theology and Christology, without taking into account all the modern questions
raised above.

In this study, I will argue in line with Bauckham that John's
Gospel, like most part of the NT, has a high Christology, i.e. 'a
Christology of divine identity, in which Jesus is understood to be
included in the unique divine identity of the one and only God ...
though also developed in distinctive ways in the most theologically reflective and creative of them.'[67] A distinctive feature of
John's Gospel is the degree of the explicitness of its Christology.[68]
This explicitness of John's Christology made John's Gospel an important source for all parties in the Christological conflicts in the
early Church.[69]

---

[65] For an overview, see Ashton, *Fourth Gospel*; see also Herman Ridderbos,
"The Structure and Scope of the Prologue to the Gospel of John," in *The
Composition of John's Gospel: Selected Studies from Novum Testamentum*,
ed. David E. Orton (Leiden: Brill, 1999), 41–62.

[66] On this issue of John's unity and differences in style, see among others
G. Van Belle, M. Labahn, and P. Maritz, *Repetitions and Variations in the
Fourth Gospel: Style, Text, Interpretation* (Leuven: Peeters, 2009); on the
issue of Jewish sources underlying the Gospel, see Ashton, *Fourth Gospel*,
2–6, 57–96. The main proponent of a Gnostic origin is Rudolf Bultmann,
The Gospel of John: A Commentary (Philadelphia, PA: Westminster Press,
1971). The first German edition was published in 1941.

[67] Bauckham, *Testimony*, 239–52, here 239; cf. Larry W. Hurtado, *How on
Earth Did Jesus Become a God? Historical Questions about Earliest Devotion
to Jesus* (Grand Rapids, MI: Eerdmans, 2005), 97–104.

[68] Jörg Frey, "Continuity and Discontinuity between «Jesus» and «Christ».
The Possibilities of an Implicit Christology," *RCatT* 36 (2011): 73–74;
John Painter, "The Point of John's Christology. Christology, Conflict and
Community in John," in *Christology, Controversy, and Community: New
Testament Essays in Honour of David R. Catchpole*, ed. David G. Horrell
and Christopher M. Tuckett, NovTSup (Leiden: Brill, 2000), 240.

[69] Pollard, *Johannine Christology*; Parvis, "Christology," 120–37.

Nevertheless, while the Gospel is very explicit about Jesus' divine status, there are several tensions or ambiguities in John's Christology. These ambiguities make it difficult to grasp John's Christology firmly, and have caused strikingly different interpretations of the Gospel. For that reason, it is impossible to give *the* definitive interpretation of John's Gospel and its Christology. Furthermore, postmodern theorists have made it clear that any interpretation of a text is influenced by the interpreting subjects, including me. My attempt to present an informed understanding of John's Christology, based on recent scholars that have addressed the issue, therefore does not claim to be a full, 'omniscient' interpretation in contrast to those of Athanasius and Arius. However, while my perspective is limited in certain ways, an overview of John's Christology adds to our understanding of Athanasius' distinctive use of the Gospel of John.

Paul N. Anderson has devoted attention to the considerable tensions within John's Christology and argues that the tensions have been resolved in basically three ways. First of all, some scholars argue that there are no real tensions within John and therefore opt for a full harmonisation of these tensions. The second way of resolving the tensions is to argue that the tensions are due to external circumstances (the use of different sources, the work of one or more redactors, and various crises in the history of Johannine Christianity such as expulsion from the synagogue). The third option is to regard the Christological tensions as '*internal* to the thinking and writing of the evangelist'.[70] According to Anderson, who favours this third option, John's Gospel is written dialogically on purpose. Hence, a polyvalent rather than a monological interpretation is required to do justice to these tensions

---

[70] Paul N. Anderson, *The Christology of the Fourth Gospel: Its Unity and Disunity in the Light of John 6*, WUNT 2/78 (Tübingen: Mohr Siebeck, 1996), 10. After completing the main text of this study, I became aware of Rheaume's monograph on this matter. His findings bear much similarity to the position defended in this study. See Randy Rheaume, *An Exegetical and Theological Analysis of the Son's Relationship to the Father in John's Gospel: God's Equal and Subordinate* (Lewiston, Lampeter: Edwin Mellen Press, 2014).

that are intentionally inserted by the author of John's Gospel.[71] I agree with him that it seems impossible to harmonise all the tensions satisfactorily, and that the theory of external circumstances cannot resolve all the tensions either. So, somehow, these tensions and ambiguities are internal and intentional to the Fourth Gospel.

I will look into three themes of John's Gospel that produce these tensions and ambiguities concerning Christology: (1) the theme of agency and mission, (2) the 'I am' sayings, and (3) the pre-existence of Christ.

The Agency and Mission of the Johannine Son

The theme of mission is very prominent and broad in John. The Gospel of John contains numerous declarations of the Son that he is sent, with two different verbs (πέμπω Jn 4:34; 5:23–24, 30, 37; 6:38–39, 44; 7:16, 18, 28, 33; 8:16, 18, 26, 29; 9:4; 12:44–45, 49; 14:24; 15:21; 16:5; 20:21; ἀποστέλλω Jn 3:34; 5:36, 38; 6:29, 57; 7:29; 8:42; 10:36; 11:42; 17:3, 8, 21, 23). Both verbs are also used in other situations for John (Jn 1:6, 33) or the Jewish leaders (Jn 1:22; 7:32). This observation raises the question in what way the author of the Fourth Gospel regarded Jesus as unique. Thomas Gaston holds that Jesus' self-references to his mission indicate that the Johannine Jesus is not considered truly divine, since many Johannine sayings of Jesus portray Jesus as being sent (see 3:34; 4:34; 5:23–24, 30, 36; 6:29, 38, 57; 7:16; 8:18, 42; 9:4; 11:42), similar to John the Baptist (1:6).[72] While Gaston's claim that Jesus understood his mission in terms similar to John the Baptist might have a parallel in some cases (Jn 4:34; 5:30; 7:16), in many other instances Gaston's examples are less convincing. In Jn 3:34, Jesus speaks 'the words of God, for he gives the Spirit without measure', and in several other instances mentioned by

---

[71] Paul N. Anderson, "From One Dialogue to Another: Johannine Polyvalence from Origins to Receptions," in *Anatomies of Narrative Criticism: The Past, Present, and Futures of the Fourth Gospel as Literature*, ed. Tom Thatcher and Stephen D. Moore, Resources for Biblical Study 55 (Leiden: Brill, 2009), 93–119, here 93.

[72] Thomas E. Gaston, "Does the Gospel of John Have a High Christology?," *HBT* 36 (2014): 137.

Gaston, Jesus' mission supersedes John the Baptist's mission (5:36; 8:18) or involves much larger claims or deeds in the context of the narrative (5:23–24; 6:39, 57; 11:42). Gaston's observations point to an ambiguity concerning Jesus' real identity in John's Christology.

Several Johannine references about Jesus' mission seem to indicate a higher claim about the Son than Gaston maintains. Jesus is 'from above' (3:31; 8:23), 'from heaven' (6:32–33, 38), and 'from God' (6:46; 8:42; 13:3; cf. 7:39; 16:28). Gaston suggests that these statements 'speak of an intimate relationship between the Father and Jesus in his temporal state; Jesus, whilst on earth, sees the actions of the Father and mimics them'.[73] This suggestion is difficult to accept in three statements that connect Jesus' origins and activity with heaven. In John 3:31–32, the evangelist reads 'he who comes from heaven is above all. He bears witness to what he has seen and heard.' In verse 35, he says further that 'the Father loves the Son and has placed all things in his hands.' In this case, it is unlikely that John is just talking about an intimate relationship between the Father and Jesus in his temporal state. At this point John's Christology indicates that the Son is uniquely connected to the Father, in a way that no human being is. While many references to Jesus' mission can be understood in a non-exclusive way, this passage creates a tension with those 'ordinary' mission statements of Jesus.

A similar tension is found in John 6. In verses 41–42, the Jews dispute Jesus' claim that he is the bread of life, because they know his human parents. For that reason, Jesus cannot be right to claim: 'I have come down from heaven' (6:42). The Jews in John's Gospel recognise the messianic claim, but argue that he cannot be the Messiah, because they know his parents. Jesus' response emphasises his unique relationship with the Father:

> No one can come to me unless drawn by the Father who sent me; and I will raise that person up on the last day. ... Everyone

---

[73] Gaston, "Gospel of John," 139; Farrell supports this view. Shannon Elizabeth Farrell, "Seeing the Father (Jn 6:46, 14:9)," *Science et Esprit* 44 (1992): 6, 12–13, 17; idem, "Seeing the Father (Jn 6:46, 14:9)," *Science et Esprit* 44 (1992): 328.

who has heard and learned from the Father comes to me. Not
that anyone has seen the Father except he who is from God;
he has seen the Father (6:44–46).

The mission motif connects Jesus in a very special way to the
Father. Jesus claims the ability and authority to raise people from
the dead at the last day and a unique mediation of knowledge
concerning the Father.[74] Gaston therefore resolves the Christological tension of the Fourth Gospel by explaining away the indicators of Jesus' divinity to maintain the humanness and earthliness
of the Johannine Jesus. While it might be a possibility in some
instances, and it indicates that the author of the Fourth Gospel
has a concern for the humanity and earthliness of Jesus, Gaston's
suggestion certainly does not do justice to all the passages of
John's Gospel.

Paul N. Anderson takes a different approach to the Christological tension in John. He understands the mission or agency
motive of the Johannine Jesus as part of the Father-Son relationship. One of the elements of the agency motive in John is his portrayal of Jesus as a Prophet-like-Moses, which goes back to Deuteronomy 18:15–22.[75] Anderson claims that Jesus' being sent
from God proves that he is a true and authentic prophet. This
Prophet-like-Moses motive is the reason Jesus does not claim to
do or say anything more or less than the Father. This sounds as if
the Son is strongly subordinate to and dependent on the Father,
but this is not true, because the 'egalitarian and subordinate relations to the Father are ... *two sides of the same coin*', according to
Anderson.[76] Paradoxically, especially because the Son does nothing on his own, but everything together with his Father, his claim

---

[74] C. K. Barrett, *The Gospel According to St John. An Introduction with Commentary and Notes on the Greek Text*, 2nd ed. (London: SPCK, 1978), 296;
Donald A. Carson, *The Gospel According to John*, The Pillar New Testament Commentary (Grand Rapids, MI: Eerdmans, 1991), 293–94.

[75] Paul N. Anderson, "The Having-Sent-Me Father: Aspects of Agency,
Encounter, and Irony in the Johannine Father-Son Relationship," *Semeia*
85 (1999): 33–57.

[76] Anderson, "Having-Sent-Me Father," 41; italics original. See also
Rheaume, *Exegetical and Theological Analysis*, 185–209.

is authentic because it honours the Father and demonstrates their unity (cf. Jn 5:17–18; 10:25–30; 11:41–43). Furthermore, Jesus as the agent of the Father even receives a prominent role in sending the Spirit (Jn 14:26; 15:26; 16:7) and the disciples (Jn 13:20; 20:21).[77] Especially in sending the Spirit, Jesus receives a role parallel to that of the Father.

Anderson further claims that the agency motive takes different forms (such as prophetic, apocalyptic and sapiential) that 'often play complementary and parallel roles'.[78]

This results in an ambiguity and tension in John's Christology that is internal to the thinking of the evangelist. On the one hand, the Son is God's agent and conveys God's words. On the other hand, 'the Son *is* the Word of God—made flesh (1:1, 14) in whom the glory of God is encountered.'[79] John describes Jesus as God's agent in different ways, without hesitation, but claims at the same time that the Son as Word of God is pre-existent and involved in creation. This tension is not fully resolved in John's Gospel, and for that reason, the Gospel contains a somewhat reciprocal relation between Jesus' declarations of being sent by the Father and his equality with the Father (see the discussions on Jn 3:31–36 and Jn 6:41–46 above). The Johannine agency motif

> functions theologically to provide a bridge between the traditional past and the eschatological present, as the God who was and is becomes connected with the God who is doing and will be doing. The Johannine Father-Son relationship ... presents the christocentric revelation of the Father as conjoined with the theocentric mission of the Son.[80]

Anderson thus argues for an intentional use of the Christological tensions by the author of the Fourth Gospel. The tensions, caused by ambiguity, function as a means of doing justice to both Jesus' divinity and humanity. In this way, the evangelist relates Jesus in

---

[77] See Carson, *John*, 528–29; David Crump, "Re-Examining the Johannine Trinity: Perichoresis or Deification?," *SJT* 59 (2006): 395–412.

[78] Anderson, "Having-Sent-Me Father," 43. Cf. Rheaume, *Exegetical and Theological Analysis*, 128–33.

[79] Anderson, "Having-Sent-Me Father," 42; italics original.

[80] Anderson, "Having-Sent-Me Father," 51.

a unique manner to the only God and highlights the salvational significance of Jesus' life, death and resurrection. Because the Son is sent, is obedient in everything and does not do anything on his own (5:30), he is not challenging the Jewish monotheistic confession that there is another God. Jesus is a prophet like Moses, and even more than that, the full revelation of the Father himself. In other words, the concept of Jesus' mission enables John to confess Jesus as God, while remaining a Jewish monotheist who accepts Jesus as Messiah and Son of God (cf. Jn 20:30–31).

The prominence of Jesus' mission in the Gospel of John demonstrates a desire for balancing the confession of Jesus as divine and his obedience in his earthly mission. In his Christology, John wants to do justice to both the profoundly earthly character of Jesus and his divine claim, signified in his teachings and deeds. The agency theme clearly indicates that John's Christology is not 'in the air', but rather 'down to earth'. Bauckham argues that Jesus' actual presence in history is essential for the author of John's Gospel. Bauckham has drawn attention to the fact that John's Gospel in particular contains many topographical and chronological references. More than in other Gospels, a reader is aware where and when Jesus is in the course of the narrative, because of the many topographical and chronological references that illustrate that '[o]rdinary history is transcended in metahistory' in the life of Jesus, which 'bursts the boundaries of space and time'.[81] Both the high Christological claims and distinctly earthly remarks come together in the theme of Jesus' mission and agency. For that reason, high Christological claims, such as the universal significance of Jesus' life, death and resurrection, as well as the awareness that he is the Word and Son of God, are complemented and balanced by the emphasis that Jesus is the Word that became flesh (1:14). After this discussion of the agency theme in John, which has demonstrated certain ambiguities and tensions in John, and a concern for Jesus' presence in real history, I will now discuss two issues relating to Jesus' divine status.

---

[81] Bauckham, *Testimony*, 103.

The Johannine 'I Am' Statements

Another theme crucial to understanding John's Christology is the use and function of Jesus' ἐγώ εἰμι (I am) sayings throughout the Gospel. The 'I am' sayings play an important role in John, and scholars recognise one or more distinct sets of 'I am' sayings. The best-known 'I am' sayings are those in which Jesus applies a variety of metaphors, such as bread of life, to himself (Jn 6:35; 8:12; 10:7; 10:11; 11:25; 14:6; 15:1). In general, this series of metaphorical 'I am' sayings puts forward high claims concerning Jesus.[82]

Other 'I am' sayings seem to stand on their own, as if used in an absolute sense. Bauckham recognises a series of such 'I am' sayings (Jn 4:26; 6:20; 8:24; 8:28; 8:58; 13:19; 18:5, 6, 8). This series is less easily discernible than the series of metaphorical 'I am' sayings, but is equally, if not more, significant in John's Gospel. Nevertheless, the words ἐγώ εἰμι seem to be an intentional parallel to the words that are spoken by YHWH in Deuteronomy (32:39) and Isaiah (41:4; 43:10, 13; 46:4).[83] In these instances, the LXX reads ἐγώ εἰμι and the Masoretic Text reads אני־הוא or הוא אני.[84] The most likely explanation of these 'I am' statements in the Gospel of John is that they suggest an identification of Jesus with the words and salvation of YHWH.[85]

---

[82] Riemer Roukema, "Jesus and the Divine Name in the Gospel of John," in *Revelation of the Name YHWH to Moses*, ed. George H. van Kooten (Leiden: Brill, 2006), 213.

[83] This use of 'I am' in these passages cannot be derived from Exodus 3:14, as is sometimes suggested; the LXX renders Ἐγώ εἰμι ὁ ὤν, which would make ὁ ὤν the divine name in this passage, not ἐγώ εἰμι. See Bauckham, *Testimony*, 246; Gaston, "Gospel of John," 135–36.

[84] In some cases either the LXX or Masoretic Text has a more emphatic form; a double ἐγώ εἰμι (Isa 43:25; 45:18; 46:4; 51:12) or אנכי אנכי הוא (Isa 43:25; 51:12). Bauckham, *Testimony*, 247. See also Rheaume, *Exegetical and Theological Analysis*, 300–323.

[85] Roukema, "Divine Name," 211–13, here 213. He refers primarily to David Mark Ball, *"I Am" in John's Gospel. Literary Function, Background, and Theological Implications*, Journal for the Study of the New Testament Supplement Series 124 (Sheffield, England: Sheffield Academic Press,

Some of these instances might be understood as a simple self-identification without Christological connotations.[86] Jesus' ἐγώ εἰμι in Jn 4:26 might be read as a natural affirmation that he is Messiah (cf. Jn 4:29), while the same words in Jn 6:20 (par. Mk 6:50; 14:62) might just be a neutral self-identification, to dispel the disciples' fears in the boat. In chapter 18, 'I am' might be understood as a response to the soldiers and Jewish leaders that were searching for Jesus; yet the group that came to arrest Jesus fell to the ground, so it might suggest more than just a natural self-reference.[87] In these three cases an ordinary sense of the word 'I am' might be possible, but a special usage is by no means ruled out either. Connected to the fact that occurrences of the words elsewhere in the Gospel seem impossible to read in an ordinary sense, these might be understood as absolute 'I am' sayings as well.

The other four 'I am' sayings (8:24; 8:28; 8:58; 13:19) are less likely to be understood as a neutral self-identification of Jesus. If the correspondence to the words of YHWH in Deut 32:39 and Isaiah 41:4; 43:10 is accepted, and no plausible natural meaning can be discerned in these 'I am' sayings, the significance of this Johannine feature must be explained as a relation that John establishes between the words of YHWH and those of Jesus. In that case the question remains whether these statements should be seen as a claim that Jesus is identified as a special agent on God's behalf, or as a claim of the Son's true divinity and identification with YHWH. Since most of the discussion focuses on the passages from chapter 8, I will quote these texts in full:

> [Jesus] said to [the Jews], 'You are from below, I am from above; you are of this world, I am not of this world. I told you that you would die in your sins, for you will die in your sins

---

1996). The idea of the 'I am' sayings as a series is advocated by Bauckham, *Testimony*, 243–50.

[86] Bauckham, *Testimony*, 244–45; cf. Barrett, *John*, 281. As a parallel usage, Jn 9:9 might be mentioned. This verse uses the words ἐγώ εἰμι as a self-identification of the blind man who is healed by Jesus.

[87] Bauckham, *Testimony*, 244–45; Roukema, "Divine Name," 213; Carson, *John*, 342–43, 578.

unless you believe that I am he (ἐγώ εἰμι).' (8:23–24) ... So Jesus said, 'When you have lifted up the Son of Man, then you will realize that I am he (ἐγώ εἰμι), and that I do nothing on my own, but I speak these things as the Father instructed me.' (8:28) ... Then the Jews said to him, 'You are not yet fifty years old, and have you seen Abraham?' Jesus said to them, 'Very truly, I tell you, before Abraham was, I am (ἐγώ εἰμι).' (8:57–58)

Thomas Gaston denies the option that these 'I am' statements contain a strong claim of divine identity, and reads a low Christology in John. Although he locates the background of 'I am' sayings in Deuteronomy (32:39) and Isaiah (41:4; 43:10; 46:4), Gaston neglects the potential implications that speak against his position. Concerning Jn 8:24, Gaston claims that the 'I am' statement is unclear, since the Jews ask 'who are you?' in verse 25. However, this reasoning is questionable. While the Jews do not understand the ἐγώ εἰμι in Jn 8:24, this cannot be used against the meaning in its absolute sense. Throughout John's Gospel, Jews and disciples alike misunderstand many deeds and words before Jesus' resurrection (cf. Jn 2:19–22), so that confusion is not a reason against the absolute meaning of 'I am'.[88] Concerning Jn 8:28, Gaston remarks that it is not an absolute 'I am' statement, because 'Son of Man' is available as a grammatical referent.[89] He is right that this is the only available grammatical referent. Nevertheless, since this grammatical referent results in a rather awkward or 'enigmatic' sentence, other scholars are inclined to opt for an absolute understanding of this ἐγώ εἰμι.[90] Gaston also proposes a reading of Jn 8:58 that obviates an absolute understanding of the 'I am' saying in this passage. He suggests that the past tense (ἤμην) would have been more appropriate than the present tense ἐγώ εἰμι in Jn 8:58. This argument is speculative and avoids the question why the present tense is used. In his explanation of the verse, the

---

[88] Cf. Donald A. Carson, "Understanding Misunderstandings in the Fourth Gospel," *TynBul* 33 (1982): 59–91.

[89] Gaston, "Gospel of John," 135–37, contra Bauckham, *Testimony*, 245–46.

[90] Bauckham, *Testimony*, 245; Barrett, *John*, 343–44; Carson, *John*, 345.

book of Jubilees (16:26–28) plays a significant role.[91] The book of Jubilees connects the festival of booths, which is the setting of John 7–8, to a vision of Abraham of the Messiah. Gaston claims: 'In Jubilees Abraham saw the coming of "a holy seed"; in John Jesus claims that what Abraham saw was him.'[92] However, the parallel is imperfect, because in Jubilees, Abraham is considered chronologically prior, whereas in John 8:56–58 Jesus is presented as prior to Abraham.

Gaston's rejection of the absolute sense of the 'I am' sayings is problematic. While he acknowledges that Jesus' words ἐγώ εἰμι point to the 'I am' self-declarations of YHWH, he considers it 'more plausible to read the resonance of Jesus' "I am" sayings with the "I am" declarations of YHWH through Jesus' repeated claims in John's gospel to manifest the Father.'[93] I doubt that this understanding is plausible, for in John 8:59 and on several other occasions, the Jews consider his words blasphemous.[94] This suggests that the author of the Fourth Gospel wants to make it clear that the Jews did not merely consider Jesus to be a human representative of God. Bauckham points out that the announcement of Judas' betrayal in Jn 13:18–19 is connected to his absolute use of ἐγώ εἰμι, as Jesus declares: 'I tell you this now, before it occurs, so that when it does occur, you may believe that I am he' (13:19). This indicates Jesus' foreknowledge, a feature that is also prominent in the 'I am' declaration in Isaiah 43:9–11.[95] The cumulative evidence of the 'I am' sayings, in combination with the absence of a weaker plausible connection between the 'I am' sayings of

---

[91] Jubilees 16:26–28. 'And he [Abraham] blessed his Creator who had created him in his generation, ... for He knew and perceived that from him would arise the plant of righteousness for the eternal generations, and from him a holy seed, so that it should become like Him who had made all things. And he blessed and rejoiced, and he called the name of this festival [of booths; cf. Jn 7:2].' Tr. R. H. Charles and G. H. Box, trans., *The Book of Jubilees Or, The Little Genesis* (London: SPCK, 1917).

[92] Gaston, "Gospel of John," 136.

[93] Gaston, "Gospel of John," 136.

[94] Rheaume, *Exegetical and Theological Analysis*, 312.

[95] Bauckham, *Testimony*, 248.

YHWH and Jesus make an absolute understanding of the I am sayings the most plausible one.

Richard Bauckham claims that the absolute 'I am' statements, which connect Jesus in a unique way with YHWH throughout the Gospel, are not a deviation from monotheism: 'Rather, Jewish monotheism and Christology had been necessarily related to each other in Christian understanding of Jesus' identity from the beginning.'[96] He discerns two types of seven 'I am' sayings: metaphorical and absolute. Both have a significant function, regardless of the precise number of both types of 'I am' sayings. Bauckham claims that both types of 'I am' sayings connect Jesus' identity with God in his work of revelation and salvation. The 'I am' sayings with predicates (6:35; 8:12; 10:7; 10:11; 11:25; 14:6; 15:1) illustrate 'the inexhaustible fullness of what salvation means', thus implicitly showing that 'Jesus can be the only Savior only because he is identified with the only God'.[97] This message is made explicit by the series of absolute 'I am' sayings. These 'identify Jesus with God, not just in an abstract way, but in a way that the Scriptures associate with the universal revelation of God's unique divinity in his eschatological act of salvation for Israel and the nations.'[98] In other words, John's Christology connects Jesus' divine status in a unique way to the God of Israel that precludes ditheism, because Jesus is accomplishing the work of the God of Israel. Randy Rheaume concludes in similar fashion, after a lengthy discussion of the ἐγώ εἰμι sayings: '[T]he absolute ἐγώ εἰμι sayings assert Jesus' deity yet also make clear that the Son does not exhaust the identity of Yahweh but shares it with his Father as a distinct person in full filial submission to him.'[99] Likewise, Barrett comments on the purpose of John's Gospel: 'The deeds and words of Jesus are the deeds and words of God; if this be not true the book is blasphemous.'[100] Jesus is portrayed as divine in a

---

[96] Bauckham, *Testimony*, 240.
[97] Bauckham, *Testimony*, 250.
[98] Bauckham, *Testimony*, 250.
[99] Rheaume, *Exegetical and Theological Analysis*, 324–25.
[100] Barrett, *John*, 156.

way that the evangelist considered compatible with his Jewish monotheistic roots.

The Pre-existence of Christ in John

A third important issue in John's Christology is the pre-existence of the Son. The prologue of John's Gospel contains several strong affirmations concerning Jesus' divine status and pre-existence.[101] John 1:1 reads 'In the beginning was the Word (λόγος), and the Word was with God, and the Word was God.' Moreover, nothing has come into existence apart from the Word (1:3). It is clear that the Word of God is uniquely connected to Jesus, for the most likely reading of Jn 1:18 is: 'No one has ever seen God. It is God the only Son (μονογενὴς θεός), who is close to the Father's heart, who has made him known.'[102] In this way, the story of Jesus, who is the Messiah or Christ (1:41), is connected in a unique way to God; he is the Word of God, who is involved in creation.

Thomas Gaston does not consider this information enough to ascribe personal pre-existence to the Johannine Jesus. He claims that Jesus is not unambiguously considered divine in John's Gospel, because the title God refers to the pre-existent Word (1:1), is textually problematic (1:18), or ambiguous (20:28). He asserts that John clearly distinguishes Jesus from God and even 'contains some of the most explicit subordinationist statements in the whole NT'.[103] Gaston sees Jn 5:17–18 and 10:30–33 as subordinationist statements that seek to distinguish Jesus and God significantly. Other subordinationist statements could be added, such as 'I can do nothing on my own. As I hear, I judge; and my judgment is just, because I seek to do not my own will but the will of him

---

[101] Regardless of the Jewish(-Christian) or Gnostic origin of the prologue, the author of the Fourth Gospel considered the words appropriate to introduce his Gospel narrative, thus clearly suggesting that the divine Word, through which creation came into existence, is intimately connected to the story of Jesus Christ.

[102] Thus Barrett, *John*, 169; Carson, *John*, 139.

[103] Gaston, "Gospel of John," 133; see also Benjamin J. Burkholder, "Considering the Possibility of a Theological Corruption in Joh 1,18 in Light of its Early Reception," *ZNW* 103 (2012): 64–83.

who sent me' (5:30) and 'The Father is greater than I' (14:28). And in John 20:17, Jesus declares himself to be on the same level as humans, when he states: 'I am ascending to my Father and your Father, to my God and your God.'

For that reason, the connection between the prologue and the rest of the Gospel must be determined. Apart from the subordinationist statements given above, there is also evidence for the pre-existence of the Son in the main body of the Gospel.[104] Jesus' statement in John 17:5 strongly suggests a notion of Jesus' personal pre-existence with the Father: 'Father, glorify me in your own presence with the glory that I had in your presence before the world existed.'[105] And Jesus is clearly confessed as God by Thomas' confession: 'My Lord and my God!' (20:28). According to Riemer Roukema, the use of κύριος in Jn 20:28 is 'far more significant than the common vocative κύριε'. If the view that 'the pre-existent Logos, who is God, corresponds with the *Kyrios* or YHWH' in John's Gospel is correct, the juxtaposition of κύριος and θεός strengthens this view.[106] These statements clearly show Jesus' special status as the divine Word, and his position as God the only Son, who is exalted as Lord and God. They also raise the question how John remained within the borders of Jewish monotheism.

When both tendencies in the Gospel, both the egalitarian and subordinationist, are taken into account, it becomes clear that the tensions and ambiguities are not easily resolved. Jesus is simultaneously considered divine and pre-existent, and obedient to God the Father, because he is the divine Son and agent of the Father. It even seems that John did so intentionally, in order to have a Christology that is compatible with his understanding of Jewish monotheism. According to Roukema, the Johannine conception of Logos is compatible with Jewish monotheism, since the Lord and Logos of John are not completely identical with God the Father. The clear statements about Jesus' pre-existence are carefully chosen, because the 'evangelist wants to preclude any ditheism;

---

[104] See also Rheaume, *Exegetical and Theological Analysis*, 216–45.
[105] Barrett, *John*, 504; Carson, *John*, 557.
[106] Roukema, "Divine Name," 216; italics original.

in his own way he testifies to the plurality in God that is already displayed in the Old Testament'.[107]

If this conclusion is correct, and Jesus uses the words 'I am' in an absolute sense, identifying himself with YHWH, the question remains how the author of the Fourth Gospel could consider himself both a monotheist and ascribe these divine characteristics to Jesus. Roukema holds that the Johannine Jesus' reveals the Father's nature 'by his teaching and by his acts'.[108] He asserts that the author of John's Gospel conceives a subtle distinction between the 'Most High God and Father' and 'the *Kyrios*—YHWH, or the Logos', which is the Son.[109] 'Jesus Christ in his capacity of Logos and *Kyrios* represents God as far as he reveals himself to mankind', while God the Father is transcendent and invisible, yet deeply involved with the world, mediated through his Son.[110] That is why John's Gospel does not conceive God the transcendent Father as distant from creation (cf. Jn 5:17), nor is the Lord of the OT or the OT as a whole devalued in Gnostic fashion. On the contrary, 'Jesus is even to be associated very closely with the *Kyrios*, that is YHWH; one may even daringly speak of his identification with the *Kyrios*, YHWH'.[111]

All in all, the theme of mission in John indicates that the author is more careful in describing Jesus' divine status than some bold Christological statements on their own might suggest. This theme functions in John's theology to justify the legitimacy of Jesus' claim to identity with the one God, and on the other hand, to incorporate the reality of Jesus' human or creaturely existence within first-century Palestine. The absolute 'I am' sayings and the divine pre-existence of the prologue, Jn 17:5 and Thomas' confession in 20:28 show that the evangelist considered Jesus to be divine, which makes for some tensions in relation to the agency theme. I understand these tensions as the result of the evangelist's

---

[107] Roukema, "Divine Name," 218.

[108] Roukema, "Divine Name," 216.

[109] Roukema, "Divine Name," 218.

[110] Roukema, "Divine Name," 219–23, here 221.

[111] Roukema, "Divine Name," 222; italics original; See also Rheaume, *Exegetical and Theological Analysis*, 325–37.

attempt to understand Jesus as somehow divine, without denying his Jewish monotheistic roots. The Christological tensions are therefore a product of the Jewish background of John's Gospel. This ambiguity is also noted by John Painter: 'Christology is John's way of speaking of God at those points where the under-standing of God is being transformed. (...) What changes is the balance amongst all the details that make up the understanding of God and the purpose of God.'[112] The Jesus that John portrays is not a God instead of Israel's God; rather, Jesus' words and deeds are God's words and deeds. In that sense, high and low Christol-ogy complement each other in John's Gospel as they dialectically engage with each other.[113]

METHODOLOGICAL REMARKS

After the discussion of these two main concepts, the means of per-suasion and my understanding of John's Christology, I will now turn briefly to some other methodological remarks. These relate to some usage in terminology and some clarification on the edi-tions and translations used in this research.

---

[112] Painter, "John's Christology," 234.

[113] Painter, "John's Christology," 240 n14. At this point, I emphasise again that I will steer clear of the modern, historical-critical questions concerning John's Christology. I have argued that the tensions in John's Christology are most likely internal, that is, intended by the author of the Fourth Gospel. This phenomenon can of course be explained along different lines of thought, but I refrain from exploring the origin of these Christological tensions. In my view, an explanation of the ambiguity in John's Christology must at least take into consideration the historio-graphical concerns of the evangelist as argued by Richard Bauckham in *Testimony*, 93–112. This chapter is a slightly revised reprint of "Historio-graphical Characteristics of the Gospel of John," *NTS* 53 (2007): 17–36. Such an explanation should further take into account the coexistence of a 'theology of Jesus' and a subsequent reflection on Jesus (that led to the development of an ontological Christology) in the canonical Gospels. See e.g. Reginald H. Fuller, "The Theology of Jesus or Christology: An Eval-uation of the Recent Discussion," *Semeia* 30 (1984): 105–16.

General Terminology

References to Scripture may take various forms such as citations and allusions. In this study, I will use terminology that is mainly indebted to the work of Ehrman, Fee and Holmes. I will distinguish between four types of references: citation, adaptation, allusion and conflation. 'A "citation" refers to a verbally exact quotation of the biblical text.' 'An "adaptation" refers to a quotation that has been significantly modified (syntactically or materially) in the light of the ... discussion.' An 'allusion' signifies a clear echo of a passage which lacks sustained verbal agreement.[114] A 'conflation' is the merging of two or more biblical texts into a new one.[115] The term 'quotations' is used to refer to all citations and adaptations; the term 'references' will denote all quotations, allusions and conflations.[116]

Concerning the use of third-person personal and possessive pronouns, I have generally avoided gender-specific pronouns. However, when I used third-person language, I have used the masculine pronoun as a reflection of the situation in fourth-century Christianity, as well as that of ancient Greek and Roman society. Dates are generally referring to ce and bce. If no specific indication is given, the addition ce is presupposed.

Note on the Editions and Translations

The *Orations* are studied in the edition of the series *Athanasius Werke* 1.1.2 (*CA* I-II) and 1.1.3 (*CA* III), cited according to their chapter, page and line number in the edition. Athanasius' *Orations* are not completely available in a modern English translation. In general, Khaled Anatolios' translation, based on the critical edition of *Athanasius Werke* (*CA* I 1, 35–52; II 2–3, 18b–82), is used

---

[114] Bart D. Ehrman, Gordon D. Fee, and Michael W. Holmes, *The Text of the Fourth Gospel in the Writings of Origen. Volume One*, SBLNTGF 3 (Atlanta, GA: Scholars Press, 1992), 22; 'significantly' is a choice in line with Ehrman's earlier definition in Bart D. Ehrman, *Didymus the Blind and the Text of the Gospels*, SBLNTGF 1 (Atlanta, GA: Scholars Press, 1986), 14.

[115] Ernest, *Bible*, 35. This type of reference is not used by Ehrman, Fee and Holmes.

[116] Ehrman, Fee, and Holmes, *Text*, 22.

if available. Moreover, William Rusch has translated *CA* I and Richard Norris *CA* III 26–41 (both published in 1980). The translation of NPNF is generally used in an adapted form for the other parts (*CA* II 1, 4–18a; III 1–25; 42–67). In these instances, I am also indebted to Meijering's German commentary on *Oration* III, Rousseau's translation in French, and de Vogel's translation in Dutch, and I received some help from the classicist Tertius Bolhuis.[117] Some harmonisation between the translations has been made for the convenience of the reader: biblical references are abbreviated and bracketed and have the layout according to Anatolios' translation, if the layout of other translations differs slightly.

The term ἀγέν[ν]ητος has two spelling variants, with a single and double ν, but their meaning seems identical.[118] While Athanasius uses both terms indifferently, this research will mainly use the spelling ἀγέννητος/*agennetos*, unless the passage under discussion explicitly mentions the alternative spelling. In both spellings, the word is commonly translated in a similar way, either as unbegotten or as unoriginated. For the sake of clarity, I prefer the translation 'unbegotten', without specifying this every time in the footnotes on the consulted translations. The concept of unchangeability is expressed by several terms (ἀναλλοίωτος and ἄτρεπτος),

---

[117] E. P. Meijering, *Athanasius: Die dritte Rede gegen die Arianer. Einleitung, Übersetzung, Kommentar*, 3 vols. (Amsterdam: Gieben, 1996–1998); Athanase, Adelin Rousseau, and René Lafontaine, *Les trois discours contre les ariens* (Brussels: Lessius, 2004); Athanasius, *Redevoeringen Tegen de Arianen*, trans. Cornelia Johanna de Vogel, Monumenta Christiana 1.2 (Utrecht: Spectrum, 1948).

[118] Leonard Prestige, "Ἀγέν[ν]ητος and Γεν[ν]ητός, and Kindred Words, in Eusebius and the Early Arians," *JTS* 24 (1923): 490–91, 495–96; Hanson, *Search*, 204, 432–33; cf. Richard Vaggione, *Eunomius of Cyzicus and the Nicene Revolution*, OECS (Oxford: Oxford University Press, 2000), 248–49. Prestige discusses problems in the textual transmission of Athanasius' manuscripts in "ΑΓΕΝ[Ν]ΗΤΟΣ and Cognate Words in Athanasius," *JTS* 34 (1933): 258–65.

and translated as unchangeable, immutable or unalterable, since the two terms cover fairly the same semantic range.[119]

The Gospel of John is consulted according to the 28th edition of Nestle-Aland. Although this is a modern eclectic text, it is sufficient as a working tool, because the critical apparatus provides the relevant variant readings. The New Revised Standard Version is generally used as English translation of the biblical texts, sometimes the Revised Standard Version is used, indicated as RSV. If Athanasius discusses the Old Testament text on the basis of the Septuagint (LXX), the text is quoted according to the New English Translation of the Septuagint, edited by Albert Pietersma and Benjamin G. Wright.[120]

In the case of references to Athanasius' contemporaries, I have used the edition of Markus Vinzent for the fragments of Marcellus and Asterius, and that of the CGS series for the works of Eusebius of Caesarea. The English translation of Eusebius of Caesarea's *Against Marcellus* and *Ecclesiastical Theology* is given according to the work of Kelley McCarthy Spoerl and Markus Vinzent.[121] They have graciously allowed me to use their translation prior to its publication. The documents of the Arian controversy are also indicated according to the edition in *Athanasius Werke*, preferably Opitz AW 3,1–2 with the abbreviation Urk., or if not found there, Brennecke et al., (AW 3.1.3), with the abbreviation Dok. Translations are indicated in the footnotes. The only English translation of the *Urkunden* in Opitz AW 3,1–2 to date is found at the website https://www.fourthcentury.com/. This website is sponsored by the History Department of Wisconsin Lutheran College and by Asia Lutheran Seminary. It is supervised by Dr. Glen L. Tomphson.

---

[119] Geoffrey William Hugo Lampe, ed., *A Patristic Greek Lexicon* (Oxford: Clarendon, 1961), s.v. ἀναλλοίωτος and s.v. ἄτρεπτος.

[120] Albert Pietersma and Benjamin G. Wright, eds, *A New English Translation of the Septuagint and the Other Greek Translations Traditionally Included under That Title* (New York: Oxford University Press, 2007).

[121] Markus Vinzent and Kelley McCharty Spoerl, *Eusebius of Caesarea. Against Marcellus and on Ecclesiastical Theology*, Fathers of the Church 135 (Catholic University of America, 2017).

CHAPTER THREE.
GENERAL REMARKS ABOUT THE *ORATIONS AGAINST THE ARIANS*

This chapter will discuss several questions that have a direct relation to the understanding of the *Orations against the Arians*: the dating and genre of the *Orations*, the addressees of the *Orations*, and Athanasius' exegetical method. Because all of these issues are important for the understanding of all three *Orations*, they will be considered prior to their actual analysis.

GENERAL REMARKS ABOUT THE *ORATIONS AGAINST THE ARIANS*

This section will focus on the dating of the three *Orations*, their internal relationship, and the genre of the *Orations*.

The Dating of the *Orations*

The manuscript tradition of Athanasius' *Orations* lists four *Orations against the Arians*. In some manuscripts, *The Letter to the Bishops in Egypt and Libya* is also called an 'Oration', but this work will not be discussed in this study. Of the four other *Orations*, the so-called *Fourth Oration* is unanimously considered to be written by another author.[1] The authenticity of the first three *Orations against the Arians* is accepted without hesitation, although the dating of them is somewhat more disputed. A majority of contemporary scholars assigns all three to Athanasius' second exile: *Orations* I and II at the beginning of his second exile (in Rome, 339–40) and

---

[1] See Vinzent, *Pseudo-Athanasius, Contra Arianos IV*, 58–88.

Oration III somewhat later in the same exile (at least not long after 345).[2] However, for many centuries scholars assigned the three *Orations* together to the third exile (356–62).[3] This alternative view has not yet been wholly abandoned, because several, mainly French, scholars still date the third *Oration* to that period.[4] However, the majority of English and German scholars view the third *Oration* as a product of the early 340s, because of close parallels with doctrinal documents of that time and the absence of the crucial theological term ὁμοούσιος.[5]

The dating to the second exile has implications for the evaluation of the work in relation to the events that led to Athanasius' first exile in 335 (and to diverging perspectives within the study of Athanasius). If the *Orations* were written in the third exile (356–362), a gap of more than 20 years exists between the writings and the events, with much freedom for Athanasius 'to invent' a theological explanation for his church-political problems. However, the firm establishment of the date of the *Orations* in the second exile implies that the dispute about theology was still relatively fresh at the time of writing the *Orations*. This increases the plausibility of interaction between theological and non-theological elements in Athanasius' work against the Arians.

---

[2] See the notes on 109 and 305 in AW 1.1.2 and 1.1.3 and Meijering, *Die dritte Rede*, I:23; Leemans, "Athanasius Research," 137–44; Barnes, *Athanasius and Constantius*, 53–55; Charles Kannengiesser, "The Dating of Athanasius' Double Apology and Three Treatises Against the Arians," *ZAC* 10 (2006): 26. Kannengiesser's thesis concerning *CA* III raised awareness of the peculiarity of this oration, compared to *CA* I–II.

[3] Kannengiesser, "Dating," 26 and notes 29–30.

[4] Martin, *Athanase*, 7, 556 n.38; Xavier Morales, *La théologie trinitaire d'Athanase d'Alexandrie*, Collection des Études augustiniennes. Série Antiquité 180 (Paris: Institut d'Études Augustiniennes, 2006), 487–90; Frances M. Young, *Biblical Exegesis and the Formation of Christian Culture* (Cambridge: Cambridge University Press, 1997), 30.

[5] Leemans provides an elaborate overview of this question in Leemans, "Athanasius Research," 138–44; see further Charles Kannengiesser, *Athanase d'Alexandrie. Évêque et Écrivain. Une lecture des traités* Contre les Ariens, Théologie historique 70 (Paris: Beauchesne, 1983), 31; Meijering, *Die dritte Rede*, I:23; Barnes, *Athanasius and Constantius*, 254 n.26.

The Relation between *Orations* I-II and III

Another unresolved question in the last few decades of Athanasius research is the relation between *CA* I-II and III. Kannengiesser rejected the authenticity of *CA* III between 1983 and 2003, but since then he has accepted its genuineness.[6] He still maintains, however, that *CA* III is quite different from *CA* I-II. In 1983, his work considered the whole of the *Orations* from a literary point of view and he suggested a gradual development of *CA* I-II as well. Kannengiesser holds that Athanasius wrote a proto-*Oration* I-II around 337, into which the bishop inserted extra material at a later stage, which resulted in the current version of *Orations* I-II.[7] Kannengiesser implicitly acknowledges that his view is more problematic than he suggests, when he states that *CA* I-II 'kept its logical and redactional unity' regardless of 'its reworking into a more extended format with documentary additions' and that *Orations* I-II are 'only two parts of one single work'.[8] His concessions make a redaction theory unlikely, if not unnecessary. In the case of *Oration* III, a redactional theory of originally individually composed documents has more potential.[9] Nevertheless, it is easier to distinguish separate sections than to explain them satisfactorily with a theory of different underlying sources, especially because *CA* III

---

[6] Kannengiesser, *Athanase*; Kannengiesser, "Dating," 27–30; his change of mind is not yet visible in Kannengiesser, *Handbook*, II:711–12. For two dissertations that, with some hesitation, excluded *CA* III from their results, see John Jay Brogan, *The Text of the Gospels in the Writings of Athanasius* (Ann Arbor: UMI, 1997); Allen L Clayton, *The Orthodox Recovery of a Heretical Proof-Text: Athanasius of Alexandria's Interpretation of Proverbs 8:22–30 in Conflict with the Arians* (Ann Arbor: UMI, 1988).

[7] Kannengiesser, "Dating," 23, 27–33; idem, *Athanase*, 89–93, 301–10, 369–74, 401–2; cf. Luise Abramowski, "Biblische Lesarten und athanasianische Chronologie," *ZKG* 109 (1998): 237–41.

[8] Kannengiesser, "Dating," 28. He is opposed by Leemans, "Athanasius Research," 140–41; Craig Alan Blaising, "Athanasius of Alexandria: Studies in the Theological Contents and Structure of the Contra Arianos with Special Reference to Method" (unpubl. diss., University of Aberdeen, 1987).

[9] See Luise Abramowski, "Die dritte Arianerrede des Athanasius: Eusebianer und Arianer und das westliche Serdicense," *ZKG* 102 (1991): 389–413.

in its present state shows signs of deliberate continuity with *CA* I-II.[10] For that reason, this research will investigate *CA* I-II as well as *CA* III with the text in its final form, considering the three *Orations* to be basically a united work, written over a span of several years.[11]

The *Orations* are structured as follows: *CA* I 1–10 functions as a general introduction to the rest of *CA* I-II. *CA* I 11–36 provides a general overview of Athanasius' theology, including a section in which he addresses four questions that Arians ask on the streets, to deny the Son's eternal deity. *CA* I 37–*CA* II 82 is mainly concerned with the exposition of biblical texts that Athanasius' opponents use in support of their theology: Phil 2:9–10; Ps 45:7–8; Heb 1:4; 3:2; Acts 2:36 and Prv 8:22. *CA* II 18b–43 provides a discussion of preliminary issues before the actual interpretation of Prv 8:22 in *CA* II 44–82. *CA* III is written several years later and forms both a continuation and an extension of *CA* I-II. In *CA* III 1–25, Athanasius explains the meaning of several Johannine texts that his opponents claim for their doctrine of God and Christ: Jn 14:10; 17:3; 10:30 and 17:11, 20–23. *CA* III 26–58a deals with the interpretation of Gospel texts that emphasise the Son's human weaknesses and cause his opponents to deny the Son's eternal divinity and likeness in essence to the Father. The final section, *CA* III 58b–67, concerns the relation between divine nature and divine will and contains thematic connections to issues addressed in *CA* I-II.

The Genre of the *Orations*

The *Orations against the Arians* do not fit neatly in one of the three genres of classical rhetoric. Christopher Stead claims that the *Orations* do not belong to the judicial genre, because there is no courtroom or suggestion of a trial, while they are not epideictic either, since the *Orations* are no 'mere displays of virtuosity'. For that reason, he states that the *Orations* are closest to the deliberative genre, even though 'they are not concerned with practical questions, except in the rather limited sense of what one ought to

---

[10] See Meijering, *Die dritte Rede*, I:18–20, 26, and *CA* III 1.

[11] Meijering, *Die dritte Rede*, I:18–19.

believe'.[12] However, the view of epideictic speeches as a mere display of verbal skills needs serious reconsideration. Robert Flower
has demonstrated that epideictic speeches such as the panegyric
and invective are far from simple displays of eloquence; they need
to be regarded 'as vital parts of the political life of the Roman
world, where authority relied on the widespread recognition and
repletion of key virtues'.[13]

So, while it is difficult to link Athanasius' *Orations against
the Arians* to one of the of three rhetorical genres, the epideictic
genre might be the closest. The *Orations* contain a clear biblical
exposition of contested passages concerning the doctrinal issue
at stake. But this exposition is clearly interwoven with epideictic
elements. There is a strong element of praise and blame and
Athanasius broadcasts his values and virtues in the *Orations*, by
promoting his understanding of Christianity and blaming his opponents for deviating from it. In this way, the *Orations against
the Arians* are firmly embedded in a tradition of Christian works
that defend an orthodox doctrinal position against heretics.[14]
The *Orations* are best characterised as a combination of doctrinal
and polemical work. In line with other writings against heretics,
Athanasius' *Orations* did not simply defend 'orthodoxy', but in a
sense created the boundaries of 'orthodox' Christian faith.[15] A
clear motive to persuade underlies Athanasius' *Orations*. In this
context, Flower argues that fourth-century Christian texts
should be viewed 'as attempts to alter or prevent certain practices and beliefs', rather than as 'authoritative descriptions of
the status quo'.[16]

Athanasius' *Orations against the Arians* share a close relationship with a work of Marcellus of Ancyra and two works of Eusebius of Caesarea.[17] In the fourth-century discourse, Marcellus of

---

[12] Stead, "Rhetorical Method," 122.

[13] Flower, *Late Roman Invective*, 8.

[14] See pp 54-56 above.

[15] See Osborne, "Literal or Metaphorical?, 148–50.

[16] Flower, *Late Roman Invective*, 13.

[17] Sara Parvis, "'Τὰ τίνων ἄρα ῥήματα θεολογεῖ?': The Exegetical Relationship between Athanasius' *Orationes Contra Arianos I-III* and Marcellus of

Ancyra had written a work *Against Asterius* (probably written in 328), in which he attacked the theology of Asterius the Sophist.[18] There is considerable overlap between the theologies of Marcellus and Athanasius; both were strongly committed to upholding the Word's divinity and the gulf between God and creation.[19] At the same time, there were some crucial differences that resulted in criticisms of Marcellus' theology that were never levelled to the same degree against Athanasius.[20] Marcellus' work *Against Asterius* evoked a response from Eusebius of Caesarea, who defended Asterius in many respects and attacked Marcellus' theology in his works *Against Marcellus* (335) and *On Ecclesiastical Theology* (c. 337).[21] Athanasius' *Orations against the Arians* (339- c.345) stand in this tradition of Christian polemical literature that attacked opponents because of heresy. As such, it contains elements of the genre of invective as well, directed against the heretical Arians.

Ancyra's *Contra Asterium*," in *Reception and Interpretation of the Bible in Late Antiquity*, ed. Lorenzo DiTommaso and Lucian Turcescu, BiAC 6 (Boston: Brill, 2008), 337; she refers to Kannengiesser, *Athanase*, 123 n.16. See also Kelley McCarthy Spoerl, "Athanasius and the Anti-Marcellan Controversy," *ZAC* 10 (2007): 34–55.

[18] See Parvis, *Marcellus*, 118–23; for the edition of the extant fragments, transmitted in the anti-Marcellan works of Eusebius of Caesarea, see Markus Vinzent, *Markell von Ankyra. Die Fragmente. Der Brief an Julius von Rom. Herausgegeben, eingeleitet und übersetzt von Markus Vinzent*, VCSup 39 (Leiden: Brill, 1997).

[19] Anatolios, *Retrieving Nicaea*, 86–92, here 92; see also Parvis, *Marcellus*; Klaus Seibt, *Die Theologie des Markell von Ankyra* (Berlin: de Gruyter, 1994).

[20] Spoerl, "Athanasius and the Anti-Marcellan Controversy," 35, 39–52.

[21] See Mark DelCogliano, "Eusebius of Caesarea's Defense of Asterius of Cappadocia in the Anti-Marcellan Writings: A Case Study of Mutual Defense within the Eusebian Alliance," in *Eusebius of Caesarea. Tradition and Innovations*, ed. Aaron P. Johnson and Jeremy M. Schott, Hellenic Studies 60 (Washington, DC: Center for Hellenic Studies, 2013), 263–87; Anatolios, *Retrieving Nicaea*, 59–69.

THE ADDRESSEES OF THE *ORATIONS*

Athanasius gives several indications of his addressees in his *Orations against the Arians*. However, it is quite unlikely that Athanasius was solely or even primarily aiming to change the minds of the formal subject of his *Orations*, the Arians. It is necessary to explore what Athanasius imagined his audience to be before we can determine how Athanasius attempts to persuade them.

Formal Addressees

The question of an intended audience or readership is very important in a rhetorical analysis, because it enables one to estimate the effectiveness of the author's self-presentation and argumentation. However, unless other supplementary documents or events after the period in question shed light on the actual readers, one must turn to the work under consideration, to reconstruct the intended audience. In the case of the *Orations*, there is no absolute certainty concerning their actual readers. Nevertheless, we can establish in general terms whom Athanasius expected to read his works and whom he addresses. The title suggests that the Arians are addressed, but in the text itself, Athanasius also addresses others than the formally addressed audience.

Some lines in *CA* I 1 illuminate Athanasius' motive for writing the *Orations*. He states:

> [U]rged by you [παρ' ὑμῶν], I have considered it necessary (...) to reveal the stink of its foolishness, so that those who are far from it may continue to flee it, while those who have been deceived by it may repent and (...) may understand that just as light is not darkness, nor falsehood truth, so neither is the Arian heresy good. Indeed, those who call these people 'Christians' are greatly and seriously deceived ...[22]

There are three groups that Athanasius addresses in his *Orations*: (1) people that are far removed from the Arian heresy, (2) people that do not regard the Arian teachings as a heresy and (3) Arians. The first group, 'orthodox' Christians and bishops, should continue to flee from it. The second and third groups are both

---

[22] *CA* I 1 (110,16–22); tr. Anatolios.

'deceived' and there are similarities between these two groups. Neither of the groups considers the Christians that Athanasius called Arians to be heretics and hence they will not accept Athanasius' account without convincing substantiation. The suggestion that several of his readers are 'deceived' is not flattering at all and deviates from the common rhetorical advice to make people well disposed towards the author. The other element, making readers attentive, might be realised by his words nonetheless, but the introduction remains uncommon.[23]

The bishop speaks in the first person plural, assuming a relationship with those in the audience that support his position in advance. He modestly claims to follow the tradition of the apostles, who faithfully transmitted the teachings of Jesus; 'although the holy apostles have become our teachers and have been ministers of the Savior's gospel, we do not take our names from them. We are from Christ and we are named Christians.'[24] His subtle use of first-person plural pronouns suggests that anyone who belongs to Christ will share his position. This is a clear example of communion building in the sense that the *New Rhetoric* indicates.[25] The persons addressed at this point are solely Christians that share Athanasius' views, and are thus invited to further sympathise with Athanasius' position. The language of 'deceiving' might be positively received by them, since they do not belong to the 'deceived ones'. I will elaborate on the different groups below.

Orthodox Christians

The group that is far removed from the Arian heresy are those who share Athanasius' belief in the eternal divinity of the Word, including the bishops who supported him at the council of Alexandria in 338. In a circular letter from this council, written on behalf of the Alexandrian bishops, his opponents are already attacked for being Ariomaniacs.[26] Athanasius himself is probably

---

[23] The orator Dio Chrysostom gives an excellent example of praise and criticism in his speech "To the people of Alexandria" (Discourse 32).

[24] *CA* I 2 (111,20–24); tr. Rusch. Cf. *CA* I 3 (111,2–3; 112,10–19).

[25] Perelman and Olbrechts-Tyteca, *New Rhetoric*, 178.

[26] See Athanasius, *Apol. c. Ar.* 3–19.

the author of this letter as the archbishop of Alexandria. The signatures of all these bishops, as well as the large group of bishops Athanasius could gather to support his case a few years before in Tyre (335), indicate that he had quite some support from other bishops. In addition, pope Julius of Rome is most likely among the addressees of the *Orations*.

Other sympathisers include Marcellus and like-minded theologians. However, Athanasius subtly criticises this group alongside the Arians in some instances as well,[27] for he wants to persuade this group to accept the title Son as a proper title for the divine Word's eternity. Several monks are also among the group that explicitly dissociate themselves from the Arian heresy.[28] It is uncertain whether the words in *CA* I 1 'urged by you' refer to the monks or to Alexandrian Christians or bishops, but Athanasius certainly expects a favourable hearing from them. Athanasius had warm ties with several monks, and even wrote the highly influential *Life of Antony* (written between 356-362). Antony even came briefly from the desert to Alexandria to support Athanasius' cause in July 337 or 338 (see *VA* 69-71).

Athanasius' style is unsophisticated and steeped in biblical language, and is therefore very acceptable to this group of addressees. It is even suggested that the monastic style of living and speech was staked as a rival claim to true *paideia* in contrast to the classical form of *paideia*.[29] Their concerns were probably less theologically sophisticated than Athanasius', but in any case, they were important and highly esteemed among Christian laypeople

---

[27] Martin Tetz, "Athanasius von Alexandrien," *TRE (4)* (Berlin: de Gruyter, 1979), 346; Anatolios, "'Christ the Power and Wisdom of God'"; Wijnand A. Boezelman, "The *Gospel of John* and Polemical Equation of Arians to Jews in Athanasius' *Orationes Contra Arianos* and Contemporary Works," in *StPatr* 72, ed. A. Brent, M. Ludlow, and M. Vinzent (Leuven: Peeters, 2014), 133–46.

[28] Brakke, *Asceticism*, 129–41, esp. 139–41; cf. Kannengiesser's hypothesis that the *Letter to the Monks* refers to an earlier version of *Orations* I-II in Kannengiesser, "Dating," 29–32; idem, *Athanase*, 375–97.

[29] See Brown, *Power and Persuasion*, 4. See also Larsen and Rubenson, *Monastic Education*, on the transformation of classical *paideia* into monasticism.

in this period.[30] Christian laypeople may also have been addressed alongside the monks, but there are no specific clues for that. However, we know that some laypersons were interested in theology, for example, Asterius the Sophist.

'Impartial' Christians

A second group of addressees, those who are not Arians and do not regard Arianism as heresy, might be identified with the monks and bishops that wanted to stay impartial in the theological conflict or were not even aware of the dispute. Monks are probably included in this group. The fact that monks were initially reluctant to take sides in the controversy suggests that there were also bishops and other Christians that did not wish to commit themselves in the debate, or declared that they did not regard Arians as non-Christians.

Likely, various bishops of the Western Church were not aware of the theological subtleties in the Eastern Church. Hilary of Poitiers, for one, was not aware of the Nicene Creed before 356, so that its fame in the early 340s cannot have been too widespread, although it must have been known to some, as two Roman presbyters participated in Nicaea to represent pope Sylvester.[31] Furthermore, many Eastern bishops may have regarded theological tenets of Arianism as compatible with Christianity. Several of them may have been open to persuasion by Athanasius.[32]

A large group of monks were indifferent to theological disagreements between Arianism and Athanasius, so that Athanasius needed to urge them to take a stand against Arianism.[33] It is unlikely that Athanasius intentionally called monks deceived, because he probably did not want to alienate them from his

---

[30] Cf. Edward Jay Watts, *Riot in Alexandria: Tradition and Group Dynamics in Late Antique Pagan and Christian Communities*, The Transformation of the Classical Heritage 46 (Berkeley: University of California Press, 2010), 175–89.

[31] Cf. Hanson, *Search*, 459–60.

[32] Ernest, *Bible*, 359. He assumes this audience for *Defence before Constantius*.

[33] Brakke, *Asceticism*, 134–42.

episcopate, but Athanasius might urge them in the *Orations* to change their minds, by suggesting that the Arians have deceived many. He wanted to prevent monks from remaining supportive to Arian-minded bishops and showing them hospitality.[34]

Athanasius wants every bishop and Christian to take sides in the controversy by suggesting that there is no middle ground between him and Arianism. He characterises everyone who desires neutrality as 'deceived'; such a person is unaware of his opposition to the Church and the Lord Jesus Christ himself.[35]

Arian Opponents

The third group are the Arians, who are formally most often addressed. This group of Arians is described by Athanasius both as a unified group and as a group of theologians that hold contradictory views.[36] His emphasis on either their unity or their inconsistency depends primarily on Athanasius' polemical purpose at hand. First, I will introduce the three individuals that are explicitly addressed, and then discuss the 'Arians' as a group and the scholarly debate surrounding this designation.

Arius

The first individual is the presbyter Arius, to whom Athanasius links the heresy in particular. Arius is the author of the *Thalia*, a work in which he presents his theological views in a poetical form devised by the pagan poet Sotades. Athanasius considers the Sotadean metre inappropriate for religious or serious works, and thus suggests the frivolous nature of Arius.[37] Arius came into conflict with his direct superior, Alexander of Alexandria, somewhere

---

[34] See Brakke, *Asceticism*, 129–41.

[35] Cf. *CA* I 7 (116,22–27).

[36] Anatolios, "'When Was God without Wisdom?,'" 117–23.

[37] The Sotadean metre was associated with obscene poetry. See Llewelyn Morgan, *Musa Pedestris. Metre and Meaning in Roman Verse* (Oxford: Oxford University Press, 2010), 40–48; by linking Arius' *Thalia* to Sotades, Athanasius characterises Arius' work as perverse, see M. L. West, "The Metre of Arius' *Thalia*," *JTS* 33 (1982): 98–105.

between 318 and 321.[38] Alexander, the predecessor of Athanasius, strongly emphasised the eternity of the Son, which probably provoked a response from Arius. It is impossible to establish with certainty how they became involved in this debate. However, two ancient historians, Philostorgius and Theodoret, leave room for the idea that Alexander and Arius were competing candidates for the episcopal nomination, which turned out in favour of Alexander.[39] Over time, Arius articulated his theological views, to the displeasure of Alexander. Alexander reprimanded Arius for his theological convictions, and in turn, Arius wrote to other bishops asking for support. This was the start of a local conflict that quickly gained an international dimension, in which Arius received the support of several bishops, most notably Eusebius of Nicomedia. In 325, a council met at Nicaea to discuss, among other things, the theological questions that arose in the conflict. Arius refused to sign the Nicene Creed and was excommunicated. We do not know much about Arius and his theology, since the documents preserved in church history are mainly those written by the orthodox, not the heretics. Moreover, Constantine decreed briefly after the council of Nicaea that all of Arius' books should be burned (Urk. 33 = Dok. 28). This reduced the chances of his books being preserved for posterity. However, a few small fragments from Arius survive, and are available in *Athanasius Werke* (Opitz 3,1). The extant works are the following:

1. A letter from Arius to Eusebius of Nicomedia (Urk. 1 = Dok. 15).
2. A letter from Arius to Alexander of Alexandria with his confession of faith (Urk. 6 = Dok. 1). This letter carries signatures of other bishops, priests and deacons as well.

---

[38] For some general studies on Arius' life and writings, see Williams, *Arius*; Winrich Löhr, "Arius Reconsidered (Part 1)," *ZAC* 9 (2005): 524–60; idem, "Arius Reconsidered (Part 2)," *ZAC* 10 (2006): 121–57. On Arius' final years, see Parvis, *Marcellus*, 96–133.

[39] See Parvis, *Marcellus*, 73, Beeley, *Unity of Christ*, 106–7.

This document is probably the earliest of Arius' extant writings.[40]

3. Fragments of the *Thalia*, a theological poem that contained his view on the Son. These fragments are presented by Athanasius in *CA* I 5–6.

4. A letter from Arius and Euzoius to Emperor Constantine after their excommunication at the Council of Nicaea (Urk. 30 = Dok. 34). In the winter of 327, they submitted a theological creed with the purpose of being accepted into the Church again.

Because Arius' writings have been preserved by authors that regarded him a heretic, it is difficult to establish his exact theological views with great certainty. He is quoted mainly for his deviant doctrine of the Son of God. Anatolios categorises Arius' theology as part of a theological trajectory that emphasised the unity of the Trinity as a unity of will.[41]

Besides the limited amount of writings by Arius, there are some surviving documents that consist of written communications to or about Arius (apart from Athanasius and other orthodox Church Fathers criticising Arius).

1. Fragments of a letter of Eusebius of Nicomedia to Arius (Urk. 2 = Dok. 16).

2. A letter of Constantine to Alexander of Alexandria and Arius, just before the Council of Nicaea (325) (Urk. 17 = Dok. 19)

3. A letter of Constantine to Arius requesting his presence at an audience as soon as possible. This letter is dated 27 November 327 (Urk. 29 = Dok. 33).

4. A letter of Constantine to Arius and his colleagues (Urk. 34 = Dok. 27). Constantine sharply criticises Arius in this letter, but also offers rehabilitation to Arius if he recognises piety and truth in Arius. This letter is traditionally

---

[40] The major part is found in a version given by Athanasius, *Syn* 16,2–5; the last paragraph, including the persons subscribing to this creed, is only found in Epiphanius, *Panarion* 69,8.

[41] Anatolios, *Retrieving Nicaea*, 30–31.

dated to 333. Despite attempts to shift the date to the 320s, this is still the most plausible reading of this letter.[42]

5. A letter of Constantine to bishops and laity, declaring that all works of Arius should be burned (Urk. 33 = Dok. 28). This letter has often been considered contemporaneous with Constantine's letter to Arius and his colleagues (Urk.

---

[42] See Barnes, "Exile,", 109–129, for the relevant positions and alternative chronology as given in AW 3.1.3. Hanns Christof Brennecke has argued that the death of Arius took place before the death of Alexander of Alexandria in 328. See "Die letzten Jahre des Arius," in *Von Arius zum Athanasianum*, ed. Annette von Stockhausen and Hanns Christof Brennecke (Berlin: de Gruyter, 2010), 63–83. He bases this on the relative silence surrounding Arius in in the years after Nicaea (Brennecke, *Arius*, 64). He asserts that Alexander of Constantinople, who was forced to receive Arius into communion, had already passed away in 336. Brennecke infers this from the fact that Paul of Constantinople, the successor of Alexander, is present at the Council of Jerusalem in 335 (Brennecke, *Arius*, 70–71). This council urged the churches of Alexandria and beyond to readmit those around Arius (τούς περὶ ᾿Αρειον) into communion. See Barnes, "Exile," 123–24, for an alternative explanation of this fact. In Barnes' view, Arius was formally reaccepted at the council. The second essential aspect is whether the phrase οἱ περὶ ᾿Αρειον (see Dok 39,5; Council of Jerusalem 335) could refer to a group that did not include Arius himself. Brennecke musters textual evidence for this view, but it remains to be seen whether his case stands (see Brennecke, *Arius*, 71–74 and Barnes, "Exile," 119–21). The third point of disagreement concerns the dating of Constantine's Letter against Arius (Urk. 34 = Dok. 27) and the mention of the prefect Paterius (Opitz, 75,6-7). It is most probable that Paterius was the prefect in 333, but Brennecke argues that this is far from certain (see Barnes, "Exile," 116–19 and Brennecke, *Arius*, 75–77). Brennecke's argument is interesting but runs against the majority of scholarship on Athanasius and the Arian controversy. If his proposal were accepted, it would demonstrate that the term 'Arians' is not a polemical invention by Athanasius, but rather a conscious self-designation taken up by a group of theologians that felt an affinity with Arius' theological views at the Council of Jerusalem in 335. This might alter our understanding of the role of Athanasius in framing this discourse on Arianism. However, while Brennecke addresses significant issues, it is still better to date the death of Arius to 336.

34 = Dok. 27) and dated together to 333. However, it is most likely that the order to destroy Arius' books was written very soon after the Council of Nicaea in 325.[43]

More correspondence could be added to this list, such as the fragment of Constantine's letter to Alexander of Alexandria to receive Arius back into communion and settle the dispute (Urk. 32 = Dok. 37).[44] But these are the sources that most clearly demonstrate the direct involvement of Arius in the theological controversy up to 336, three years before Athanasius writes his *Orations against the Arians*.

The small fragment of the letter of Eusebius of Nicomedia does not shed much light on Arius, except that Arius was in communication with at least one influential bishop who found it worthwhile to correspond with Arius. The communication from Constantine demonstrates that Arius was taken seriously enough to receive imperial attention. The key interest of Constantine was to ensure peace and harmony, first by convening the Council of Nicaea in 325 and then by accepting a modified theological position. At that point, Constantine urged bishop Alexander to receive Arius back into communion (see Urk. 32 = Dok. 37). In 327, Arius was readmitted into the Church by Constantine, but Alexander and his successor Athanasius refused to accept him. In 333, Constantine's anger with Arius was rekindled and he excommunicated him again. A council of bishops readmitted him, but he soon died an undignified death in a toilet near the church in 335 or 336. This disgraceful death has sometimes been considered an invention, but Barnes argues that it was most likely the sudden death of Arius that enabled Athanasius to use this situation for polemical purposes.[45]

All in all, it is safe to conclude Arius was not the primary leader of an ecclesiastical party in his time, but he definitely exerted some influence and was protected by influential bishops. In

---

[43] See Barnes, "Exile,", 127–128.

[44] For the complete correspondence of Constantine, see P. R. Coleman-Norton, ed., *Roman State and Christian Church: Volume 1* (London: SPCK, 1966).

[45] Barnes, "Exile,", 109–113.

the *Orations*, Arius mainly features in the introduction of *CA* I 1–10, in connection with the *Thalia*. After that, his role in the *Orations* is rather limited. He is referred to several times, but Athanasius does not include more detailed information on the content of Arius' theological views. This is not completely surprising, since Arius died in 336, three or four years before the writing of the *Orations*.

Asterius

Asterius was a layman, highly interested in theology and a clever thinker and probably a leading theologian within his circle.[46] However, due to his sacrifice to the pagan gods during the Diocletian Persecution (303–311), he was disqualified from being a clergyman for life. When looking at the prominence of Asterius' work *Syntagmation* in Athanasius' *Orations,* we can assume that Athanasius regarded Asterius as his main opponent.[47] The *Syntagmation* is explicitly quoted six times in the main body (*CA* I 30; 32; II 37; 40; *CA* III 2; 60), and it has been argued that several other unidentified portions of Arian theology derive from Asterius as well.[48] DelCogliano has recently argued that Arius' *Thalia* was written soon after Asterius' *Syntagmation*. He asserts that both works were written in an attempt to win over bishops to their theological cause in 323 to support Arius and like-minded bishops in his struggle with Alexander.[49] In contrast to Arius, whose name features most conspicuously in the introductions of *CA* I and II and fades away afterwards, Asterius is absent in the introductory

---

[46] Markus Vinzent, *Asterius von Kappadokien. Die Theologischen Fragmente. Einleitung, Kritischer Text, Übersetzung und Kommentar*, VCSup 20 (Leiden: Brill, 1993), 20–32.

[47] Kannengiesser, *Athanase*, 122.

[48] Kannengiesser, *Athanase*, 128–80; See e.g. frs. 18, 20, 41–42 and Vinzent's comments in Vinzent, *Asterius*, 186–92, 194–95, 239–44. Besides the *Thalia*, Athanasius only refers to Asterius' *Syntagmation* and otherwise unspecified sources.

[49] He bases this understanding of the relationship between both works on the reading of *Decr* 8 and 20. See Mark DelCogliano, "How Did Arius Learn from Asterius?: On the Relationship between the Thalia and the Syntagmation," *JEH* 69.3 (2018): 477–92.

chapters, but features more prominently in the main body of the *Orations*.

Eusebius of Nicomedia

The third individual from the Arian party mentioned in the *Orations* is Eusebius (of Nicomedia).[50] He is only identified as Eusebius, but there is no doubt that Eusebius of Nicomedia is addressed, instead of Eusebius of Caesarea or another namesake. Eusebius of Nicomedia was an outspoken supporter of Arius (see Urk. 1–2, 8, 31 = Dok. 15, 16, 4, 36) and initially refused to sign the Nicene Creed, or at least its condemnations. He is mentioned three times in the *Orations*, always together with Arius.[51]

Arians

The three individuals mentioned above are the only opponents named in the *Orations*. Much more frequently, Athanasius refers to his opponents as Arians (Ἀρειανοί), Arian heresy (ἀρειανῆς αἵρεσις), Ariomaniacs (Ἀρειομανῖται) and 'those around Arius' (οἱ περὶ Ἄρειον). 'Arians' is the term most commonly used to refer to Athanasius' opponents, but it is also hotly debated and often criticised in the literature. Two aspects are debated in this regard. The first aspect is the correctness or incorrectness of Athanasius' labelling of his opponents as such, and the second, whether there existed a coherent ecclesiastical party that opposed Athanasian theology.

The first aspect in the literature on Athanasius has to do with fair representation of the opponents, whose writings are very sparsely preserved in comparison to the writings of their 'orthodox' counterparts. Maurice Wiles asserts that Arius held little influence within the movement often labelled as 'Arianism': 'The dead Arius was not even a whipping boy, but a whip', while Athanasius 'real quarrel was with the living'.[52] Wiles and others have

---

[50] On his life, see David Morton Gwynn, "Constantine and the Other Eusebius," *Prudentia* 31 (1999): 94–124.

[51] *CA* I 22; I 37; II 24.

[52] Wiles, "Attitudes," 43; Maurice F. Wiles, *Archetypal Heresy: Arianism through the Centuries* (Oxford: Clarendon, 1996).

concluded that the term 'Arians' is rather an imposition from outside than a term that they might have embraced. Some attempts
have been made to substitute the term 'Arians' by 'Eusebians' (οἱ
περὶ Εὐσέβιον).[53] However, this substitution has not been completely successful. Athanasius employs both categorisations
throughout his writings, but only the term 'Arians' features in the
Orations. For nearly 1500 years, this classification of Athanasius'
opponents as 'Arians' remained standard, and even today,[54] although criticised and rejected by scholars, it has not been abol-
ished, if only for want of alternatives.[55] In a sense, Wiles' criticism
is correct. It is unlikely that Arius was a leading figure in the theological debates. He was a presbyter, not a bishop, so in that
sense, he would not have had such an authoritative role in the
debate. At the same time, Arius as an individual had some significance in the movement. The fact that Constantine wrote Arius
several letters means that Constantine perceived Arius as important from either a theological or a political perspective. Arius
also gained the support of several prominent bishops in his clash
with Bishop Alexander of Alexandria. He corresponded with Eusebius of Nicomedia (Urk. 1–2 = Dok. 15-16), and in response,
Eusebius of Nicomedia exhorted Paulinus of Tyre to speak up for
the cause as well. In this letter, Eusebius of Nicomedia expresses
his gladness that Eusebius of Caesarea is being vocal for the theological cause created by the dispute between Alexander of Alexandria and Arius. He states:

> The zeal of my lord Eusebius [of Caesarea] in the cause of the
> truth, and likewise your silence concerning it, has not failed
> to reach our ears. Accordingly, if, on the one hand, we re-
> joiced on account of the zeal of my lord Eusebius; on the other

---

[53] Gwynn, Eusebians, 103–15. However, see also the declaration of the
Council of Jerusalem in 335 (Dok. 39) for the use of οἱ περὶ Ἄρειον by a
synod that spoke in favour of Arius, and footnote 319 above.
[54] Parvis, "Christology," 120 n.1.
[55] Gwynn, Eusebians, 6–8; Hanson, Search, xvii–xxi.

we are grieved at you, because the mere silence of man like you appears like a defeat of our cause (Urk. 8,2–4 = Dok. 4).[56]

This language of Eusebius of Nicomedia is clearly an attempt to gather support for Arius' theology, probably not because Arius espoused it, but because it was championed by a significant group of bishops in the fourth century. Eusebius of Caesarea wrote several letters in support of Arius (Urk. 3, 7 = Dok. 10, 9). Eusebius of Nicomedia, Theognis of Nicaea and a few other bishops were willing to side with Arius despite Constantine's pressure to condemn Arius. And after the excommunication of Arius and some others, a larger group of bishops was willing to be associated with Arius to revoke Arius' excommunication. This is evident from a letter of Constantine to Alexander of Alexandria. In this letter, Constantine mentions that Arius and Euzoius were heard about their faith in the presence of many (παρόντων πλειόνων) when they were accepted into communion in the winter of 327 (Urk. 32; = Dok. 37).

Added to that, Arius did not present a creed by himself alone. The creed he presented in an early phase of the Arian controversy was endorsed by several bishops, such as Secundus of Ptolemais (Urk. 6 = Dok. 1) Also, Eusebius of Nicomedia and a few others were willing to face excommunication in the wake of their refusal to sign the Nicene Creed in 325. While it is highly unlikely that Arius was considered a key leader in a movement of self-confessing 'Arians', Athanasius did not just invent the role of Arius in the theological controversy. The fact that Constantine had a significant amount of correspondence with Arius, and the fact that many bishops were willing to be associated with Arius' theology, even in the face of potential imperial wrath, indicate that Arius as an individual was by no means unimportant in this ecclesiastical party.

The second aspect debated with regard to Athanasius and the Arians is the question whether there was actually a coherent ecclesiastical party that could be identified as 'Arians' or

---

[56] "Letter of Eusebius of Nicomedia to Paulinus of Tyre," *Fourth Century Christianity*, 27 October 2020, https://www.fourthcentury.com/ urkunde-8/ (tr. Glen L. Thompson).

'Eusebians', or whether this was a 'rhetorical invention,' imposed upon the situation by Athanasius. David Gwynn takes issue with the concept of an 'ecclesiastical party'. While he acknowledges that 'associations between bishops did exist', and that creeds composed at councils unified individual bishops, he argues that there is a serious polemical dimension to the concept of an Arian party.[57] He registers that none of the participants in the fourth-century debate ever suggested they were a party, because that would separate them from the true Church. Gwynn asserts that this would rather be an Athanasian distortion of the situation than a realistic representation of the actual situation, though he does not want to challenge Athanasius' sincerity.[58]

Other scholars disagree with Gwynn's argument. Around the same time as Gwynn, Sara Parvis put forward evidence for two theological alliances in the period immediately leading up to the council of Nicaea.[59] She contends that Arius gained support primarily from bishops from Palestine, Phoenicia, Syria and Cilicia; all of these envisioned a gulf between the Father and the Son. While Alexander of Alexandria had much in common with Eusebius of Caesarea and Asterius, Alexander sided with Marcellus, despite their many theological differences, because they shared the belief in the Son's eternity.[60] Arius appealed to Eusebius of Nicomedia and like-minded bishops, while Alexander of Alexandria wrote a circular letter to gain support from as many bishops as possible to ensure Arius' condemnation in the letter *He Philarchos* (Urk. 14 = Dok. 17).[61]

Along the same lines, Ritter criticises the strong doubts concerning Athanasius' personal influence on the theological debate of the fourth century. He argues that a polemical imposition of the conflict by Athanasius is not likely, because he 'was hardly

---

[57] Gwynn, *Eusebians*, 106.
[58] Gwynn, *Eusebians*, 245–49.
[59] Parvis, *Marcellus*, 39–67.
[60] Parvis, *Marcellus*, 47–54.
[61] Parvis, *Marcellus*, 74.

able to impose his will on anybody'.[62] In other words, it is more plausible that Athanasius by his writings genuinely convinced others of his theological views than that he was able to 'invent' such a construct. The arguments of Parvis and Ritter seem to have influenced Gwynn, for in 2012 he takes a more nuanced position. At this point, Gwynn asserts that Athanasius' attack on the Arians is not 'merely a device of polemical rhetoric', since the 'theological issues at stake were real and fundamental'.[63] His work of 2012 thus attempts to bring together a more coherent perspective on Athanasius' life and career, which allows room for giving due weight to the theological argument in the *Orations against the Arians*.

All in all, distinct ecclesiastical parties, one of which was willing to defend Arius, did exist. This ecclesiastical party could be labelled as Eusebian or 'Arian' in contrast to Athanasius and like-minded theologians. These ecclesiastical parties might show some fluidity but are nonetheless important for understanding the dynamics of fourth-century Christianity and Athanasius' ecclesiastical career. No doubt there is a process of simplification happening in Athanasius' writings that is polemically motivated. Athanasius was under pressure and did not have the luxury to spell out all the positive aspects of the theology of Arius and like-minded theologians. There was an actual struggle going on with clear theological interests and motivations.

That Athanasius only speaks of 'Arians' in his *Orations against the Arians* is significant for another reason. Although the distinction between 'Arians' and 'Eusebians' is not generally satisfying, there is a subtle but important distinction between the Arians and Eusebians. While Athanasius considers many Arians to belong to the Eusebian party, he does not openly call all Eusebians heretics. In the case of Eusebius of Caesarea, the first Church historian, who held a position that showed an affinity with Arius and Asterius, it is quite unclear whether Athanasius considered him a

---

[62] Adolf Martin Ritter, "Athanasius as Trinitarian Theologian," in *StPatr* 52, ed. A. Brent and M. Vinzent (Leuven: Peeters, 2012), 103. Cf. Flower, *Late Roman Invective,* 220.

[63] Gwynn, *Athanasius,* 9; cf. Gwynn, *Eusebians,* 245–49.

heretic, and whether Athanasius dared to attack this Eusebius openly.[64] I will use normally use the term Arians whenever Athanasius attacks his opponents, but I will use the term Eusebians when a larger group, most notably Eusebius of Caesarea, is included.

Patristic Method of Biblical Interpretation

Prior to the discussion of Athanasius' use of the Gospel of John in the *Orations*, I will give a brief overview of Athanasius' method of biblical interpretation. In order to get a better grasp of Athanasius' exegetical method, I will first discuss the strategies that Christian authors before Athanasius used in their conflicts with heretical opponents. Secondly, I will discuss his exegetical remarks in his work *On the Incarnation*, which was written before Athanasius' polemic against the Arians started. After that, I will discuss some explicit exegetical remarks in the *Orations*.

Irenaeus and Tertullian on Biblical Interpretation against Heretics

As noted, Athanasius' *Orations* stand in a tradition of Christian authors that refuted heretics. From early on, the question concerning truth arose in Christianity and how it was to be distinguished from heresy. While there are different views on the initial phase of Christianity, it is clear that there was a desire within Christianity to decide or defend the boundaries of authentic or 'orthodox' Christianity.[65] Two of the most influential early Christians that shaped the discourse of orthodoxy versus heresy are

---

[64] On the influence of Eusebius on Athanasius, see Bouter, *Athanasius*, 24.

[65] Bauer argued that orthodoxy was a later imposition upon an earlier diverse and multifaceted group of Christian sects. See Walter Bauer, *Rechtgläubigkeit und Ketzerei im ältesten Christentum*, 2nd ed. (Tübingen: Mohr Siebeck, 1964). The first edition was published in 1934. An English translation appeared in 1971 as *Orthodoxy and Heresy in Earliest Christianity*; for a critique of Bauer's line of thinking, see Andreas J. Köstenberger and Michael J. Kruger, eds, *The Heresy of Orthodoxy: How Contemporary Culture's Fascination with Diversity Has Reshaped Our Understanding of Early Christianity* (Wheaton: Crossway, 2010).

Irenaeus and Tertullian. A very practical problem within Christianity concerned the claim that the Sacred Scriptures of the Old and New Testament contained the divine revelation. However, the Scriptures needed interpretation, and because of the subjective element of every interpretation, it remained virtually impossible to refute satisfactorily interpretations that contradicted crucial Christian views.[66] Both Irenaeus and Tertullian discovered that an appeal to the Scriptures alone was not enough to defeat a heretical view, and proposed a solution to this dilemma.[67]

In Irenaeus' time, his struggle for the correct biblical interpretation was mainly directed against the Gnostics, who doubted the legitimacy of the Old Testament as divine revelation.[68] Irenaeus attacks the views of the Valentinians, who considered themselves Christians, and therefore needs to defend the view that the Old Testament Scriptures belong to the biblical canon.[69] In this situation, Irenaeus argues that a sound person can understand the sacred Scriptures unambiguously.[70] In 'regular' cases, there is no problem in understanding Scripture, because 'the entire Scriptures, the prophets, and the Gospels, can be clearly, unambiguously, and harmoniously understood by all'.[71] However,

---

[66] See Arie Wilhelm Zwiep, *Tussen tekst en lezer. Een historische inleiding in de bijbelse hermeneutiek. Deel I: De vroege kerk – Schleiermacher* (Amsterdam: VU University Press, 2009).

[67] See Dietrich Schleyer's introduction on this theme in Tertullian, *De Praescriptione Haereticorum. Vom prinzipiellen Einspruch gegen die Häretiker. Übersetzt und Eingeleitet von Dietrich Schleyer*, ed. Dietrich Schleyer, Fontes Christiani 42 (Turnhout: Brepols, 2002), 152–211. Irenaeus' view is discussed at 178–183. See also Osborne, "Literal or Metaphorical?," 148–52.

[68] Kannengiesser, *Handbook*, I:448.

[69] See Irenaeus, *AH* III 15.2 and Anne Pasquier, "III. The Valentinian Exegesis. A Special Contribution," in *Handbook of Patristic Exegesis*, ed. Charles Kannengiesser, vol. I, BiAC 1 (Leiden: Brill, 2004), 454–70.

[70] Irenaeus, *AH* II 27.1.

[71] Irenaeus, *AH* II 27.2; tr. ANF. This does not exclude an emphasis on certain biblical books over certain other biblical books, for John's Gospel played a prominent role in Irenaeus' theology. See on this topic Bernhard Mutschler, *Irenäus als johanneischer Theologe: Studien zur Schriftauslegung*

since his heretical opponents appeal to 'ambiguous expressions' in Scripture that distract from the truth, Irenaeus takes refuge in the 'rule of truth'.[72] The rule of truth is a summary of crucial Christian beliefs that cannot be doubted by Christians and are consistent with the divine revelation in the Scriptures of the OT and NT. In his time, the confession that God, the Father of Jesus Christ, is the Creator of the world was crucial. Irenaeus argues that unclear passages should be understood in the light of clearer passages,[73] and locates the truthfulness of the 'rule of truth' in the Church's faithful transmission of it.[74] Irenaeus thus acknowledges the impossibility of defining heresy by interpretation of Scripture alone. He conceives of harmony between the rule of truth and Scripture; a heretical interpretation of Scripture can be adequately rejected, because the rule of truth and the teachings of Scripture coincide. The application of the rule of truth is Irenaeus' tool for maintaining the unity of the Old and New Testament and the proper interpretation of the Scriptures. The concept that Irenaeus calls the rule of truth is used by many other writers, including Tertullian. They refer to it as the 'rule of faith'.

Tertullian wrote against different heretics, such as Marcion and Praxeas. At least in the case of Marcion, the dispute included the boundaries of the scriptural canon, i.e. the inclusion or exclusion of the Old Testament.[75] He was equally aware of the impossibility of winning an argument against heretics from Scripture alone, and proposed an even more rigid solution than Irenaeus: the rule of faith must be placed above the exegesis of Scripture.

---

bei *Irenäus von Lyon*, Studien und Texte zu Antike und Christentum 21 (Tübingen: Mohr Siebeck, 2004); Bernhard Mutschler, *Das Corpus Johanneum bei Irenäus von Lyon: Studien und Kommentar zum dritten Buch von Adversus Haereses*, WUNT 189 (Tübingen: Mohr Siebeck, 2006).

[72] For Irenaeus' view on Scripture and the rule of faith, see Lee Martin McDonald, *The Biblical Canon. Its Origin, Transmission, and Authority* (Peabody, MA: Hendrickson, 2007), 289–301.

[73] Irenaeus, *AH* II 10.1; II 27.1; cf. *AH* III 2.1; IV 5.1.

[74] *AH* I 10.2.

[75] For literature on Marcion, see Kannengiesser, *Handbook*, I:450–53.

Tertullian thus asserts *a priori* that the heretics are wrong.[76] In his work the *On Prescriptions against heretics*, he says:

> Our appeal, therefore, must not be made to the Scriptures; nor must controversy be admitted on points in which victory will either be impossible, or uncertain, or not certain enough. (...) The natural order of things would require that this point should be first proposed: ... With whom lies that very faith to which the Scriptures belong? ... For where it shall be evident that the truth of doctrine and Christian faith is, *there* will likewise be the true Scriptures and expositions thereof, and all the Christian traditions.[77]

At first sight, Tertullian's solution seems circular and excludes the possibility of proper exegesis, for he claims to have won the battle against heretical interpretation before it has begun. However, these words do not imply that Tertullian is uninterested in exegesis. Nor does he deny Scripture as the ultimate source of revelation, for he wrote much about the proper interpretation and exegesis of the Scriptures.[78] His words must be understood in the light of a realistic evaluation of the nature of appeal to authority. If two parties turn to the Scriptures with conflicting views, the argument can never be decisively won, and he therefore appeals to the rule of faith to assert the right knowledge *a priori*.

Athanasius on Biblical Interpretation

Athanasius' stands in the tradition of Irenaeus and Tertullian. One of the earliest works of Athanasius is his double work *Against the Pagans-On the Incarnation*. In this work, he gives some remarks on his understanding of exegesis and biblical interpretation. The dating of *Against the Pagans-On the Incarnation* is complex, but needs to be discussed in order to determine the status of this text in relation to the *Orations against the Arians*.[79] The occasion of its

---

[76] Tertullian, *Praesc.* 13.6.

[77] *Praesc.* 19; tr. ANF, adapted. Italics original.

[78] Geoffrey D. Dunn, "Tertullian's Scriptural Exegesis in *de Praescriptione Haereticorum*," *JECS* 14 (2006): 141–55.

[79] See Athanasius, *Contra Gentes, and De Incarnatione*, ed. Robert W. Thomson, Oxford Early Christian Texts (Oxford: Clarendon, 1971); E. P.

writing and its date have been connected to various events: before
the condemnation of Arius (318–325),[80] during Athanasius' prep-
aration for the episcopate (325–328),[81] in his early episcopate
(before 335), during the first exile to Trier (335–337),[82] or even
as late as the third exile.[83] The dating has of course implications
for the extent to which this work, including its exegetical method,
is already influenced by the theological dispute with Arius. Proponents of the early dating emphasise that there are no explicit
references to the Arians, while advocates of a later dating assert
that its theology is influenced by the Arian controversy. I follow
the scholars who date the treatises before 335. This means that
the theological conflict might already have been present when he
wrote these works. However, the treatises contain Athanasius'
view on the interpretation of Scripture before he started his explicit polemic against Arianism in the late 330s.

At the end of *On the Incarnation*, Athanasius speaks of the accuracy of Scripture in a quite general sense. A large part of this
work consists of a demonstration of the superiority of Christian
faith over the pagan Greek philosophers in terms of rationality and
reasonableness. Athanasius then says:

> If you ... read the words of the Scriptures and really apply
> your mind to them, you will learn from them more completely
> and more clearly the accuracy (ἀκρίβειαν) of what has been
> said. For the Scriptures were spoken and written by God
> through men versed in theology; and we have learned from
> the teachers of theology who are found therein, who were also
> witnesses of the divinity of Christ, and we pass on our
> knowledge to your own love of learning.[84]

Meijering, *Athanasius: Contra Gentes. Introduction, Translation, Commentary*, Philosophia Patrum 7 (Leiden: Brill, 1984); E. P. Meijering, *Athanasius: De Incarnatione Verbi* (Amsterdam: Gieben, 1989).

[80] Meijering, *Contra Gentes*, 1–2.

[81] Barnes, *Athanasius and Constantius*, 12–13.

[82] Kannengiesser, "Dating," 22.

[83] Martin, *Athanase*, 485 n.128.

[84] *DI* 56 (272,3–10); tr. Thomson.

In this passage, Athanasius asserts that the Scriptures are the primary source of knowledge concerning God. He presupposes that the Scriptures clearly teach Christ's divinity, for the Scriptures were written by witnesses of Christ's divinity. This might be considered a form of dogmatic exegesis that settles the matter of Christ's divinity. Since the Scriptures were written by witnesses of Christ's divinity, any interpretation that questions this key feature cannot be correct. Besides the study of the Scriptures, a person's disposition should be sound, for 'without a pure mind and a life modeled on the saints, no one can apprehend the words of the saints'.[85] In short, Athanasius assumes both an objective quality, i.e. accuracy, as well as a subjective quality, i.e. piety and awareness of Christ's divinity, in biblical interpretation. Piety and a right understanding of Scripture are therefore inseparable.[86] Already in *On the Incarnation*, the core message of the Scriptures hinges on the eternity of Christ. This conclusion is affirmed by P. F. Bouter, who states three hermeneutical principles of Athanasius: (1) Christ can be found in the whole of Scripture, (2) Scripture has its own distinctive (divine) speech, and (3) understanding Scripture presupposes piety.[87] This implies that Athanasius' focus on Christ and the necessity to approach Scripture in a pious way was formed before his systematic polemic against Arianism that started at the end of the 330s.

Athanasius further describes his method of biblical interpretation in the *Orations*. In *CA* I 54, he says:

> [I]t is necessary, ... to expound faithfully the time (καιρός) when the apostle spoke and the person (πρόσωπον) and subject

---

[85] *DI* 57 (274,5–7); tr. Thomson.

[86] Cf. Peter Widdicombe, *The Fatherhood of God from Origen to Athanasius* (Oxford: Clarendon, 1994), 155–58.

[87] See Bouter, *Athanasius*, 42–67. Some caution concerning this conclusion is necessary because Bouter establishes it partly on the possibly inauthentic *Expositions on the Psalms*. See Bouter, *Athanasius*, 20–35. A main opponent of its authenticity is Christopher Stead. See "St Athanasius on the Psalms," *VC* 39 (1985): 65–78. However, Bouter's outline of Athanasian hermeneutics is by and large supported by Thomas F. Torrance, *Divine Meaning: Studies in Patristic Hermeneutics* (Edinburgh: T&T Clark, 1995), 179–288, 272–88.

(πρᾶγμα) about which he wrote, lest the reader, being ignorant of these and other matters, might miss the true meaning
(διάνοια). (...) When someone has an accurate knowledge of
these things he has an accurate and sound notion (διάνοια) of
the faith. But if someone misunderstands such things, he falls
into heresy immediately.[88]

Athanasius presents a general rule in this passage. He mentions
three necessary elements for a correct understanding of a passage
from Scripture: (1) time (καιρός) (2) person (πρόσωπον) and (3)
thing/subject (πρᾶγμα). Without a correct understanding of all of
these three elements, the exegesis will surely lead to heresy.[89]
Athanasius speaks of the true, accurate and sound διάνοια in the
singular, here and in many other instances.[90] Donald Fairbairn
traces an overarching narrative in Athanasius' view on Scripture,
which starts with God's existence and moves to God's work on
behalf of humanity's salvation.[91]

In *CA* III 28–29, Athanasius makes another exegetical remark. He speaks about 'the basic meaning' (σκοπός) of Christian

---

[88] *CA* I 54 (164,1–5); tr. Rusch, adapted.
[89] *CA* I 54 (164,14–16). See also Hermann J. Sieben, "Hermeneutik der
dogmatische Schriftauslegung des Athanasius von Alexandrien," in
"Manna in deserto". Studien zum Schriftgebrauch der Kirchenväter, ed. Hermann J. Sieben, Edition Cardo 92 (Köln: Koinonia-Oriens, 2002), 35–60,
especially 39–48. This is a translation of "Herméneutique de l'exégèse
dogmatique d'Athanase," in *Politique et théologie chez Athanase d'Alexandrie*, ed. Charles Kannengiesser (Paris: éditions Beauchesne, 1974), 195–
214. Stead notes that other Church Fathers argued for another scope of
Scripture, thus emphasising the particularity of Athanasius' scope of
Scripture. Christopher Stead, "Athanasius als Exeget," in *Christliche Exegese zwischen Nicaea und Chalcedon*, ed. Johannes van Oort and Ulrich
Wickert (Kampen, Netherlands: Kok Pharos, 1992), 174–84. Ernest notes
the same and mentions that a rule is only applied "when the resulting
interpretation is theologically satisfactory". Ernest, *Bible*, 176–77.
[90] Twomey, "St Athanasius," 85.
[91] Donald Fairbairn, "Context, Context, Context: Athanasius' Biblical Interpretation in *Contra Arianos*," *Perichoresis* 12 (2014): 134. See also Torrance, *Divine Meaning*, 229–88.

faith and defines the σκοπός of Scripture with an exclusive focus on Jesus Christ:

> we take hold of the basic meaning (σκοπόν) of the faith which belongs to us Christians, use it as a standard, (ὥσπερ κανόνι) and, as the apostle says, 'apply ourselves to the reading of the inspired Scripture' (1 Tim 4:13). The enemies of Christ, who are ignorant of this, 'have been led astray off the path of truth' (Wisd. of Sol. 5:6) and 'have stumbled over the stone of stumbling' (Rom 9:32), thinking 'other than what they ought to think' (Rom 12:3).
>
> What is the basic meaning and purport of Holy Scripture? It contains, as we have often said, a double account of the Savior. It says that he has always been God and is the Son, because he is the Logos and radiance and Wisdom of the Father. Furthermore, it says that in the end he became a human being, he took flesh for our sakes from the Virgin Mary, the God-bearer.[92]

Athanasius argues that the σκοπός of Scripture can be reduced to the double account of the Saviour. Scripture speaks of both his pre-existence as God and of his time as a human being during the Incarnation. Thomas F. Torrance accepts Athanasius' claim in this respect and argues that Athanasius' understanding of the σκοπός of Scripture takes into account 'the economical nature of God's acts and words' and is 'in accordance with the rule of faith'.[93] However, Athanasius' view on the σκοπός of Scripture seems clearly motivated by the main doctrinal issue addressed in the *Orations*. Athanasius' outline of the σκοπός of Scripture is established by means of a circular reasoning, not by means of an objective point of reference.

After quoting some passages from John and Philippians, Athanasius boldly states that '[a]nyone who makes his way through the whole of Scripture with the meaning of these texts in mind will, on the basis of what they [the whole of Scripture] say', conclude that Father and Son were both involved in creation and

---

[92] *CA* III 28–29 (339,29–340,33; 340,1–4); tr. Norris, adapted.
[93] Torrance, *Divine Meaning*, 234–35.

salvation.[94] As the formal principle, Athanasius holds, one must look to the double account of the Saviour, both his divinity and humanity. It is quite clear that two axioms are crucial for Athanasius' reading of Scripture. (1) It is his *a priori* conviction that the Scriptures univocally speak about the eternal divinity of both Father and Son, as taught in the Church from the beginning. (2) Divine knowledge given in the Scriptures is superior to knowledge achieved through reason. These Scriptures contain the words of the Lord Jesus Christ himself and saints who wrote about him. If someone considers the context (time, person, subject) and the σκοπός of Scripture (the double account of the Son of God) appropriately, and lives piously as well, he will not err in understanding the Scriptures. This element of piety is confirmed by Michael Haykin, when he argues that Athanasius soon realised the danger of reading Scripture 'literalistically'. Because of that, Athanasius focused his exegesis on 'the revelation of God in Jesus Christ, and a life lived in obedience to that revelation'.[95] In his reading of Scripture, Athanasius focuses on the person of Christ, but that does not mean that he frequently used allegory in his interpretation of the Scriptures. In this respect, Haykin asserts that 'theological principles certainly determine the questions which Athanasius asks of the Scriptural text ... [b]ut this delimitation does not mean that they determine the exact content of this exegesis'.[96] Athanasius' appeal to the accuracy of Scripture is also qualified by Karin Metzler's study on Athanasius' use of Scripture.[97] His custom of referring to Scripture is typical of early Christian authors; he feels free to make grammatical changes, or to change the tenses of a text, to clarify the salvational-historical

---

[94] *CA* III 29 (340,14–15); tr. Norris.

[95] Michael A. G. Haykin, *The Spirit of God: The Exegesis of 1 and 2 Corinthians in the Pneumatomachian Controversy of the Fourth Century*, VCSup 27 (Leiden: Brill, 1994), 63.

[96] Haykin, *Spirit of God*, 66. See also Torrance, *Divine Meaning*, 229–88.

[97] See especially Karin Metzler, *Welchen Bibeltext benutzte Athanasius im Exil? Zur Herkunft der Bibelzitate in den Arianerreden im Vergleich zur* ep. ad epp. Aeg, Abhandlungen der Nordrhein-Westfälischen Akademie der Wissenschaften 96 (Opladen: Westdeutscher Verlag, 1997), 18–27.

perspective.[98] Also, he does not hesitate to conflate different biblical texts and often alludes to biblical texts, without bothering too much about the exact rendering of the biblical text.[99]

Irenaeus' and Tertullian's solution for safeguarding biblical interpretation against heretical positions already demonstrated that disagreement on interpretation of the Scriptures with opponents that appeal to the same Scriptures is highly problematic. The absence of an 'objective' tool that can function as a neutral and independent arbiter to solve such interpretive disagreements led Irenaeus and Tertullian to appeal to a predefined core of Christian faith that functions as an arbiter that settles the disagreement in their favour. In their cases, the dispute with the Gnostics and Marcion included the extent and size of the Christian Scripture. Because their opponents were highly critical of the Old Testament, the rule of faith included a Christian commitment to both the OT and NT. In the fourth century, the inclusion of the OT was a common feature in mainstream Christianity, shared by Athanasius and his opponents.[100] Athanasius emphasised the importance of piety in studying and interpreting the Scriptures. From early on, he highlighted the crucial role of Scripture in testifying to the divinity of Christ and this remained the same in the debate of the *Orations*. Although he attempted to provide some additional parameters, his argument in the *Orations* that the core of Scripture is summarised in the double account of the Son's divinity and humanity contains a degree of circularity, because the

---

[98] Metzler, *Bibeltext*, 19–20.

[99] Metzler, *Bibeltext*, 23–24.

[100] Athanasius quoted several deutero-canonical documents alongside canonical Old Testament texts. See Johan Leemans, "Athanasius and the Book of Wisdom," *ETL* 73 (1997): 349–68; Johan Leemans, "Canon and Quotation: Athanasius' Use of Jesus Sirach," in *Biblical Canons*, ed. Jean-Marie Auwers and Henk J. de Jonge (Leuven: Leuven University Press, 2003), 265–77. On Athanasius' contribution to the formation of the biblical canon, see David Brakke, "A New Fragment of Athanasius's Thirty-Ninth Festal Letter: Heresy, Apocrypha, and the Canon," *Harvard Theological Review* 103 (2010): 47–66. Athanasius considered the book Baruch canonical and the book Esther pious but deutero-canonical in *Festal Letter* 39,17.

crucial issue between Athanasius and his opponents is precisely how and in what sense Christ can be called divine. But such a degree of circularity was unavoidable from the outset.

To get a better view on his practice of biblical interpretation, now that his formal view on Scripture and biblical interpretation has been established, this research will proceed to investigate whether Athanasius is faithful to his method.[101] The focus in this research on John's Gospel will shed more light on Athanasius' actual practice of biblical interpretation. This will be explored in the next chapters.

---

[101] Cf. Stead, "Exeget," 178.

CHAPTER FOUR.
ANALYSIS OF *ORATION* I

In the first chapter, we pointed out that modern scholars interpret Athanasius' work and life in strikingly different ways. Some claim that he was an impeccable theologian, who relentlessly fought for the truth, while others regard his theological arguments (at least partly) as a smokescreen for other affairs. This disagreement calls for a rhetorical reading of Athanasius' *Orations* that is sensitive to both 'theological' and 'non-theological' dimensions. Since Scripture is crucial in Athanasius' method of persuasion, the Gospel of John has been singled out as the most cited biblical book in the *Orations*. Investigating Athanasius' reception of John allows an evaluation of both Athanasius' theological positioning and the argumentative and non-argumentative moves he made in the circumstances of the fourth century. This chapter will thus investigate the use of John in *CA* I as an important part of his strategy of persuasion.

CA I can be divided into three parts: (1) introduction (*CA* I 1–10), (2) exposition of Athanasius' theology (*CA* I 11–36) and (3) counter-exegesis of specific texts (*CA* I 37–64). I will discuss the three sections subsequently.

CA I 1–10: INTRODUCTION TO THE *ORATIONS*

In the introductory section of the *Orations against the Arians*, Athanasius hardly refers to the Gospel of John, but biblical references are present, often as part of the establishing of *ethos* and negative *ethos*. According to Athanasius, the heretics are inventors of heresies, and it is possible to distinguish between Christians and

heretics. He separates the heretics from Christians in the opening
lines of the *Orations*:

> It has become evident that all the heresies which have turned
> aside from the truth were manufacturing madness, and their
> impiety has become manifest to all long ago. For the fact that
> the inventors of these heresies have 'gone out from among us'
> (1 Jn 2:19) makes clear, as the blessed John has written, that
> their minds neither were nor are now with us. Therefore, as
> the Savior has said, 'they do not gather with us but scatter'
> with the devil (Lk 11:23), and they are on the lookout for
> those who are sleeping so that, by sowing their own poison of
> destruction, they may have companions to die with them.[1]

In his introduction, Athanasius wants to establish two things: his
own trustworthiness and the wickedness of his opponents. His
Orations are presented as a response to requests from fellow bishops: 'Therefore, urged by you [προτραπεὶς παρ' ὑμῶν], I have considered it necessary to pierce through the "folds of the breast-
plate" (Job 41:5) of this loathsome heresy.'[2] By indicating that he
is writing in response to others, he shows that he does not engage
in unnecessary discussions, while the biblical references illustrate
that the evil of heretics is already predicted in Scripture. Focusing
on this negative side might alienate some readers, but he also uses
first plural pronouns to create communion between himself and
sympathetic readers.

Although Athanasius associates his opponents with all sorts
of madness and evil, he implicitly acknowledges that the heresy
of the Arians is not as easily discernible as other heresies. The
Arian heresy has disguised itself as true Christianity, by shrouding
'itself in the language of the Scriptures.' Scripture, then, is a fundamental source for all participants in the conflict.[3] Athanasius
concedes that some people regard Arians as Christians, but argues
that this is wrong and a result of the deceptive appearance of the
Arians. His aim in demonising his opponents is therefore twofold:
to keep Christians who are not close to his opponents far away

---

[1] *CA* I 1 (109,1–110,5); tr. Anatolios.
[2] *CA* I 1 (110,16–17); tr. Anatolios.
[3] *CA* I 1 (110,10); tr. Anatolios.

from their teachings and to change the mind of those Christians who do not see any harm in the Arian teachings. It seems improbable that Athanasius expects to bring about a change of mind in the Arians; his tone is too aggressive, and several times he states that the Arians are not open to persuasion and devise new arguments for impiety.[4]

The introductions to the three *Orations* are utilised by Athanasius to connect the Arian view to madness (μανία), thus undermining their good sense (φρόνησις). *CA* I and II both mention the word madness in the opening line, while *CA* III starts with the word Ariomaniacs (οἱ Ἀρειομανῖται).[5] The prominence of madness at the start of all three *Orations* seems intentional, in order to slander the opponents from the start.

Second, Athanasius portrays the Arians as enemies of the Church who closely align themselves with the devil, the ultimate source of evil and amorality. He concurs that heresies ultimately derive from the devil himself, who is the arch-enemy of Christ, the Church and the truth. This suggestion is not unique to Athanasius, for Tertullian had stated the same in his work *Against Praxeas* (written ca. 213–220).[6] The association with the devil is conspicuous in *CA* I 1–10. Besides the remark that the Arians "'do not gather with us but scatter" (cf. Lk 11:23) with the devil',[7] he

---

[4] Cf. *CA* II 1 (177,1–6); *CA* III 59 (371,1–7).

[5] See *CA* I 1 (109,1–2); II 1 (177,1–2); III 1 (305,1–306,2). Robertson translates it as 'Ariomaniacs' because of the wordplay between Arians and madness. See his note in the translation of the NPNF series at *CA* I 4, 308 n.3.

[6] Tertullian, *Against Praxeas* 1; tr. ANF. 'In various ways has the devil rivalled and resisted the truth. (…) Here the old serpent has fallen out with himself, since, when he tempted Christ after John's baptism, he approached Him as "the Son of God;" surely intimating that God had a Son, even on the testimony of the very Scriptures, out of which he was at the moment forging his temptation: "If thou be the Son of God, command that these stones be made bread (Mt 4:3).'" See also Opelt, *Polemik*, 62–65, cf. 146–50; see further Karlheinz Deschner, *Kriminalgeschichte des Christentums. Die Alte Kirche. Fälschung, Verdummung, Ausbeutung, Vernichtung* (Reinbek bei Hamburg: Rowohlt, 1990), III:491–97.

[7] *CA* I 1 (110,5); tr. Anatolios.

also mentions that the heresy 'hypocritically shrouds itself in the language of the Scriptures, as did its father the devil (cf. Mt 4:1ff.), and forces itself again into the paradise of the church'.[8] Athanasius thus presents his opponents in close association with the devil in order to discredit them. Constantine's letter, written in rebuke of Arius in the 330s, also links wrong interpretation of Scripture with the devil, wickedness and madness. He mentions the devil four times and madness seven times in this letter. The following statement illustrates Constantine's criticism on Arius clearly: 'As the Devil has desired, so he had made Arius a manufactory of iniquity for us. (...) Oh, you possessor of a mouth perverted and a nature quickly roused to wickedness.'[9]

In *CA* I 2, Athanasius asserts a relation between the Arians and several negative biblical prototypes. To call Arians Christians is equal to arguing that Caiaphas is a Christian and to including 'the traitor Judas with the apostles'. It is also 'like saying that those who asked Barabbas instead of the Savior did nothing wrong, and that the apostates Hymenaeus and Alexander should be commended for their fine thought' (cf. 1 Tim 1:20).[10] Athanasius carefully selects these persons in Scripture, who denied Christ, to emphasise their difference from authentic Christianity. Right at the start of his theological defence, he relates the Arians to the unbelieving first-century Jews, whereas he and true Christianity follow Christ, suggesting that the Arians have relapsed into the unbelief of those first-century Jews who rejected Christ. Athanasius thus constructs a dichotomy between heresy and the true faith. Two counter-genealogies are presented to the reader. This is not just associating by linking heretics to known impious persons. It is creating a re-enactment of Scripture by connecting the biblical past and the present into one seamless continuum.[11] On

---

[8] *CA* I 1 (110,7–8. 10–12); tr. Anatolios. See further *CA* I 6: Arius is 'a successor of the devil's reckless haste' (115,6–7); tr. Rusch, and *CA* I 8 (116,6–117,9).

[9] Urk. 34 (70,27–30); tr. Coleman-Norton. See also Urk. 34 (69,2; 73,33–34; 74,3; 75,1).

[10] *CA* I 2 (110,2–6); tr. Rusch.

[11] See Flower, *Late Roman Invective*, 179.

the one hand, there are the Arians, who put Arius in place of Christ, and the poet Sotades instead of Moses and the other saints.[12] On the other hand, there are the Christians, who are named after Christ, not after a bishop who is (legitimately) in office. The implicit dichotomy that runs through the introduction is made more explicit at the end of *CA* I 2, where Athanasius associates naming with belonging. Thus Athanasius states: 'After Christ we are and are named Christians, but since they have from others the beginning of what they regard as faith, it is fair that they have their name.'[13] The reader is thus forced to choose sides, black or white, and to choose to which community they want to belong.

In *CA* I 3, this argument is enhanced in Athanasius' delineation of two genealogies of both heretics and true Christians in ecclesial history. Athanasius acts here in line with Justin and Irenaeus, as well as with polemicists in ancient philosophical schools who distinguished between true and false teachers.[14] In this way, opponents are excluded as outsiders. Athanasius argues that the followers of sects are named after their leader, while Christians follow no one but Jesus Christ. He claims that while 'we all are Christians ..., Marcion, an inventor of a heresy, was long ago expelled. Those who stood fast with the expellers of Marcion remained Christians. But the followers of Marcion were no longer Christians. Thereafter they were called Marcionites.'[15] He similarly refers to the Valentinians, Basilidians, Manichees, Simonians, Cataphrygians, Novatians and Melitians and states about the Arians:

> So after blessed Alexander had cast out Arius, those who stayed with Alexander remained Christians. Those who united with Arius bequeathed the name of the Savior to us who were with Alexander. Thereafter they are called Arians. See then,

---

[12] *CA* I 2 (110,7–111,10).

[13] *CA* I 2 (111,23–25); tr. Rusch, adapted.

[14] Lyman, "Topography of Heresy," 46–48; See further Robert Lee Williams, *Bishop Lists: Formation of Apostolic Succession of Bishops in Ecclesiastical Crises* (New Jersey: Gorgias, 2005).

[15] *CA* I 3 (111,1–4); tr. Rusch.

after Alexander's death, those who are in fellowship with Athanasius, who succeeded Alexander, and those with whom Athanasius is in fellowship–all have the same standard (τύπος).[16] They do not have the name of him (τὸ τούτου) and he (αὐτός) does not take his name from them, but rather, as is the custom, they are all called Christians.[17]

Athanasius' presentation of the heretics is tendentious; the naming was often an imposition from outside rather than a self-conscious appropriation of the name of their founder, but it is an excellent tool for establishing a negative *ethos* concerning his opponents.[18] Most heresies that are named in this list were commonly rejected, so if Athanasius' presentation of the facts is accepted, it disqualified his opponents from the start. Athanasius presents himself as a follower of Christ, in contrast to all heretics who follow their heresiarch. All heresies ultimately boil down to the same: rejection of Jesus Christ. Interestingly, Arius had been anxious to dissociate himself from any heresy in his *Letter to Alexander* (Urk. 6 = Dok. 1).[19] If a successful link between a theological position and heresy could be established, that position was untenable. For that reason, both parties emphasise their orthodoxy by rejecting heretical views.

Besides undermining his opponents' *ethos*, Athanasius shows his own modesty, obedience to Christ and legitimate authority as

---

[16] See William Rusch, "Some Comments on Athanasius's *Contra Arianos* I, 3," in *Arianism: Historical and Theological Reassessments*, ed. Robert C. Gregg, PMS 11 (Cambridge, MA: Philadelphia Patristic Foundation, 1985), 223–32.

[17] *CA* I 3 (112,10–17); tr. Rusch.

[18] For a discussion of the problems of Manichaeism, which to a large extent pertain to other labels as well, see Nicholas J. Baker-Brian, *Manichaeism: An Ancient Faith Rediscovered* (London: T&T Clark, 2011), 15–24.

[19] Arius dissociates himself from Valentinus, who 'pronounced that the offspring of the Father was an issue'; the Manichees, who 'taught that the offspring was a portion of the Father, consubstantial', Sabellius, who 'dividing the Monad speaks of a Son-and-Father' and Hieracas, who speaks 'of one torch from another, or as a lamp divided into two'. Urk. 6 (12,10–13,1); tr. Stevenson.

bishop. The references in the citation above are Athanasius' only self-references in the *Orations*, and present him as a modest follower of Christ. His authority as bishop of Alexandria is not presented as a right he deserves, and he does not boast about his own qualities but portrays himself as obedient and humble. This enhanced the contrast with heretics, who want to claim their name instead of keeping that of Christ, and implicitly he thus locates the legitimacy of his episcopate in his serving of Christ. He reinforces this dichotomy between Christians and heretics, between the Arians and himself, at the end of *CA* I 3. Everyone who remains with the Church remains a Christian, but 'those who go over to heretics ... forsake the name of Christ and thereafter are called Arians'.[20]

In *CA* I 4, Athanasius reiterates the mutual exclusiveness of being either Arian or Christian, impious Arians in contrast to pious believers, by asking rhetorically: 'How then can they be Christians, who are not Christians, but Ariomaniacs?'[21] Athanasius claims that the Arians even have a different canonical text: the *Thalia*, with the inappropriate style of the Greek poet Sotades, functions as heretical counterpart to the divine Scriptures of Old and New Testament.[22] In introducing the *Thalia* of Arius, Athanasius equates Arius with the Jewish Pharisees, who

> were hypocrites in naming God. Blaspheming, they were refuted in saying, 'Why do you, being a man, make yourself God?' (cf. Jn 10:33), and you [i.e. Jesus] say, 'I and the Father are one' (Jn 10:30). Thus the base and Sotadian Arius is a hypocrite, speaking about God, introducing the style of Scripture.[23]

Athanasius constructs an imaginary dialogue between Jesus and the Pharisees. The Pharisees object to two of Jesus' statements in the Gospel of John, and Arius equally opposes Jesus Christ's divinity. However, both Johannine texts are slightly reformulated

---

[20] *CA* I 3 (112,25–27); tr. Rusch.
[21] Πῶς τοίνυν Χριστιανοὶ οἱ μὴ Χριστιανοί, ἀλλὰ Ἀρειομανῖται; *CA* I 4 (112,1).
[22] On the Sotadean metre, see Morgan, *Musa Pedestris*, 40–48.
[23] *CA* I 4 (113,17–23); tr. Rusch.

to bring out the contrast between the Pharisees/Arius and Jesus. Jn 10:33 is rephrased as a question, where the original contains a statement; Jn 10:30 becomes an angry statement that the Pharisees repeat after Jesus, and understand as an unambiguous indicator of divinity. The changes are subtle, but ignore the Christological tension of the original.[24] The imaginary dialogue with its subtle changes to John's Gospel suggests a direct refutation of the Arian position, since the similar position of the Pharisees evidently rejected Jesus Christ's true identity. The fact that many views of the Pharisees are rejected by his Arian opponents is neglected, for Athanasius is solely interested in asserting the fundamental similarity between both groups: failure to acknowledge that Jesus is truly God and united with Him. All nuances in depicting his opponents are absent. Athanasius thus suggests that although Arius included scriptural phrases in the *Thalia*, Christians should not be deceived, because it rejects Jesus' testimony about himself. Flower's description of the phenomenon of literary re-enactment in fourth-century polemical literature is illuminating at this point.[25] Athanasius' literary re-enactment here builds a bridge between biblical times and the present. He places himself directly in the footsteps of biblical *exempla* and puts his adversaries in the position of negative biblical figures. He thus establishes *ethos* for himself and negative *ethos* for his opponents at the same time.

CA I 5–6 presents excerpts from the *Thalia*, and probably also fragments from other Arians, such as Asterius. These fragments support his argument that there are two opposite genealogies and bodies of literature – the Scriptures for the Christians versus the *Thalia* for the Arians. Athanasius mentions three slogans that he will attack several times in the main body of the *Orations*. The opponent's impiety leads to the following slogans:

> 'The Son was not always,' for since all things came into being from nothing, and all existing creatures and works came into

---

[24] In a comment on Jn 10:30, Barrett notes that 'John's language comes somewhat nearer to metaphysics, but ... is by no means purely metaphysical'. Barrett, *John*, 382.

[25] See Flower, *Late Roman Invective*, 23–32, 181

being, even the Word of God himself 'came into being from nothing,' and 'there was once when he was not;' and 'he was not before he came out of nothing'.[26]

These slogans have a strong rhetorical effect of constructing a negative *ethos* of his opponents. He suggests that all nuances can be reduced to a small set of slogans that illustrates their impiety. He thus arouses anger against his impious opponents, for Athanasius asks, immediately after the quoted material from the *Thalia*: 'Who, hearing such things and the melody of the *Thalia*, does not justly hate Arius's jesting about such things as if he were on a stage? ... Will not all human nature be struck speechless at Arius's blasphemies and shut its ears and close its eyes?'[27] Athanasius thus closely relates Arius to the *Thalia*, which is presented as a most irreligious work, both in content and style; even 'serious Greeks' cannot take it seriously.[28] Athanasius adds that Arius' *Thalia* caused his excommunication by the 'ecumenical synod' of Nicaea (325).[29] Nevertheless, while Athanasius clearly portrays Arius unfavourably, William Harris considers it likely that the *Thalia* was indeed designed to be sung: 'Arius wrote a popular presentation of his doctrine in the poem *Thaleia*, but much of its effectiveness apparently derived from the fact that it could be sung.'[30] In that case, Arius' strategy to make the *Thalia* accessible to a wider audience is employed by Athanasius for the purpose of establishing Arius' negative *ethos*.

Charlotte Roueché has demonstrated that slogans or acclamations gained significantly in prominence in the Later Roman Empire. In antiquity, acclamations were important in both religious and secular meetings. Acclamations were a regular part of

---

[26] *CA* I 5 (114,12–15); tr. Rusch. See further the comments at *CA* I 12 below.

[27] *CA* I 7 (115,1–2. 116,10–11); tr. Rusch.

[28] *CA* I 4 (113,5–11).

[29] *CA* I 7 (116,19–20).

[30] William V. Harris, *Ancient Literacy* (Cambridge, MA: Harvard University Press, 1989), 305.

public life.[31] At least from the second century CE, reports of acclamations increased and from the fourth century onwards, acclamations were commonly heard. Inscribed acclamations became widespread.[32] Acclamations initially functioned simply as a way of giving assent, but in the fourth century, provincial rulers had to report acclamations uttered by groups of people to the emperor himself.[33] Acclamations or slogans thus possessed persuasive power and were politically significant. Peter Brown asserts that this phenomenon also entered the church; church services 'provided weekly parade-grounds for the use of slogans,' with the liturgy owing 'much to the secular tradition of chanted acclamations'.[34] This form of persuasion is far removed from the persuasive power exerted by individual eloquent rhetors with their classical *paideia*. Nonetheless, the power of acclamation allowed the masses to have a voice in important decisions.[35] Roueché and Brown primarily see evidence for this use of slogans in the fifth century. However, it seems plausible that Athanasius is describing here a custom that was visible in the theological controversy of his time. The question is then whether Athanasius has invented these slogans to portray the Arians negatively, or, more plausibly, that those with theological views like Arius had designed these catchphrases and used them to promote their theological views. In this way, Athanasius takes up these slogans to demonstrate their inadequacy and to present his sound theological alternative.

After the attack on Arian theology, and Arius in particular, Athanasius presents himself as modest and fair-minded. He invokes the Lord's assistance in refuting the heresy and announces that he will reveal the heresy's villainy by asking the opponents

---

[31] Charlotte Roueché, "Acclamations in the Later Roman Empire: New Evidence from Aphrodisias," *Journal of Roman Studies* 74 (1984): 181–84.

[32] Roueché, "Acclamations," 184–86.

[33] Roueché, "Acclamations," 186.

[34] Brown, *Power and Persuasion*, 149.

[35] Brown, *Power and Persuasion*, 149–50.

questions.[36] In *CA* I 9, he then presents his orthodox Christian faith, in opposition to that of Arius:

> Behold, we speak freely about the religious faith on the basis of the divine Scriptures; we place it as a light on the lampstand saying, 'He is by nature true Son and legitimate from the Father, peculiar to his substance, the only-begotten Wisdom and true and only Word of God.' (...) The Lord also said, 'He who has seen me has seen the Father' (Jn 14:9).[37]

Athanasius uses the plural form 'we' to interact with his readers and to construct implicitly an orthodox communion that opposes Arianism. The subsequent citation of the Gospel of John is used to contrast the words of Jesus to those of Arius and supports his trustworthiness and good sense. In this way, it functions as a legitimation for his doctrine of the Son. Athanasius' view is disputed by his opponents. His appeal to Jn 14:9 suggests a natural closeness between Father and Son, but the context of the verse qualifies the statement in Jn 14:9 in several ways. The direct relation between Father and Son is not clear to the disciples (Jn 14:8–9a) and in Jn 14:10–12 Jesus states that he does not speak on his own, and he does not expect his disciples to believe him because of his words, but because of his deeds. The phrase 'peculiar to his substance (ἴδιος τῆς οὐσίας αὐτοῦ)' demonstrates Athanasius' theological thinking, rather than being a direct appeal to Scripture itself. Οὐσία is a term that in the biblical sources referred to wealth or property (Lk 15:12–13; cf. Tob 14:3; 3 Macc 3:28), but in fourth-century theological discourse, the term had come to refer to God's substance. In other words, the reference to Jn 14:9 illustrates that his theological reasoning goes beyond direct inferences from the biblical text alone.

On the whole, the Gospel of John plays a limited role in the introduction; Athanasius rather appeals to the general categories of Scripture versus impious literature in *CA* I 1–10. In *CA* I 10, he contrasts the words of Scripture and Arius again:

---

[36] *CA* I 7 (116,26–27). Cf. *CA* I 10 (120,30).
[37] *CA* I 9 (117,1–4; 118,9–10); tr. Rusch.

> Whose words discourse about God and show that Jesus Christ
> our Lord is God and Son of the Father? These words that you
> have disgorged or these that we have spoken and state from
> the Scriptures? If the Savior is not God or Word or Son, you
> may ... say whatever things you wish. But if he is Word of the
> Father and true Son ... is it not worthy to obliterate and ex-
> punge both the other words and the Arian *Thalia* as an image
> of evil?[38]

Athanasius thus suggests that the Arians, despite the clarity of
Scripture's testimony on the Son's eternity, wish to believe something else, with the *Thalia* as a counter-text of Scripture. He presents himself implicitly in the role of a philosopher who dares to
speak the truth. He states that his opponents posses 'the patronage
of friends and the fear of Constantius'; their heresy is to be hated
since their dependency on patronage and fear of emperor Constantius demonstrates their lack of freedom of speech
(παρρησία).[39] The image of a philosopher with freedom of speech
was commonplace. However, Athanasius reverses this image
here. His opponents are fearful of the emperor and do not dare to
speak the truth. Athanasius nowhere uses the concept of *parréshia*
in a positive way. He only employs the concept in its reverse form
to inflict negative *ethos* upon his opponents. He concludes the introduction of *Oration* I with linking the Arians with madness and
the devil:

> Therefore, since all that remains to say is that their [i.e. the
> Arian] mania came from the devil (for he alone is the sower
> of such opinions), let us resist him. For against him is our real
> conflict, and they are but instruments, so that ... they may be
> ashamed, when they see him who sowed the heresy in them
> without resource.[40]

Athanasius obviously relates the Arians to the devil to classify
them as enemies of Christ. He alludes to the parable of the weeds
among the wheat (cf. Mt 13:24–30) to depict the Arians as misled
by the devil. This image excuses the Arians partly for their

---

[38] *CA* I 10 (119,1–8); tr. Rusch, adapted.
[39] *CA* I 10 (119,15–19); tr. Rusch.
[40] *CA* I 10 (120,27–31); tr. Rusch.

impiety, because they are not aware of their deception, but it does present them as morally weak and impious people, for God-fearing persons would have recognised the works of Satan. An important element in establishing negative *ethos* in Athanasius' *Orations* is therefore his presentation of his opponents as instruments of the devil, and as impious people who err in interpreting Scripture.

In the rest of the *Orations*, both the devil and Arius as an individual who wrote the *Thalia* feature less prominently. Whereas the Arians are initially portrayed as instruments of the devil, in the main body of the *Orations* the Arians' madness is described as equal to the devil's or even exceeding it.[41] Just as association with the devil fades away after the introduction, so the prominence of Arius as an individual becomes less distinct. Most of the hostile words towards Arius occur in this introduction. Indeed, the fragments of his *Thalia* feature exclusively in this introductory section of the *Orations*.[42] Moreover, the material attributed to Arians quite probably goes back to Asterius rather than Arius in many instances.[43] In other words, Arius becomes less prominent as an individual in the rest of the *Orations*.[44] While

---

[41] See *CA* I 22 (132,12); II 17; II 38; III 59; III 67.

[42] *CA* I 5–6, 9. Cf. *Syn* 15 and the discussion on their relation. Rowan Williams, "The Quest of the Historical *Thalia*," in *Arianism: Historical and Theological Reassessments*, ed. Robert C. Gregg, PMS 11 (Cambridge, MA: Philadelphia Patristic Foundation, 1985), 1–35; Charles Kannengiesser, "Les 'Blasphèmes d'Arius' (Athanase d'Alexandrie, De synodis 15): un écrit néo-arien," in *Mémorial André-Jean Festugière*, ed. Enzo Lucchesi and H. D. Saffrey (Geneva: Patrick Cramer, 1984), 143–51; Christopher Stead, "Thalia of Arius and the Testimony of Athanasius," *JTS* 29 (1978): 20–52; the discussion is also considered unresolved by Peter Leithart, *Athanasius* (Grand Rapids, MI: Baker Academic, 2011), 178 n.10.

[43] Vinzent, *Asterius*, 283–301 cf. Asterius, frs. 43, 63, 65 (Vinzent).

[44] See *CA* II 1 (177,1–6); II 22 (199,23); II 24 (201,29); II 37 (214,8); III 28 (339,13). Schmitz remarks that relatively few polemical utterances are directed against Arius himself, as compared to utterances against the Arians in general. See "Schimpfwörter in Athanasius' Reden gegen die Arianer," in *Roma Renascens. Ilona Opelt von ihren Freunden und Schülern zum 9.7.1988 in Verehrung gewidmet*, ed. Michael Wissemann, Beiträge

Arius has been portrayed as the arch-heretic for centuries, his direct influence on a movement decreased quickly after his death. Arius died in 336, before Athanasius launched his attack on Arianism (ca. 338 in his tenth *Festal Letter*).[45] Athanasius' strategy of describing the movement as mainly indebted to Arius is thus a conscious attempt to establish a negative *ethos* of his opponents. Arius featured in quite some communication with Constantine in the early stages of the controversy. However, Arius was not seen as a real leader of the movement, during his lifetime, let alone after his death. The Council of Antioch (341), which expressed views that Athanasius would label as 'Arian', explicitly states: 'We have not become followers of Arius – for how could bishops follow a presbyter?'[46] At the same time, it should be noted that there were also bishops that did not wish to dissociate themselves from the theological thinking that Arius represented. The reference at the Council of Antioch might well have been an effect of Athanasius' *Orations* or other works that argued for a monolithic Arianism, to ensure that their theological views and the formally condemned position of Arius were equated.

To Athanasius, it is clear that he is in line with Christianity and therefore in line with the truth, whereas the Arians are not genuine Christians, either by ignorance or by hypocrisy. This indicates that he is mainly writing to Christians who keep away from Arianism and those who do not consider Arians heretics, but not to Arians themselves. He expects his audience to adhere to the Christian Scriptures and above all to God. He presents himself as sensible, because he follows the divine words of Scripture and avoids other worldviews that conflict with it (pagan, Jewish and heretical). Athanasius' language is illustrative of the fourth-

---

zur Spätantike und Rezeptionsgeschichte (Frankfurt am Main: Lang, 1988), 310.

[45] See Rudolf Lorenz, *Der zehnte Osterfestbrief des Athanasius von Alexandrien. Text, Übersetzung, Erläuterungen*, BZNW 49 (Berlin: de Gruyter, 1986); even while it seems likely that *Henos somatos* is written by Athanasius, there is a gap of more than 10 years in which the term Arianism is absent in Athanasius' work.

[46] See Dok. 41.5 (149,1–3) in: Athanasius, *Syn* 22,3–7 (248,29–30).

century discourse that was harsh against ecclesiastical opponents.[47] Although Justin (*First Apology* 58) regards Marcion as
driven by a devil, and Tertullian in *Against Praxeas* associates
Praxeas with the devil several times (chapters 1, 10, 23), Athanasius' overall tone is even harsher than that of most before and
after him.[48] The only source that shows a fair resemblance to the
tone of Athanasius in his *Orations* is Constantine's letter on Arianism (Urk. 34). The difference is that Constantine wrote as the emperor to Arius as an unruly subject. In this context, Peter Brown's
remark about the relationship between power and persuasion is
illuminating: 'Power, not persuasion, remains the most striking
characteristic of the later Roman Empire.'[49]

CA I 11–36: ATHANASIUS' REBUTTAL OF ARIAN TEACHINGS

In the second part of Oration I (11–36), Athanasius focuses on the
content of the Arian teachings. He singles out several slogans and
key questions that his opponents appeal to and counters their
views with a combination of reasoning, appeal to Scripture and
polemic.

---

[47] One of the strongest statements of Eusebius of Caesarea is 'Let every
mouth reject the impious and godless men [i.e. most of all Marcellus]
who have suffered the error of polytheism, those men who, having cast
down into the multitude the special and unique begetting of the only-
begotten Son, have addressed him as Father "of gods and men," [Homer,
Iliad 8.1,52] both mixing together men with gods, and introducing the
same Father as being of one nature with the former. But with demonic
energy they uttered this impious and godless statement...'. *ET* I 12
(Kl./H. 72,26–32); tr. McCarthy Spoerl and Vinzent, adapted. What is
quite exceptional in Eusebius' *Ecclesiastical Theology* is more common and
frequent in Athanasius' *Orations*.
[48] Lucifer of Calaris must be excepted from this judgment. 'Lucifer had
written attacks upon the Emperor which would have richly justified Constantine had he cut off his head or had him strangled. His works consist
of almost no arguments in favor of N [i.e. the Nicene Creed], which he
scarcely understands, but rather of one continued shrill monotone of
abuse.' Hanson, *Search*, 323.
[49] Brown, *Power and Persuasion*, 7.

CA I 11–13: Eternity of the Son

In *CA* I 11–13 Athanasius focuses on the Arian slogan 'There was a time that the Son was not', introduced in *CA* I 5.[50] Athanasius constructs an imaginary dialogue between himself and the Arians and points to an ambiguity in the slogan. He asks what it was that existed 'once', when the Son was not. He excludes the possibilities (1) Father (because it ascribes temporality to the Father) and (2) Son (as self-contradictory) and concludes that 'once' must necessarily mean 'a time' (χρόνος). Time is intentionally avoided by Arius, because he does not want to attribute temporality to the Son explicitly. However, Athanasius points out that Arius is comfortable with the expression that the Father pre-exists (προϋπάρχει) the Son without beginning (ἀνάρχως), which entails a temporal connotation.[51] Although Athanasius simplifies the debate by using a slogan, he engages with crucial concepts of Arian theology as well. He shows awareness of this subtlety and he undergirds this with his reasoning that Arius' words imply a timeless time before the Son, thus attacking the subject matter of the dispute between him and 'Arian' theologians. Athanasius backs up his argument with several appeals to the Scriptures and inductive reasoning to establish the necessity of the Son's eternity. The Son is 'always, everlasting, and always coexisting with the Father', for the Scriptures speak nowhere (οὐδεμία) of the Son's temporality. He cites Jn 1:1: 'In the beginning was the Word, and the Word was with God and the Word was God' and several other passages as proof of the wide gulf that separates God from creation, whereas nothing separates the Father and the Son.[52]

In *CA* I 12, Athanasius provides another proof of the Son's eternity. God's creation is established by the 'Word of God, through whom "all things have come into existence"' (cf. Jn 1:3; 1 Cor 8:6; Col 1:16–17; Nicaenum).[53] If this is accepted as an indicator of divinity, the Son cannot be counted among the

---

[50] See *CA* I 11 (120,1–2); cf. *CA* I 5 (114,14).
[51] See *CA* I 11 (120,9–11). For Arius's words, see Urk. 1 (2,6. 2,9–3,3) and Urk. 6.
[52] *CA* I 11 (120,13–16); cf. *CA* I 11–12.
[53] *CA* I 12 (121 (2–3); tr. Rusch.

creatures. And if the Son is not a creature, he must be eternal. The specific diction of Scripture further indicates the Son's eternity, for the Father is known through the Son (cf. Mt 11:27), and 'when Philip said: "show us the Father" (Jn 14:9) he said not "See creation" but "He who has seen me has seen the Father"'.[54] The diction of Jesus' 'I am' sayings serves as proof of the Son's eternity: '[t]he Lord himself says, "I am the truth" (Jn 14:6), and he does not say, "I became the truth," but he always says, "I am": "I am the shepherd," "I am the light," "Do you call me Lord and teacher? You call me well, for I am." (Jn 10:14; 8:12; 13:13)'.[55] Since the 'Word of the Father himself' has said this, who 'still has doubts about the truth and will not immediately believe that in the expression "I am" is indicated that the Son is everlasting and without beginning for every age?'[56] Athanasius thus asserts the Son's eternity on scriptural grounds and he employs reason to arrive at his conclusion. Several Johannine passages are claimed to be self-evident in their proof of the Son's eternity.

To see what Athanasius actually does, the distinction between necessary and non-necessary signs is illuminating. In fact, the 'I am' sayings function as non-necessary signs of the Son's eternity. This is in particularly clear in the case of Jn 14:6, for Athanasius is careful to mention only one of the three attributes of this verse. According to John 14:6, Jesus calls himself 'Way', 'Truth' and 'Life'. Although it seems quite natural to regard all three attributes on the same level, Athanasius carefully distinguishes between these three titles, to support his strong emphasis on the eternity of the Son. The title 'Way' (ὁδός) is inappropriate to the Son's eternity and would run counter to Athanasius' objective, whereas the titles 'Truth' and 'Life' are perfectly suitable in this respect.[57] Athanasius thus breaks up the connection in the original setting of John, to highlight only those elements that

---

[54] *CA* I 12 (121,7–9).

[55] *CA* I 12 (122,31–35); tr. Rusch, adapted. His reference to John 10:4 is incorrect. See Jn 10:11 and 14.

[56] *CA* I 12 (122,35–37); tr. Rusch.

[57] "Way" (ὁδός) is an attribute that Athanasius does not assign to the Son's ontology, but to his humanity. Cf. *CA* II 61.64–65.

support his argument. Other contemporaries dealt differently with this text. Marcellus of Ancyra only accepts the title 'Word' to refer to the eternal Son of God, and applies not only the title 'Way', but also 'Truth' and 'Life' to the incarnate Son.[58] Eusebius of Caesarea criticises Marcellus' view, with an appeal to Jn 8:12 and 14:6. However, in his quotation, he substitutes 'Way' for 'Light' to suit his argument in *ET* I 20: 'And that he himself is also "Light", the Savior shows, when he says in agreement with what has been recounted before concerning light: "I am the light of the world," (Jn 8:12) and again: "I am the light, and the truth and the life," (Jn 8:12 and 14:6).'[59] He argues that 'Truth' and 'Life' and numerous other titles pertain to the divine Son, and harshly criticises Marcellus for selecting just one attribute of the Son and neglecting all the other ones.[60] Eusebius is also selective, for in the quotation just mentioned, he substitutes 'Way' for 'Light'. Later in the same chapter, he cites Jn 14:6 in full on one occasion, but neglects the implications of the title 'Way' in the subsequent discussion. He states in *ET* I 20:

> one of the prophets called him 'Life' and 'Light' in addressing God and saying, 'For with you is the fountain of life; in your light we shall see light (Ps 36:9).' For who was the fountain of life from God and the light, other than he who said in the gospels, 'I am the light of the world,' (Jn 8:12) and 'I am the way (ὁδός) and the truth and the life' (Jn 14:6)? For this reason again, approaching God as a suppliant in prayer, the prophet says, 'Send out your light and your truth; they will lead me (ὁδηγήσει) (Ps 43:3).'[61]

He connects the three attributes of Jn 14:6 to Psalm 43:3 (LXX), where the nouns φῶς (light) and ἀλήθεια (truth) appear alongside the verb ὁδηγέω (to lead upon the way). While he quotes three

---

[58] Marcellus, fr. 3 (Vinzent) and Vinzent, *Markell*, xxix, xxxiv. See also Marcellus, fr. 38 and his *Letter to Julius of Rome* (Vinzent 126,2–3. 9. 13; 128,4–5. 11–12) on the pre-existent Son.

[59] *ET* I 20 (Kl./H. 84,35–85,1); tr. McCarthy Spoerl and Vinzent. He quotes all three titles together in *ET* I 20 (Kl./H. 94,7).

[60] *ET* II 10 (Kl./H. 110,25–30).

[61] *ET* I 20 (Kl./H. 94,3–9); tr. McCarthy Spoerl and Vinzent.

attributes on one occasion together, the titles 'Light' (Jn 8:12) and 'Truth' are related to the Son ontologically, the title 'Way' is not considered appropriate in the same sense.[62] Athanasius' view is situated somewhere between that of Eusebius and Marcellus. Although Marcellus' approach caused several theological difficulties that both Athanasius and Eusebius reject, Marcellus' approach is in a way more consistent than Athanasius' one, for Athanasius had to break up the logical unity of Jn 14:6 in order to safeguard the eternal equality of Father and Son. However, at this point it is clear that not all scriptural notions can be taken into account to arrive at a theological position; a process of reasoned selectiveness is inevitable.

In *CA* I 13, Athanasius again emphasises the words of the Lord himself as a proof of the Son's eternity in contrast to humanity's created and ephemeral state of being. He quotes some passages about creation and contrasts these words to those of the Son himself from John's Gospel. The first is used to emphasise the Son's foreknowledge, the other to sustain the Son's eternal existence. 'The Lord through his own person said, "If you loved me, you would rejoice, because I said, 'I go to the Father, because the Father is greater than I' and now I have told you before it happened that when it happens, you will believe." (Jn 14:28–29)'[63] A few sentences later, he cites Jn 8:58: 'Before Abraham came into existence, I am'.[64] Athanasius is not interested in the further context at this point, but he just assumes the self-evident meaning of the 'I am' texts to exclude any temporality related to the Son's existence. Hence, Athanasius stresses capacities of the Son such as being eternal and having foreknowledge, while the part of Jn 14:28, 'The Father is greater (μείζων) than I' is just mentioned in

---

[62] With regard to the titles in Jn 14:6, Eusebius' preferred title for the Son is 'Truth'. See *CM* I 4 (Kl./H. 23,18); *ET* I 20 (Kl./H. 94,18); II 14 (Kl./H. 118,18), combined with 'Life' in *ET* I 20 (Kl./H. 85,1; 94,7); II 10 (Kl./H. 110,25–29). 'Way' is not mentioned, except for the passage quoted *ET* I 20 (94,3–9).

[63] *CA* I 13 (122,8–10); tr. Rusch.

[64] *CA* I 13 (123,13).

passing, without any comment.[65] Athanasius merely uses this
verse to point to the foreknowledge of the Son, while he must
have been aware of the problematic potential of this verse for his
own theology; Eusebius of Caesarea's *Letter to Euphration of Bala-
nea* in the early 320s induces from the word μείζων that the Son
is subordinated to the Father.[66] Athanasius decides to ignore this
issue altogether and concludes this section by stating: 'How did
time or age subsist at all, when according to you [i.e. the Arians]
the Word had not yet appeared through whom all things came
into existence and without whom not one thing came into existence? (Jn 1:3)'[67] In this way, Athanasius suggests that Jn 1:3 supports his position that the Son is not a creature at all because
everything has come into existence through the Word or Son
without any trace of ambiguity. The notion of the creation
through the Word safeguards the eternity and uncreatedness of
the Son, since it is logically impossible that the Son is both Creator and creature. In this section, Athanasius is highly selective in
discussing Johannine texts and their implications. Two notions
from the Johannine prologue together with the words of Jesus
himself that support his theology are understood to be self-evident in favour of the Son's eternity. However, in the case of Jn
14:6 and 14:28–29, Athanasius glosses over several ambiguities
and potential problems concerning the interpretation of these passages.

---

[65] Simonetti argued that Jn 14:28 did not receive much attention in the
early stages of the Arian controversy. Manlio Simonetti, *Studi sull'Aria-
nesimo*, Verba seniorum 5 (Roma: Editrice Studium, 1965), 128; cf. idem,
"Giovanni 14:28 Nella Controversia Ariana," in *Kyriakon*, ed. Patrick
Granfield and Josef A. Jungmann (Münster: Aschendorff, 1970), 152–55;
Hanson opposes this view in *Search*, 836.

[66] Urk. 3 (5,3), 'The Father who has sent me is greater than me' (ὁ πατὴρ
ὁ πέμψας με μείζων μού ἐστι) (e.g. Jn 4:34 and 14:28). See idem, *ET* I 11;
II 7.

[67] *CA* I 13 (123,25–27); tr. Rusch.

CA I 14–16: Father, Son, Spirit

In *CA* I 14, Athanasius discusses the Arian objection to his theology that his doctrine of the Son's eternity makes Father and Son brothers. This idea might lead to the acceptance of two first principles (ἀρχαί) and divine brotherhood of Father and Son. Athanasius records the objection of his opponents thus: "'If there was not once when he was not, but the Son is everlasting and coexists with the Father, you say no longer that he is the Father's Son but that he is the Father's brother.'"[68] In response, Athanasius attacks both the integrity of his opponents and the soundness of their argumentation. He argues that the objection has not come from ignorant people, but 'is a Jewish "pretext" (πρόφασις) shared by those who wish, as Solomon said "to be separated" from the truth (Prv 18:1).'[69] Moreover, because 'they do not discern how God is of the Father's origin, they deny him, for these senseless ones (οἱ ἄφρονες) measure the offspring of the Father by themselves.'[70] Therefore, they 'must be questioned and refuted, so that they might perceive the true state of things.'[71] A maxim, a proverb from the book of Proverbs, undergirds his suggestion of his opponent's negative *ethos*, and because his opponents are impious, their arguments deserve close consideration. Athanasius interweaves these polemical remarks in a reasonable account to attack the content of his opponents' argument. This twofold attack might be a result of his varied readership. He wants to attack his opponents' argument on its own merits, but he also warns those who

---

[68] *CA* I 14 (123,1–3); tr. Rusch. Twenty years before, Arius had blamed Alexander's teaching of 'always God, always Son' (Urk. 1 (2,1. 3)), and claimed that the Son did not exist before he was begotten or created or founded (cf. Prv 8:22–25), because the Son is not unbegotten (Urk. 1 (3,3–4); cf. Urk. 6 and Eusebius of Caesarea, Urk. 3).

[69] *CA* I 14 (124,9–10); tr. Rusch.

[70] *CA* I 15 (125,7–9); tr. Rusch, adapted. Most often, the expression οἱ ἄφρονες is used in the context of their understanding of the Son's divinity and Athanasius' assertion that they hold a human conception of the Son's existence. Cf. *CA* I 22 (132,10); I 29 (138,3) I 55 (165,4); II 29 (205,2). In *CA* II 27 (204,25); II 63 (240,6) he refers to them without the definitive article.

[71] *CA* I 15 (125,9–11); tr. Rusch.

do not care about theological subtleties (certain monks?) to assert that neutrality is impossible. Maxims, such as the slogans that represent the core of Athanasius' presentation of Arianism and appeals to proverbs that suggest the senselessness of the Arians are effective in establishing a negative *ethos* of his opponents, but not in providing a solid basis for sustaining beliefs.[72] For a particular group, the use of maxims was the most effective way to gain support for his orthodox position, yet Athanasius does not reduce the matters to such simplicity only.

In the argumentative part of his response, Athanasius defends himself against the accusation of teaching two ἀρχαί. The Son is not merely an offspring (γέννημα), but Son: 'If our faith is in the Father and Son, what sort of brother is there between them? How is the Word able to be called the brother of him whose Word he is?'[73] This, according to him, avoids the possibility of the existence of two first principles. Athanasius switches from the term Son (υἱός) to Word (λόγος) to respond to the Arian criticism. Word is an impersonal term and therefore less likely to attract human associations that Athanasius wants to avoid. He asserts that the distinctive names of Father and Son safeguard the genuine distinction between them, and that this is sufficient for maintaining one, simple, first principle (ἀρχή). If there were a pre-existing principle (ἀρχὴ προϋπάρχουσα) that begot both Father and Son, they would rightly be called brothers, but the Father is the source (ἀρχή) and begetter (γεννητής) of the Son and nobody's son, while the Son is Son and not a brother of the Father.[74] Athanasius thus rejects the existence of two ἀρχαί in speaking of Father and Son, by accepting that only the Father is the source. The Son is begotten from eternity, but not fully identical to the Father (He is not Father) to avoid both theogony (a hierarchical chain of being of

---

[72] Perelman and Olbrechts-Tyteca, *New Rhetoric*, 167.
[73] *CA* I 14 (123,6–124,8); tr. Rusch. Cf. *Syn* 51, where Athanasius also refutes the charge that *homoousios* makes the Father and Son brothers.
[74] *CA* I 14 (124,10–13). Cf. Eusebius, *ET* II 7.

Father, Son and Spirit) and two first principles.[75] The Son is eternal offspring of the Father, not a later addition that complements the Father's substance; for the substance (οὐσία) of the Father is never incomplete (ἀτελής), just like light is never without radiance or a source without water.[76] This argument works if the opponents accept the appropriateness of immaterial images to inform about the Father-Son relationship.[77] Athanasius reinforces this probability by stating that the Son's generation is incomparable to human generation. The comparison with human generation is of limited value, due to the incompleteness of the nature (τὸ ἀτελὲς τῆς φύσεως) of humans, while 'the offspring of God is eternal, because of the eternal perfection of his nature.'[78]

Successively, he describes in an affirmative sense how Father and Son are ontologically related by demonstrating the different relation of Son and creation to the divine Spirit.[79] Creatures are in need of the Spirit, while the Son is the Giver of the Spirit. The Son cannot be inferior to the Father, because he sends the divine Spirit. Athanasius states: 'All other things partake of the Spirit; according to you, then, of what is he [i.e. the Son] a partaker? Of the Spirit? Rather the Spirit itself receives from the Son (cf. Jn 16:14), as he himself said.'[80] The Son, who is the Giver of the Spirit

> is the Wisdom and Word of the Father, in whom and through whom he creates and makes all things. And this is his reflection, in whom he enlightens all things (Cf. Jn 1:9) ... This is his character and image, in whom he is contemplated and known. Therefore both 'he himself and the Father are one' (Jn

---

[75] See E. P. Meijering, "Athanasius on the Father and the Son," in *God, Being, History. Studies in Patristic Philosophy*, ed. E. P. Meijering (Amsterdam: North-Holland Publishing, 1975), 4–5.

[76] *CA* I 14 (124,13–14. 25–27).

[77] Asterius distinguishes between the innate Word and the Son-Word. Cf. frs. 64, 66 (Vinzent) = *CA* II 37.

[78] *CA* I 14 (124,18–19).

[79] Cf. Leithart, *Athanasius*, 57–88.

[80] *CA* I 15 (125,15–18); tr. Rusch. Cf. Jn 16:13–14: 'When the Spirit of truth comes ... he will not speak on his own, but will speak whatever he hears ... He will glorify me, because he will take what is mine.' (NRSV)

  10:30), and 'he who sees him also sees the Father' (Cf. Jn 14:9)...[81]

This argument shows that a Trinitarian notion was not disputed between Athanasius and his opponents.[82] Both groups commit to it, and therefore Athanasius' argument that the Son is the Giver of the Spirit and hence eternal must have had some force. The claim that the Son is Giver of the Spirit is sustained with reference to John 16:14. Jn 10:30 and 14:9 are referred to together with Jn 1:9 to establish that the Son is eternal light and image of the Father. Jn 10:30 and 14:9 are both modified, from a statement by Jesus himself in the first person singular to the third person singular, thus offering a perspective on the subject that is subtly influenced by Athanasius. In the Gospel of John, both are expressions of Jesus himself, which are qualified in the setting of the narrative. In Athanasius' presentation, the expressions are *about* Jesus, who is already introduced as the Wisdom and Word of the Father, which are understood self-evidently. This modification of the biblical texts suggests stronger ontological implications in Athanasius' presentation than modern exegetes generally discern from these Johannine texts itself.

CA I 17–21: The Trinity is Eternal and Creator

In *CA* I 17–18, Athanasius quotes the Arian slogans 'There was once when he was not' and 'He was not before he was begotten' in order to refute them afterwards.[83] Athanasius takes for granted that God creates through his Son-Word (cf. Jn 1:3). If the Son-Word is not eternal, (1) God cannot truly be Creator.[84] (2) If the Son is not eternal with the Father, the Trinity itself would not be eternal, but instable and expanding.[85] Athanasius' position differs from both Marcellus and the 'Arians'.[86] Marcellus refused to call the Word of God

---

[81] *CA* I 16 (126,20–24); tr. Rusch, adapted.
[82] Anatolios, *Retrieving Nicaea*, 36, 43–44.
[83] *CA* I 17 (127,9–10).
[84] *CA* I 17 (126,2–5).
[85] *CA* I 17 (127,10–19). Cf. *CA* II 37, contra Marcellus, fr. 48 (Vinzent).
[86] Anatolios, *Retrieving Nicaea*, 87–89, 92, 108–9, 145; Morales, *La théologie trinitaire*, 493–94, 497–513.

Son before the Incarnation and argued that in the end of times, the Son would again subject himself to God (cf. 1 Cor 15:28). He conceives the Godhead as a Monad expanding (πλατυνομένη) in a Triad.[87] Athanasius rejects this view of the Trinity in terms of contraction and expansion. The Arians argued in a different way for a Trinity with unequal divine hypostases: the Son and Spirit are inferior to the Father and thus constitute an unequal Trinity.[88] In contrast to both positions, Athanasius argues that the Trinity must be equal in honour and therefore, as Trinity, be eternal and Creator. Although this implicitly corrects the position of Marcellus of Ancyra, he only attacks the Arians explicitly. Athanasius argues that 'no Christian would endure' the Arians who teach a developing Triad: 'It is peculiar to the Greeks to introduce an originated Triad and to equate it with originated things. (...) But the Christian faith (...) worships the individual oneness of its Godhead and flees the blasphemies of the Arians.'[89] Athanasius confidently claims all the evidence (that is, the authority from Scripture and reason) on his side.[90] He speaks about the Christian faith as rejecting the Arian position in very general terms. The Arian view is incompatible with his – authentic – Christian view, because it leads to an unstable, God-unworthy conception of the Trinity.

In *CA* I 19, Athanasius provides scriptural evidence that the Son is Creator together with the Father, in order to identify the Son with the titles Wisdom, Word and Life. He first establishes that God is the spring of Wisdom and Life, based on Jn 14:6 and

---

[87] Marcellus, fr. 48 (Vinzent 42,10–12).

[88] Even Eusebius of Caesarea, who sometimes criticises Asterius' views, states: 'For we neither deem them equally worthy of honor, nor both without source and unbegotten, but deem the one [hypostasis] as unbegotten and without source, while [we deem] the other as begotten and having the Father as his source.' *ET* II 7 (Kl./H. 104,14–16); tr. McCarthy Spoerl and Vinzent.

[89] *CA* I 18 (128,15–18. 21–23); tr. Rusch.

[90] Cf. *CA* I 17, where Athanasius concludes an argument thus: 'The above is enough to overthrow the Arian heresy. Nevertheless, from what follows someone might observe its heterodoxy.' (126,1–2); tr. Rusch. Wiles claims that Athanasius perceived the nature of the conflict in this way from the beginning of his episcopate, in "Attitudes," 32.

a text from Proverbs: 'The Son is these things, who says "I am the life" (Jn 14:6) and "I Wisdom have encamped with prudence" (Prv 8:12).'[91] Athanasius correlates the Christological titles Wisdom and Word: 'Solomon says, "God by Wisdom founded the earth ..." (Prv 3:19). And this Wisdom is the Word, and "through him" as John says, "all things came into existence" (Jn 1:3).'[92] The expression 'all things' is seen by Athanasius as proof that the Son cannot be counted among 'all things'.[93] Since the Son is the offspring of the Father, this indicates that the Son 'is peculiar (ἴδιον)... in relation to the Father (cf. Jn 5:18), and this shows that the Father is peculiar to the Son'.[94]

In CA I 20–21, Athanasius elaborates on the notion that the Son is peculiar (ἴδιον) to the Father and hence eternal. The Arian view has tremendous consequences for the Father's eternity as well, for 'let the thoughtful person note how the perfection and fullness of the Father's substance is deprived.'[95] If the Son is not eternally peculiar to God, truth is not always in God.[96] On top of that, the statement 'the Son was not before he was begotten' is incorrect, because the Son himself is the Truth:

> Since the Father exists, there is always in him truth, which is the Son who says, 'I am the truth' (Jn 14:6) (...) Let us look at the characteristics of the Father, that we may decide if the image is his. The Father is everlasting, immortal, powerful, Light, King, almighty God, Lord, Creator, and Maker. These characteristics are necessarily in the image, so that truly 'he who has seen the Son has seen the Father.' (Jn 14:9)[97]

Since the Son is truth and the Father's image, he must co-exist with God's substance. Athanasius thus attributes many divine titles to the Son, to argue that he is ontologically the Son of God. In this exposition on what he perceives as the Christian truth,

---

[91] CA I 19 (128,7–8); tr. Rusch. Rusch refers to Jn 16:6 instead of 14:6.
[92] CA I 19 (129,19–22); tr. Rusch.
[93] CA I 19 (129,24–25).
[94] CA I 19 (129,32–33); tr. Rusch, adapted.
[95] CA I 20 (130,8–9).
[96] CA I 20 (130,15).
[97] CA I 20 (130,16–17); CA I 21 (130,1–5); tr. Rusch, adapted.

Athanasius also attacks his opponents' dishonesty again in *CA* I 21.

> The Arians, ... designed for themselves conclusions such as 'If the Son is the Father's offspring and image and is like the Father in all things, then just as he is begotten, the Son necessarily ought to beget, and he becomes father of a son' (...) Inventors of evils, truly enemies of God, in order that they do not confess the Son as the image of the Father think corporeal and earthly things about the Father himself, accusing him of segments, emanations and influxes.[98]

Athanasius suggests that the reasoning of his opponents is a deliberate attempt to attack the truth. He asserts that his opponents' concern that an eternal Son must be a Father as well is a smokescreen for their impiety, and leads to an unstable Trinity. Against their impiety and dishonesty, Athanasius places Scripture and scriptural argumentation. Athanasius argues that the characteristics of God the Father are by necessity displayed in the Son as well, grounded on a modification of Jesus' saying that who sees the Son, sees the Father (cf. Jn 14:9). These words have to be taken at face value and he asserts that virtually all attributes of the Father belong to the Son with an appeal to the Gospel of John. He closely aligns the Johannine theological notions that 'everything has come into existence through the Word' (Jn 1:3) and two Christological titles of John 14:6. As a pre-modern theologian, he directly infers doctrinal conclusions from scriptural notions without a strong concern for the historical context in which the words originally functioned. This leads to the disappearance of the subtle irony and ambiguity that is involved in Jn 5:18. Whereas John's Gospel evades the question how Jesus conceived his identity precisely, because the Jews object to Jesus' claim of divinity, in *CA* I 19, it is reduced to a plain description of Jesus as the offspring of the Father.[99] Nevertheless, his argument cannot be reduced to polemical distortion, for his opponents had to come to

---

[98] *CA* I 21 (131,11–18); tr. Rusch.
[99] Cf. Gaston, "Gospel of John," 134; Barrett, *John*, 256; Carson, *John*, 249–50.

terms with the consequences of the non-eternity of the Son for their own conception of the Trinity.

CA I 22–36: Four Arian Questions

Athanasius does not engage extensively with philosophical matters, but he is anxious to demonstrate the reasonableness of his position. Meijering notes that Athanasius attacks the Arian arguments 'as both unbiblical and conflicting with reason; …in fact he often produces Biblical texts in order to prove his reasonable arguments'.[100] Scripture and reason are complementary in Athanasius' defence of the eternal divinity of the Son of God. As Anatolios aptly summarises the situation in fourth-century Christianity: 'There was a shared sense both of the primacy of faith and of the necessity of applying reason to faith.'[101]

In CA I 22–36, Athanasius mainly uses logical argumentation to counter some views of his opponents. In CA I 21, he had refuted his opponents' argument that if the Son is like the Father in all things, he must be a father as well and beget a son. Central to his counter-argument is that the divine Father-Son relation is only partly reflected in the human father-son relation, because human parenthood does not qualify the divine, but vice versa.[102] Athanasius claims that the Arians ask four types of suggestive questions: questions on (1) the difference between the Maker and the Son, (2) the meaning of the term unbegotten, (3) changeability or unchangeability in God and (4) the implications of the birth metaphor.[103]

---

[100] E. P. Meijering, "ΗΝ ΠΟΤΕ ΟΤΕ ΟΥΚ ΗΝ Ο ΥΙΟΣ. A Discussion on Time and Eternity," in God, Being, History. Studies in Patristic Philosophy, ed. E. P. Meijering (Amsterdam: North-Holland Publishing, 1975), 166.

[101] Anatolios, Retrieving Nicaea, 36.

[102] CA I 21 (131,31–132,33). See also Widdicombe, The Fatherhood of God; cf. Marcellus, fr. 1 (Vinzent), who accuses Asterius of speaking in a rather human way (ἀνθρωπικώτερον) about the Father and Son. Vinzent, Markell, xxxii–xxxiii. All references to Marcellus will be given according to this edition.

[103] CA I 22 (132,17–23); cf. CA II 18 (195,20–23).

Difference between the Father and Son

In *CA* I 23, Athanasius blames his opponents for inconsistency: 'why if they hear that God has a Son they deny him by looking at themselves? But if they hear that he creates and makes, do they no longer oppose their human notion?'[104] He asserts that 'if anyone would reasonably examine them, they will be found to provoke much laughter and scoffing.'[105] He then comes to the subject matter: the first Arian question is: 'He who is, did he make him who is not, from that which was not, or him who was? Therefore did he make the Son who is or who is not?'[106] Athanasius asserts that the Arians anticipate that people will answer to the first question of the Arians 'He who is [made] Him who is not',[107] which would render the Son inferior to the Father. Athanasius blames his opponents for stating the question without qualification (ἁπλῶς) and thus using confused and vague terminology. He argues that the referents of 'He who is' (ὁ ὤν) and 'the things that are not' (τὰ μὴ ὄντα) must be specified before the question can be answered.[108] Athanasius asserts that God 'who is (τόν ὄντα), is able to make things which are not and which are and which were previously'.[109] His opponents' reasoning is confused (ἀσύστατος), since both 'what is' and 'what is not' come into existence, and he gives an example to illustrate the problem of their question. Craftsmen work with material that previously existed (τῆν οὖσαν ὕλη), but God made creation that did not exist before it was made.[110] Athanasius argues that the Arians should add the question: 'Was the God who is, once Wordless? Being Light, was he

---

[104] *CA* I 23 (133,8–11); tr. Rusch, adapted; cf. *CA* I 26 (136,16–22).
[105] *CA* I 23 (133,19–21); tr. Rusch. Cf. *CA* I 26 (135,1–136,10).
[106] *CA* I 22 (132,17–19); tr. Rusch.
[107] *CA* I 24 (133,3); cf. *CA* II 74 (251,17–18).
[108] Of course, this is a discussion technique that also shows the establishment of a negative *ethos*, because his opponents ask wrong questions. A clear-cut distinction between both *logos* and negative *ethos* seems impossible.
[109] *CA* I 24 (133,4–5); tr. Rusch.
[110] *CA* I 24 (133,5–134,12).

lightless (ἀφεγγής), or was he always the Father of the Word?"[111] By situating this imaginary dialogue, Athanasius takes the privilege to supplement the Arian questions with his own ones, and thus illustrate the irrationality of the Arian question. He asserts that the Arians are refuted by his argumentation above and three biblical passages that he quotes: 'John said: "The word was" (Jn 1:1). Paul wrote "Who being the reflection of his glory" (Heb 1:3) and "The God who is over all blessed forever" (Rom 9:5).'[112] His use of Scripture backs up his reasoning on this point; the reference to John is the primary scriptural reference: it comes first and is terminologically most closely connected to the actual discussion.

In *CA* I 25, Athanasius asks another counter-question to demonstrate the Arian contradiction: 'the God who is, not existing, has he come into existence or is he even before he came into existence? And because he exists, did he make himself?'[113] Anatolios asserts that all participants in the fourth-century doctrinal debate affirmed both the worship of Jesus Christ in the Church, and that 'the preexistent Christ was the Creator of the world and in some sense the paradigm of creation, or at least contained the paradigms of creation'.[114] On those premises, Athanasius suggests that the Arian question concerning the Son also harms the Father. For while creation comes into existence by the Word, the Son-Word is Creator as well (cf. Jn 1:1; Col 1:16). The Arians can only maintain that the Son-Word is not truly God and yet worship him, if they (1) deny the notion of creation through the Word, (2) admit that they worship a creature, or (3) suggest that God created himself.[115] The first position contradicts the divine revelation, the second one is blasphemous, and the third one is self-contradictory. Their position is therefore inconsistent (ἀσύστατος) and must be rejected. Athanasius states that the orthodox answer to the first

---

[111] *CA* I 24 (134,14–15); tr. Rusch, adapted. Rusch's translation omitted the word always (ἀεί).

[112] *CA* I 24 (134,23–25); tr. Rusch.

[113] *CA* I 25 (134,5–6). Not a precise translation of: ὁ ὢν θεὸς οὐκ ὢν γέγονεν; ἢ καὶ πρὶν γένηται ἔστιν; ὢν οὖν ἑαυτὸν ἐποίησεν; cf. *CA* I 26 (135,3–136,11).

[114] Anatolios, *Retrieving Nicaea*, 37.

[115] Cf. *CA* I 25 (134,4–9).

question is 'that the Father who is, made the Son who is, "for the Word became flesh" (Jn 1:14)' in the consummation of times.[116] The reason of the Arian confusion is thus located in their failure to understand that 'the Word became flesh'. Athanasius suggests that his opponents separate the Son from 'the God who is', because of the attributes of the incarnate Son that are inapplicable to the divinity. His solution is that the incarnation, the becoming flesh of the Word, provides sufficient explanation to maintain both the identity of the Son and God the 'Father who is', and the distinction of Father and Son, especially due to the subordinate and God-unworthy attributes of the incarnate Son.

According to his use of Scripture, Athanasius' primarily suggests that his opponents err because they fail to understand the significance of Jn 1:14. While Jn 1:14 indeed affirms that the Word became flesh, the co-eternity of the Son which is crucial to Athanasius' idea discussed in this section cannot properly be derived from this passage as such. At this point, Athanasius evades the later Chalcedonian question how the Son can both have divine and human attributes. He attacks his opponents for ignoring the incarnation, while they are mainly concerned to maintain the unity and singularity of the supreme divine Being. He ignores the tensions in the Johannine Christology, and claims an overall perspective indicated by this appeal to Jn 1:14, which proves his opponents wrong.

Birth Metaphor

The second question Athanasius discusses is a question to women: 'Did you have a son before you gave birth? And just as you did not, thus the Son of God was not before he was begotten.'[117] He challenges the applicability of the birth metaphor to the Father-Son relation.[118] Whereas the Arians deduced temporality of the Son's generation from this metaphor, Athanasius asserts that

---

[116] *CA* I 25 (135,26–28); tr. Rusch, adapted. Cf. Rousseau's translation of the passage: 'Le Père qui est a fait le Fils alors que celui-ci était, car «le Verbe a été fait chair» (Jn 1:14). Cf. further Heb 9:25.

[117] *CA* I 22 (132,21–23); tr. Rusch.

[118] *CA* I 26–29 (137,10–139,28).

God's begetting is incomparable to human procreation. He asserts that one should not ask women but men a question, to emphasise another element of the birth metaphor. If men are asked whether they buy their sons externally or receive them from themselves, a man will answer that a son belongs to his own substance (τῆς ἐμῆς οὐσίας ἴδιος καὶ ὅμοιος).[119] Although time avoids an immediate re-alisation of the potential of human nature (φύσις), when this bar-rier is removed, it can be realised instantly. Athanasius asserts that the metaphor preserves the identity of substance of Father and Son, while its human limitations are not applicable to the divine Father-Son relation. In that respect, non-human metaphors like sun radiance and source water better illustrate the eternal coexistence of Father and Son.[120]

Besides his appeal to reasonableness, Athanasius' habit of re-ferring back to what he has already established is noteworthy, because he thus suggests that he consistently presents all the evi-dence completely. In CA I 28, Athanasius states: 'In anticipation we have said in the above material that it is not necessary to com-pare the generation of God with the nature of men .... Now we say the same thing.'[121] Some lines further he likewise states: 'It has been proved (ἀποδέδεικται) sufficiently above that the off-spring from God is not an affection (οὐκ ἔστι πάθος), and now it is also proved (δέδεικται) that the Word has not been begotten ac-cording to affection (οὐ κατὰ πάθος).'[122] He thus indicates that God is not subject to affections or passions, and meanwhile underlines the consistency of his arguments.

This strategy of referring back is especially useful if Athana-sius assumed his work to be heard rather than read by many, be-cause listeners do not have the luxury of rereading passages for a detailed comparison.[123] In the case of written communication, the effectiveness of the strategy is less clear, but it is quite likely that

---

[119] CA I 26 (136,22–27); cf. CA III 67 (381,10–21).
[120] CA I 27 (137,10).
[121] CA I 28 (137,1–3); tr. Rusch.
[122] CA I 28 (138,22–23); tr. Rusch, altered. Cf. καθὰ προείπομεν in CA II 3 (179,4).
[123] Cf. Watts, Riot in Alexandria, 262.

his work was not just read, but also heard. In any case, this recurring phenomenon might be caused by the importance of orality in the Arian controversy.[124] Athanasius mentions that the four Arian questions, discussed in *CA* I 22–36, are asked to 'boys at the market place' and to women. He does not explicitly state what the implications of the location, the market place, are, but since he states that the Arian questions are not from the Scriptures but from their own hearts, and moreover, impious, it might be meant pejoratively as an antithesis between discussing holy questions in the profane setting of the market versus the sacred place of the church.[125]

Athanasius' remarks are far from gender-sensitive, which shows that he envisaged an exclusively male audience. Athanasius stated that it is unnecessary to respond to the foolish views of the Arians, but 'it might be fitting to converse with them ... especially because silly women (γυναικάρια) are readily tricked by them'.[126] Athanasius' remarks about women are not atypical of the ancient world.[127] Aristotle remarked for example that 'the relation of male to female is by nature a relation of superior to inferior and ruler to ruled' (*Politics*, 1245b12).[128] The women-men distinction might subtly be employed to discredit the Arian

---

[124] Harris, *Ancient Literacy*, 300, 305.

[125] See *CA* I 22 (132,15–17); *CA* I 37 (147,10–12).

[126] *CA* I 23 (133,2–4); tr. Rusch. Cf. *CA* I 22 (132,21); I 26 (136,11). Athanasius probably alludes to 2 Tim 3:6 at this point. The word γυναικάρια is used in 2 Timothy 3:6. In both instances, the γυναικάρια are deceived by false teachers.

[127] For the position of women in the patristic era, see Gillian Clark, *Women in Late Antiquity. Pagan and Christian Life-Styles* (Oxford: Clarendon, 1993); for the freedom of speech in ancient Greece and Rome, see Kennedy, *Christian and Secular Tradition*, 15–19, 119–21; for a critique of the whole concept of the status of women in ancient Greece, see Marylin A. Katz, "Ideology and 'the Status of Women' in Ancient Greece," in *Women in Antiquity: New Assessments*, ed. Richard Hawley and Barbara Levick (Routledge, 2002), 21–43.

[128] Aristotle further states: '[T]he male, unless constituted in some respect contrary to nature, is by nature more expert at leading than the female, and the elder and complete than the younger and incomplete.' (1259a41)

position, for it is amoral and an indication of incompetence if one attempts to persuade women if men could not be persuaded by one's arguments.[129]

Unbegotten

The third market question, attributed to Asterius, concerns the meaning of the term unbegotten (ἀγέννητος). The meaning of God's *agennesia* already features in an early stage of the controversy. In outlining their concern of divine simplicity, the Eusebians put the word ἀγέννητος to the fore. Arius' *Confession to Alexander* mentions it as God's primary attribute.[130] Athanasius discusses the term ἀγέννητος in *CA* I 30–34. He suggests that the Arian question 'Is the unbegotten one or two?'[131] anticipates the answer 'one' to count the Son among the originated beings.[132] Athanasius points to the ambiguity of the term to avoid this consequence. He first downplays its importance, by indicating that ἀγέννητος has a Greek (non-scriptural) origin. The Greeks use the term for (1) that which not yet has 'come into existence, but being able to come into existence', (2) 'that which neither has come into existence nor is able ever to come into existence' and (3) 'that which exists but has not come into existence from anything and does not have a father of its own'.[133] Asterius added (4) 'that "unbegotten" is that which has not been made but always is'.[134] The first two options are soon dismissed, while he asserts that in the fourth sense, attributed to Asterius, 'the Son is ἀγένητος too', for

---

[129] Cf. *CA* II 30 on Athanasius' subordination of women to men. Moreover, in the new state, humans shall no longer 'be on guard against the beguilement of woman'; *CA* II 69 (246,22); tr. Anatolios.

[130] Urk. 6. (12,4–5); tr. Williams. 2001, 270. 'We acknowledge one God, the only unbegotten, the only eternal, the only one without cause or beginning, the only true, the only one possessed of immortality, the only wise, the only good, the only sovereign.'

[131] See *CA* I 22 (132,19); tr. Rusch. Reiterated in *CA* I 30 (139,3); I 31 (141,1); I 32 (142,14); II 18 (195,22). *CA* I 22; I 31; I 32 read ἀγένητον; *CA* I 30 and II 18 read ἀγέννητον.

[132] *CA* I 30 (139,6–140,7).

[133] *CA* I 30 (140,16–23); tr. Rusch.

[134] *CA* I 30 (141,25); tr. Rusch.

the Son is not made either.[135] Athanasius is willing to grant that the Father alone is unbegotten in the (third) sense of 'existing but not having been begotten from anyone, not having a father of his own'.[136] This definition does not relegate the Son to the realm of created beings, because the Word (λόγος) is similar (οἷος) to his begetter (ὁ γεννήσας).[137] The rationale behind Athanasius' argument is the ambiguity of ἀγέννητος. Asterius' question cannot be answered properly, and when the sense is specified, it offers no support for the inferiority of the Son.

In *CA* I 32, Athanasius attacks another inconsistency in Asterius' thought: Asterius claims both that the Unbegotten is one and that God's Wisdom is unbegotten and without beginning.[138] According to Athanasius, Asterius distinguished between Gods own (ἴδιον) power and Christ, on the basis of 1 Cor 1:24, which lacks a definite article.[139] This true and eternal power and Wisdom of God (cf. Rom 1:20) coexists without beginning (ἄναρχος) and is unbegotten with God.[140] Athanasius therefore blames Asterius for being inconsistent and he produces a reasonable *tu-quoque* argument. Athanasius was accused of teaching two first principles (cf. *CA* I 14), but Asterius cannot speak unambiguously of one unbegotten principle either.[141] Since Asterius holds that God's power and Wisdom coexists (συνυπάρχει) eternally with God, the Unbegotten is not unambiguously one, Athanasius concludes that the Arians employ the term ἀγέννητον to qualify the Son as originated (γενητόν).[142] The extensive interaction with Asterius, and absence of Arius at this point suggests strongly that Athanasius regarded Asterius as his main opponent. Asterius is introduced in

---

[135] *CA* I 31 (141,5).

[136] «κατὰ τὸ ὑπάρχον μέν, μήτε δὲ γεννηθὲν ἔκ τινος μήτε ἔχον ἑαυτοῦ πατέρα» *CA* I 31 (141,9–10); tr. Rusch.

[137] *CA* I 31 (141,14).

[138] *CA* I 32 (142,3–4). Cf. Asterius, frs. 64 and 66 (Vinzent).

[139] 'Christ, power of God and wisdom of God'. Unfortunately, both the RSV and NRSV add the definite particle (the) in their translation of this verse. Cf. Asterius, fr. 64 (Vinzent).

[140] Fr. 66 (Vinzent).

[141] Cf. *CA* I 32 (142,14–17).

[142] *CA* I 32 (142,14–17. 20–21).

CA I 30–32 as 'the villainous sophist Asterius, the advocate (συνήγορος) of the heresy',[143] and soon afterwards as 'Asterius the Sophist', who zealously defends (συνηγορεῖν) the 'Arian heresy'.[144] The nickname 'Sophist' seems to be used pejoratively, because Athanasius contrasts Asterius' wisdom with his actual inconsistency.[145] The label 'advocate of heresy' is also solely used for Asterius, and depicts him as a conscious defender of impious views.[146]

After several chapters with hardly any scriptural references, Athanasius includes them from *CA* I 33 onwards. He argues that the term unbegotten can be used appropriately, but is employed dishonestly by his opponents, in accordance with their heresy. They do not understand 'that he who honors the Son honors the Father and that "he who dishonors the Son dishonors the Father" (Jn 5:23)'.[147] This text, that functions in John to show that there is in fact no competition between God and Jesus and that whatever honour is bestowed upon Jesus is not comparable to that of idol worship, but rather results in the glorification of God, is reconfigured in this new setting as a strong catchphrase against the impiety of the Arians. In *CA* I 34, Athanasius expresses his preference for scriptural language, ending up by citing John:

> Unbegotten was discovered by the Greeks, who do not know the Son. But 'Father' was known by our Lord, and he rejoiced in it. He himself, knowing whose Son he is, said, 'I am in the Father and the Father is in me' (Jn 14:10) and 'He who has seen me, has seen the Father' (Jn 14:9) and 'I and the Father are one' (Jn 10:30) and nowhere does he appear to call God 'unbegotten'.[148]

---

[143] *CA* I 30 (140,23–141,24).

[144] *CA* I 32 (141,1–2). The predicate 'the Sophist' is reiterated in *CA* II 28, 37 and III 2.

[145] See in *CA* I 32 and II 37.

[146] *CA* I 32 (141,2); III 2 (307,1); *CA* III 60 (373,18–19). Cf. Guido Müller, *Lexicon Athanasianum* (Berlin: de Gruyter, 1952), 1378; Lyman, "Topography of Heresy," 45–48.

[147] *CA* I 33 (143,18–20); tr. Rusch.

[148] *CA* I 34 (144,9–14); tr. Rusch, adapted.

Subsequently, Athanasius states that Father is the name that Jesus has 'taught us to pray' in Matthew 6, and locates 'the main point (κεφάλαιον) of our faith' in the baptismal commandment in Mt 28:19, which mentions Father, Son and Holy Spirit (and not Unbegotten).[149] The Christological material of John proves helpful in this setting to rebut the Arian argument that unbegotten clearly separates the Father from the Son.

His rejection of Asterius' conception of unbegotten is not unwillingness to use theological vocabulary outside the Bible as such. Athanasius is willing to accept the term ἀγέννητος despite its absence in Scripture; he even states that the bishops of Nicaea 'employed unscriptural words' against 'impiety'.[150] Nevertheless, when an unscriptural term endangers his theology, he feels free to argue from the three Johannine texts that 'Father' is a more appropriate term. The material cited above shows that the use of ἀγέννητος testifies to a genuine difference in theology, and is not mere polemic on Athanasius' part.[151] Besides reasoning and argument by example and from implication, Jn 10:30 and 14:9–10 are crucial in this section. The Christological statements, attributed to Jesus himself, serve as the evidence for his theological position that closes all discussion. The subtlety about what these expressions originally meant in John's Gospel is less important than its actualisation in the controversy. Jn 10:30 has most certainly a strong (though not necessarily exclusive) functional meaning.[152] The proof-text setting is even clearer in the case of Jn 14:9–10. Both are treated as individual sayings that are closely connected because of their content rather than their original context. The rabbinic principle that 'a man's agent is like to himself (Mishnah *Berakoth* 5:5)' is not adequate as a full explanation of Jn 14:9, that Jesus represents the Father, for Jesus' claim in this section is more

---

[149] *CA* I 34 (144,14–16); tr. Rusch.

[150] *CA* I 30 (140,9–11); tr. Rusch.

[151] Hanson, *Search*, 60, 204–205; see also Mark DelCogliano, "The Influence of Athanasius and the Homoiousians on Basil of Caesarea's Decentralization of 'Unbegotten,'" *JECS* 19 (2011): 197–223.

[152] Barrett, *John*, 382; Carson, *John*, 394–95.

than just that,[153] but Athanasius takes the implications of Jn 14:9 further than John would have imagined. Athanasius' observation at this point is correct, in so far as Jesus calls God Father, but his selection suggests that these texts unequivocally support his view. However, the often quoted Jn 14:10 is part of a question and a qualification: 'Do you not believe that I am in the Father and the Father is in me? The words that I say to you I do not speak on my own; but the Father who dwells in me does his works. Believe me that I am in the Father and the Father is in me; but if you do not, then believe me because of the works themselves. Very truly, I tell you, the one who believes in me will also do the works that I do and, in fact, will do greater works than these, because I am going to the Father (Jn 14:10–12).' In its original setting, this text indicates both Jesus' dependence on and reciprocity with the Father. Jesus locates the trust for his reciprocity with the Father in the works he does; he even claims that the works are matched or even superseded by believers in him. These works of the disciples are only possible by virtue of believing in him, but at any rate, they qualify the words of Jn 14:9–10 that Athanasius used in a self-evident way for his theology. Athanasius claims the obvious clarity of the diction of these Johannine texts for his position, conveniently bracketing the context of the Christological statements that call for a more cautious evaluation. In that way, the Johannine texts receive a new meaning in the theology of Athanasius.

Changeability

In CA I 35–36, Athanasius addresses the question of the Word's changeability and free will: 'Is he good by choosing to be good through his free will and so is able to change, if he wills it, as one who is changeable by nature? Or is he like a rock or a piece of wood, not having a choice that is free to be moved and to incline toward this or that?'[154] The question whether the Son is unchangeable is already present at an early stage of the controversy; Arius

---

[153] Carson, *John*, 494–95; contra Barrett, *John*, 459.
[154] *CA* I 35 (144,4–145,6); tr. Anatolios. Cf. *CA* I 22 (132,19–21); Asterius, fr. 44 (Vinzent).

holds that the Son ... is unchangeable (ἀναλλοίωτος) and adds in the same breath that the Son 'was not, before he was begotten, or created, or purposed, or established'.[155] Most likely, this means that Arius regarded the Son as changeable in theory, while unchangeable in a practical sense.[156] Athanasius vehemently disagrees with Arius on this aspect and asks somewhat pejoratively 'who could imagine a more disgusting thing than this teaching'.[157]

In *CA* I 35, Athanasius quotes the three Johannine touchstone texts again and deliberates on the consequences of an alterable and changing Word. He argues that the Son cannot even be in theory changeable, by framing several rhetorical questions in language resembling these Johannine texts. He takes for granted that the Father is unchangeable, and he alludes to Jn 14:9 that he who sees the Son must see the Unchangeable. Since the Father is utterly unchangeable, there cannot be any kind of change in the Word or Logos of God either.[158] For

> if the Son is changeable, according to them, and is not always the same but rather is always alterable by nature, how can such a one be the 'Image' of the Father, if he lacks the likeness of the Father's unchangeability? Or how can he be wholly 'in the Father' (Jn 14:10) if he has a faculty of choice that is ambivalent in its inclination? (...) For how can what is not perfect be 'equal to God' (Phil 2:6; cf. Jn 5:18)? Or how can he not be unchangeable who is 'one with the Father' (Jn 10:30) and who is the Father's Son and belongs to his essence?[159]

Athanasius asserts the inappropriateness of ascribing changeability to the Son and its problematic consequences for knowing the Father on the ground of Johannine notions and logical contradictions. If the Son is changeable, he cannot display the Father, and neither could he have been 'in the Father'. He further asserts that his opponents' reason (λόγος) is in danger 'if they falsely ascribe change to the truly existent Word/Reason (τοῦ ὄντως ὄντος λόγου) ... For

---

[155] Urk. 1 (3,3); tr. Stevenson.
[156] Hanson, *Search*, 92–93.
[157] *CA* I 35 (145,11–12); tr. Rusch.
[158] *CA* I 35 (145,15–20).
[159] *CA* I 35 (145,21–24.26–29); tr. Anatolios.

"the tree is recognised by its fruit" (Mt 12:33), and so the one who "has seen the Son has seen the Father" (Jn 14:9) and the knowledge of the Son is knowledge of the Father."[160] The text of Matthew is in line with the polemical tone in this passage and Jn 14:9 provides the theological rationale for the claim that the view on the changeability of the Word has impact on the opponents' view of God and affects their sanity.

The theological concept 'Image' (εἰκών; cf. Col 1:15) is crucial in asserting the similarity between Father and Son. Concerning this theme, it is relevant to consider Origen's view. His position on the changeability of the Word-Son was taken in two different ways in the fourth century.[161] Origen held that no rational creature is unchangeable 'except for the nature of God'.[162] The soul of Christ is therefore changeable in practice, but he consistently chose the good.[163] At the same time, Origen upheld the Word's and the Spirit's immutability.[164] Athanasius derives other

---

[160] CA I 35 (145,29–32); tr. Anatolios, adapted. Anatolios refers to CG 9, 19, 34, DI 12 and Decr 2 for more claims of Athanasius that those who do not honour the divinity of the Logos become irrational.

[161] For the importance of Origen, see Williams, Arius, 131–157; Ayres, Nicaea and Its Legacy, 20–30; Anatolios, Retrieving Nicaea, 15–20.

[162] Origen, DP I 8.3.

[163] DP II 6.4. The human or rational soul of Christ 'possessed immutability from its union with the Word of God'; tr. ANF.

[164] DP I 2.10; 'But the Wisdom of God, which is His only-begotten Son, being in all respects incapable of change or alteration, and every good quality in Him being essential, and such as cannot be changed and converted, His glory is therefore declared to be pure and sincere.' DP I 6.2 'For in the Trinity [God, his Christ and the Holy Spirit] alone, which is the author of all things, does goodness exist in virtue of essential being; while others possess it as an accidental and perishable quality'; DP I 8.3 'There is no nature, then, which may not admit of good or evil, except the nature of God—the fountain of all good things—and of Christ; for it is wisdom, and wisdom assuredly cannot admit folly; and it is righteousness, and righteousness will never certainly admit of unrighteousness; and it is the Word, or Reason, which certainly cannot be made irrational; nay, it is also the light, and it is certain that the darkness does not receive the light. In like manner, also, the nature of the Holy Spirit, being holy,

conclusions from the concept of εἰκών than Origen. Origen regarded Christ, the Image of God as a representation in a limited
way. Origen is careful to limit the implications of the comparison,
and holds that Christ represents the Godhead to a certain extent,
'so that we, who were unable to look upon the glory of that mar-
vellous light when placed in the greatness of His Godhead, may,
by His being made to us brightness, obtain the means of behold-
ing the divine light by looking upon the brightness'.[165] In this context, Origen also cites the three Johannine texts (Jn 14:9; 10:30
and 14:10) that are frequently used by Athanasius in the same
context.

The Eusebian strand of thinking emphasised the subordinate
aspects of Christ as Image, but that has consequences for the representation of God by Christ. They compromise the accuracy of
Christ's representation of the Godhead. Athanasius upholds the
accuracy of Christ's representation, by downplaying the subordinate elements; he focuses on the importance of Christ's divine attributes that are perfect, and therefore, perfectly accurate, when
Christ is rightly called Image of God. Athanasius claims that reason and Scripture prove the Arians wrong in their emphasis on
Christ's subordination and limited representation of the Godhead.
He asserts on the basis of the consequences of these three Johannine verses (10:30; 14:9–10) that the Son is unchangeable and
similar to the Father.

Informed by Scripture and reason, Athanasius posits a gulf
between the Son and creation. Τά γενητά are changeable and unstable in nature, but the Son is of the Father and of his substance
and therefore unchangeable and immutable (ἀναλλοίωτος καὶ
ἄτρεπτος) like the Father himself.[166] If he is the Word and Wisdom
of God, he must be unchangeable, unless the Arians regard him
as accidental (συμβεβηκός) to God's substance.[167] If this line of

---

does not admit of pollution; for it is holy by nature, or essential being.'
tr. ANF.

[165] *DP* I 2.8; tr. ANF.

[166] *CA* I 36 (146,18–20); tr. Anatolios.

[167] *CA* I 36 (146,22). Cf. Meijering, *Orthodoxy and Platonism*, 68; Christopher Stead, *Divine Substance* (Oxford: Clarendon, 1977), 60, 141–42.

reasoning is accepted, the Son is unchangeable. Argumentation and an appeal to Scripture go hand in hand in this passage. Besides his argument, Athanasius claims that the saints (the biblical books), or rather the Lord, are more reliable than the words of the heretics. At the end of *CA* I 36, he provides a word from the Lord (Jn 14:6) that supports the Son's unchangeability. He remarks that since the Son is Truth, he never changes:

> For how can that be true which changes and alters and does not stand in one and the same state? But the Lord says, 'I am the Truth' (Jn 14:6). If then the Lord himself says this about himself and shows his inalterability, ... from where did these impious people conceive such inventions?[168]

The word of the Lord himself cuts short the whole argument. The rationale behind these words is that if the Son is Truth, he must be unchangeable. Again, Athanasius employs this Johannine verse in a selective way by choosing only one of the three attributes. Another attribute of Jn 14:6, 'Way', would be an inappropriate substitute in this context, and is conveniently ignored by Athanasius. It seems that the citation is more motivated by rhetorical than exegetical value, which nevertheless might have appealed to Christians less interested in theological subtleties.[169]

CA I 37–64: Refuting the Arian interpretation of Scripture

In the third part of *Oration* I, several 'Arian' interpretations of biblical texts are discussed, refuted and supplied with an 'orthodox' exposition. In this section, the Gospel of John provides Athanasius with logical means for criticising the Arian exegesis of these biblical texts, while it simultaneously supports his own exegesis.[170] Athanasius singles out six proof-texts, to be discussed in *CA* I-II. He opens his defence in strongly polemical terms. His opponents 'violently distort [the divine sayings] to accommodate them to their own minds'. Athanasius wants to show that these passages

---

[168] *CA* I 36 (146,27–31); tr. Anatolios.
[169] See the comments made at *CA* I 12 above.
[170] Pollard, *Johannine Christology*, 185.

of Scripture 'have a right sense, while' his opponents 'understand them badly'.[171]

CA I 37–45: Phil 2:9–10

Athanasius first discusses Philippians 2:9–10: 'Therefore (διό) God also highly exalted him and gave him the name that is above every name, so that (ἵνα) at the name of Jesus every knee should bend, in heaven and on earth and under the earth.' He asserts that the Arians regard 'therefore' and 'so that' as an indication that the Son received exaltation as a reward (μισθός), and therefore, he must be changeable (τρεπτός).[172] Athanasius remarks that Eusebius (of Nicomedia) and Arius not only said that Christ received exaltation as a reward, but also dared (τετολμήκασιν) to write it down, while 'their followers have not drawn back from saying these statements in the middle of the marketplace, oblivious of the insanity of what they are saying'.[173] Athanasius continues to discuss Phil 2:9–10 and then states: 'It is necessary to address the question to them yet again, so that the final consequence of their impiety may be made evident.'[174]

Athanasius claims that his opponents understand the passage as if the Son received his position as a reward, which would be a form of adoptianism. He sketches his opponents' argument in a way that they would never accept it; that his opponents would think that the Son needed the incarnation as improvement for his own sake; Athanasius proposes instead that the human flesh needed improvement, not the Son.[175] 'For if he [i.e. the Son] did not exist prior to becoming human—or even if he did exist but

---

[171] *CA* I 37 (146,1–147,4); tr. Anatolios, adapted.
[172] Cf. *CA* I 37 (147,8–10). It is very probable that this is not an Arian teaching per se, but a logical inference from Athanasius' point of view. On the reception of this text and Ps 44,7–8 in the first centuries, see Mariette Canévet, "La théologie au secours de l'herméneutique biblique: l'exégèse de Phil. 2 et du Ps. 44 dans le Contra Arianos I, 37–52 d'Athanase d'Alexandrie," *OCP* 62 (1996): 185–95.
[173] *CA* I 37 (147,10–12); tr. Anatolios, adapted.
[174] *CA* I 38 (148,12–14); tr. Anatolios.
[175] *CA* I 38 (147,1–148,12).

was promoted later—how is it that "all things were made through Him", and "in him" (cf. Col 1:16, Jn 1:3)?"[176] Several OT epiphanies (Abraham, Moses), as well as citations from Daniel 7:10, John 17:5 and Psalm 18:10, 14 prove Athanasius' point. John 17:5 is the most prominent text in Athanasius' thought. He states: 'If, according to them, he only now attained advancement, how is it that he makes mention of his own glory that was before the world and transcends the world? For the Son himself said, "Glorify me, Father, with the glory which I had with you before the world was" (Jn 17:5).'[177] Some lines further, he summarises: 'Therefore, if even before the world came to be, the Son possessed glory, ... then he was not promoted on account of having descended but rather he himself promoted those things which were in need of advancement.'[178] John 1:3 and 17:5 articulate thus most clearly Athanasius' theological point. The other passages are far from embellishments, but the force of the argument depends heavily on the Johannine Gospel.

In *CA* I 39, one of Athanasius' most famous statements reveals his general approach concerning texts on Jesus' humanity: The Son 'being God, later became a human being in order that we may be divinized'.[179] He argues that if others are called 'son' and 'gods' (Ex 7:1; cf. Ps 82:6) before the incarnation and the Son is not truly God, 'how then were "all things through him" (Jn 1:3; Col 1:16) and "he was before all things" (Col 1:17)? Or how is he "the firstborn of all creation" (Col 1:15) when there were others before him who were called "sons" and "gods"?'[180] With this rhetorical question, he suggests the implausibility of the Arian position. He further qualifies this as 'a false invention of these present-day Judaizers'.[181] Athanasius argues in this imagined dialogue that deification cannot occur without the Word, because Jesus said to the Jews: '"If he calls these gods, to whom comes the Word

---

[176] *CA* I 38 (147,21–22); tr. Anatolios.
[177] *CA* I 38 (148,26–28); tr. Anatolios.
[178] *CA* I 38 (148,30. 32–33); tr. Anatolios.
[179] *CA* I 39 (149,1–2); tr. Anatolios.
[180] *CA* I 39 (149,6–8); tr. Anatolios.
[181] *CA* I 39 (149,8–9); tr. Anatolios.

of God ..." (Jn 10:35; cf. Ps 82:6). But if all who are called sons and gods ... are adopted and deified through the Word ... then it is clear that all is through him'.[182] Athanasius thus understands the Word (λόγος) of God in Jn 10:35 to be a self-reference to Jesus. However, according to Barrett, this text is 'a difficult passage for convinced monotheists'.[183] The reference to 'gods' in Psalm 82 is most likely addressed to the Israelites that received the law at Sinai. The argument in John thus does not show that Jesus is truly God, but seems to respond to the Jews' objection against Jesus' claim of unity with the Father.[184] The ambiguity of John is substituted by the undoubted affirmation that Jesus as the Word divinised humanity.

In *CA* I 40, Athanasius states with even more confidence that he is not only able to counter 'their irrational fabrications by providing correct conceptions about the Son' but that he will also demonstrate from Scripture 'the unchangeableness of the Son and his inalterable nature, which is that of the Father'.[185] He quotes Philippians 2:5–11 in full to undergird his interpretation: the Son did not benefit from the incarnation, but he became a servant for humanity's sake. In his first explanation (*CA* I 41–43), he wonders how the Son can receive what he possessed in advance already. This is difficult to understand, yet it is

> not a riddle but a divine mystery! 'In the beginning was the Word and the Word was with God, and the Word was God' (Jn 1:1); but, later, for our sakes, 'the Word became flesh' (Jn 1:14). And to refer to him now as 'highly exalted' is not to signify that the essence (*ousia*) of the Word is exalted. For he always was and is 'equal to God' (Phil 2:6); but the exaltation pertains to the humanity. These things were not said of him before but only when the Word became flesh (cf. Jn 1:14), so that it may be evident that 'humbled' (Phil 2:8) and 'exalted' (Phil 2:9) are spoken of the humanity.[186]

---

[182] *CA* I 39 (149,13–16); tr. Anatolios.
[183] Barrett, *John*, 384.
[184] Carson, *John*, 397–99.
[185] *CA* I 40 (149,1–4); tr. Anatolios.
[186] *CA* I 41 (150,5–10); tr. Anatolios.

A twofold paradigm of understanding the Son as eternal Word and human being (Jn 1:1, 14) is apparent in this passage. Athanasius illustrates the double viewpoint of eternal Word (Jn 1:1) and human being (Jn 1:14) and explains Philippians 2:9–10 within this paradigm; hence this passage cannot mean that the Son received his glory because of his incarnation. The Gospel of John, or better: Athanasius' way of reading it, safeguards the 'proper' interpretation of Philippians, the attribution of the words of exaltation to Christ's incarnated status.

This twofold paradigm, or double account of the Saviour (cf. *CA* III 29), is also evident when Athanasius asserts that it is humanity that benefits from the Son's incarnation. Athanasius states that

> the Image of the Father and Immortal Word 'took the form of a servant' (Phil 2:7) and, for our sakes (δι' ἡμᾶς), subjected himself to death as a human being, so that through death, he may thus offer himself for our sakes (ὑπὲρ ἡμῶν) to the Father. (...) himself sanctifies all things and yet says to the Father that he sanctifies himself for our sake (Jn 17:19) - not in order that the Word may become holy, but in order that he may make us all holy in himself - thus also it is now said that '[God] highly exalted him' (Phil 2:9).[187]

Athanasius repeatedly uses the words 'for our sakes' in this section; it transforms a somewhat abstract reasoning into an existential reality for the readers. The interpretation of Scripture and theological opinion on the eternity of the Son cease to be something abstract, but are of immediate concern to his addressees. In this process, Jn 17:19 is slightly adapted to contain a more intense pastoral tone, for the Son 'sanctifies himself for our sakes'.[188] Athanasius links both passages to each other, to make clear that the exaltation has to be understood in view of Jn 17:19 (for their sakes I sanctify myself, so that they also may be sanctified in truth). Jesus' words about sanctification 'for their sakes' lead Athanasius to conclude that the words of Philippians 2 are written

---

[187] *CA* I 41 (151,13–16. 23–26); tr. Anatolios, adapted.
[188] Jn 17:19: 'And for their sakes I sanctify myself, so that they also may be sanctified in truth.'

'on our behalf and for us' (δι' ἡμᾶς καὶ ἡμῶν);[189] humans can be children of God, because of the Son's incarnation and exaltation. Athanasius further mentions in favour of his claim that

> John also says in the Gospel: 'But as many as received him, he gave them power to become children of God' (Jn 1:12). (…) It is not he who attained an advancement from us, for the Word of God is full and without need. Rather, it is we who were promoted through him. For he is 'the light which enlightens every man who comes into the world' (Jn 1:9).[190]

The prominence of John in this interpretation of Phil 2:9–10 – the exaltation of Jesus took place for humanity's sake – is obvious. In the history of interpretation of John 1:9, the part 'who comes into the world' is either connected to 'light' or 'every man', which results in either a Christological or soteriological focus. Although Athanasius does not dwell on the different implications, the context as well as the citation of verse 12 suggests a soteriological focus. Athanasius stresses that humans receive grace from Jesus in his divine capacity. This is not contested by his opponents – they just derive different conclusions from this fact with regard to the Son's exact divine status. In the flow of the argument, however, Athanasius' appeal to it adds to his overall case. After his interpretation of the intrinsic value and meaning of the passage, Athanasius states therefore: 'So it is useless for the Arians to lean upon that conjunction, "therefore".'[191]

Athanasius employs his exegetical principle of time (καιρός), person (πρόσωπον) or thing/subject (πρᾶγμα) quite flexibly. In explaining Philippians 2:9–10, he regards the incarnation as the time of the passage. However, as long as the eternal divinity of the Son is maintained, he is pragmatic concerning the precise qualification of time. Athanasius also offers an alternative explanation of the text, which states 'the same thing in a parallel way' in *CA* I 44–45.[192] In this second explanation, Athanasius focuses on another aspect of the exaltation: the Son's exaltation might

---

[189] *CA* I 42 (152,3–4).
[190] *CA* I 43 (153,13–14. 20–23); tr. Anatolios.
[191] *CA* I 43 (153,23–26); tr. Anatolios.
[192] *CA* I 44 (153,2–154,3); tr. Anatolios.

refer to his resurrection from the dead, as Origen had taken it before him.[193] John 1:14 in particular is prominent in this explanation of the passage. Athanasius asserts that the Son is both the one who is descended and ascended (cf. Eph 4:10) and the second Adam (cf. 1 Cor 15:45). He claims that 'therefore' (διό) in Philippians 2:9 is used because all humans died and remained dead, but only the Son rose from the dead.

> And this cause, as he previously said, is that, being God, he became human. (...) [H]e is the 'second human being from heaven' (1 Cor 15:47), for the 'Word became flesh' (Jn 1:14). (...) And although he 'humbled himself' (Phil 2:8) ... nevertheless he was 'highly exalted' (Phil 2:9) and raised up from the earth, since he was the Son of God in the body.[194]

The framework of 'being God – becoming human' is asserted, and ultimately grounded in the notion that the Word became flesh (Jn 1:14). Athanasius reads Jn 1:14 as a parallel of Phil 2:8 to assert that Phil 2:9 speaks of the resurrection of the Son; exaltation after his humble state on the earth before his resurrection. Athanasius time and again claims that the Son and Word are one and the same. Jesus Christ, the Son of God is not different from the eternally existing Word of God. Athanasius concludes that both the death and exaltation occurred to no one other than the Word:

> Since the body was his, and was not external to the Word, it is fitting that when the body was highly exalted, (Phil 2:9) he himself, as a human being, is said to be highly exalted on account of the body. If he had not become human, these things would not have been said of him. But if 'the Word became flesh' (Jn 1:14), it is necessary that both the exaltation and the resurrection are referred to him[.][195]

Athanasius himself favoured the conclusion that the words in Phil 2:9–10 referred to the resurrection of the Son. The first explanation (in *CA* I 37–43) was regarded as acceptable and

---

[193] Canévet, "La théologie," 187.

[194] *CA* I 44 (154,12–21); tr. Anatolios.

[195] *CA* I 45 (155,6–10); tr. Anatolios, adapted.

ecclesiastical, but the second explanation (in *CA* I 44–45) removed any connection between exaltation and the Son's ontological status as well. Athanasius thus allows for two moments in the
exaltation of Jesus, because both result in an orthodox interpretation. The crucial Johannine text to interpret the passage is Jn
1:14. By reading Philippians 2 through the lens of John 1:14, the
connection between reward and exaltation and the Son's divine
status is avoided. Athanasius can therefore summarise at the end
of *CA* I 45: 'For he received the humanity in such a way as to
grant it exaltation and this exaltation was its deification. But the
Word himself was forever in possession of this, according to his
own divinity and perfection, which are of the Father.'[196] He then
concludes after having given his own interpretation: 'This is the
meaning of what is written by the apostle and serves to refute the
impious.'[197]

John 1:14 is prominent in the explanation of this verse. Obviously, Athanasius only quotes a small part of the full passage
(And the Word became flesh and lived among us, and we have
seen his glory, the glory as of a father's only son, full of grace and
truth 1:14). This is a reduction of the question what John 1:14 as
such meant, but understandable given the status of the pressing
question. Barrett asserts that in the words ὁ λόγος σὰρξ ἐγένετο,
ἐγένετο does not mean (1) 'became', 'since the Word continues to
be the subject of further statements', (2) 'was born' as flesh, man,
and proposes (3) instead that 'the Word came on the (human)
scene – as flesh, man'.[198] This seems most plausible; in the flow of
the passage, it is clear that he lived among humans and is wit-
nessed as a unique human being, 'full of grace and truth'. Bauckham points to the many chronological and topographical remarks
that are connected to John's theology: 'Nothing keeps readers
more constantly aware that the story is that of the Word made
flesh than the topographical and chronological precision of the
narrative.' And although '[o]rdinary history is transcended in metahistory, ... this can only happen through Jesus' real presence'

---

[196] *CA* I 45 (155,24–26); tr. Anatolios.
[197] *CA* I 46 (155,1–2); tr. Anatolios.
[198] Barrett, *John*, 165.

in this ordinary history.[199] But the weight Athanasius puts on this verse in the *Orations* can only be maintained by claiming that the evangelist intended to proclaim the complete equality of the Son with the Father's οὐσία. John's Gospel contains elements that support Athanasius' view on the equality of Father and Son, but balances this with clear subordinationist tendencies.[200] For that reason, Athanasius needs to be selective in handling the Christological material of this Gospel to maintain his understanding of Jn 1:14, since he derives stronger consequences from this text than the text itself warrants.

CA I 46–52: Ps 45:7–8

The next biblical passage that Athanasius discusses is Ps 45:7–8 (LXX: Ps 44:7–8; cf. Heb 1:8–9).[201] Athanasius quotes it according to the LXX text: 'Your throne, O God, is forever and ever. A rod of equity is of [sic!] your rule; you loved righteousness and hated lawlessness. Therefore God, your God, anointed you with oil of rejoicing beyond your partners.'[202] Origen applied this text to the human soul of Christ, envisaging the unity between the Word and the human soul, while Eusebius of Caesarea applied it to Christ's divinity, to regard Christ as a second God.[203] For the Arians, this text provided evidence for the Word as theoretically mutable, but practically immutable Word, distinguishing him from God the Father. In Grünbeck's estimation, their method was accurate, with attention to the grammatical and syntactical context of the

---

[199] Bauckham, "Historiographical Characteristics," 26–27.

[200] Barrett, *John*, 92; Crump, "Johannine Trinity"; cf. Frey, "Continuity and Discontinuity," 96–98; for the use of Jn 1:14 in the early Church, see Christian Uhrig, *"Und das Wort ist Fleisch geworden": zur Rezeption von Joh 1,14a und zur Theologie der Fleischwerdung in der griechischen vornizänischen Patristik*, MBTh 63 (Münster: Aschendorff, 2004).

[201] See Canévet, "La théologie," 188–91, 193–95; see also Elisabeth Grünbeck, *Christologische Schriftargumentation und Bildersprache: zum Konflikt zwischen Metapherninterpretation und dogmatischen Schriftbeweistraditionen in der patristischen Auslegung des 44. (45.) Psalms*, VCSup 26 (Leiden: Brill, 1994).

[202] Pietersma and Wright, *Septuagint*, 569.

[203] Grünbeck, *Christologische Schriftargumentation*, 74–85, 159–65.

verse.[204] According to Athanasius, the Arians used this text to argue that the Son was anointed for his task to redeem humanity. From this point, he derives the in his eyes impious conclusion that the Arians have to draw: the Son's anointment then improves him, just as kings of Israel were promoted after their anointment. If this is granted, the Son is not equal to the Father, for someone who is in need of anointment cannot be eternally divine.[205] His opponents did not go to the extreme of saying that the Son was promoted in the same way as earthly kings. However, in Athanasius' view, an anointed and promoted Son cannot be truly divine, so he assigns this text to the incarnate Christ. The Arians applied this text to the pre-existent Son. However, since they also conceived three divine *hypostaseis*, they cannot maintain that all three are divine in the same way.[206] In reality, they must have considered the three divine *hypostaseis* to be unequal to each other, in that way compromising on the divine aspect of the Son (and Spirit).[207] This provides a rationale behind Athanasius' counter-interpretation at this point.

Athanasius disconnects this correlation between the Son's anointment and promotion by outlining the differences between the anointment of earthly kings and that of the Saviour. The earthly kings received the Holy Spirit, whereas the Saviour is the Giver of the Spirit. The Son does not only give the Spirit, he is also the supplier of the Spirit (τοῦ τε πνεύματος τοῦ ἁγίου χορηγὸς ὢν αὐτός), so the Spirit can only give to creatures after receiving it from the Son.[208] The Son's anointment by the Spirit can

---

[204] Grünbeck, *Christologische Schriftargumentation*, 169.

[205] Cf. *CA* I 46 (156,7–21); I 47 (156,1–5; 157,8–12).

[206] See Arius, *Letter to Alexander* (Urk. 6 (13,7)) and Anatolios, *Retrieving Nicaea*, 42–44.

[207] Reflection on the divinity of the Holy Spirit is already found in Irenaeus, Tertullian and Origen, but was not a subject of systematic reflection before the late 350s, Anatolios, *Retrieving Nicaea*, 24–26, 133–155; see also Mark DelCogliano, "Basil of Caesarea, Didymus the Blind, and the Anti-Pneumatomachian Exegesis of Amos 4:13 and John 1:3," *JTS* 61 (2010): 644–58.

[208] *CA* I 46 (156,18–19).

therefore only refer to the time he was a human. As a human, he received the Spirit, in order that

> he may provide us human beings with the indwelling and intimacy of the Holy Spirit, just as he provides us with exaltation and resurrection.[209] The Lord himself provides this meaning when he says, in his own person, in the gospel according to John: 'I have sent these into the world, and I sanctify myself for their sakes, that they may be sanctified by the truth' (Jn 17:18–19). (…) [H]e is not sanctified by another, but he sanctifies himself, in order that we may be sanctified in the truth.[210]

This conclusion is crucial to Athanasius' view that the Son is not dependent on someone else for sanctification. The Son sanctifies others, even in his incarnate state, so there is no relation between his anointment and promotion. In his explanation of Psalms 45:7–8, he returns to his emphasis on the Son as the giver of the Spirit.[211] He and his opponents agree that the Son is anointed by the Spirit, but by identifying the Son as the giver of the Spirit – an almost exclusively Johannine theme – he counters the problematic implications of the Son's anointment. According to Crump, the evangelist John could emphasise the role of the Son as the Giver of the Spirit, because John does not regard the Spirit as a divine person, but as the Son's representative.[212] This is an overstatement, because the Spirit comes upon Jesus in Jn 3:34, which means that the Spirit is more than just the Son's representative.[213] Nevertheless, it is clear that the Spirit has a less prominent

---

[209] Anatolios mentions that Athanasius' view is closely related to Irenaeus. See Khaled Anatolios, "The Influence of Irenaeus on Athanasius," in *StPatr* 36, ed. M. F. Wiles and E. J. Yarnold (Leuven: Peeters, 2001), 474–75; see also Johannes Roldanus, *Le Christ et l'homme dans la théologie d'Athanase d'Alexandrie: étude de la conjonction de sa conception de l'homme avec sa christologie* (Leiden: Brill, 1968), 236–52.

[210] *CA* I 46 (156,19–27); tr. Anatolios.

[211] Cf. *CA* I 14–16.

[212] Crump, "Johannine Trinity," 408.

[213] Crump, "Johannine Trinity," 399; See contra Crump, Barrett, *John*, 226; Carson, *John*, 213.

role than the Son in John's Gospel.[214] Athanasius gratefully uti-
lises this aspect, because confession of Father, Son and Holy Spirit
as divine is common in his fourth-century context, rather than its
coherence with the theology of the Gospel as such.[215]

Athanasius implicitly assumes, as is illustrative for an enthymeme, that there is an either/or relation. The Son must either
give to or receive from the Spirit. Since the Gospel of John explicitly mentions the Son as the giver of the Spirit, Athanasius asserts
that he is other than all of creation, which receives its subsistence
from the divine Spirit. All of creation receives from the Spirit, but
the Son, as Creator, gives the Spirit to others and to himself in the
incarnate state. Since the incarnation happened for the sake of
humanity, all that the Saviour has experienced has happened for
humanity's sake. Athanasius therefore concludes that the Son is
not sanctified by another, but by himself, and Ps 45:7–8 has to be
understood in the light of his redemptive work.

In *CA* I 46, Athanasius emphasises the Son as the supplier of
the Spirit. Athanasius then calls Jesus 'Lord of sanctification' and
adapts the words of Jn 17:18–19. He states:

> How does he [i.e. Jesus] speak the way he does, except as if
> to say, 'I, being the Word of the Father, give the Spirit to my-
> self, having become a human being. And, in the Spirit, I sanc-
> tify myself, having become human, so that henceforth all may
> be sanctified in me by the truth, "For your word is truth" (Jn
> 17:17)'.[216]

Athanasius clearly indicates that these are not the actual words
of Jesus, but that there is no other way to understand these words
than the way he does, with the figure of *sermocinatio*. This figure
brings a feeling of presence; it seems that it is not an ancient text
that is interpreted, but that Jesus himself clarifies the ambiguity
of this text in favour of Athanasius' interpretation. By this figure
of speech, Athanasius presents a literary re-enactment of the

---

[214] Barrett, *John*, 88–92; Carson, *John*, 499–500.
[215] Anatolios, *Retrieving Nicaea*, 36–38, 133.
[216] *CA* I 46 (156,27–30); tr. Anatolios.

biblical story. He seamlessly connects the biblical past with the present Christological controversy.[217]

Athanasius' emphasis on the Son as giver of the Spirit demonstrates his preference for this Johannine notion. In the discussion of Ps 45:7–8, Athanasius addresses the meaning of Jesus' baptism. In all accounts of this event, as well as some other New Testament passages, Jesus receives the Spirit,[218] a notion that is problematic to Athanasius' case that the Son is the giver of the Spirit and therefore eternally and equally divine with the Father. The portrayal of the Son as receiving the Spirit is more dominant in the synoptic tradition, while John emphasises the Son's giving of the Spirit. In Jn 1:32–33, Jesus' actual baptism is not mentioned, but the descending of a dove on him is maintained. This element correlates well, however, with the synoptic accounts. The Son as giver of the Spirit is stressed later on in the same Gospel (cf. 16:7, 14; 20:22). To reconcile both notions, Athanasius argues that the Son is by nature the giver of the Spirit, while the Son received the Spirit during the Incarnation, which took place for humanity's sake.[219] Therefore, everything the Spirit gives to the Son during the incarnation is what the Spirit has received from the Son in the first place. In this way, the Son's receiving from the Spirit does not separate him from the Father. Athanasius explains it thus:

> In fact, the Lord himself says to his disciples, 'the Spirit will take from what is mine' (Jn 16:14), and 'I will send him to you' (Jn 16:7) and 'Receive the Holy Spirit' (Jn 20:22). And he who provides for others as Word and Radiance of the Father is nevertheless now said to be 'sanctified' (Jn 17:19), because he has become human and the sanctified body is his own.[220]

After this string of Scripture quotations, including many Johannine ones, he concludes: 'Therefore it is because of us and for our

---

[217] See Flower, *Late Roman Invective*, 23–32.

[218] See Jn 3:34; Mt 3:16–17; Mk 1:10–11; Lk 3:21–22; cf. Lk 4:18 and Isa 61:1, Acts 10:38.

[219] Cf. *CA* I 47 (156,2–3).

[220] *CA* I 47 (157,14–18); tr. Anatolios.

sakes that the Scriptures speak in this way.'[221] Athanasius already alluded to the Son's supplying to the Spirit (in *CA* I 15–16), but now he undergirds the notion with three Johannine texts and the introductory marker: 'the Lord himself says'. In practice, Athanasius claims that every deed that comprises the deity of the Word must be understood in the light of his incarnation for humanity's sake (cf. Jn 17:19). He thus connects other parts of Psalm 45 (LXX 44) to the humanity of the Lord as well:

> Likewise, David hymns the Lord as the Eternal God and King who was sent to us and assumed our mortal body. He signifies this when he sings in the psalm: 'Myrrh and aloes and cassia from your garments' (Ps 45:9); and this is indicated also by Nicodemus and the companions of Mary, when the one came carrying 'a mixture of myrrh and aloes, weighing about a hundred pounds' (Jn 19:39).[222]

Athanasius, as a pre-modern theologian, has no difficulty in connecting this verse from Psalm 45:9 to the myrrh and aloes in John as a proof for the Psalm's reference to the incarnate rather than the pre-existent Christ. In combination with this line of reasoning, it is clear to Athanasius that the Lord's baptism (Mt 3:13–17) and anointment (Ps 45:8) have taken place for the benefit of humans. Athanasius argues against any form of progress in the Son, and clothes it in highly personal, existentially engaged language when he speaks about progress in the immortal, divine Son to accept the mortal flesh. These words about the Lord's incarnation must be 'written because of us and for our sakes', because no reward is greater than being 'in the bosom of the Father (Jn 1:18).'[223] The anointment was not for Christ's benefit, but for human beings: 'us'. Grünbeck remarks that Athanasius does not meet the content of the Arian exegesis, but rather gives catechesis at this point.[224] In this way, he relates to the audience, creating a strong sense of communion. It is also obvious in the following words:

---

[221] *CA* I 47 (157,21); tr. Anatolios.

[222] *CA* I 47 (157,34–38); tr. Anatolios.

[223] *CA* I 48 (158,2–4); tr. Anatolios.

[224] Grünbeck, *Christologische Schriftargumentation*, 178–82, here 182.

The Savior makes clear all these things when he says to the
Father: 'And the glory which you have given to me, I have
given to them, so that they may be one, as we are one' (Jn
17:22). So it is because of us that he is glorified (Jn 17:5) and
because of us that it is said that 'He took' (Phil 2:7) and 'was
anointed' (Ps 45:8) and 'highly exalted' (Phil 2:9). It was so
that we may receive, that we may be anointed, that we may
be highly exalted in him, just as he sanctifies himself for our
sakes, so that we may be sanctified in him (Jn 17:19).[225]

This passage illuminates Athanasius' conviction and his handling
of those passages: all attributes that could compromise the Lord's
divinity are attributed to the Incarnation that took place for man's
benefit. Three passages from the Gospel of John are highlighted
to substantiate his massive claim, namely that all human characteristics can be attributed to the incarnation. Athanasius' two natures exegesis that anticipates Chalcedon relies for its substantiation on the Gospel of John. He achieves this by reading John's
Gospel highly selectively. John's balancing between strong Christological claims (5:17–18; 10:18; 14:9–10; 20:28) with clear affirmations of Jesus' weakness as a human (crying (11:35), fear
(12:27)) and of obedience (4:34) seems intended by John to make
sense of the Christological claims within the borders of Jewish
monotheism. However, in Athanasius' thought, the affirmations
of Jesus' weakness and obedience must be explained in such a
way that they do not harm his theological axiom of how Jesus as
the Word of God is anointed and exalted. The creatureliness of
Jesus is embraced by John, but disguised by Athanasius, seemingly because John's concern is primarily historical, whereas Athanasius' concern is primarily metaphysical, supplemented with a
pious application: incarnation for the sake of humanity.

Athanasius asserts that the Arian view of the Son's anoint-
ment must imply a reward ($\mu\iota\sigma\theta\acute{o}\varsigma$). This is impossible according
to Athanasius, for 'the one who was sitting on the Father's throne'
lacks nothing (cf. Jn 16:14, 7, 13).[226] In CA I 48, Athanasius elaborates on this framework of the eternity of the Word and his

---

[225] CA I 48 (158,23–159,27); tr. Anatolios.
[226] CA I 47 (157,25–32); tr. Anatolios.

becoming human, in which he cites a variety of biblical texts to support his statements. Athanasius asks rhetorically what the Immortal benefits from taking up mortality, clearly suggesting that the answer is: none. He subsequently states that it is the Son who sanctifies all humans by the Spirit, by appealing again to Jn 20:22: 'Receive the Holy Spirit' and the promise of Jesus in Jn 15:26a: 'I will send you the Paraclete, the Spirit of truth'.[227] These promises of the Son are fulfilled, because they are promised by the Word of God. That Athanasius only cites this part of Jn 15:26 is significant, for in John's Gospel, Jesus states: 'When the Advocate comes, whom I will send to you from the Father, the Spirit of truth who comes from the Father, he will testify on my behalf (NRSV).' Athanasius thus downplays the role of the Father in the procession of the Spirit, by handling this Johannine passage very selectively, leaving out the part that runs counter to his emphasis on the procession of the Spirit by the Father. While he himself is selective, Athanasius contends that the Arians 'falsify the divine sayings'.[228] Their understanding of the word 'therefore' (Ps 45:8; Heb 1:9) is a 'pretext', and he states polemically: 'let these amateurs in Scripture and experts in impiety understand that ... the word "therefore" does not signify any reward for the virtue or conduct of the Word.'[229] Athanasius constructs a negative *ethos* of his opponents by providing scriptural proof of his own position, while ascribing his opponent's position to personal desires, amateurism in Scripture and deliberate impiety. This link between wrong biblical interpretation and impiety is not wholly without a close parallel. Constantine, writing a letter against Arius in 333, links faulty biblical interpretation to impiety. He states

> 'A wicked interpreter is really an image and a statue of the Devil ... Lend your ears and listen a little, impious Arius, and understand your folly (ἄνοιαν)... Wash yourself, then, in the Nile, if possible, you fellow full of absurd insensibility; and

---

[227] *CA* I 48 (158,10–13. 15–16).
[228] *CA* I 48 (158,6–7); tr. Anatolios.
[229] *CA* I 49 (159,1–6); tr. Anatolios. Cf. *CA* I 52 (163,27–30).

indeed you have hastened to disturb the whole world by your impieties.'[230]

However, Athanasius' hostile language against the Arians remains quite exceptional in comparison to other contemporaneous sources. Athanasius might have borrowed the polemical of Constantine's language. Athanasius certainly knew about this letter, for he has preserved it in his work *On the Council of Nicaea*.

In *CA* I 50, Athanasius discusses another aspect of the relation between Jesus and the Spirit that does not fit easily into his theology. Matthew reports that Jesus announces that he will cast out demons by the Spirit of God (Mt 12:24–28; cf. Lk 11:15–20). This fact runs contrary to Athanasius' emphasis on the Son's giving to the Spirit and the subsequent Spirit's receiving from the Son. Both Marcellus and Eusebius of Caesarea probably had less difficulty with this verse, since they emphasise the procession of the Spirit from the Father (cf. Jn 15:26b). This would suggest a mutual giving of Son and Spirit. Athanasius wants to emphasise the equality of Father and Son, and therefore, he attributes the casting out of demons by the Spirit to Jesus' humanity. He envisages a difference between Jesus' presentation to outsiders (in this case the Jews) and his disciples.

> The Lord spoke ... to the Jews, as a human being. But to the disciples he showed his divinity and greatness; and no longer manifesting himself as less than the Spirit, he indicated rather that he was equal to the Spirit when he gave them the Spirit and said, 'I will send him' (Jn 16:7) and 'he will glorify me' (Jn 16:14) and 'whatever he hears he will say' (Jn 16:13). As in that case, the Lord who is Giver of the Spirit did not shrink from saying, as a human being, that he 'casts out demons in the Spirit' (Mt 12:28), so also in the same way, he ... said this because of his having become flesh, as John says (Jn 1:14).[231]

Again, a selection of Johannine notions determines Athanasius' interpretation of texts that deal with dependence of the Son upon the Spirit. Athanasius solely emphasises the Son as sender of the

---

[230] Urk. 34 (69,3; 71,18; 74,9–11); tr. Coleman-Norton.

[231] *CA* I 50 (160,14–22); tr. Anatolios.

Spirit to argue for the co-eternity of Father and Son. Besides that, he wants to avoid any emphasis on the Son's dependency, despite the fact that the Son is often described as sent by the Father in John.[232] One citation of Jn 6:38–40 contains the word πέμπω, but without any comment on this element.[233] Only parts of the Gospel of John function as a hermeneutical key for Athanasius, while other parts are downplayed. Whereas the notion of the Son as sent is ignored, the Son as the sender or supplier does feature several times in *CA* I-II.[234] Both elements result in a subtle distinction between God and Jesus that is crucial in John's Gospel for maintaining Jewish monotheism and the claim that the 'deeds and words of Jesus are the deeds and words of God'.[235] While a subtle distinction between Father and Son is also important in Athanasius' thought, the primary emphasis of Athanasius is on claiming the Son's eternity, without regarding him as a second ἀρχή, thus changing the content of the statement, even while maintaining Johannine language. For that reason, all subordinationist elements in the Gospel of John and other biblical texts are regarded as a result of the Son's Incarnation for humanity's benefit: 'The [human] flesh was first sanctified in him and ... and so we have the Spirit's grace that follows from his reception, receiving from his fullness (Jn 1:16).'[236]

Athanasius' interpretation of Christ's anointment in Ps 45:7–8, and his view on the relation between Son and Spirit might be

---

[232] See also the discussion in *CA* III 7 (below). Twenty years later, in *Ser* I 20 (503,31–504,41), Athanasius acknowledges that 'the Son is sent from the Father'. Cf. *Ser* I 2 (453,25–454,28); *Ser* I 15 (489,5–490,7).

[233] *CA* II 54. See further allusions to Jn 4:34, cf. Jn 17:4; (*CA* I 50; 59), Jn 5:23 (*CA* I 18; 33). Jn 6:38 (*CA* I 44), all without πέμπω in Athanasius' work.

[234] Jn 15:26 (*CA* I 48 (158,15–16); Jn 16:7 (*CA* I 47 (157,15); *CA* I 50 (160,17).

[235] Barrett, *John*, 156; see also idem, "'The Father Is Greater than I' (Jo 14, 28): Subordinationist Christology in the New Testament," in *Neues Testament und Kirche: für Rudolf Schnackenburg [zum 60. Geburtstag am 5. Januar 1974, von Freunden und Kollegen gewidmet]*, ed. Joachim Gnilka (Freiburg: Herder, 1974), 144–59.

[236] *CA* I 50 (161,31–33); tr. Anatolios. *CA* II 53; III 27.

contrasted to Eusebius of Caesarea's to show that Athanasius does not just take up the evident meaning of Scripture, but lets his understanding be controlled by rational considerations and views defended by contemporaries. Whereas Athanasius attributed Christ's anointment to his incarnate state, Eusebius relates this passage to Christ's pre-existent state in his *Proof of the Gospel* (written ca. 318). Eusebius – in line with Origen – says that Ps 45:7–8 is

> referring to the highest power of God, the King of kings and Lord of lords, ... the Christ and the Anointed, Who is the first and only one to be anointed with this oil in its fullness, ... and is declared to be God of God by His communion (μετοχῇ) with the Unbegotten that begat Him, both the First and the Greater.[237]

Eusebius regards the Christ as the highest power, solely-begotten and declared to be God by his communion (cf. Ps 44:8 (45:8 LXX), μετόχους), a view that is rejected explicitly by Athanasius.[238] However, Eusebius' *Proof of the Gospel* was written before the start of the Council of Nicaea. His view might have changed after the turbulent period of Nicaea. Eusebius was probably even examined at the Council of Antioch, early in 325, to be provisionally excommunicated.[239]

Athanasius appealed to Jn 15:26b, 16:14, 17:19 and 20:22 to assert the importance of the Son's role in the Spirit's procession, instead of focusing on the Father's role in the Spirit's procession (Jn 15:26a). If one compares Athanasius' discussion of the topic to the discussion of Eusebius of Caesarea in his *Ecclesiastical Theology* (ca. 337) and Marcellus' fragments, it is interesting to see that of the three of them, only Athanasius appeals to Jesus' words 'for their sakes I sanctify myself' (Jn 17:19). Eusebius quotes Marcellus extensively, but neither of them quotes this text. Athanasius, Eusebius and Marcellus all refer to Jn 16:14 and

---

[237] Eusebius, *DE* IV, 15 (Heikel 175,23–29); tr. Ferrar.

[238] *CA* I 46 (156,7–13). Cf. *CA* I 14–16.

[239] See Urk. 18 (= Dok. 20) on the statement of this council and Hanson, *Search*, 146–51; Luise Abramowski, "Die Synode von Antiochien 324/25 und ihr Symbol," *ZKG* 86 (1975): 356–66.

20:22,[240] but whereas Athanasius emphasises the Son's role in the Spirit's procession, the latter two discuss those two texts in relation to the Spirit's procession from the Father (cf. Jn 15:26b).[241] Marcellus argues that both the Son and Spirit proceed from the Father, so that they are fundamentally and indiscriminately one and later expand into a Trinity (τριάδα).[242] Eusebius of Caesarea and Athanasius favour a more differentiated account within the Trinity. Athanasius clearly and primarily defends the eternity of the Son, which presupposes a distinction between Father and Son, while Eusebius clearly regards the existence of Father, Son and Holy Spirit as distinctive as well. 'The only-begotten Son of God teaches that he himself has come forth from the Father because he is always together with him, and likewise about the Holy Spirit, who exists as another besides the Son.'[243] Although Eusebius primarily emphasises the Spirit's procession from the Father, he cites the part about the Son's involvement in Jn 15:26 several times.[244]

Asterius' fragments do not contain Jn 16:14, 17:19 or 20:22, but this is not decisive for how he used these texts. However, he does appeal to Jn 15:26, holding that the Spirit proceeds from the Father. He thus argues that the Son (as non-sender of the Spirit) must be inferior to the Father from whom the Spirit proceeds.[245] Athanasius completely ignores the notion that the Spirit proceeds from the Father in the *Orations*, and only quotes Jn 15:26a, which

---

[240] Eusebius, ET III 4–6 (Kl./H. 159,6.30; 162,25.33; 163,5); Marcellus, fr. 48–49 (Vinzent). See also Holger Strutwolf, *Die Trinitätstheologie und Christologie des Euseb von Caesarea. Eine dogmengeschichtliche Untersuchung seiner Platonismusrezeption und Wirkungsgeschichte* (Göttingen: Vandenhoeck und Ruprecht, 1999), 224–30.

[241] Marcellus, fr. 48 (Vinzent); cf. Asterius, fr. 59 (Vinzent). Eusebius, *ET* III 5 (Kl./H. 161,7).

[242] Fr. 48 (Vinzent 42,16–18).

[243] *ET* III 4 (Kl./H. 159,30–32); tr. McCarthy Spoerl and Vinzent, adapted. Cf. *ET* III 5 (Kl./H. 160,29–161,14).

[244] Eusebius, *Comm. Isa.* II 3 (Ziegler 211,6–8); II 16 (Ziegler 247,31–32); II 49 (Ziegler 367,35–36).

[245] See Asterius, fr. 59 (Vinzent) transmitted in Eusebius of Caesarea, *ET* III 4.

emphasises the Son's role in sending the Spirit. Both Athanasius and Asterius emphasised one element, resulting in an impasse on this point. The Gospel of John did not give unequivocal support to any of their positions. They reached the limits of what this biblical document in the first century proclaimed about Jesus Christ, and they argued about the implications of these views for their questions in the fourth century.[246]

Athanasius also bases his interpretation of Ps 45:7–8 on the premise of the Son's immutability. Athanasius asserts that his opponents use the words of the Scriptures as a pretext (ὑπόνοια).

> For the Word of God is unchangeable and is forever the same; and not merely (οὐχ ἁπλῶς) the same, but the same as the Father is. For otherwise how is he 'like the Father' (cf. Jn 14:10)? Or how is it that all which belongs to the Father belongs to the Son (Jn 16:15, 17:10) if he does not have the Father's unchangeability and inalterability?[247]

Athanasius grounds the unchangeability of the Son in an allusion to two passages from the Gospel of John: Jn 16:15a 'All that the Father has is mine' and 17:10a 'All mine are yours, and yours are mine', instead of focusing on the texts that suggest a hierarchical relation between Father and Son. In passing, he criticises Origen's solution that the Christ was inclined to both good and evil, and wilfully chose the good, 'for in that case changeability would again be introduced'.[248] According to Athanasius, the Word of the Father is the 'giver of virtue' (χορηγὸς ἀρετῆς) and 'being just and holy by nature ... he is said to "love righteousness and hate injustice" (Ps 45:8).'[249] He cites several OT passages that declare that the Father also loves righteousness and hates injustice (Ps 11:5, 7; 87:2; Mal 1:2; Isa 61:8), and argues that both sets of expressions

---

[246] Cf. Xavier Morales, "La préhistoire de la controverse filioquiste," *ZAC* 8 (2004): 317–31.

[247] *CA* I 52 (162,2–5); tr. Anatolios.

[248] *CA* I 52 (162,6–7); tr. Anatolios. On Origen's view, see *DP* II 6.5 (SC 252. 318–19) and J. Rebecca Lyman, *Christology and Cosmology. Models of Divine Activity in Origen, Eusebius, and Athanasius* (Oxford: Clarendon, 1993), 58–81.

[249] *CA* I 52 (162,8–9); tr. Anatolios.

must be applied equally to Father and Son. Either 'let them take the former words in the same sense as these latter, for the former also were written about the Image of God; or else, misunderstanding these latter words as well as those former, they will contrive the notion that the Father too is changeable'.[250] Although he presents his case against the Arians as a case that is supported by the whole of Scripture, he bases himself on a small set of Johannine notions, conveniently ignoring Johannine notions that run counter to his argument.

CA I 54–64: Heb 1:4

In *CA* I 53, Athanasius announces the texts that he will discuss in the continuing part of *CA* I-II. He mentions Proverbs 8:22 first, but will discuss it as the final one (in *CA* II 18b–82). He further announces that he will discuss Hebrews 1:4 (*CA* I 54–64), Hebrews 3:1–2 (*CA* II 1–11) and Acts 2:36 (*CA* II 12–18a). After the full quotation of these texts, Athanasius states hostilely about his opponents that 'they tricked the foolish, quoting the words as a pretense instead of the true meaning,' and that they sow the 'poison of heresy.'[251] He asserts that his opponents secretly side with Caiaphas and the Jews and that they therefore should appeal neither to the OT nor to NT documents. This is clear construction of negative *ethos* that denies his opponents the right to interpret the Christian Scriptures. Since their theology suggests that they do not understand that God will truly 'dwell on the earth (1 Kg 8:17),'[252] they should not read the apostolic sayings and openly side with Caiaphas and the Jewish party. And because they in practice seem to deny the statement '"the Word became flesh" (Jn 1:14) and his incarnate presence,' as do the Manichees, there is no need for them to cite from the book of Proverbs.[253] Athanasius asserts suggestively that the reason 'they do not dare to deny "the Word became flesh,"' but explain the Saviour's incarnate presence

---

[250] *CA* I 52 (162,16–19); tr. Anatolios.

[251] *CA* I 53 (163,10–11); tr. Rusch, altered.

[252] *CA* I 53 (163,14–15); tr. Rusch. Other references to Caiaphas are found in *CA* I 2; II 40; III 28; III 67.

[253] *CA* I 53 (163,15–17); tr. Rusch. This probably refers to Proverbs 8:22.

wrongly is because of their love for money and apparent hon-our.[254] In other words, Athanasius suggests that his opponents have no genuine concern for the interpretation of the Scriptures, and are only motivated by money and power. Since his opponents' interpretation deviates from his own, he suggests that they should not argue from the New Testament, because they are liable to Jewish tendencies, and neither from the Old Testament, because of their Manichean tendencies. Neither suggestion would be accepted by the Arians, but they might have had some rhetorical force for Athanasius' audience, in which Jn 1:14 functions as the crucial proof of Athanasius' suggestive depiction of his opponents.

In *CA* I 54–64, Athanasius discusses Hebrews 1:4, in particular the part 'Having become so much better (κρείττων) than the angels'. He claims that 'it is necessary, as it is fitting to do for all of divine Scripture ... to expound faithfully the time when the apostle spoke and the person and subject about which he wrote' to uncover the right meaning.[255] In this context, Athanasius outlines his exegetical principle of time (καιρός), person (πρόσωπον), and thing/subject (πρᾶγμα),[256] all three of which need to be understood correctly to arrive at a sound interpretation.[257] He continues to outline exegetical principles and presents negative biblical examples (Hymenaeus and Alexander; 1 Tim 1:20) who misunderstood certain texts (*CA* I 54) and states in the subsequent chapter that 'the enemies of Christ ..., have fallen into abominable heresy', because they neglected 'the person, the facts, and the time of the apostle's word'.[258]

---

[254] *CA* I 53 (163,16–164,21); tr. Rusch.

[255] *CA* I 54 (164,1–4); tr. Rusch.

[256] Sieben asserts that Athanasius uses this rule sometimes more loosely (cf. *CA* II 7–8), but that this does not contradict the statement in *CA* I 54. "Hermeneutik," 39–40.

[257] See chapter 3.3 and *CA* I 54 (164,14–16). Stead notes that other Church Fathers argued for a different scope of Scripture, thus emphasizing the particularity of Athanasius' scope of Scripture. Stead, "Exeget," 177–78; Ernest notes the same and mentions that application of the rule is dependent on the result of theological implications: Ernest, *Bible*, 176–77.

[258] *CA* I 55 (165,1–3); tr. Rusch.

Athanasius concurs that the Arians use the words of Hebrews 1:4 to argue for a gradual difference between the Son and the angels,[259] while the Scriptures – Heb 1:4 included – teach the difference between the Son and angels. He develops two arguments to sustain his conviction: (1) κρείττων signifies a qualitative difference between the Son and the angels and (2) Hebrews 1:4 speaks about the time of the Lord's incarnation.

Athanasius first asserts that the word better (κρείττων) is not used to compare the Son to the angels, but to distinguish him from them and other created beings. He strongly distinguishes between the originated things, which are called begotten 'by participation of the Son in the Spirit', and the naturally begotten Son.[260] In *CA* I 56, Athanasius states: "'All things came into existence through him, and without him nothing came into existence" (Jn 1:3) (...). [And] if the Son is other than originated things, only the peculiar offspring of the Father's substance, the pretext of the Arians about "having become" (γενόμενος; Heb 1:4) is in vain."[261] Athanasius further points to the context of Hebrews for this interpretation, as he cites Hebrews 1:5a and 7 with approval at the end of *CA* I 57,[262] but his discussion of the word 'better' (κρείττων) is more central in his interpretation. He argues that comparisons are always made between equal terms (ὁμογενέσιν) instead of unequal terms (ἑτερογενέσιν). In comparisons, it is not customary to use the word κρείττων, but rather μᾶλλον or πλέον. This claim shows that Hebrews 1:4 does not compare the Son to the angels, but distinguishes him from them.[263] In the course of this argument, he subtly provides an interpretation of Jn 14:28 – 'The Father is greater (μείζων) than I' – that is acceptable to his theology. In *CA* I 58, he argues that because the Son is the Maker of things, he is

---

[259] *CA* I 53 (163,8–13); cf. *CA* I 55 (166,34–40); I 56 (166,1–4).

[260] *CA* I 56 (166,9–167,13).

[261] *CA* I 56 (167,13–15. 17–19); tr. Rusch. See also *CA* II 3–4, where Athanasius reiterates the point of the indifference of terminology, as long as the nature of things is clear.

[262] *CA* I 57 (168,20–22).

[263] Cf. *CA* I 57 (167,8–9.12–168,16).

different in kind and substance from originated things... For this reason the Son himself did not say, 'My Father is better [κρείττων] than I' (cf. Jn 14:28), lest someone suppose that he is foreign to his Father's nature, but he said 'greater,' (μείζων), not in some greatness of time, but because of the generation from his Father.[264]

This is one of the few occasions where Athanasius deals with this text from the Gospel of John, which suggests a superiority of the Father to the Son: Jn 14:28.[265] In *CA* I 13, he glossed over the words, by highlighting Jesus' foreknowledge in the context; here he argues that the word greater (μείζων) is compatible with his Christological view. He asserts that κρείττων is used in comparisons of unequal subjects, while μᾶλλον, πλέον and – implicitly – μείζων are used in a comparison between equal subjects. With this claim, he assumes to have solved the difficulties in interpreting both Heb 1:4 and Jn 14:28: the distinction between Son and angels is clear, so that the word κρείττων must be understood in a different sense. However, it is a circumstantial argument that might be contradicted by other examples; for example, Jn 5:36 speaks of Jesus' teaching as 'greater' (μείζω) than that of John, but it seems unlikely that Athanasius would say that there is just a gradual difference between the teachings of Jesus and John. Yet Athanasius might hold that there is a correspondence between the teaching of the biblical writers, and by inference, of John the Baptist.[266] Nevertheless, Jesus' words that 'more (μείζων) than Jonah is here' (Mt 12:41) seriously undermines Athanasius' argument on the meaning of κρείττων.[267] If Athanasius had applied his explanation consistently, he would have had to acknowledge the equality between Jesus' and John's teaching and between Jesus and Jonah. This is clearly not assumed in the Gospels, or by either Athanasius or his opponents, but would be the logical consequence of his

---

[264] *CA* I 58 (169,21–25); tr. Rusch.

[265] See Barrett, "'The Father is greater than I' (Jo 14, 28)". For Athanasius' use of Jn 14:28, see also *CA* I 13; III 1; 7; *Syn* 28.

[266] Cf. *CA* III 10.

[267] Only in *CA* III 23 Athanasius does refer to Mt 12:41, however without μείζων. See further Meijering, *Die dritte Rede*, I:209–11.

argumentation. Athanasius ignores the potential implications of Jn 14:28 altogether in *CA* I-II, but addresses Jn 14:28 in more depth in *CA* III (1; 7), his use of this text will therefore be discussed more elaborately at that place.

In *CA* I 59, Athanasius develops his second line of argument in the explanation of Heb 1:4. 'Having become greater than the angels' does not concern the being of the Word (*Logos*) – the ontology –, but the appearance of the Word in the flesh (τὴν ἔνσαρκον ἐπιδημίαν τοῦ λόγου) – the soteriology.[268] He illustrates the qualitative difference between angels and the Son by stating that '[t]he Law "was spoken through angels" and "has perfected no one,"' (Heb 2:2; 7:19) ... but the sojourning of the Word "has perfected the work" of the Father (Jn 17:4).'[269] Athanasius elaborates on this interpretation with a reference to Heb 7:22 and Jn 1:14. In *CA* I 60, he states that the Lord Jesus Christ secured our salvation by his incarnation:

> The statement 'He has become a surety (ἔγγυος)' (Heb 7:22) indicates the security (ἐγγύην) on our behalf which has occurred through him. As being Word, 'he became flesh,' (Jn 1:14) and the 'becoming' we infer to the flesh. (...) Here too the ministry through him has become better (κρείττων). (...) [For] 'the Son of God came into the world not to judge the world but that he might redeem all and that the world should be saved through him' (Jn 3:17 and Tt 2:14). (...) Seeing this, John cried out, 'The law was given through Moses, grace and truth happened through Jesus Christ' (Jn 1:17).[270]

The notion of surety (Heb 7:22) is intuitively connected to the mixed reference to Jn 3:17 and Tt 2:14, thus embedding it more emphatically into the soteriological framework that the Son became incarnate 'on our behalf'. This is emphatically enhanced by John's exclamation that Jesus Christ, the incarnate one, brought a 'better' covenant than the old covenant of Moses (Jn 1:15, 17). Athanasius reads the words of the evangelist (1:16–18) as words of John the Baptist (mentioned in 1:15) to increase the effect of the

---

[268] *CA* I 59 (169,1–3).
[269] *CA* I 59 (170,23–25); tr. Rusch, adapted.
[270] *CA* I 60 (171,1–3. 9–10. 15–21); tr. Rusch, adapted.

words in Jn 1:17. This reading of the prologue is technically possible, but quite unlikely.[271]

According to Athanasius, the word κρείττων is thus not used to separate the Father from the Son. He mentions the symbolic nature of the Son sitting at the right hand of the Father (Col 3:1), and argues that there is one God with an appeal to Jn 1:1 and Jn 14:9.[272] Athanasius continues and states: 'whatever is of the right hand of and precious in the Father this the Son also has as he says, "All things as many as the Father has, are mine." (Jn 16:15) (...) And again this shows that he is in the Father as the Son is in the Father and the Father in the Son (cf. Jn 14:10).'[273] Jn 1:1, 14:9 and 10 assert the Son's divinity and Jn 16:15 ensures his equality to the Father. Athanasius further contrasts angels and the Son, thus arguing that Heb 1:4 must be related to the Son's incarnate state:

> When angels minister, they say 'I have been sent to you' (Lk 1:19) and 'the Lord commanded.' And the Son though he speaks in human fashion, 'I have been sent' (ἀπεστάλην; Jn 17:3), and comes 'to complete the work' (Jn 17:4) and 'to minister' (Mt 20:28, cf. Jn 5:38), nevertheless he says, since he is Word and image, 'I am in the Father and the Father is in me' (Jn 14:10) and 'He who has seen me has seen the Father' (Jn 14:9) and 'The Father remaining in me does the works.' (Jn 14:10) (...) Thus this is sufficient to win over those who fight against the truth itself.[274]

These words show the vast impact of the Gospel of John on Athanasius' theologizing and his conviction that Heb 1:4 should be applied to the incarnate state of the Son. Jn 14:9–10 and 17:3–4 function prominently in this passage, both as a support of the human and divine in Jesus Christ.

Athanasius' choices in portraying the contrast between the Son and angels become more clear when compared to Eusebius of Caesarea's view in the *Ecclesiastical Theology* (ca. 337). In *ET* II 7,14, Eusebius quotes Jn 5:22–23 to assert that the Son 'clearly

---

[271] Barrett, *John*, 168.

[272] *CA* I 61 (171,3–172,6).

[273] *CA* I 61 (171,6–172,8; 172,10–11); tr. Rusch, adapted.

[274] *CA* I 61 (172,14–23); tr. Rusch.

commanding [the Church] to honor him not like the prophets nor like the angels or the powers that are distinct from these, but very nearly like (παραπλησίως) the Father himself'.[275] He further states in *ET* III 5: 'But given that the Holy Spirit is another alongside the Father and the Son, the Savior, showing his unique characteristic (τὸ ἰδίωμα), has called him Counselor, distinguishing him from the common run of similarly titled [spirits] through the title "Counselor." For the angelic powers also are "spirits." For it has been said: "He who makes his angels spirits." (Heb 1:7).'[276] Eusebius does construe more than just a gradual difference between angels and the Son, and quotes Hebrew 1:7 to indicate the qualitative difference between them. Athanasius' emphasis on the equality goes too far for him, however. Jn 16:15, a text often quoted by Athanasius, which strongly expresses the equality between Father and Son, is never quoted by Eusebius, while his familiarity with this verse is visible in his quotes of Marcellus of Ancyra.[277] All in all, Eusebius offers some subtle criticism to Asterius, whom he mainly defends against Marcellus' accusations in his *Ecclesiastical Theology*. Both Asterius and Eusebius distinguished the Son from the eternal God. However, Eusebius rejects the title κτίσμα for the Son in his later work altogether (cf. *ET* I 9), while Asterius probably used this term for the Son, thus regarding the Son as a creature that excels the others in glory, but is creature nonetheless.[278]

The last three chapters (I 62–64) contain some further remarks about Heb 1:4, but Athanasius is not adding new lines of argument, as he reiterates what he has said already and employs intimate language to relate himself to sympathetic readers. Very pointedly, Athanasius states in *CA* I 64: 'When "the Word became flesh and dwelled among us" (Jn 1:14) ... then he became deliverance for us and he became life and propitiation.'[279] Jn 1:14 reads the personal pronoun 'us' to emphasise this pronoun in his soteriological explanation of Heb 1:4. The language that he uses

---

[275] *ET* II 7,14 (Kl./H. 105,35–106,6); tr. McCarthy Spoerl and Vinzent.
[276] *ET* III 5,21 Kl./H. (163,12–16); tr. McCarthy Spoerl and Vinzent.
[277] *CM* II 2 (Kl./H. 37,22–39,26); cf. Marcellus, frs.74–75 (Vinzent).
[278] See Asterius, fr. 35 and Vinzent, *Asterius*, 222–24.
[279] *CA* I 64 (175,6–8); tr. Rusch.

for communicating with his opponents is completely opposite to the intimate words he uses for communicating with readers sympathetic to him. At no point in his exposition does he allow any sympathy for his opponent's character. The very last words of the *First Oration* are indicative of that. For the text of Hebrews 1:4 does not suggest 'that the substance of the Word is originated (Heaven forbid!) ... although heretics might be ungrateful and contentious in regard to their impiety'.[280]

CONCLUSION

Oration I demonstrates a strong selectivity in scriptural argumentation and conflation with polemical argumentation. The Gospel of John functions both as an ethical and logical means of persuasion. Throughout *Oration* I, it is clear that Athanasius does not just appeal to John for logical argumentation, but also attempts to win trust by building up his character. The opposite holds true as well: Athanasius often employs polemical language, intertwined with argumentation, to construct a negative *ethos* of his opponents. The Gospel of John functions often as the obvious mirror text that contains a 'clear' or unambiguous meaning that is deliberately neglected by the Arians. In *CA* I 1–10 Athanasius focuses heavily on Arius and his impiety. Athanasius argues for two opposing genealogies and bodies of Scripture, those of the Christians and heretics, pious and impious. He discredits both the content and style of Arius' *Thalia*, and selects a few slogans that demonstrate Arius' impiety.

In the second part, *CA* I 11–36, polemical argumentation addresses several genuine theological differences concerning the Son's identity. Two texts from the Johannine prologue (1:1, 14) and several key texts from Jesus in John concerning his identity feature prominently in his argument. Athanasius does not formally distinguish between John and other parts of Scripture, but employs Johannine texts as the most convenient ones. In a sense, a small selection of passages of Scripture, including many Johannine ones, function as catchphrases of Athanasius' theology and oppose the impious Arian slogans.

---

[280] *CA* I 64 (175,12–15); tr. Rusch.

In *CA* I 37–64, Athanasius discusses three texts that pose difficulties to his view concerning the eternal divinity of the Son. To counter these difficulties, he appeals to several Johannine key texts and notions, while neglecting other chapters and crucial Johannine notions, such as the mission of Jesus. Even on the level of verses, he shows great selectivity, Jn 14:6 and 15:26. One time, in *CA* I 46, he employs the figure of *sermocinatio*, which transforms the understanding of Jn 17:17–19 and enhances the plausibility of his interpretation of the passage. His exegetical rule in *CA* I 54 that a correct interpretation takes into account time (καιρός), person (πρόσωπον), and thing/subject (πρᾶγμα) is employed with flexibility; as long as it does not run counter to his main theological convictions, he allows room for alternative interpretations.

Athanasius emphasises certain proof-texts, and downplays several other theological notions that are essential to John's theology. While John constantly balances statements about closeness between God and Jesus with statements about the Son's obedience to the Father, and Jesus confesses that the Father is greater (14:28), the fourth-century position of Athanasius cannot easily incorporate subtleties that are crucial within John's theology. Jn 1:14 is employed for a two natures exegesis that is not – certainly not in the way Athanasius suggests – present in John. Besides that, Athanasius' appeal to Johannine verses is in several cases clearly different from his contemporaries, Eusebius of Caesarea, Asterius and Marcellus (Jn 15:26; 17:19), further illustrating the selective use of the Gospel of John by Athanasius and other fourth-century authors. At times, Athanasius sides either with Marcellus or Eusebius of Caesarea, with clear criticism of theological choices of the one or the other, which indicates that the theological trajectories contained more nuances than suggested by Athanasius' polemic, which is exclusively directed against the Arians. However, in terms of polemical language, the *Orations* stand closer to Constantine's letter against Arius (Urk. 34 = Dok. 27) than to the works of Eusebius of Caesarea and Marcellus.

CHAPTER FIVE.
ANALYSIS OF *ORATION* II

Oration II continues where *Oration* I ended. The division into two *Orations* is without doubt because of practical reasons, for Athanasius already announced the discussion of these texts in *CA* I 53. Furthermore, Athanasius' opening words of *CA* II show that he does not expect his opponents to have changed their minds in the meantime:

> I did indeed think that enough had been said already against the hypocrites of Arius' madness both about their refutation and on the truth's behalf, and to ensure an end to and repentance of their evil thoughts and words about the Saviour. However, they still do not yield; but ... they rather bring in new conceptions of their impiety.[1]

Athanasius continues his explanation of biblical texts in the second *Oration*, asserting that his opponents use the keywords from Prv 8:22 (ἔκτισε) and Heb 3:2 (τῷ ποιήσαντι) to regard the Son of God as a work and creature (ποίημα καὶ κτίσμα).[2] He blames his opponents for shutting themselves up in unbelief and appeals to Jn 1:1 and 1:14 for the correct understanding of these texts. Otherwise, the Arians 'would have learned that "In the beginning was the Word, and the Word was with God, and the Word was God" (Jn 1:1). But when the Word had become human at the good pleasure of the Father, it was suitably said of him by John: "the

---

[1] *CA* II 1 (177,1–6); tr. NPNF, adapted.

[2] *CA* II 1 (177,6–9). See also Gwynn, *Eusebians*, 231–44.

Word became flesh" (Jn 1:14).'[3] Jn 1:1 and Jn 1:14 provide again the glasses through which he will examine the texts he cites immediately afterwards. He claims that Jn 1:1, 14; Acts 2:36; Prv 8:22; Heb 1:4; Phil 2:7; and Heb 3:1–2 'all ... have the same meaning, a pious one, which declares the divinity of the Word, even those that speak humanly concerning him, because he has become Son of man'.[4] This is consistent with Athanasius' outline of his exegetical principle of relating everything in Scripture to Christ's divinity and humanity. Athanasius asserts that the divinity of the Word is not challenged by biblical passages that speak humanly about Jesus. These texts just have to be applied properly, by understanding that they relate to the incarnate state of the Son (cf. Jn 1:14). The divinity of the Word of God is unquestioned, because 'the creation "has come to be through him" (Jn 1:3).'[5] Athanasius therefore reasons that if willing belongs to God, and 'his Word is producer and creator, then it is beyond doubt that this Word is the living will of the Father, and Essential Energy, and True Word, in whom also he constitutes and governs all things excellently'.[6] John 1:1, 1:3 and 1:14 thus shape the understanding of all the other biblical texts.

---

[3] *CA* II 1 (177,18–22); tr. Newman, adapted.

[4] *CA* II 1 (178,27–30); tr. Newman, adapted. The biblical texts cited after Jn 1:1, 14 are given in *CA* II 1 (177,22–178,27): 'Let all the house of Israel therefore know assuredly that God has made him both Lord and Christ, this Jesus whom you crucified.' (Acts 2:36; *CA* II 11b–18a); 'The Lord created me as the beginning of his ways, for his works.' (Prv 8:22; *CA* II 18b–82); 'having become as much superior to angels' (Heb 1:4a; *CA* I 53–64); 'taking the form of a slave' (Phil 2:7) (all NRSV) and 'Therefore, holy brothers, who share in the heavenly calling, fix your thoughts on Jesus, the apostle and high priest whom we confess. He was faithful to the one who appointed him.' (Heb 3:2; *CA* II 1–11a), (RSV). Phil 2:7 seems to refer to Athanasius' discussion of Phil 2:9–10 in *CA* I 37–45. That would mean that Athanasius considered the discussion of *CA* I 37 – II 82 to be a unit.

[5] *CA* II 2 (179,20–21); tr. Anatolios.

[6] *CA* II 2 (179,24–26); tr. Anatolios. See further *CA* III 58b–67 on Athanasius' view on the divine will.

CA II 1–11 A: HEB 3:2

After this brief transitional section, Athanasius mentions that the Arians misuse Hebrews 3:1–2 for their heretical understanding of the Son. He cites Heb 3:1–2 to discuss it subsequently: 'Therefore, holy brothers, who share in the heavenly calling, fix your thoughts on Jesus, the apostle and high priest whom we confess. He was faithful (πιστός) to the one who appointed him (τῷ ποιήσαντι αὐτόν).' Athanasius focuses on the latter part: 'He was faithful to the one who appointed him', to assert that the Son is not ontologically faithful to his maker/appointer (τῷ ποιήσαντι) and therefore not made. He gives several arguments to assert that the Son is not a creature or work (ποίημα): (1) the priority of the nature of things over terminology, combined with the clarity of the creation through the Word (Jn 1:3), (2) the Son is πιστός in the active sense, and (3) a comparison between the ministry of the Son and Aaron the high priest.

Athanasius first asserts that the nature of things is more important than terminology; once the nature of things is clear, terminology must be understood in accordance with the nature of things. Athanasius claims therefore that a 'term is indifferent … as long as the nature is confessed. For terms do not take anything away from the nature' of substances.[7] Of course, this is somewhat tautological, because the disagreement between Athanasius and Arius concerned the Son's nature or mode of existence. Yet Athanasius claims that he already understands the nature of things beforehand. Nevertheless, though he argues for the indifference of terminology, Athanasius argued at length in *CA* I 54–64 that μείζων and κρείττων are not just indifferent terms. Athanasius' statement on this point cannot therefore be taken as if he applied the priority of nature over terminology without any consideration for the actual wording of the biblical text. In *CA* II 3–4, he argues that a concept must fit within a larger complex of thought. James D. Ernest speaks of Athanasius' concept of a meta-narrative within Scripture in this respect.[8] Athanasius argues for the priority of

---

[7] *CA* II 3 (179,6–8); tr. Anatolios. See also Osborne, "Literal or Metaphorical?"

[8] See pp 103–110 above and Ernest, *Bible*, 131–51.

nature over the actual wording by claiming that no one is confused about the real status of that person if a human person calls
a child 'a servant' or a servant 'a child'. Athanasius complains that
his opponents have no difficulty applying this rule when it comes
to human creatures. However, whenever the Arians 'hear "Offspring," and "Word," and "Wisdom," they ... deny the generation,
natural and genuine, of the Son from the Father' because of other
texts.[9] Athanasius' application of the priority of nature over terminology aims to provide a rationale for the custom that biblical
texts that might imply a creaturely status of the divine Son (such
as Heb 3:2) require an alternative explanation for that biblical
expression.[10]

In this way, Athanasius prioritises the notion of the Son as
Word, Wisdom and Creator. The words 'He was faithful to him
who appointed (τῷ ποιήσαντι) him' (Heb 3:2) cannot mean that
the Son is made; that the Father is the appointer or maker of the
Son must relate to the Son's soteriological purpose. He cites Ps
104:24 and Jn 1:3 to prove that 'all the works were made through
the Word and the Wisdom'. After the citation of these two biblical
passages, Athanasius concludes: 'And if He is the Word and the
Wisdom, by which all things come to be, he is not one of the
works, nor at all a creature, but the Offspring of the Father.'[11]
Athanasius thus rejects the option that the Father is the maker of
the Son's being on the basis that 'nothing came into being' without Him (Jn 1:3).

In CA II 6, Athanasius argues that the word πιστός in Hebrews 3:2 should be understood in the active sense. The word
πιστός has both an active sense (faithful, obedient) and a passive
sense (trustworthy). Athanasius considers the active sense of
πιστός to be divinely unworthy, and he therefore claims that the
Son is πιστός in the passive sense. The Son 'remains unchangeable
and inalterable (ἄτρεπτος μένων καὶ μὴ ἀλλοιούμενος) in his human

---

[9] CA II 4 (10–11); tr. NPNF, adapted.
[10] CA II 5 (181,3–7).
[11] CA II 5 (182,18–21); tr. NPNF, adapted. Athanasius also cites Ps 104:24
and Jn 1:3 together at CA I 56 and II 27.

economy and fleshly presence'.[12] In this way, Athanasius asserts that Heb 3:2 does not imply a comparison with others. However, this is clearly the train of thought in Heb 3:2, because the latter part of the verse reads: 'just as Moses also was faithful in God's house.' While Hebrews 3:2 does not indicate that Jesus is a creature (κτίσμα) or work (ποίημα), it must be noted that his claim concerning πιστός runs counter to the flow of Hebrews 3:2. The obvious reason seems to be that a truly divine Son cannot be actively trusting, so that he must be trustworthy in the passive sense.

After Athanasius' argument on the active and passive sense of πιστός, Athanasius relates Heb 3:2 to the ministry of the Son and compares it to Aaron's ministry as high priest. He mentions two elements of his exegetical rule (cf. *CA* I 54; time, person, subject): time (καιρός) and circumstances (χρεία) as an equivalent of πρᾶγμα. He uses these concepts to assert that Hebrews 3:2 must not be applied to the time 'before the creation' but to the time when 'the Word became flesh (Jn 1:14)'.[13] He compares the Son with Aaron, who is mentioned in the Epistle to the Hebrews as well (cf. Heb 5:4). Athanasius' twofold paradigm of eternal Word – human being appears again (cf. Jn 1:1, 14) in the comparison between Aaron and the Son. Aaron was born as a human, who became the high priest 'when God wanted it (ὅτε ὁ θεὸς ἠθέλησε)'.[14] Likewise, the Lord was 'in the beginning the Word: "and the Word was with God, and the Word was God" (Jn 1:1). But when the Father willed (ὅτε δὲ ἠθέλησεν ὁ πατήρ) that ransoms should be paid for all and grace should be given to all, then truly the Word, as Aaron his robe, took his earthly flesh.'[15] Athanasius compares Aaron and the Son to demonstrate the priority of ontology over having a ministry. Consistent with his argument that the nature of things controls the terminology, he suggests that a ministry does not alter ontological status. Therefore, the word τῷ ποιήσαντι in Heb 3:2 does not suggest that the Son's being is made by the

---

[12] *CA* II 6 (183,27–28); tr. NPNF, adapted Cf. *CA* II 6 (182,12–183,24).
[13] *CA* II 7 (183,6–7).
[14] *CA* II 7 (184,18–19); tr. NPNF, adapted.
[15] *CA* II 7 (184,24–27); tr. NPNF, adapted.

Father, but that the Father made the Son flesh when the need was
there to save the world.

In *CA* II 8, Athanasius reiterates that the incarnation of the
Lord is crucial for the understanding of the disputed texts:

> If indeed the Lord had not become human, the Arians can bat-
> tle; but if 'the Word became flesh (Jn 1:14)' what else ought
> to have been said concerning him when become man, but
> 'Who was faithful to Him that made him?' For just as it is
> proper to say about the Word: 'In the beginning was the Word
> (Jn 1:1)', likewise it is proper to man to 'become' and to be
> 'made'. Who would then not have asked, if one had seen the
> Lord walking as a human and demonstrating himself to be
> God from His works: 'Who made him human?' And who again,
> on such a question, would not have answered that the Father
> made him man, and sent him to us as high priest?[16]

John 1:1 and 1:14 reappear in this passage. Athanasius inserts the
opinion of an imaginary first–century spectator to present his distinction between the ontology and ministry of the Son as ex-
tremely plausible. As in *Oration* I, Athanasius constructs a negative *ethos* of his opponents by ascribing disagreements in interpretation to deliberate Arian distortion of the passage. He states that
the Arians would have had a case to battle if the Lord had not
become human, but since it is clear that the Word was in the beginning (Jn 1:1) and became flesh (Jn 1:14), the Arians ignore the
facts and are deliberately resistant to a central truth of Christianity.[17] He concludes with an extended citation of Hebrews 2:14–
3:2 to establish the correctness of this interpretation of Heb 3:2.[18]

CA II 11B–18A: ACTS 2:36

In *CA* II 11–18a, Athanasius discusses Peter's statement that 'God
has made (ἐποίησεν) him both Lord and Christ, this Jesus whom
you crucified (Acts 2:36, RSV)'. The text in general, and the word

---

[16] *CA* II 8 (184,12–185,19); tr. NPNF, adapted.

[17] *CA* II 8 (184,12–185,15). A similar remark occurs in *CA* II 16 (192,15–
17). See further *CA* II 1 (178,30–34).

[18] *CA* II 8 (185, 23–32). Cf. *CA* I 40 for the same strategy in the interpretation of Phil 2:9–10.

'has made' (ἐποίησεν) in particular, are discussed by Athanasius. Athanasius asserts that these words should be applied to the ministry (οἰκονομία) of the Son, to preclude the suggestion that the Son is ontologically *made* Lord and Christ. He argues that (1) the Son is not a ποίημα, but that Acts 2:36 must be read alongside Acts 2:22, (2) is best explained as an accommodation of Peter's speech for evangelistic purposes and (3) must be explained with the acknowledgement that the Son gives the Spirit.

The crucial word, ἐποίησεν, is derived from the verb ποιέω. Athanasius claims that the Arian point of view comes close to that of the pagan Stoics. This incorrect view of Acts 2:36 is caused by their wrong attitude and lack of elementary Christian education. If they search in Scripture for words of the verb 'to make', such as ἐποίησε and πεποίηται, they will even end up like the Stoics, with the slight difference that the Stoics 'extend God into all things' while the Arians 'rank God's Word with each of the works (ποιήματα)'.[19] Athanasius asserts that his opponents hold that the Son is a 'work' (ποίημα), which in Athanasius' eyes is an equivalent of the term 'creature' (κτίσμα).[20]

Athanasius asserts that Peter's precise diction indicates how to interpret this verse correctly. In Acts 2:36 the term 'make' (ἐποίησεν) is not used in an absolute sense, because 'it is not said "God made himself a Son" or "He created himself a Word"'.[21] First of all, the Son is not made Word, but Lord in Acts 2:36. Secondly, Athanasius appeals to Acts 2:22: 'You that are Israelites, listen to what I have to say: Jesus of Nazareth, a man attested (ἀποδεδειγμένον) towards you by God with deeds of power, wonders, and signs that God did through him among you.' This verse indicates that the Lord is not just 'made' in absolute terms, but

---

[19] *CA* II 11 (188,25–26); tr. NPNF, adapted. In other instances, Athanasius associates his opponents with polytheism (*CA* III 15 (323,3–4); 16 (325,21–22)) and atheism (*CA* II 43 (219,4–5); *CA* III 67 (381,37))).

[20] See *CA* II 12 (188,1–2). At this point, Athanasius misrepresents his opponents; the word 'work' (ποίημα) is an inference by Athanasius, because the Arians solely used the word 'creature' (κτίσμα), and with several qualifications. See the discussion at *CA* II 19 below and Gwynn, *Eusebians*, 235–36.

[21] *CA* II 11 (188,16–17); tr. NPNF, adapted.

'towards you', and 'among you' (Acts 2:22).[22] Athanasius argues
that Jesus, by the things and wonders he performed, 'was shown'
(ἀπέδειξεν), that is, was made (ἐποίησεν), to be

> God in a body and Lord ... This is also phrased in the Gospel
> of John: 'For this reason the Jews were persecuting him, be-
> cause he was not only breaking the sabbath, but was also call-
> ing God his own Father, thereby making himself equal to God'
> (Jn 5:16,18). For the Lord did not make (ἔπλαττεν) himself
> God at that moment, (...) but he showed it through the works,
> saying, 'Even though you do not believe me, believe my
> works, that you may know that I am in the Father, and the
> Father in me" (Jn 10:38 and 14:10). In this way, the Father
> has 'made Him Lord and' King 'in the midst of' (Acts 2:36, 22)
> us.[23]

Athanasius thus suggests that Jesus manifested himself to be Lord
among humans. This is clear from John 5:16–18; the Jesus-oppos-
ing Jews persecuted Jesus for making himself the equal of God.
He infers that 'making' in John's Gospel indicates that the Jews
were angry with Jesus, because of his manifestation of his Lordship. Furthermore, Athanasius connects Jesus' claim that his
works prove his divinity (Jn 10:38) with the signs and wonders
that are mentioned in Acts 2:22. He thus contends that, both in
Acts and John, the Lord manifested himself to be God, and asserts
that the Lord displayed his divinity through his works.[24] However,
John's Gospel itself allows for more ambiguity in this respect than
Athanasius suggests, because the conflation of Jn 5:16, 18 is followed by Jn 5:19–30, which demonstrates the Son's obedience to
the Father, not his eternal divinity.

Athanasius also neutralises the suggestion of the Son as a
ποίημα (work), by referring to anthropomorphic concepts in the
OT. He cites 'Become to me a protector-God' (Ps 31:3 (LXX:30:3))
and 'I will be their God' (Ezek 37:27; 2 Cor 6:16), claiming that
no one would infer a change in God's being on the ground of these

---

[22] *CA* II 12 (188,12–13).

[23] *CA* II 12 (189,18–26); tr. Newman, adapted.

[24] The difference in Christology between the Gospels is rather gradual
than absolute. See Barrett, *John*, 70; Carson, *John*, 58.

passages.[25] He asserts that parallel statements about the Son must be understood likewise: 'While the Word is everlasting Lord and King, ... Peter did not say that the being of the Son was made, but instead spoke of his Lordship over us.'[26] This reasoning might have been convincing to sympathetic readers, but the point of dispute with his opponents is exactly whether the Son is divine in the same sense as the Father. He discredits his opponents, suggesting that their foolishness (ἀφροσύνη) causes their worship of 'the creature instead of the God over all (cf. Rom 1:25)'.[27]

In *CA* II 15–18, Athanasius points out that the language in Acts 2:36 is adapted, because it is Peter's evangelistic speech on Pentecost to convince the Jewish audience. Athanasius intimates that Peter adapted his speech to the Jewish expectations. A citation of John 12:34 illustrates that the Jews were unaware of Christ's suffering, and that the Jews therefore did not expect him 'as the Word coming in flesh, but as a mere man'.[28] Jesus himself corrected them in this respect, because he taught the Jews 'that God dwelled among them, saying: If those to whom the word of God came were called "gods"—and the scripture cannot be annulled—can you say that the one whom the Father has sanctified and sent is blaspheming because I said: "I am God's Son"?' (Jn 10:35–36)[29] The Johannine citations thus function to illustrate the usefulness of Acts 2:36 in relation to the Jewish ignorance concerning the divinity of Christ. The statement in John 10:34–36 might be a Jewish riddle that suggested that the Jews could not accuse Jesus of claiming to be God's Son, because the term 'gods'

---

[25] See *CA* II 13 (190,22); *CA* II 14 (190,9; 191,25). All three passages contain the reference to Ps 31:3.

[26] *CA* II 13 (190,10–12); tr. NPNF, adapted.

[27] *CA* II 14 (191,33–36); tr. NPNF. *CA* II 28 (205,27); cf. *CA* II 40 (216,6–8).

[28] *CA* II 15 (191,5–6); tr. NPNF, adapted. (Jn 12:34: 'We know that when the Messiah comes, he remains forever. How can you say that the Son of Man must be lifted up?' Athanasius has substituted 'We have heard from the law' by 'We know'.

[29] *CA* II 15 (192,9–11); tr. NPNF, adapted. Athanasius omits 'into the world' after 'sent' in Jn 10:36. Only Jn 10:35 reappears at other places in Athanasius' oeuvre. Cf. *CA* I 39; *Ser* II 4; *EpAfr* 7.

is not used exclusively for the true God in the OT (cf. Ex 7:1).[30] However, Athanasius ignores the ambiguity in John 10:34–36 and assumes instead that it supports his theology unequivocally. While the section surrounding this statement in John's Gospel contains several indications of equality between the Father and the Son (Jn 10:30, 33, 38), and the term 'Son of God' (10:36), Athanasius neglects the context in John's Gospel and suggests that the text clearly teaches that Jesus is the Son of God.

In *CA* II 16, Athanasius freely retells the speech of Peter at Pentecost. He takes the liberty of pulling together material from OT and NT in this reconstructed speech to sustain his claim that Acts 2:36 must be understood in relation to the non-believing Jews in Peter's audience. Towards the end of the speech, Athanasius makes Peter say that

> since we men would not acknowledge God through his Word, nor serve the Word of God as our natural Master, it pleased God to show in man his own Lordship, and so 'to draw all men to Himself' (Jn 12:32). But to do this by a mere man was not fitting, [and] (…) therefore the Word himself became flesh, (cf. Jn 1:14) and the Father called his name Jesus, and so 'made' him Lord and Christ, (Acts 2:36) as much as to say: 'He made him to rule and to reign.'[31]

The meaning of Acts 2:36 is related to two passages from the Gospel of John in order to align the meaning of Acts more closely to Athanasius' theology. John 1:14 functions as the proof that the eternal Lord became a human and John 12:32 further highlights the soteriological context of Acts 2:36. Athanasius describes the result of Peter's speech for the non-believing Jews: 'The Jews then, most of them, hearing this, came to themselves and immediately acknowledged the Christ, as it is written in the Acts. But the Ariomaniacs on the contrary choose to remain Jews, and to

---

[30] For the original setting of John 10:34–36, see Tom Thatcher, *The Riddles of Jesus in John: A Study in Tradition and Folklore*, SBLMS 53 (Atlanta, GA: SBL, 2000), 219, 226–29. Ex 7:1 reads 'The LORD said to Moses, "See, I have made you like God to Pharaoh"'.

[31] *CA* II 16 (193,41–48) tr. NPNF adapted.

contend with Peter.'[32] The rhetorical nature of this imaginary speech of Peter at Pentecost in *CA* II 15–17 must be noted. John J. Brogan has described Athanasius' use of Acts 2:36 as an example of textual corruption, as 'wholesale invention' of a biblical text.[33] James D. Ernest disputes this description, since readers would understand the difference between such a speech and actual biblical text.[34] The observations of both of them are right, but they do not point to the effect of this rhetorical figure. The imaginary speech of Peter is an instance of the style figure *sermocinatio*, which need not be 'historically true', but just 'in agreement with the character of the person speaking' to be effective.[35] The literary re-enactment allows Athanasius to align the interpretation of Acts 2:36 more closely to other authoritative texts. Furthermore, Athanasius' presentation suggests that it is not Athanasius himself who is speaking, but the apostle Peter who is explaining his own speech at Pentecost, which adds trustworthiness to his argument.

The effect of this rhetorical figure is twofold. First of all, it allows Athanasius to redirect his interpretation of Acts 2:36, by reading it in the light of John 1:14, 12:32 and other texts, through the voice of Peter the great apostle. Secondly, it urges Christians who do not regard Arians as heretics to make a choice. Athanasius discredits the Arians by accusing them of Judaising tendencies in the voice of an authoritative apostle.[36] These two dimensions, theology and polemic, interact smoothly in Athanasius' use of the imaginary speech of Peter. John's Gospel is not used to establish the polemical assertion: Jn 1:14 and Jn 12:32 function in the attempt to clarify the fourth-century theological concern that the Son is in no way a ποίημα or κτίσμα. However, this question was irrelevant for the writer of Acts. In John's Gospel, the 'high' and

---

[32] *CA* II 17 (193,1–3); tr. NPNF, adapted.

[33] Brogan, *Text*, 280–282, here 280.

[34] Ernest, *Bible*, 180 n149.

[35] See pp 47–49 above and Lausberg, *Handbook*, 367 (par 821).

[36] See *CA* I 39 (149,12–14); cf. *CA* I 55 (165,18–20); *CA* II 15 (191,7–192,9); *CA* III 30 (341,11–14). For the contrast between revelation to the disciples and revelation to non-believing Jews, see *CA* I 50 (160,14–15); cf. *CA* III 55 (367,16–24).

'low' elements of Christological discourse are both intended to clarify how Jesus' deeds and words are really the deeds and words of God, and how Jesus is the Father's agent in the world. This serves the purpose of remaining within the boundaries of Jewish monotheism. In the *Orations*, the issue is redirected to the question of how 'low' Christological expressions are compatible with the eternal divinity of the Son. The explicit statements in John are used in this setting to elicit the rather implicit Christology of Acts and other New Testament documents.[37]

In conclusion, Athanasius appeals to the notion of the Son as the Giver of the Spirit to sustain his interpretation of Acts 2:36. Because Acts 2:33 describes Jesus as receiving the Spirit, he discusses the relation between the Son and Spirit.[38] He asserts first of all that the Son is like (ὅμοιος) God, and 'being like Him, He is both Lord and King, for he says himself, "He that has seen me, has seen the Father (Jn 14:9)"'.[39] Furthermore, the Son is not a creature, but equal to the Father, since he gives the Spirit:

> For creatures are sanctified (ἁγιάζεται) by the Holy Spirit. The Son, however, is not sanctified (οὐκ ἁγιαζόμενος) by the Spirit (cf. Jn 17:19), but rather he is the Giver of it to all (cf. Jn 16:7), which shows that he is not a creature, but the true Son of the Father. And yet he who gives the Spirit, is himself (αὐτός) also said to be made. Although he has been made Lord among us (cf. Acts 2:36) because of his humanity, he gives [the Spirit], because he is God's Word. For he always was and is, as Son, also as Lord and Sovereign of all, similar to the Father in all things, and having all that is the Father's, as he himself said (Jn 16:15).[40]

The texts that are used in this fragment to apply Acts 2:36 to Christ's incarnate state undergo a significant shift of interest in this way. In its original setting, the word ἐποίησεν (he was made) is used as an expression of Jesus' Messiahship, without bothering about the precise terminology. In the fourth century, this 'low'

---

[37] On this issue, see Frey, "Continuity and Discontinuity," 69–98.
[38] See also *CA* I 46–52 and pp 160–173 above.
[39] *CA* II 17 (194,7–8); tr. NPNF, adapted.
[40] *CA* II 18 (194,7–195,13); tr. NPNF, adapted.

Christological statement of Acts 2:36 no longer functions as an acknowledgement that Jesus is Lord and Messiah. In Athanasius' *Orations*, Jesus' Messiahship and his divine status are presupposed, so that this 'low' Christological statement points to Christ's incarnate state. At the same time, the references to Jn 14:9; 16:7 and 16:15 are indicative of Jesus' eternal divinity. Significantly, the references to Jn 16:7 and 16:15 are allusions rather than citations, thus allowing Athanasius to highlight his interpretation of the texts. In the *Orations*, the tension between 'low' and 'high' Christological statements is removed, and the 'high' Johannine Christological statements are assumed more clearly than is warranted by the Fourth Gospel.

CA II 18B–43: PROLEGOMENA TO PROVERBS 8:22

The largest part of the second *Oration* is devoted to Proverbs 8:22 (LXX): 'The Lord created me as the beginning of his ways, for his works.' The interpretation of Proverbs 8:22 was disputed from the earliest stages of the controversy. Epiphanius of Salamis (c. 315–403) even states that the whole controversy arose because of this text.[41] Three out of four expressions concerning the divine Son in Arius' *Letter to Eusebius of Nicomedia* are derived from Proverbs 8: 'Before he was begotten (γεννηθῇ, 8:25), or created (κτισθῇ, 8:22), or defined, or established (θεμελιωθῇ, 8:23), he did not exist.'[42] It is therefore safe to state that Proverbs 8 was crucial to both Athanasius and his opponents. Furthermore, Proverbs 8:22 is one of the most challenging passages to Athanasius, who therefore devotes most of the second *Oration* to this text.[43] In *CA* II 18b–43,

---

[41] Epiphanius, *Panarion* 69,12.1. See further Urk. 8 (16,11–12); Socrates, *Historia Ecclesiastica* II 21. See further Simonetti, *Studi sull'Arianesimo*, 9–87, esp. 56–67; Young, *Biblical Exegesis*, 37–40; Luise Abramowski, "Das theologische Hauptwerk des Athanasius: die drei Bücher gegen die Arianer (Ctr. Arianos I–III)," *Communio Viatorum* 42 (2000): 5–23; Clayton, *Orthodox Recovery*; Parvis, "Christology," 123–37.

[42] Urk 1 (3,3) and Abramowski, "Hauptwerk," 15.

[43] In *CA* II 18, he discusses the text after having referred to it already five times in advance, in *CA* I 53 (163,1–2); I 62 (173,25); II 1 (177,7); II 4 (180,5); II 11 (187,7).

Athanasius refutes several theological insights of the Arians that relate to the question whether the Son is a κτίσμα, and defends his alternative that the Son belongs truly and genuinely to the Father.

Throughout the whole of CA II 18–43, Athanasius is first and foremost concerned with the disconnection of the verb ἔκτισε from the noun κτίσμα in relation to the Son's natural state of being. Everything Athanasius says in this passage is aimed to support his central argument that the word ἔκτισε in Prv 8:22 does not justify the inference that the Son is ontologically a 'creature' (κτίσμα).[44] At the beginning, Athanasius constructs a negative *ethos* of the Arians, to explain why his opponents do not arrive at the same conclusion. This is very obvious in CA II 18b, where he attributes the Arian understanding of Prv 8:22 to their impiety and fantasy.[45] Athanasius remarks that he writes to avoid the impression that the Arians are right. To avoid that they might deceive many of the ignorant, Athanasius deems it 'necessary to examine the words ... "he created" (Prv 8:22), in order to show that in this case, as in everything, they are in possession of nothing more than fantasy'.[46] This is a rhetorical remark, because Athanasius downplays in this way the genuine difficulty that he has with this text. In fact, he stated in CA I 1 that he was requested by fellow bishops to write a treatise against the Arians, so it is likely that his lengthy exposition on Proverbs 8:22 is also for the edification of orthodox believers.

In the rest of the section, appeals to reason are prominent, with some scriptural (often Johannine) passages backing it up. We will follow Athanasius' train of thought in this section. The Son is (1) not a special creature, (2) the Maker of creation and completely like the Father, (3) worshipped, (4) not an

---

[44] On the views of Dionysius of Alexandria and Eusebius of Caesarea on κτίσμα, see Uta Heil, *Athanasius von Alexandrien De sententia Dionysii: Einleitung, Übersetzung und Kommentar* (Berlin: de Gruyter, 1999), 236–246; Vinzent, *Asterius*, 221 n.55; Anatolios, *Athanasius*, 6–11, 244 n.37.

[45] '[T]hese people ... invent pretexts for themselves, for the sake of impiety' CA II 18 (195,18–19); tr. Anatolios.

[46] CA II 18 (195,30–34); tr. Anatolios.

intermediate being; and (5) God and his Word are inseparable. He concludes with an excursus on the implications for baptism.

CA II 19: The Son is Not a Creature Like Any of the Creatures

In *CA* II 19, Athanasius presents the Arian position to his readers. He first quotes a fragment of Arius' *Letter to Alexander* (Urk. 6): "'He is a creature (κτίσμα), but not as one of the creatures, he is made (ποίημα), but not as one of the things made, he is an offspring (γέννημα), but not as one of the offsprings.'"[47] Athanasius shows awareness of subtleties concerning the Arian position: the Son is not just a creature, but a very special creature. However, whereas Arius added that the Son is a 'perfect creature of God' (κτίσμα τοῦ θεοῦ τέλειον) in the *Letter to Alexander*, Athanasius ignores the addition of 'perfect'.[48] Athanasius considers any nuance concerning the predicate creature in relation to the Son to be misleading, because the Arians view the Son not as 'the only-begotten Son, but as one of many brothers'.[49]

In his demonstration of the problematic consequences of the Arian position, Athanasius not only neglects the nuances regarding their use of the predicate 'creature', he also claims that the predicates 'creature' (κτίσμα) and 'work' (ποίημα) are interchangeably used. However, this equation is an imposition on the Arian teaching by Athanasius, for Arius himself consciously avoided the term ποίημα in relation to the Son and used the term κτίσμα with some nuances.[50] It is clear that Athanasius distorted Arius' words for his aim of refuting and disqualifying his opponent. Though Athanasius misrepresents his opponents' theological view, it does not alter Athanasius' basic argument. The Word as actively

---

[47] *CA* II 19 (195,2–4); tr. Anatolios, altered. Anatolios' translation lacks the word 'not' in the clause on ποίημα. Cf. Arius, Urk. 6 (12,9–10): 'perfect creature of God, but not as one of the creatures; offspring, but not as one of [the] things that have come into existence'; tr. Stevenson, adapted. The middle part in Athanasius' description: 'He is made (ποίημα), but as one of the things that are made' is not present in the text of Arius.

[48] Urk. 6 (12,9–10). For Arius' words, see the previous note.

[49] *CA* II 19 (195,5; 196,11–14).

[50] Gwynn, *Eusebians*, 235–6. Cf. *CA* II 18 (195,15–18).

involved in the creation of the cosmos cannot be a (perfect) creature.[51]

In *CA* II 22, Athanasius returns to this issue. Athanasius objects to the suggestion that the Son could be a creature, because the Son knows the Father in an exclusive way. If the Son were a special creature, all creatures could have known the Father. He cites Ex 33:20 and Mt 11:27 to counter this suggestion of a special creature and asks rhetorically concerning the Son: 'how is it that he alone reveals the Father and he alone and no one else knows the Father (Jn 6:46, 10:15)?'[52] Athanasius, and probably his opponents as well, would assign this saying to the pre-existent state of Jesus. Therefore, this text represents a strong argument against the Arian position.[53] He cites Jn 6:46 again in answer to his own rhetorical question, that the Word is unique and completely different from all of creation: 'He alone knows the Father and he alone sees the Father, as he has said, "No one has seen the Father except the one who is from the Father" (Jn 6:46), and "No one knows the Father except the Son" (Mt 11:27), though Arius does not think so.'[54] In this way, he suggests that Scripture proves Arius and the Arians wrong.[55]

For that reason, Athanasius does regard any use of the term 'creature' in relation to the Son of God as an indication of inferiority. His most fundamental claim, and the reason for refuting the Arians, is that any theology that understands the term 'creature' in relation to the Son's divinity will ultimately err. Athanasius holds that creatures are qualitatively different from God, so the Son is either ontologically divine or a creature. An intermediate

---

[51] See Meijering, *Die dritte Rede*, I:76–77.

[52] *CA* II 22 (198,13–15); tr. Anatolios.

[53] Several commentators agree. See Barrett, *John*, 169, 296; Carson, *John*, 134, 294. Others disagree, see Farrell, "Seeing the Father," 6, 12–13, 17; idem, "Seeing the Father," 328.

[54] *CA* II 22 (199,20–23); tr. Anatolios.

[55] This is one of the rare occasions that Arius is mentioned as individual in the main body of the *Orations*, for Athanasius primarily interacts with the theology of Asterius. Arius is also mentioned in *CA* I 1–10 and II 24. In *CA* III, Arius is only mentioned in chapter 28 to urge Christians to stay away from Arius' madness (339,12–14).

category is no option. His simplification of the Arian theology thus determines the ultimate consequences of the concept 'creature'. In this way, Athanasius both creates a straw man to defeat and represents a voice in a genuine theological debate.[56]

CA II 20–22: The Son as Maker of Creation

In *CA* II 20, Athanasius provides an important argument for his view that the Son cannot be a special creature. While all creatures differ only gradually among each other, the Son is the Maker of creation, because Father and Son work together in creating. All of the earth acknowledges its Maker and the Truth, so if

> its Maker is the Word, who says himself, 'I am the Truth' (Jn 14:6), then the Word is not a creature, but he alone belongs (*idios*) to the Father. As he himself says, 'For I was arranging beside Him' (Prv 8:30); and 'My father works until now and I work' (Jn 5:17). So the 'until now' shows his eternal existence in the Father, as Word. For it belongs to the Word to work the works of the Father, and not to be external to him.[57]

Athanasius cites Jn 5:17 to argue that the Son is the divine Maker and the Truth (Jn 14:6). Because the 'works' (cf. Prv 8:22) are performed by both the Father and the Word according to Jn 5:17 and Prv 8:30, the Word cannot be created for the sake of these works. No one should therefore infer from ἔκτισε in Prv 8:22 that the Son is a κτίσμα.

Second, Athanasius emphasises the difference between the verb 'created' (ἔκτισε) in Proverbs 8:22 and the 'Arian' term 'creature' (κτίσμα). Only God creates (out of nothing), while human beings create things out of existing matter. Elaborating on the co-operation of Father and Son (Jn 5:17), he states:

> But if what the Father works, the Son also works, and what the Son creates is the creation of the Father, then if also the Son himself is a work and creature of the Father, it turns out

---

[56] Cf. Anatolios, *Retrieving Nicaea*, 41–98; Rudolf Lorenz, "Die Christusseele im Arianischen Streit: nebst einigen Bemerkungen zur Quellenkritik des Arius und zur Glaubwürdigkeit des Athanasius," *ZKG* 94 (1983): 43.

[57] *CA* II 20 (197,15–22); tr. Anatolios.

> that he makes himself and thus will be creator of himself
> (since the Father's works are also works of the Son), which is
> senseless and impossible.[58]

Athanasius excludes the possibility of the Son as a creating creature. Because the Son is Maker, according to Jn 5:17, this leaves
two possibilities: the Son either makes himself or is not a creature
at all. The first option is self-contradictory, and can therefore be
ruled out. Therefore, the Son is not a creature, but ἴδιος to God the
Father.[59] The allusion to Jn 5:17 removes all ambiguity about the
cooperation of Father and Son within John's narrative. In John,
Jesus performs a healing on the Sabbath, which Athanasius applies to their cooperation in the creation of everything. C. K. Barrett remarks that John's argument in Jn 5:17 presupposes the
claim that 'God is essentially and unchangeably creative'.[60] Although Athanasius' inferences from this passage therefore seem
justified, the fact remains that the consequences of John's argument are made more explicit by Athanasius, to decide whether
Jesus Christ could be considered ontologically a κτίσμα or not.

In the next step of thought, Athanasius claims that the Word
is an efficient cause: 'None of the things that have come to be is
an efficient cause (ποιητικὸν αἴτιον): "for all things have come to
be through the Word" (Jn 1:3). The Word would not be maker of
all things if he himself was one of the things created.'[61] His frequent appeal to Jn 1:3 highlights the crucial role that the concept
of the Word (λόγος) has in Athanasius' *Orations*. Pollard comments
that the subject in John's Gospel 'is Jesus Christ, not the Logos'.[62]
In contrast, the fourth-century question makes Athanasius consider the role of the Word in its own right, as an efficient cause
(ποιητικὸν αἴτιον). The term efficient cause is also discussed by Aristotle. In *Physics* 3–7 and *Metaphysics* 1–2, Aristotle outlines his
perspective on causes and why things change. He distinguishes
between the formal cause, the material cause, the efficient cause

---

[58] *CA* II 21 (197,1–4); tr. Anatolios, adapted. Cf. *CA* II 42 (218,1–3).
[59] Cf. Morales, *La théologie trinitaire*, 407–61.
[60] Barrett, *John*, 256.
[61] *CA* II 21 (198,13–16); tr. Anatolios.
[62] Pollard, *Johannine Christology*, 12–14, here 13.

and the final cause; the efficient cause is also described as the moving cause; the cause that initiates change.[63] Athanasius inserts the term 'work' (ποίημα) to highlight the problematic consequences of Arian theology and the reason why the Son cannot be regarded as a κτίσμα. In this way, the Aristotelian concept helps Athanasius to draw a clear distinction between the Son and creatures. Whereas creatures are not able to initiate change, because they are not efficient causes, the Word, through whom all things have come into existence (cf. Jn 1:3), is an efficient cause that initiates changes, and is therefore not a creature. This is also suggested in John's Gospel, but the evangelist does not address Jesus Christ by the title Word after the prologue. In contrast, Athanasius discusses the term Word extensively; the incomparability of the Word and creatures plays a crucial role in Athanasius' argument that the Son-Word cannot be a κτίσμα.

Polemically, Athanasius claims that the Arians imitate the heretics Valentinus, Marcion and Basilides, who all held that not only God, but also beings lower than the true God were able to create.[64] Athanasius seems to suggest that all these heretics blur the line between the efficient cause, which is God himself, and creatures, who cannot be an efficient cause. This is the reason for his association of the Arians with the heretic Valentinus, even though Arius and his fellows explicitly dissociated themselves from Valentinus in Arius' *Letter to Alexander*.[65] Other

---

[63] Vasilis Politis, *Routledge Philosophy Guide Book to Aristotle and the* Metaphysics (London: Routledge, 2004), 53–55, mainly 54.

[64] *CA* II 21 (198,17–18); tr. Anatolios. See also *AH* II 2.1–4; II 3.1 and Anatolios, "Influence," 470–71. On Athanasius' comparison to the Valentinians, see further *CA* I 3; I 56; II 70.

[65] See Urk. 6 (12,10–11). The only-begotten Son is not 'as Valentinus pronounced that the offspring of the Father was an issue'; tr. Stevenson. A fragment of this letter is cited in *CA* II 19. See further Athanasius' defence in Syn 52. Christof Markschies questions the heretical nature of Valentinus' thought. In his view, the heresy of Valentinianism is the product of his pupils, rather than that of Valentinus himself, in *Valentinus Gnosticus? Untersuchungen zur valentinianischen Gnosis mit einem Kommentar zu den Fragmenten Valentins*, WUNT 65 (Tübingen: Mohr Siebeck, 1992), 388–407. On Valentinus' use of John's Gospel, see Kyle Keefer,

contemporaries acted similarly; Eusebius of Caesarea associates Marcellus with the known heretic Sabellius, by suggesting that Marcellus 'is clothing himself in the mantle of Sabellius, and has made himself a stranger to both the knowledge and the grace in Christ'.[66]

Athanasius also associates the Arians with pagan Greek thought by contrasting the Greek and Christian conceptions of creation. The Greeks consider God to be a craftsman (τεχνίτης), whereas Christians regard God as the Maker (ποιητής), who creates through his own Word (cf. Jn 1:1).[67] The Son

> is the Word of the Creator God; and from the works of the Father, which the Word himself works, (cf. Jn 5:17) one recognizes that he is in the Father and the Father is in him (Jn 14:10–11) and that the one who has seen him has seen the Father (Jn 14:9) because of the identity of essence and the complete likeness (τὸ ἴδιον τῆς οὐσίας καὶ τὴν κατὰ πάντα ὁμοιότητα) of the Son to the Father.[68]

Athanasius asserts that the Son possesses identity of essence and complete likeness to the Father, with allusions to Jn 5:17 and Jn 14:9–11. By using allusions, Athanasius is able to derive stronger conclusions from these Johannine notions than seems warranted. He intimates that the Scriptures portray the complete likeness between Father and Son unequivocally. However, while these crucial elements of his theology do not appear as such in Scripture,

---

The Branches of the Gospel of John: The Reception of the Fourth Gospel in the Early Church, The Library of New Testament Studies 332 (London: T&T Clark, 2006), 26–32.

[66] CM I 1 (Kl./H. 4,26–28); tr. McCarthy Spoerl and Vinzent. In ET I 1, the name Sabellius also appears three times, next to several other places in this work.

[67] CA II 22 (198,1–3); cf. CA II 28 (205,27). See ET I 10 on Eusebius' view of the contrast between Creator and craftsman.

[68] CA II 22 (198,7–10); tr. Anatolios. Jesus' words 'I in the Father and the Father in me' of John 14:10 are repeated in John 14:11 with a different nuance. Athanasius frequently quotes only this part of John 14:10. For convenience, references to these words from John's Gospel are indicated always as stemming from John 14:10, although the same words are also found in John 14:11.

they are effective in excluding the Arian view. Athanasius asserts the meaning of Jn 14:9–10 as self-evident, leaving out the setting in John's Gospel, which was more careful in presenting Jesus as the unique representative of the Father. While John presents Jesus as God's unique representative, he is also obedient and completely dependent on the Father: 'The words that I say to you I do not speak on my own; but the Father who dwells in me does his works (Jn 14:10b)'. With the original ambiguity of John's statements removed, Athanasius asserts that Jn 14:9–10 unambiguously proves that the Word, Wisdom, and Son of the Father is rightly called Maker and Creator, and hence is not a κτίσμα.

CA II 23–24: The Son Is Worshipped

In *CA* II 23, Athanasius collects biblical material to demonstrate that God is qualitatively distinct from all creatures, because only God is worshipped. While creatures reject worship from fellow creatures (Acts 10:26; Rev 22:9), the Word is worshipped in the OT (e.g. Ps 97:7 (quoted in Heb 1:6); Isa 45:14). Worship is thus a necessary sign of divinity, and the Son accepts it from his disciples. The Son

> receives the disciples who worship (προσκυνοῦντας) him and assures them of who he is, saying, 'Do you not call me 'Lord and Teacher'? You speak well; for so I am' (Jn 13:13). And when Thomas calls him 'my Lord and my God' (Jn 20:28), he lets him say it; instead of preventing him, he approves of him.[69]

Athanasius considers Jesus' acceptance of worship in Jn 20:28 as a proof of his divinity, even though he is careful not to claim that Jesus commanded or encouraged his disciples to worship him (cf. Mk 10:17–18). The worship makes the Son unique, and rules out the possibility that he is an exalted creature. For the created angels, who are superior to humans, consistently reject worship from other creatures while they worship the Son (Heb 1:6).[70] The

---

[69] *CA* II 23 (200,26–29); tr. Anatolios.
[70] *CA* II 23 (200,14–23); cf. Rev 22:9; Judg 13:16.

worship to the Son therefore proves that Father and Son are both equally and fully divine, because the Son

> would not be worshipped nor would these things be said of him if he were one of the creatures at all (εἰ ὅλως). But ... he is not a creature, but ... he also, like the Father, is worshipped ... [f]or he has said: 'All things that the Father has are mine' (Jn 16:15). Indeed, it is proper to the Son to have whatever belongs to the Father and to be such that the Father is seen in him (cf. Jn 12:45), and all things are made through him (cf. Jn 1:3).[71]

While the Arians did not hold the Son to be simply one of the creatures, the worship to the Son makes any conception of the Son's ontological creatureliness impossible. It is noteworthy that the three references of Athanasius' claim to illustrate the equality of Father and Son are derived from John's Gospel (1:3; 12:45; 16:15).

Jn 1:3 is frequently brought to presence in this part, and occurs again in an imagined debate between himself and the Arians. Because Athanasius directly addresses his opponents, he creates an engaged debate in which the citation of Jn 1:3 in the form of a question is the end of all possible objections. He suggests that the Arian teaching bluntly contradicts the creation through the Word, by saying:

> If all things are creatures and all things have their subsistence from non-being, and the Son also, according to you, is a creature and a work and one of those that once were not, how is it that God has made all things through him alone and 'without him not one thing came to be' (Jn 1:3)? Or why is it the case that when reference is made to 'all things,' no one understands the Son as signified among the 'all' but one restricts the reference to the things that have come into being?[72]

Athanasius challenges the Arians on their inconsistency of understanding the Word as a creature on the one hand, while they also must accept that everything came through the Word on the other.

---

[71] *CA* II 24 (200,1–201,7); tr. Anatolios, adapted.
[72] *CA* II 24 (201,9–13); tr. Anatolios.

John's Gospel provides Athanasius with the most suitable statements on the unity between God the Father and the Son. Nevertheless, Athanasius is highly selective in presenting the words of
John's Gospel. While these statements in John are clearly interrelated with statements of Jesus' submission to the Father (Jn 4:34;
6:38), Athanasius hardly ever refers to such indicators of Jesus'
obedience and submission in the *Orations*. The name Jesus without an addition, such as Lord, Christ or Saviour, does not appear
outside Scripture citations in the *Orations*. Athanasius' concern for
the humanity and earthliness of Jesus has by and large disappeared (cf. *CA* I 42–43; II 14, 16; III 53), in favour of his argument
concerning the worship to the Son.

CA II 25–31: The Son Is Not an Intermediate Being

After the argument concerning the Son's worship, Athanasius
moves to the point that the Son is not an intermediate being between God and creation that was taught to create. Although they
might phrase it somewhat differently, his testimony can be
trusted that some Arians held this view. Before Athanasius attacks
their arguments, he questions the integrity and sanity of his opponents, mentioning that 'Eusebius and Arius and Asterius, the
one who sacrificed, have not only said these [i.e. senseless and
impious] things but have dared to write them'.[73] Writing is performed more consciously than speech, and the addition of the
verb τολμάω further increases the suggestion of deliberate impiety,[74] so that their theological views and understanding of Scripture are not to be trusted.[75] In *CA* II 28, Athanasius further attacks
Asterius' integrity. He refers back to Asterius' sacrifice during the
Diocletian persecution (303–311), when Asterius 'learned to deny

---

[73] *CA* II 24 (201,28–29); tr. Anatolios. Cf. *CA* I 37 (147,10–12). The views
of Arius and Asterius are not only uttered in speech, 'but Arius inserted
them into the composition of his *Thalia* and Asterius the Sophist wrote
these very things which he have reported above'; *CA* II 37 (214,7–9); tr.
Anatolios.
[74] Meijering, *Die dritte Rede*, I:110–11.
[75] *CA* II 25 (201,1–3); tr. Anatolios. Cf. *CA* I (110,18); II 26 (203,16).

the Lord'.[76] Athanasius thus discredits Asterius' piety to undermine the credibility of the views proposed by Asterius. Although personal attacks are a rhetorical *topos* for discrediting the opponents, Athanasius uses it more frequently, not only for attacking their ideas, but also discrediting them as individuals. In contrast, Eusebius of Caesarea solely describes Marcellus' ideas as madness.[77]

According to Asterius, God created everything through a mediator, because creatures 'would not be capable of withstanding his immediate hand and creative activity'.[78] Asterius distinguishes between the innate Reason (λόγος) of God (which exists eternally in God) and the Son (who is created before all ages) to maintain the singularity of God.[79] Because of that, the Word of God is not as divine as the Father, nor a creature, but an intermediate being between God and creation. According to Athanasius, this begs the question how this somehow created intermediate Word could bear God's direct influence, in contrast to all other creatures, and he suggests that this position is problematic.

Athanasius attacks Asterius' use of human analogies for the conception of the Son. Asterius had argued that the Son could have been a servant or instrument to create the other creatures, just as God delivered Israel from Egypt through the help of Moses.[80] Athanasius ridicules the comparison of the Son's and Moses' mediation. Moses was a servant, while the Son is the Creator, which is evidenced in two biblical statements concerning God's Word and Wisdom: "'all things have come to be in wisdom" (Ps 104:24) and "apart from the Word not one thing came into being" (Jn 1:3).'[81] Athanasius therefore repeats that the Son is Word and

---

[76] CA II 28 (205,18–19); cf. CA II 24 (Asterius ὁ θύσας) and Opelt, *Polemik*, 47–50.

[77] Eusebius describes Marcellus' view as containing ἀτοπία CM I 1 (Kl./H. 6,6); μανία ET II 7 (Kl./H. 105,22); ἠλίθιος ET III 5 (Kl./H. 161,16).

[78] CA II 24 (201,25–26); tr. Anatolios. Cf. Asterius, fr. 26 (Vinzent).

[79] Asterius, frs. 64–73 (Vinzent).

[80] CA II 27 (203,1–3); cf. Asterius, fr. 47 (Vinzent).

[81] CA II 27 (203,7–11); tr. Anatolios.

Wisdom, truly divine and source of creation, and hence not a mediating being between God and creation.[82]

In *CA* II 28, Athanasius cites a fragment from Asterius concerning the Son thus: 'Although he is a creature and of those that come into being, he has learned to create from the Master and Maker and thus has come to serve the God who taught him.'[83] Athanasius refuses this view of the Son on the ground that God is not indifferent to the material realm and is self-sufficient.[84] Athanasius asserts that 'the Word did not become creator through teaching', because 'the Father is seen to be still working even while the Son exists, as the Lord himself says: "My Father is working until now and I also am working" (Jn 5:17)'.[85] Jn 5:17 functions to prove that God did not need an intermediate being to create, because the Father remains involved in the act of creation. He thus claims that Asterius' suggestion that the Word was taught to create makes the Son superfluous (περιττός).[86] In that case, it 'appears that the Son has come into being for our sake, and not we for his, since we were not created on his account but he has been made for us.'[87] According to E. P. Meijering, Athanasius' attack on the consequences of his opponent's theology 'seems justified' on this point.[88] Athanasius' appeal to Jn 5:17 rightly points to the problematic consequences of considering the Son to be merely the mediating agent in creation.

In *CA* II 31, Athanasius reiterates the primacy of the creative Word of God in contrast to the secondary nature of creation. Even if God had not willed and decided to create, the Word would

---

[82] *CA* II 27–28 (204,25–205,16).

[83] *CA* II 28 (16–18); tr. Anatolios. See also fragment 34 (Vinzent) and Vinzent, *Asterius*, 445–50.

[84] See *CA* II 29 (205,1–8); cf. *CA* II 25, the citation of Mt 10:29 and 6:25–30, that God even cares about the sparrows, the grass and the hairs of human beings.

[85] *CA* II 29 (205,8–206,11); tr. Anatolios.

[86] *CA* II 29 (206,12–14).

[87] *CA* II 30 (206,1–2); tr. Anatolios.

[88] Meijering, "ΗΝ ΠΟΤΕ," 165 n.21.

still be 'with God' (Jn 1:1) and the Father 'in him' (Jn 10:38, 14:10). But the things that come into being are incapable of becoming apart from the Word. They came to be through him and this makes sense because the Word is the Son of God who belongs (*idios*) to the essence of God by nature and is from him and 'in him' (Jn 10:38), as he himself said.[89]

The presence of Johannine references is unmistakable in Athanasius' argument that the Son is in no way part of creation, but dwells in the Father eternally. Jn 1:1; 10:38 and 14:10 refer to the Son's indwelling, the creation through the Word is vaguely alluded to, but nevertheless present again in Athanasius' basic argument that the Son cannot be a κτίσμα.

CA II 32–40: The Father and the Word are Inseparable

In *CA* II 32–40, Athanasius argues that the Word is inseparable from the Father. Athanasius starts polemically, claiming that his opponents, the heretics, 'are not waging the battle (μάχην) … against us, but in fact are waging war on the divinity itself (θεότητα μάχονται)'.[90] Athanasius cites ten passages, including Jn 1:1, and asserts that all these biblical texts refute the Arian heresy, because they are 'indicating the eternity of the Word and signifying that he is not foreign but proper to the essence of the Father'.[91] He further appeals to the analogy of light and its radiance: just as light is not seen without its radiance, so no sane person can consider God to be ever without reason (λόγος) or without wisdom.[92] This remark is prompted by the Arian denial that God's innate reason (λόγος) is identical with the Son-Word revealed in Jesus Christ.

---

[89] *CA* II 31 (207,6–9); tr. Anatolios. Cf. 'when the Word himself works and creates, then there is no question and answer, for the Father is in him and the Word is in the Father (cf. Jn 10:38).' *CA* II 31 (208,29–31); tr. Anatolios.

[90] *CA* II 32 (208,1–3); tr. Anatolios.

[91] *CA* II 32 (209,15–17); tr. Anatolios. Mt 3:17; Prv 8:25; Heb 1:3; 1 Cor 1:24; Ps 36:10; Ps 104:24; cf. Jer 1:11; Jn 1:1; Lk 1:2 and Ps 107:20.

[92] *CA* II 32 (209,17–19).

Athanasius admits that his opponents do not suggest that God has Reason or Wisdom as an accidental attribute, because he claims that his opponents teach two Words or Wisdoms.[93] Stead and Williams argue that these are not the words of Arius, but more likely an inference of Athanasius.[94] However, on this point Athanasius attacks Asterius, who did distinguish between an eternal, innate Word of God and the Son-Word that became flesh in Jesus Christ.[95] Athanasius disputes this distinction, because he holds that creatures cannot reflect the Father accurately, while he regards the Son as an accurate expression of the *hypostasis* of the Father. If Athanasius is to be trusted on this issue, the Arians considered the Father-Son language, which is liable to change because of the birth metaphor, philosophically inadequate for maintaining the unity within God.[96]

Athanasius asserts that Scripture and images derived from Scripture make their position untenable.[97] The biblical passages he cites are shaped by the image of light and its radiance, to maintain that the Son is from the being of the Father.

> [T]he Father remains whole, the expression of his subsistence (χαρακτῆρα τῆς ὑποστάσεως; cf. Heb 1:3) always endures and preserves an unvarying likeness and image to the Father, so that one who sees him sees in him also the subsistence of which he is the expression. (...) The Savior himself also teaches us this, saying: 'The Father who abides in me is doing the works which I do' (Jn 14:10; cf. Jn 10:25), and 'I and the

---

[93] See *CA* I 5 (114,18–21); *CA* II 37 (214,9–28). Cf. Asterius, frs. 64, 66 (Vinzent).

[94] Stead, "Thalia," 33; Rowan Williams, "The Logic of Arianism," *JTS* 34 (1983): 59.

[95] See frs. 64, 66 (Vinzent). Athanasius quotes these fragments in *CA* II 37.

[96] *CA* II 32 (209,29–210,33); tr. Anatolios. See Asterius, fr. 76 (Vinzent) and Osborne, "Literal or Metaphorical?," 166–69.

[97] '[T]he exactness (ἀκρίβεια) of these scriptural phrases and the meaning indicated by the scriptural symbols ... refute the ramblings of their defiled doctrine.' *CA* II 33 (210,2–4); tr. Anatolios.

Father are one' (Jn 10:30), and 'I am in the Father and the
Father in me' (Jn 14:10).[98]

The image of light and its radiance (ἀπαύγασμα; Heb 1:3) explains
in fourth-century terminology the absence of change and division
within the unity of Father and Son.[99] However, as soon as Athanasius appeals to Scripture, he returns to the relational language
of Father and Son, more specifically to Jesus' words from John's
Gospel. He conflates the words of Jn 14:10 'the Father who dwells
in me does his works' and Jn 10:25 'The works that I do in my
Father's name testify to me' to the phrase 'The Father who abides
in me is doing the works which I do' to demonstrate the unity of
the 'works' of Father and Son. This is the only time in the three
Orations that Athanasius refers to another element of Jn 14:10
than his beloved words 'I in the Father and the Father in me'. On
this point, Athanasius appreciates the agency theme in John, to
assert the inseparability of Father and Son. However, John's
agency theme is interpreted as the relation between the heavenly
Father and the earthly Jesus, but within the divine Father-Son
relationship.

Athanasius also discusses the inseparability of Father and
Son in relation to the concept of λόγος. He points to the incomparability of the human and divine λόγος, and backs his view with
reference to Jn 1:1 and 1:3. Whereas a human word is different
from the person itself and it disappears immediately after it is
uttered, God's Word is like the radiance of light; the divine λόγος
'is the perfect offspring of one who is perfect; therefore he is God
and Image of God. For "the Word" it says, "was God" (Jn 1:1).'[100]
Furthermore, while the words of humans do not act, God's Word
'is Creator and "without him nothing came into being" (Jn 1:3),
nor can anything come into being without him'.[101]

---

[98] CA II 33 (210,9–16); tr. Anatolios.

[99] Morales, *La théologie trinitaire*, 42–46, 529–42; Cf. Jaroslav Pelikan, *The
Light of the World. A Basic Image in Early Christian Thought* (New York:
Harper, 1962).

[100] *CA* II 35 (212,19–20); tr. Anatolios.

[101] *CA* II 35 (212,27–28); tr. Anatolios.

In *CA* II 37, Athanasius quotes two fragments of his opponent Asterius that distinguish between an eternal power and wisdom of God and the Word. Asterius distinguished between Christ as *a* power of God (cf. 1 Cor 1:24) and *the* eternal power that is identical with God (cf. Rom 1:20).[102] Asterius' concern was to maintain God's unity by distinguishing between the eternal Word and Wisdom of the Father and the Son.[103] While he considered the Son to be God (θεός), he only referred to the Son as *a* God, without the definite article ὁ (the). In contrast, he called God the Father ὁ θεός with a definite article (*the* God). In that way, he could confess the Son God, but also maintain the ultimate singularity of *the* God; according to Markus Vinzent, Asterius wants to safeguard both 'the absoluteness and exclusivity of the being of *the* God, as well as his freedom, paternal ability to beget, and agency as Creator'.[104] In order to emphasise God's singularity, Asterius stated that Christ is not identical with God's eternal Power (δύναμις) and Wisdom, but the firstborn and only-begotten of many created powers. To remove all ambiguity, Asterius asserts that all the individually created powers are dependent on God, even suggesting that the grasshopper (ἡ ἀκρίς) is called a great power (δύναμις μεγάλη) in Joel 2:25 as well.[105] The authenticity of these Asterius

---

[102] *CA* II 37 (214,7–19); see Asterius, fr. 64 (Vinzent).

[103] Vinzent, *Asterius*, 44–48; See also idem, "Gottes Wesen, Logos, Weisheit und Kraft bei Asterius von Kappadokien und Markell von Ankyra," *VC* 47 (1993): 174–80.

[104] 'Durch die Unterscheidung von ausschließlichen und wesensdefinierenden Begriffen und nichtausschließlichen wesenhaften, aber nicht notwendigen Bezeichnungen gelingt es Asterius, einerseits die relationslose Absolutheit und Nichtmitteilbarkeit des Wesens »des« Gottes, andererseits aber auch dessen Freiheit, väterliche Zeugungsfähigkeit und schöpferische Wirksamkeit zu begründen.' Vinzent, "Gottes Wesen," 175.

[105] *CA* II 37 (20–26) = fr. 66 (Vinzent). 'Although "his eternal power and wisdom," which the logic of truth manifests as without beginning and unbegotten, is indeed one and the same, yet many are those which are individually created by it, of which Christ is firstborn and only-begotten. Yet all are equally dependent on the one who procures them. And all are justly called "powers" of the one who creates and makes use of them. Thus the prophet says that the locust, which comes to be as a divinely

fragments is not doubted,[106] so that Athanasius' attempt to construct a negative *ethos* of his opponents is not just his inference, but the product of Asterius' opinions as well. Many pious believers would consider the comparison between Christ and a grasshopper offensive, so Athanasius' exclamation: 'Do they not deserve to be completely hated for merely saying this?' would probably be answered affirmatively by readers sympathetic to him.

In contrast, Athanasius asserts the inseparability of Father and Son. He argues that Asterius' view of unbegotten 'Wisdom, which coexists eternally with God', is inconsistent. 'For what coexists does not coexist with itself but with another.'[107] Athanasius thus demonstrates that his opponents' denial of the Son's eternity, out of a concern for the singularity of God's unbegottenness, is not solved by their alternative. If there were a coexisting Wisdom with God, other than the Son, this would also conflict with God's absolute singularity. While Asterius most likely would have answered that this λόγος would not be a distinct *hypostasis*, but an attribute of *the* God, Athanasius' objection demonstrates the problems of conceiving an ultimate singularity in God, and to what extent that is undesirable for (Christian) monotheism. Athanasius argues therefore that only one Word of God exists, and that all other existing words and powers are different and inferior to the Word and Son of God.

> The Savior indicates that such words are other than himself when he says in his own person: 'the words, which I have spoken to you' (Jn 6:63). Such words are not offsprings (...) [n]or was it one of these many words which, according to John, 'became flesh' (Jn 1:14), but it is as the only Word of God that he is preached by John: 'The Word became flesh' (Jn 1:14), and 'everything came to be through Him' (Jn 1:3). (...) The works that are accomplished through him are also declared, for 'all things visible and invisible' (Col 1:16) 'came to be

---

sent judgment for the sins of human beings, is called by God not only "power" but also "great power" (cf. Joel 2:25).' Tr. Anatolios.

[106] Vinzent, *Asterius*, 302–8. See also Athanasius, *Syn* 18.

[107] *CA* II 38 (215,17–18); tr. Anatolios.

through him and apart from him not one thing came into being' (Jn 1:3).[108]

The first reference to John (6:63) is clearly included because of
its diction, not because of a serious argumentation that the Arians
would consider spoken words to be equivalent to the Word. Nevertheless, where Asterius distinguished between the Word that
became flesh in Jesus Christ and God's innate Word, Athanasius
disagrees with him, asserting that the Son is identical with the
Word and innate Reason of God on the basis of scriptural reasoning.[109] Because the eternal Creator-Word, through whom everything exists (Jn 1:3; Col 1:16), is the one who became flesh (cf.
Jn 1:14), Asterius draws an incorrect and inappropriate distinction between God the Father and his Son-Word. Again, the Johannine prologue is crucial for Athanasius in maintaining that the
Son is the true and genuine Word that is inseparable from the
Father.

That leads Athanasius in *CA* II 40 to confront his readers with
Asterius' inconsistency, demonstrating the negative *ethos* of his
opponent. Athanasius claims that where Asterius first spoke of
many powers and of the comparison to the grasshopper or cater-
pillar (here: ἡ κάμπη), he is 'acting inadvertently, like Caiaphas
(Jn 11:51), ... and ends up confessing only one power. Thus he
writes, "God the Word is one but rational beings are many; and
the being and nature of Wisdom is one but the things that are
wise and good are many."'[110] The comparison with Caiaphas at
the trial of Jesus is polemical, but Athanasius is able to point to
Asterius' inconsistency. Whereas Asterius denies that this Word
and Wisdom is the genuine Son of the Father, the Arians do not
maintain the Father's singularity either. Furthermore, by their
separation of the Son from the Father they have ended up like the
heretics, who conceive of another god than the one and only true
God. So the Arians

---

[108] *CA* II 39 (215,7–9. 10–13); tr. Anatolios.
[109] Anatolios, "'When Was God without Wisdom?'"; see idem, "'Christ the
Power and Wisdom of God.'"
[110] *CA* II 40 (216,6–210,10); tr. Anatolios, adapted. See Asterius, fr. 32
(Vinzent).

end up in a complete fuddle about everything and deny the
true Wisdom while they invent one that does not exist, just
like the Manichees who deny the true God and make for themselves another one. But let the Manichees and the other heresies hear that the Father of Christ is one, who, through his
own Word, is also Lord of creation and its Maker. For their
part, let the Arian fanatics also hear that there is one Word of
God, who is the only proper and genuine Son from the Father's
being and who possesses an indivisible unity with his Father.[111]

In this fragment, Athanasius suggests that the Arians and Manichees both reject, each in their own way, the inseparability of the
genuine Word with the Father.[112] He contends that the view that
the Son is not the eternal Word of God virtually equates the Arians
to the Manichees. While E. P. Meijering calls the comparison to
the Manichees purely rhetorical in order to show that all heresies
belong together,[113] Anatolios contends that Athanasius' remark is
not merely rhetorical. According to Anatolios, Athanasius could
rightly exploit the comparison between Arians and Manichees.
Since both positions results in a 'hidden God' (Deus absconditus),
whose Word is not active in creation, the Manichean and Arian
positions ultimately boil down to the same basic problem.[114] According to the Manichees, the true God is not the God present and
active in creation; while the Arians separate the Son-Word of the
Scriptures from the Father by introducing a true and innate Word
of God that is the true agent in creation instead of the Son-Word
of the Scriptures. Athanasius' suggestion does not of course do
justice to all nuances of the Arian position and conveys a rhetorical potential that carries further than the actual parallels. Nevertheless, although the Arians are not Manichees and even dissociate themselves from the Manichees, it might have discredited
them in the eyes of some 'neutral' Christians at that time, since

---

[111] CA II 40–41 (217,21; 217,1–4); tr. Anatolios.
[112] See CA I 23 (133,11–13). See also CA II 39 (216,22–26); III 35;
EpAeg.Lyb 16.
[113] Meijering, Die dritte Rede, II:211.
[114] Anatolios, Athanasius, 262 n.116.

Manichaeism was one of the largest enemies of Christianity.[115] By engaging with rational aspects of Arianism, and associating his opponents with the Manichees, Athanasius voices his crucial core insight that the Word is inseparable from the Father as a logical inference from biblical (Johannine) passages and images of the Father-Son relationship.

CA II 41–43: Excursus on Baptism

In *CA* II 41–43, Athanasius tightly relates the view of the Word as the eternal Son of God, and hence not a creature (κτίσμα), to the sacrament of baptism. Baptism represents the divine grace and can only be received through a truly divine mediator, according to Athanasius. He refers back to the discussion in *CA* II 25–40 as a demonstration of the appropriateness 'that "all things came to be through him" (Jn 1:3)', and remarks that the 'flow of the argument has moved us to mention holy baptism'.[116] In the sacrament of baptism,

> the Son is named along with the Father not as if the Father were insufficient, nor as if haphazardly or by chance, but because he is the Word of God and his proper Wisdom and Radiance, who is always with the Father. Therefore it is not possible for the Father to bestow grace except in the Son.[117]

---

[115] Lyman even suggests that Arius' teaching originated against a group of Manichees, which might shed light on Athanasius' use of polemic, in J. Rebecca Lyman, "Arians and Manichees on Christ," *JTS* 40 (1989): 502–3; see also Jacob Albert van den Berg, *Biblical Argument in Manichaean Missionary Practice: The Case of Adimantus and Augustine*, Nag Hammadi and Manichaean Studies 70 (Leiden: Brill, 2010); on the dissociation of Arius from the Manichees, see Arius' *Letter to Alexander*, Urk. 6. On the missionary activities of the Manichees, see L. Koenen, "Manichäische Mission und Klöster in Ägypten," in *Das römisch-byzantinische Ägypten: Akten des internationalen Symposions 26.–30. September 1978 in Trier*, ed. G. Grimm, H. Heinen, and E. Winter, Aegyptiaca Treverensia 2 (Mainz am Rhein: Philipp von Zabern, 1983), 93–108.

[116] *CA* II 41 (218,18–20); tr. Anatolios.

[117] *CA* II 41 (218,20–23); tr. Anatolios.

Athanasius asserts that the baptism in the name of the Father, the Son and the Holy Spirit (Mt 28:19) makes the belief in the eternal divinity of the Son of God crucial for salvation. Because all grace is mediated through the divine Son, there is no divine grace for a Christian without a divine Son. Athanasius already emphasised the cooperation of Father and Son (CA II 22; 29; cf. Jn 5:17), and returns to the mutual work of Father and Son in the sacrament of divine grace: baptism. Whatever the Father does,

> he does through the Son and the Lord himself says, 'the things that I see my Father doing, these things I also do' (Jn 5:19), so also when baptism is given, the one whom the Father baptizes the Son also baptizes, and the one whom the Son baptizes is perfected in the Holy Spirit.[118]

The saving act of baptism is only effective if both Father and Son are divine. The baptism formula in Matthew 28:19 does not presuppose the fourth-century doctrine of the Son or Trinity, but an exalted status of the Son seems to be presupposed in the baptism formula 'in the name of the Father, Son and Holy Spirit'.[119] While the Matthean words should not be read as an unequivocal statement of a coexisting Trinity, Athanasius can rightly argue that the status of the Son has implications for the salvation in baptism. Furthermore, according to Carson, Jesus' claims in Jn 5:19 that 'the only one who could conceivably do "whatever the Father does" must be as great as the Father, as divine as the Father', so Athanasius' appeal must have been convincing to many sympathetic and 'impartial' readers.[120]

Athanasius further illustrates the cooperation of Father and Son with the image of sun and radiance and two Johannine passages: 'Thus, when he bestowed his promise to the saints, he said: "My Father and I will come and make our dwelling with him" (Jn 14:23), and again, "that they may be one in us, as You and I are

---

[118] CA II 41 (218,26–31); tr. Anatolios.

[119] Robert Horton Gundry, Matthew: A Commentary on His Handbook for a Mixed Church Under Persecution, 2nd ed. (Grand Rapids, MI: Eerdmans, 1994), 51–53, 596.

[120] Carson, John, 251; the italics in the original are replaced by quotation marks.

one" (Jn 17:21, 10:30).'[121] These Johannine verses and the image of sun and radiance prove for Athanasius that the Father and Son are one in being and work, and indicate that the Son is the true Word of the Father.

Successively, he blames the Jews – and implicitly the Arians – for their wrong view of the Son. While the Jews removed 'from their midst the wisdom which is from the fountain, our Lord Jesus Christ' by rejecting Jesus as king and instead choosing Caesar (cf. Jn 19:15) and lost Jerusalem and their reasoning because of their denial, the Arians 'end up endangering the very fullness of the mystery ... of baptism'.[122] Athanasius uses the term 'Jews', a term that is emphatically utilised in John's Gospel, without concern for the nuances that modern interpreters are careful to point out.[123] Just as Athanasius takes some Christological statements out of their first-century setting in John, he also employs the term Jews in this way. The Arians are juxtaposed with the disbelieving Jews in that neither of them receives salvation in baptism; neither of them conceived of the Son in the correct way. Athanasius extends this reasoning to the heresies of the Manichees, Phrygians, and followers of Paul of Samosata as well and concludes that 'those who think the way of Arius, although they read what is written and say the names [in baptism]', do not receive the effects of their baptism. Everyone who considers the Son to be 'unlike (*anomoion*) and other than the Father in being, ... will not be conjoined with the Father, not having his proper Son who is from him by nature, who "is in the Father, and in whom the Father is" (Jn 14:10), as he himself said.'[124] With a strong warning, Athanasius cautions Christians who are uninterested in the theological, for they will not 'be able to call to their aid any of those who now deceive

---

[121] *CA* II 42 (218,1–3); tr. Anatolios.

[122] *CA* II 42 (218,6–7. 10–13); tr. Anatolios.

[123] See Urban C. Von Wahlde, "The Johannine 'Jews': A Critical Survey," *NTS* 28 (1982): 33–60; Reimund Bieringer, Didier Pollefeyt, and Frederique Vandecasteele-Vanneuville, eds, *Anti-Judaism and the Fourth Gospel. Papers of the Leuven Colloquium, 2000* (Leiden: Westminster John Knox Press, 2001).

[124] *CA* II 43 (220,27–29); tr. Anatolios.

them when they see the Lord whom they denied sitting upon the throne of his Father and judging the living and the dead.'[125] This excursus on baptism might catch the attention of those without interest in theological subtleties. He thus warns that the explanation of ἔκτισε in Prv 8:22 is not a neutral event, for even the effect of the sacrament of baptism depends on the confession of a truly divine Son of God.

In this way, Athanasius already prepares the correct interpretation of Proverbs 8:22 before the actual discussion of this text. In this preliminary discussion, he depends heavily on several carefully selected Johannine notions and a few images of non-living nature, alongside a demonstration of the inconsistency and impiety of his opponents and the implications of theology for the effect of baptism.[126]

CA II 44–82: ATHANASIUS' EXPOSITION OF PROVERBS 8:22

After several announcements (CA I 53; II 1; II 4; II 11; II 18) of the text and a long preliminary discussion in CA II 18b–43, Athanasius finally discusses Proverbs 8:22: 'The Lord created (ἔκτισε) me as a beginning of His ways, for his works.' He acknowledges that he in fact decided upon the correct interpretation of the verse already: 'We have taken up these points at such length ... before dealing with the passage of the Proverbs, so that they may recognize that it is not fitting to call the Son of God a creature and may thus learn to read correctly the passage in the Proverbs, according to its right sense.'[127] Athanasius' discussion in CA II 44–82 contains six elements: (1) the proverbial nature of Prv 8:22, (2) the custom of Scripture, (3) the determination of the priority of clear sayings about the Son, (4) the explanation of the terms 'ways' and 'works', (5) an excursus on Prv 8:23, and (6) an alternative interpretation of Prv 8:22.

---

[125] CA II 43 (220,31–33); tr. Anatolios.
[126] See also the comment of Anatolios, Athanasius, 138 n.126.
[127] CA II 44 (220,1–4); tr. Anatolios. See further CA II 46 (223,19–22; 29–31) and CA II 50 (226,1–3).

CA II 44–52: Prv 8:22 as a Proverbial Text

Athanasius argues in *CA* II 44–52 that Proverbs 8:22 should be understood metaphorically, because other biblical texts literally predicate that the Son is truly divine, hence not a creature. He appeals to a distinction between clear and unambiguous sayings, proposing that his frequently quoted texts from the Johannine prologue are unambiguous. In his argument, he has to establish the plausibility of his view that distinguishes two sets of referents within the speech of the divine Wisdom in Proverbs 8:12–31.

Proverbs 8:22 stands in the context of Proverbs 8:12–31, which deals with a speech of the divine Wisdom, who describes herself as created (ἔκτισε). In Eastern theology, there was a long tradition of reading Proverbs 8:22 ('He created'); 8:25 ('He begets me'); and 8:30 ('I daily rejoiced in his presence') in relation to the ontology of the Wisdom or Word. Origen understood Proverbs 8:25, 30 as a proof of the Son's 'eternal hypostatic existence' and subordination to the Father. He ambivalently states about Proverbs 8 that it suggests both a beginning and a non-beginning of the Son: 'For he [the Son] is beginning, as we have learned in Proverbs, in so far as he is Wisdom, as is thus written: "God created me, the beginning of his ways, for his work" (Prv 8:22). But in so far as he is Word, he is not beginning, for "In the beginning was the Word" (Jn 1:1).'[128] Origen's approach to this section was therefore interpretable in different directions. In the Western Christian tradition, this section of Proverbs 8 was interpreted differently. Tertullian and many others distinguished two separate events in Prv 8:22 and Prv 8:25; 8:30, and related both types of texts to separate events.[129]

In the fourth century, the divine Wisdom is commonly related to the divine Word and Jesus Christ. Eusebius of Caesarea asserts that the whole section contains one referent: the divine

---

[128] Origen, *Comm. Ioh.* I 222. Cf. *Comm. Ioh.* I 102; 111; 244 and Joseph W. Trigg, *Origen*, The Early Church Fathers (London: Routledge, 1998), 262 nn38, 41. For a general study on Origen's exegesis, see Peter W. Martens, *Origen and Scripture: The Contours of the Exegetical Life*, OECS (New York: Oxford University Press, 2012).

[129] Clayton, *Orthodox Recovery*, 132–42.

pre-incarnate Christ.[130] He advocated this basic unity of Proverbs 8:12-31 over against Marcellus of Ancyra, who held that it was possible to distinguish between statements concerning the pre-existent and incarnate Christ in this chapter. Both solutions have their problems. For Eusebius of Caesarea, the difficulty of inter-preting ἔκτισε (created) was how it could be applied to the pre-incarnate, divine Wisdom. Eusebius argues that the Son is not a creature, because the Hebrew word in Prv 8:22 should not be translated as ἔκτισε, but as ἐκτήσατο (he possessed him).[131] In this way, Eusebius avoided the problematic consequences of the word ἔκτισε in Prv 8:22 (LXX). The Arians radicalised Origen's emphasis on ἔκτισε in verse 22 at the cost of reading verse 25 in a secondary sense.[132]

Athanasius did not know Hebrew and was less interested in such a technical argument than Eusebius. He does not appeal to the different translation options from Hebrew to Greek and pro-vides another solution to avoid the teaching that the Son is a crea-ture (κτίσμα), in line with Marcellus of Ancyra.[133] Athanasius dis-cerns two sets of referents in Proverbs 8:12-31 and provides an explanation why not all expressions in this section should be un-derstood in the same way. Athanasius distinguishes between (1) proverbial and (2) clear or unambiguous texts in Scripture. He reworks the elaborate argument of Marcellus on proverbial

---

[130] Eusebius of Caesarea quotes the passage in full and states: "I have deliberately laid these out in their entirety out of necessity, having shown that the one who says these is one person, since there is no change of speaker in the middle [of the passage]." *ET* III 2 (Kl./H. 138,1-4); tr. McCarthy Spoerl and Vinzent. Cf. Meijering, *Orthodoxy and Platonism*, 98-101; see further Clayton, *Orthodox Recovery*.

[131] *ET* III 2 (Kl./H. 143,19; cf. 141,30-142,5; 143,3-21).

[132] See Origen, *In Jer.* 9.4, *DP* IV 4.1. Cf. Eusebius of Caesarea, *ET* III 2 (138,31-34) and Clayton, *Orthodox Recovery*, 144-48, 166-98.

[133] Clayton, *Orthodox Recovery*, 215-16. Marcellus of Ancyra separates between Prv 8:22-26 (see frs. 26-29, 31-32, 34-42, 44-45) (Vinzent) and Prv 8:27-30 (see frs. 88, 110) (Vinzent). Athanasius partly shares his approach to this section with Marcellus, but whereas Marcellus relates Prv 8:25 to the incarnate state of the Son, Athanasius relates it to the divine state of the Son.

sayings. Whereas Marcellus dwells elaborately on examples from Greek literature (τῶν ἔξωθεν) to demonstrate that the genre of Proverbs cannot always be taken at face value (fr. 23),[134] Athanasius only gives a scriptural warrant for his distinction – a citation of Jn 16:25. It suggests that Athanasius' primary audience in the *Orations* are Christians with meagre interest in study of the pagan classics.[135]

Athanasius claims that the title of the book of Proverbs indicates that Proverbs 8:22 must be interpreted proverbially. His argument is quite unsophisticated and straightforward, compared to Marcellus' one: 'For what is spoken in the Proverbs (Παροιμίαι) is not spoken plainly but proclaimed in a hidden manner, as the Lord himself taught in the Gospel according to John, saying: "I have spoken to you these thing in parables (ἐν παροιμίαις)" ... (Jn 16:25).'[136] While Athanasius claims that his distinction is based on the correspondence between the title of the book Proverbs (Παροιμίαι) and Jesus' words ἐν παροιμίαις in Jn 16:25, the real reason is that a literal reading of Proverbs 8:22 would contradict the Son's eternal divinity. Sayings from the book of Proverbs that correspond with his theology are considered 'literal' without hesitation.[137] This is visible in his discussion of Proverbs 9:1: 'Wisdom has built herself a house.' After citing this text, Athanasius remarks:

---

[134] See Marcellus, frs. 23, 25, 29, 40 (Vinzent). Abramowski, "Hauptwerk," 17; Simonetti further points to Eustathius of Antioch as a possible source for Athanasius' interpretation: *Studi sull'Arianesimo*, 38–56. Parvis and Clayton show more awareness of both the similarities and differences between Marcellus' of Ancyra and Athanasius: Parvis, "'Τὰ τίνων ἄρα ῥήματα θεολογεῖ?,'" 353–59; Clayton, *Orthodox Recovery*, 220–22.

[135] Ernest, *Bible*, 363, 366; see also John Vanderspoel, *Themistius and the Imperial Court: Oratory, Civic Duty, and Paideia from Constantius to Theodosius* (Ann Arbor: University of Michigan Press, 1995), 17–18, 72–76.

[136] *CA* II 44 (221,7–11); tr. Anatolios. Cf. *CA* II 77 (255,18–20): 'The Word did not say of himself that he was a creature by nature, but was speaking in proverbs when he said, "the Lord created me" (Prv 8:22).'

[137] Clayton, *Orthodox Recovery*, 297–98. Cf. Marcellus, see frs. 88, 110 (Vinzent). See further Osborne, "Literal or Metaphorical?," 152–55.

> Clearly (δῆλον), the house of Wisdom is our body, in the taking of which Wisdom became human. So it is fittingly said by John: 'The Word became flesh' (Jn 1:14), and through Solomon, Wisdom speaks about herself with precision inasmuch as she does not say, 'I *am* a creature,' but only that 'the Lord created me as a beginning of his ways, for his works' (Prv 8:22); not 'He created me into being,' nor 'I have the beginning and generation of a creature.'[138]

Athanasius asserts that Wisdom is not created in an ontological sense by reading Proverbs 8:22 through the glasses of Proverbs 9:1 and John 1:14. He then suggests some alternatives that would clearly indicate the Son's non-existence, inferring that this is not meant by ἔκτισε in Prv 8:22. By defining Proverbs 9:1 as a 'clear' statement, he claims that these three texts, Prv 9:1, Prv 8:22 and Jn 1:14, all suggest 'that the Word himself is wholly flesh but that he has put on flesh and become human'.[139]

In *CA* II 50, Athanasius asks 'how did all things come to be through him (Jn 1:3) and have their consistence in him (Col 1:17)' if the Son were a creature (κτίσμα)?[140] Quotations and allusions to Jn 1:3 featured prominently in *CA* II 18b–43 and are repeated at this point.[141] Athanasius brings this biblical notion of creation through the Word clearly into presence by asserting its clarity, thus arguing that the word ἔκτισε is said of the Son when he came to 'complete the work' (Jn 4:34).[142] He asserts that his objection to a 'literal' reading of Proverbs 8:22 is similar to the custom of calling God 'Father', which does not annul human servanthood by nature.[143] He urges his opponents not to deny the Son's eternity, because the word ἔκτισε should not be used to 'deny the eternity

---

[138] *CA* II 44 (221,20–26); tr. Anatolios. Cf. *CA* II 46 (223,24–29).

[139] *CA* II 47 (223,6–7); tr. Anatolios. Cf. Marcellus, frs. 80, 119 (Vinzent).

[140] *CA* II 50 (226,9–11); tr. Anatolios.

[141] Words of Jn 1:3 are found in *CA* II 21 (198,14–15); II 24 (201,10–12); II 27 (203,10–11); II 31 (207,21); II 35 (212,27–28); II 39 (216,13–18); II 41 (218,18–19). In *CA* II 39, Jn 1:3 and Col 1:16 are conflated. Col 1:16 is also mentioned in *CA* II 27; II 41. In *CA* II 41, Athanasius indicates his purposiveness in referring to Jn 1:3.

[142] *CA* II 50 (226,19–20).

[143] *CA* II 51 (227,6–8).

of his divinity and that "in the beginning was the Word" (Jn 1:1) and "all things came to be through him" (Jn 1:3) and "in him all things were created" (Col 1:16)'.[144] For 'the Word did not come into being by being created but "in the beginning was the Word" (Jn 1:1) and after this he was sent "for the works" [cf. Jn 4:34] and the economy pertaining to them'.[145] Athanasius thus asserts that no expression in Scripture can mean that the being of the Word – the ontology – is created, because this can only be said in relation to his redemptive work – the soteriology. His conception of the content of the Scriptures, voiced most notably by John 1:1, 3 and Colossians 1:16 in this passage, is so dominant that he does not allow these notions to be overruled. Hence Athanasius establishes that ἔκτισε in Proverbs 8:22 should not be read in the obvious or literal way, but in relation to the Son's incarnate state. The Gospel of John is prominently present as the mirror text of Proverbs, which counters any conception of Proverbs 8:22 that would deny his doctrine of the Son. At this point, Perelman's remark about the importance of the presentation of the data must be remembered. The strong emphasis on certain scriptural verses, many of them Johannine, asserts the self-evident nature of those texts, and hence the metaphorical nature of another text, that is, Proverbs 8:22.[146]

CA II 53–55: The Custom of Scripture

Athanasius asserts that his distinction between clear and unambiguous sayings in Scripture is justified, because of the 'custom of Divine Scripture' (ἔθος ... τῇ θείᾳ γραφῇ).[147] While the expressions created (ἔκτισε), formed (ἔπλασε), and appointed (κατέστησε), that suggest a beginning are used in relation to the Son,[148] 'he nevertheless also taught that he existed before all that when he said: "Before Abraham came to be, I am" (Jn 8:58) and "When he

---

[144] *CA* II 51 (227,6–11); tr. Anatolios.
[145] *CA* II 51 (228,22–23); tr. Anatolios. See also *CA* II 52 (228,6–7), where Athanasius cites Jn 1:1 in contrast to ἔκτισε.
[146] See Perelman and Olbrechts-Tyteca, *New Rhetoric*, 116.
[147] *CA* II 53 (230,16–17). See also Twomey, "St Athanasius," 85–118.
[148] Cf. *CA* II 53 (229,1–3).

prepared the heavens, I was with him" (Prv 8:27) and "I was ar-
ranging with him" (Prv 8:30)."[149] These two types of texts are mir-
rored in Jn 1:14 and 1:1: attributes pertaining to the fleshly state
of the Word (cf. Jn 1:14) are always qualified and supplemented
with a reason, but attributes pertaining to his divinity (cf. Jn 1:1)
are used without qualification. He uses an enthymeme to assert
that what is evident for the Father is evident for the Son as well:

> For he is the radiance of the Father. Just as the Father does
> not exist for a certain reason, so also one must not seek a rea-
> son for his radiance. 'In the beginning was the Word and the
> Word was with God, and the Word was God' (Jn 1:1); so it is
> written and no 'why' is given. But when 'the Word became
> flesh' (Jn 1:14), then the reason is given why he came, saying,
> 'and he dwelt among us.'[150]

With this appeal to the custom of Scripture, Athanasius suggests
that it is not only possible but also necessary to understand ἔκτισε
in Prv 8:22 in relation to the Son's humanity. While Prv 8:22 is a
problematic text for his theology, Athanasius 'triumphantly' turns
this 'problem into a polemical weapon' against his opponents.[151]

Athanasius' distinction between the absence or presence of
purpose about the Son is strongly shaped by the difficulties he
encounters in relation to the Arians.[152] Clayton criticises Athanasius for tracing a 'latent' meaning in the first instance and omit-
ting it in the other. While there is nothing in Prv 8:22–23 'that

---

[149] *CA* II 53 (229,4–6); tr. Anatolios, adapted.

[150] *CA* II 53 (230,20–24); tr. Anatolios. Anatolios mentions that Athanasius shares this interpretation of Prv 9:1 with Marcellus, Hilary of Poitiers
and Gregory of Nazianzus (*Oration* 30:2). Eusebius of Caesarea rejects it
(*ET* I 10; III 2).

[151] Rowan Williams, "Baptism and the Arian Controversy," in *Arianism
after Arius. Essays on the Development of the Fourth Century Trinitarian Conflicts*, ed. Michel R. Barnes and Daniel H. Williams (Edinburgh: T&T
Clark, 1993), 154; cf. Anatolios, "'When Was God without Wisdom?,'"
119–21.

[152] Stead argues that although Athanasius accuses the Arians of disre-
garding the context of biblical texts, he himself does the same. Stead,
"Exeget," 177–81; Clayton, *Orthodox Recovery*, 296–98.

would elicit such a connection', he 'violated the rule of latent meaning' in his reading of Prv 8:25.[153] Clayton's remark shows the circumstantial nature of Athanasius' strategy on this point.

The Gospel of John plays a crucial role in the illustration of the general custom of Scripture in *CA* II 54. Athanasius illustrates his claim concerning unqualified sayings about the Son's nature with five texts from the Gospel of John. In contrast to the 'hidden', proverbially spoken words of Prv 8:22 (cf. *CA* II 44), the Son speaks openly and without qualification (ἀπολελυμένος εἴρηκεν) about his being:

> The Lord himself has said many things in proverbs, but in referring to himself, he spoke without qualification: 'I am in the Father and the Father in me' (Jn 14:10) and 'I and the Father are one' (Jn 10:30) and 'The one who sees me has seen the Father' (Jn 14:9) and 'I am the light of the world' (Jn 8:12) and 'I am the truth' (Jn 14:6).[154]

Athanasius' distinction between 'plain' or 'unqualified' sayings about the Son's nature and 'proverbial', 'hidden' or 'qualified' sayings about the incarnate state of Christ is also found in Christian writers before him, such as Irenaeus.[155] To identify the Gospel of John as especially illustrative of this distinction seems original to Athanasius. All five 'plain' sayings are derived from the Gospel of John. Athanasius also points to three Johannine sayings of Jesus to illustrate that the purpose of the Son's becoming human is supplemented by additional reasons:

> What this need was, for the sake of which he became human, the Lord himself indicates, saying: 'I have come down from heaven, not in order to do my will but the will of the one who sent me. And this is the will of the one who sent me, that I may not lose anything of what he has given me, but may raise it up on the last day. For this is the will of my Father, that everyone who sees the Son and believes in him should have eternal life and I will raise him up on the last day' (Jn 6:38–40). And again, 'I have come as light into the World, so that

---

[153] Clayton, *Orthodox Recovery*, 297.
[154] *CA* II 54 (230,1–4); tr. Anatolios.
[155] *AH* II 10.1; II 27.1.

everyone who believes in me may not remain in darkness' (Jn 12:46). Yet again he says: 'For this I have been born and for this I have come into the World, to witness to the truth' (Jn 18:37).[156]

The Gospel of John is thus extensively brought into presence again to advocate the plausibility of his statements. However, Athanasius handles the content of John selectively as well. The profoundly Johannine notion of Jesus' submission to the Father's will is not commented upon. The verses that Athanasius selects, he selects with a specific purpose. And even when he cites a biblical text, he is only foregrounding the elements that contribute to his argument concerning the general custom of Scripture.[157]

In *CA* II 55, Athanasius musters additional material for his claim that the Son's incarnate presence is always accompanied by an expression of purpose. He cites Heb 2:14–15, 1 Cor 15:21 and Rom 8:3–4, and two passages from John's Gospel (3:17 and 9:39). He quotes these verses, distinguishing between John and a word from the Saviour himself and returns in a summary to the five citations: 'So he did not come for his own sake but for our salvation [cf. Jn 3:17] and for the banishment of death [cf. Heb 2:14–15] and the condemnation of sin [cf. Rom 8:3–4] and for the renewal of sight to the blind [cf. Jn 9:39] and the raising of all from the dead.'[158] These texts together illustrate the custom of Scripture. The reason that Athanasius extracts these biblical passages is that the Son is not created for his own sake, but for 'our sakes' and 'our need'.[159] The general custom of Scripture, which distinguishes between those texts about the Son's being and the Son's incarnate state, enables him to explain why the Word, whom he

---

[156] *CA* II 54 (230,12–231,21); tr. Anatolios.

[157] In *Oration* III 7, Athanasius discusses this issue in more detail.

[158] *CA* II 55 (231,17–232,19); tr. Anatolios. 'And John says, "God did not send his Son into the world in order to condemn the world but so that the world may be saved through him" (Jn 3:17). Again, the Savior says himself: "I have come into the world for judgment, so that those who do not see may see and those who see may become blind" (Jn 9:39).' *CA* II 55 (231,14–17); tr. Anatolios.

[159] *CA* II 55 (232,19–21); cf. *CA* II 56 (232,9–12).

acknowledges to be the Creator (κτίστης), described himself as being created (ἔκτισε): he is created as a human, to save humanity. Athanasius is not interested in the meaning of the Johannine passages as such, for example what Jesus' submission to the Father's will means exegetically, but John's Gospel gives him the most convenient material for illustrating the custom of Scripture.

CA II 56–64: The Priority of 'Clear' Sayings

In the subsequent chapters of *CA* II, Athanasius uses the custom of Scripture to prioritise certain clear sayings. He discusses the priority of (1) γεννάω (to beget; cf. Prv 8:25) over κτίζω (to create; cf. Prv 8:22) and (2) the Christological title only-begotten over firstborn.

The priority of γεννάω over κτίζω

In *CA* II 56–60, Athanasius discusses the relation between Prv 8:22 and 25 to determine the logical priority of begetting over creating. Prv 8:25 (LXX) states: 'before the mountains were established and before all the hills, he begets me (πρὸ δὲ πάντων βουνῶν γεννᾷ με).' Athanasius primarily discusses the verbs γεννάω (8:25) and κτίζω (8:22) to assert that γεννάω has logical priority over κτίζω.

While the book of Proverbs contains sayings that should be taken literally, Athanasius regards Prv 8:25 as illuminating and truthful sayings that shed light on the proverbial term ἔκτισε of Prv 8:22.[160] Athanasius justifies his reading of Prv 8:25 ('Before all the hills, he begets me (γεννᾷ με)') as a 'clear' expression about the Son's ontology because no reason is added.[161] In contrast, 'created (ἔκτισε) for the works' (Prv 8:22) is not a clear expression, because the reason is added: the divine Wisdom is created 'for the works'. Therefore, 'even if the works had not been created, the Word of God still was and the "Word was God" (Jn 1:1) but his

---

[160] Prv 8:30 is also a 'clear saying': 'The Father is everlasting, and his Word is also everlasting and, being everlasting, he says: "I was his delight every day, rejoicing before him" (Prv 8:30) and "I am in the Father and the Father is in me" (Jn 14:10).' *CA* II 56 (232,12–233,14); tr. Anatolios.
[161] *CA* II 56 (233,25).

becoming human would not have taken place if the need of humanity had not become a cause.'[162] Jn 1:1 is thus crucial for Athanasius to disconnect the relation between Prv 8:22 and 8:25 that was maintained by the Eusebians.

Athanasius further asserts the priority of γεννάω over κτίζω in Prv 8:22–25 by discussing Deuteronomy 32 (LXX), which also contains both verbs. Deut 32:6b reads: 'Did not he himself, your father, acquire you and make (ἐποίησεν) you and create (ἔκτισεν) you?' and Deut 32:18 reads: 'You abandoned God who bore (θεὸν τὸν γεννήσαντα) you, and you forgot your God who nurtures you.' In this chapter, the verb κτίζω (Prv 8:22; Deut 32:6) also occurs earlier in the text than the verb γεννάω (Prv 8:25; Deut 32:18). Athanasius does not suggest that both terms might be equivalents for describing Israel's relationship to YHWH, as modern readers might do, but he argues for a general custom of speech within Scripture concerning the use of γεννάω and κτίζω. Whereas his opponents assert the priority of κτίζω over γεννάω, because of their prior occurrence in the biblical text in both Deuteronomy and Proverbs, Athanasius provides a rationale for the priority of γεννάω over κτίζω. He asserts that God first *made* his people (32:6), and only after that did he *beget* them by loving them as his people (32:17–18). He discerns the same dynamic between γεννάω and κτίζω in the Gospel of John, for 'John says: "He granted them authority to *become* children of God, begotten not from blood nor from the will of the flesh nor from the will of man, but from God" Jn 1:12–13)'.[163] These words are very precise, for humans are able,

> by receiving the Word, [to] receive authority from him 'to become children of God' (Jn 1:12). Being creatures by nature, they would not become 'sons' except by receiving the Spirit of the natural and true Son. So it was in order to bring this about and to make humanity receptive of divinity that 'the Word became flesh' (Jn 1:14).[164]

---

[162] CA II 56 (233,25–27); tr. Anatolios.
[163] CA II 59 (236,5–7); tr. Anatolios. italics original.
[164] CA II 59 (236,13–17); tr. Anatolios.

The Gospel of John thus functions as a mirror text for a pattern he detects elsewhere in Scripture. Creatures are first created, and only then begotten as sons, but the Son is Son, before he becomes a creature, to save humanity. In that way Athanasius concludes: '[t]he phrase "begets me," (Prv 8:25) closely following upon "created," (Prv 8:22) makes the meaning coherent and shows that, while "created" is said with a view to a cause, "begets me" precedes "created."'[165]

On this point, a remark of Charles Kannengiesser must be challenged. He asserts that Athanasius' reference to John 1:14 is a typical lesson of Athanasian exegesis devoid of any polemical intention.[166] This statement is only partly right and raises a question concerning the audience and original dimensions of the *Orations*, and about Athanasius' use of Jn 1:14. For Kannengiesser, the difference between the fierce polemic in *CA* II 18b–43 and the relative absence of polemic in *CA* II 44–61 is one of his arguments for discerning different layers in the text of the *Orations*.[167] However, even in *CA* II 58 Athanasius addresses the Arians, and Kannengiesser acknowledges this as a 'rupture de l'élan', without offering an explanation of it.[168] This indicates that the existence of an original, purely catechetical treatise is difficult to prove. For that reason, the difference in polemical and more friendly language shows that Athanasius' frequent suggestion that he writes primarily for the sake of refuting his opponent is a rhetorical construct.[169] In fact, the primary purpose might be the edification of pious believers, supplemented with the wish to convince those who did not have a firm opinion on the theological issues. Athanasius might have considered his attack on the Arians in *CA* II 18–43 to be sufficient and therefore allows himself a more modest

---

[165] *CA* II 60 (237,9–11); tr. Anatolios.
[166] 'La leçon d'exégèse démunie de tout élément polémique, amorce l'exposé narratif, de manière à le centrer sur une citation larvée de *Jn* 1,14, enrobée dans une formule typique de la catéchèse athanasienne.' Kannengiesser, *Athanase*, 294 n.22.
[167] Kannengiesser, *Athanase*, 255–404, esp. 288–309.
[168] Kannengiesser, *Athanase*, 294 n.21.
[169] Cf. *CA* II 1 (177,1–6). II 18 (195,29–34); II 20 (196,1).

tone in the second part, elaborating on the soteriological concerns he genuinely has in the subsequent part.[170]

This might also explain why the soteriological interpretation of Proverbs 8:22 seems a genuine concern of Athanasius, which simultaneously has a polemical intent. Since an appeal to Jn 1:14 frequently serves to refute his opponents, polemical intentions certainly coexist alongside pastoral and theological intentions. While Jn 1:14 is and can be used for Athanasius' theology, it should not be overlooked that his opponents had much more in common with Athanasius than his polemic suggests. Moreover, Barrett suggests that the paradox of John's Gospel is that the glory (δόξα) is only 'to be seen in the flesh (σάρξ) and nowhere else'.[171] While Athanasius provides a legitimation of his theology in which Jn 1:14 features prominently, his basic argument is that the flesh does not compromise the Son's divine glory. It is impossible to decide *the* interpretation of Jn 1:14, but it is clear that the original sense is less evidently in favour of Athanasius' interpretation than Athanasius intimates.

Firstborn and Only-begotten

Athanasius next discusses the relation between two Christological titles: 'firstborn' of all creation (πρωτότοκος; Col 1:15) and 'only-begotten' (μονογενής; Jn 1:14, 18; 3:16, 18; 1 Jn 4:9).[172] The relation between those titles was construed in different ways in the fourth century, with profound implications. Asterius argued that if the Son is the firstborn of all of creation (cf. Col 1:15), he is also part of creation.[173] Marcellus of Ancyra advocated the priority of

---

[170] See for some exceptions *CA* II 58; 64; 70; 74; 82 and the milder criticism in *CA* II 71–72.

[171] Barrett, *John*, 165.

[172] For 'firstborn', see also Rom 8:29; Col 1:18; Heb 1:6; Rev 1;5. Origen relates Prv 8:22 to Jn 1:1, Col 1;15 and 1 Cor 1:24 in *DP* I.2.1 and *Comm. Ioh.* I.100–1 and Parvis, "'Τὰ τίνων ἄρα ῥήματα θεολογεῖ?,'" 354. See further Eusebius of Caesarea, *ET* I 10; III 1–3 and Mark DelCogliano, "Basil of Caesarea on Proverbs 8:22 and the Sources of Pro-Nicene Theology," *JTS* 59 (2008): 183–90.

[173] Fr. 25 (Vinzent) = *CA* II 63.

only-begotten, because 'it is clear that the only-begotten, if he were really only-begotten, can no longer be firstborn, and if the firstborn were [really] firstborn, he cannot be only-begotten'.[174] Athanasius holds with Marcellus that firstborn and only-begotten cannot be true in the same sense and argues for the logical priority of only-begotten.

Athanasius asserts that the title 'firstborn' is equivalent to brother (cf. Rom 8:29; Heb 2:11): the Son 'became for us a human being and brother through the likeness of the body (...) In this body the Lord becomes our guide into the kingdom of heaven and to his own Father, saying "I am the way" (Jn 14:6) and "the door" and all must "enter through me" (Jn 10:9).'[175] For that reason, firstborn is a non-exclusive term and concerns the Son's relation to creation, while only-begotten is an exclusive term that concerns his relation to the Father: "'only-begotten" and "Son" and "Word" and "Wisdom" are terms that refer back to the Father and indicate the fact that the Son belongs to the Father. So, "we have seen his glory, glory as of the only-begotten from the Father" (Jn 1:14) ... and "the Word was with God" (Jn 1:1).'[176] Similarly, the Son is called 'without qualification ... "the only-begotten Son who is in the bosom of the Father" (Jn 1:18).'[177] The contrast with the title firstborn is clear in Athanasius' mind. Since firstborn is supplemented with a reason, this title pertains to the incarnate Christ. The difference is succinctly summarised in an opposition: 'Before the Son was called "firstborn of all creation" (Col 1:15) he

---

[174] See Marcellus, fr. 10 (Vinzent) = Eusebius of Caesarea, *CM* I 4 (Kl./H. 20,4–7); tr. McCarthy Spoerl and Vinzent.

[175] *CA* II 61 (238,13–14. 18–20); tr. Anatolios. Cf. *CA* II 74 (251,14–17).

[176] *CA* II 62 (239,6–11.13–14); tr. Anatolios, adapted.

[177] *CA* II 62 (239,22–24); tr. Anatolios. In *CA* II 37 (214,18), Athanasius quotes a fragment of Asterius with the variant 'the only-begotten God'. See Andrew T. Lincoln, *The Gospel according to Saint John*, Black's New Testament Commentaries 4 (Peabody, MA: Hendrickson, 2005), 108; Carson, *John*, 139; Barrett does not really choose, see *John*, 169; Barnabas Lindars favours the reading only-begotten Son, in *The Gospel of John*, The Century Bible (London: Oliphants, 1972), 99; On the textual difficulties, see Burkholder, "Possibility of a Theological Corruption in Joh 1,18," 64–83.

himself was none the less "the Word with God, and the Word was God" (Jn 1:1)'.[178] The emphasis on the Johannine prologue (which mentions only-begotten two times) is thus clearly supportive in asserting the logical priority of only-begotten.

Athanasius borrows his argumentation for the priority of only-begotten from Marcellus of Ancyra, who argues that even someone with great difficulty to learn understands that both terms cannot be applied in the same way.[179] Whereas Marcellus was very hesitant to ascribe the Christological title Son to the pre-incarnate Word,[180] Athanasius makes this a major topic in his defence in his *Orations against the Arians*. In Athanasius' list of titles for the Pre-incarnate, the titles only-begotten and Son precede the titles Word and Wisdom. The contrast between only-begotten and firstborn enables him to relate firstborn to the Son's incarnate state. This provides him with another reason for understanding ἔκτισε in Prv 8:22 in relation to the Son's creation in God's plan of redemption as an equivalent of the title firstborn.

CA II 65–72: The Ways and the Works

In *CA* II 65–72, Athanasius discusses another part of Proverbs 8:22: 'The Lord created me as the beginning of his ways, for the sake of his works.' He now focuses on the part of the verse: 'the beginning of his ways for the sake of his works' (ἀρχὴν ὁδῶν αὐτοῦ εἰς ἔργα αὐτοῦ). He connects the 'ways' (ὁδῶν) of Proverbs with Jesus' declaration that he is the 'way' (ὁδός; Jn 14:6). Athanasius says: 'He "was created a beginning of ways" so that we may walk on that way and enter through the one who says "I am the way"

---

[178] *CA* II 63 (239,2–240,4); tr. Anatolios.

[179] See fr. 10 (Vinzent).

[180] Vinzent points to fr. 3 and comments upon it to assert that Marcellus rejected the title Son. See *Markell*, lxxi; Lienhard, however, argues that Marcellus changed his mind in his *Letter to Julius of Rome*, so that Marcellus sincerely addressed the Preincarnate as Son, although the title Word remained his preferred terminology. "Did Athanasius Reject Marcellus?," in *Arianism after Arius. Essays on the Development of the Fourth Century Trinitarian Conflicts*, ed. Michel R. Barnes and Daniel H. Williams (Edinburgh: T&T Clark, 1993), 71.

(Jn 14:6) and "the gate" (Jn 10:9)."[181] He suggests that the Son's attribute 'way' in Jn 14:6 provides a clue to the 'ways' in Proverbs 8:22. Proverbs 8:22 points to God's love for humanity:

> [I]n his love for humanity (φιλανθρώπως), none other than the Lord is created 'a way,' as the beginning of the new creation. He fittingly says, 'The Lord created me as the beginning of His way for His works' (Prv 8:22), so that humanity may no longer live according to the old creation. But since there is now the beginning of a new creation and we have Christ as the beginning of its ways, we may henceforth follow the one who says, 'I am the way' (Jn 14:6).[182]

This interpretation of Proverbs 8:22 is speculative and suggestive, but religiously satisfying for Athanasius. This understanding acknowledges the relation between ἔκτισε and κτίσμα, but the Son of God is not ontologically a κτίσμα. Athanasius continues: by becoming created, the 'perfect Word of God put on the imperfect body and is creature himself' and hence, humanity is provided with immortality and access to paradise.[183]

Athanasius next discusses the works (ἔργα) of Proverbs 8:22, arguing that the works for which Wisdom is created are the works fulfilled by Jesus according to John's Gospel (Jn 4:34; 5:36; 17:4). He links the works of Proverbs and John at the end of *CA* II 66:

> This is exactly what the Savior says, 'I glorified you upon the earth. I perfected the work that you have given me to do' (Jn 17:4), and again, 'The works which the Father has given me to perfect, these works which I do, bear witness to me' (Jn 5:36). The works which he here says that the Father has given him to

---

[181] *CA* II 64 (241,22–25); tr. Anatolios. Cf. *CA* II 61 (238,18–20); *CA* II 37 (214,4). Athanasius disagrees with Asterius' identification of Word as a similar attribute to vine, way, door and tree of life (cf. Jn 15:5; 14:6; 10:9; Rev 22:5. Cf. *CA* II 37. Athanasius is roughly in line with Marcellus in this respect, fr. 3 (Vinzent). The difference between them is that Marcellus does not reckon 'life' (Jn 14:6) to be part of the eternal nature of the Son, while Athanasius does so (cf. *CA* I 19 (128,7–8)). See also pp 126–29 above.
[182] *CA* II 65 (242,14–18); tr. Anatolios. Cf. Marcellus, fr. 30 (Vinzent).
[183] *CA* II 66 (243,20–23); tr. Anatolios.

perfect are those for which he is created, saying in the Proverbs, 'the Lord created me as the beginning of his ways for his works' (Prv 8:22). For it is the same thing to say, 'The Father has given me the works' (cf. Jn 5:36), and 'He created me for the works' (Prv 8:22).[184]

This citation illustrates clearly how Athanasius interprets the Proverbs text in the light of the Gospel of John. God's love for humanity made it necessary that the Son had to perform works to set humanity free and lead them on the way to immortality. By linking the Johannine submission texts to ἔκτισε from Prv 8:22, he provides a solution for understanding these Johannine texts as well. He does not explicitly discuss the Johannine submission texts in *CA* I-II (Jn 4:34; 6:38), but provides in a subtle way an explanation of these texts that do not easily fit with Johannine texts about the equality of Father and Son that Athanasius frequently appeals to.

Athanasius claims that only a divine Saviour might release humanity from its mortality and conquer the devil,[185] so that the reason the 'Word became flesh is to restore the works of the human race, that have been lost due to sin'.[186] Because the consequences of sin could not be absolved by originated beings, 'it was the Lord himself who absolved it, as he himself said: "... unless the Son will set you free" (cf. Jn 8:36).'[187] All the fruits of divinisation, the remission of sin, and salvation require the Word's divinity, who was created as a human being. Since the Word was created as a human being, humans remain no longer 'upon the earth, but as he himself said, where he is, we will be also (Jn 14:3)'.[188] In Athanasius' allowance for an interpretation that the

---

[184] *CA* II 66 (243,23–29); tr. Anatolios.

[185] For Athanasius' description of the consequences if the Son would be a creature, see *CA* II 67 (244,20–245,32); II 70 (247,1–3; 17–248,22); II 73 (250,10–14).

[186] *CA* II 67 (244,1–20).

[187] *CA* II 67 (244,26–28); tr. Anatolios. References to Jn 1:14, Jn 14:30 (The prince of this world is coming and he finds nothing in me) and 1 Jn 3:8 follow. See *CA* II 69 (246,11–16).

[188] *CA* II 69 (246,17–19); tr. Anatolios. Cf. *CA* I 39 (149,1–2): 'He ... became a human being in order that we may be divinised.'

Son was created as a human being, Jn 1:3 is brought into presence again by a citation. For 'if the things that were made were worked by ... God, while it is written that "all things came to be through the Word, and without him not one thing came to be" (Jn 1:3) ... then clearly the Son must not be a work.'[189] Time and again, Athanasius ascertains that the Word's creation for the sake of salvation does not annul his rightful position as Creator. In this setting, Athanasius discusses Romans 8:22, which says that all creation groans to be liberated 'from the slavery of corruption', in connection with Jn 8:35–36. The Son is the one who liberates creation from slavery, as is said in Jn 8:35–36. Because the Son

> grants sonship (ὁ υἱοποιῶν) and freedom to all (as he said to the Hebrews then: 'The slave does not remain in the house forever, but the Son remains forever. Therefore if the Son sets you free, you shall be free indeed' (Jn 8:35–36)) ... it is clearer than light that the Word of God is not a creature but the true and genuine Son of the Father by nature.[190]

Thus, because the Son is the true and genuine Son of the Father, ἔκτισε cannot mean that the Son is an ontological κτίσμα, but must mean that the Son became a κτίσμα during his incarnation. In his conclusion, Athanasius expresses himself modestly, in contrast to the more polemical style in the rest of his work, by concluding: 'it seems to me that these words, even if they are meagre, are sufficient to provide a basis for those who are more eloquent to prepare further refutation of the Arian heresy.'[191]

CA II 73–77: Excursus on Prv 8:23

In *CA* II 73–77, Athanasius briefly explains the subsequent verse: Proverbs 8:23 – 'He established me [Wisdom] before the ages' – to argue that this text must be attributed to the Word's incarnate presence. The primary question is whether the Word is the Son of God. Peter affirms this in Mt 16:16 and 'the father of the Arian heresy' also asked in the beginning of Jesus' ministry: '"If you are the Son of God..." (Mt 4:6).' The devil asked this with a reason:

---

189 *CA* II 71 (248,19–22); tr. Anatolios.
190 *CA* II 72 (249,19–250,23); tr. Anatolios.
191 *CA* II 72 (250,23–25); tr. Anatolios.

if Jesus was the Son, the diabolical tyranny would end, but if he was a creature, the devil would not have to worry about his presence on earth. It was also clear for the Jews in Jesus' time that Jesus considered himself the Son of God, for 'the Jews of that time were angered because the Lord called himself the Son of God and "called God his own Father" (Jn 5:18)'.[192] Athanasius suggests that if even the devil and Jews (Jewish leaders) attached meaning to the title Son, the Arians too must acknowledge that the Son is the true and genuine Son of God. The allusion to Jn 5:18 functions as the clearest marker of the Son's identity, resulting in an anti-Judaistic remark (cf. CA II 42).

Athanasius discusses Prv 8:23 in line with his argument concerning Prv 8:22, but does not insert other Johannine material. In CA II 77, Athanasius finishes his discussion of Prv 8:22 and gives a general remark about Prv 8:22–23. Somewhat surprisingly after so many chapters of explanation of this text, Athanasius holds that the reason for the word ἔκτισε remains ultimately an enigma (cf. Prv 12:5–6).[193]

CA II 78–82: Prv 8:22 Revisited

Athanasius gives an alternative explanation of Prv 8:22 in CA II 78–82.[194] In the first explanation of Prv 8:22, the part 'for the works' (εἰς ἔργα αὐτοῦ) is related to the Son's work of salvation (CA II 44–72). In the second explanation, this phrase is related to Wisdom's imprint in all of creation (CA II 78–82): '[T]he Word is not a creature by essence, but the saying in the Proverbs refers to that within us which is called wisdom.'[195] Athanasius illustrates this explanation with the case of a king's son, whose father imprints his name on each work of the city. Athanasius inserts a *prosopopoeia*, to explain that Proverbs 8:22 must be understood in

---

[192] CA II 73 (250,10–15); tr. Anatolios. For other references to Jn 5:18, see CA I 15; II 12; III 27. Cf. CA I 19; III 20.

[193] CA II 77 (255,23–26).

[194] For an argument on this section as a later redaction, see Kannengiesser, *Athanase*, 369–74; Blaising deems this view unnecessary. Blaising, "Athanasius," 9.

[195] CA II 78 (256,24–25); tr. Anatolios.

relation to the imprint of the divine Wisdom in all the works of creation. Wisdom says: 'For my imprint (*typos*) is in them and thus have I condescended in the act of creating.'[196] Thus, ἔκτισε in Prv 8:22 might point to the imprint of Wisdom in the works of creation. For if someone fears the Lord (Prv 1:7) 'and then ascends by intelligence and understanding and perceives in creation the Creator Wisdom, he will perceive in her also her Father, as the Lord himself has said, "The one who has seen me has seen the Father" (Jn 14:9)'.[197] This alternative interpretation of Prv 8:22 is no problem at all for Athanasius' theology, so that he can accept it by reasoning that if God created everything in Wisdom (cf. Ps 104:24), Wisdom, Jesus Christ, is displayed in everything. Though this might be satisfying to Athanasius, it is a clear deviation from the text and from the potential meanings that could reasonably be derived from John 14:9.

In a somewhat more plausible part of this section, Athanasius relates Jn 1:3 to Prv 8:25–28. In Prv 8:25, Wisdom claims to be an offspring in the words 'He begets me'.

> Now, since she goes on to say, 'When he fashioned the heavens, I was there with him' (Prv 8:27), we must understand that she is saying that the Father did not fashion the heavens or 'the clouds above' (Prv 8:28) except through her. For it is beyond doubt that all things were created in Wisdom, and apart from her not one thing was made (cf. Jn 1:3).[198]

According to this interpretation, everything is made by the Word and Wisdom of God, and this Wisdom is by condescension imprinted in all the works of the whole universe, connecting the creative Wisdom of Proverbs 8 to the Word in Jn 1:3.[199] Wisdom was thus displayed in the works and divine knowledge was accessible for humans from the beginning of creation.[200] Athanasius' rationale for the incarnation in this proposal is that God desired himself to be revealed more clearly, and has therefore made 'the

---

[196] *CA* II 79 (257,27–28); tr. Anatolios.
[197] *CA* II 80 (258,14–16); tr. Anatolios.
[198] *CA* II 81 (258,1–4); tr. Anatolios.
[199] Cf. *CA* II 81 (258,5–7).
[200] Cf. *CA* II 81 (258,8–259,15) and *CG* 1.

true Wisdom herself take flesh and become a mortal human being and endure the death of the cross'.[201] This Wisdom, the Word of God, has become the fullest way of divine revelation in becoming flesh for humanity's sake.

> [I]t is the same Wisdom of God, who previously manifested herself, and her Father through herself, by means of her image in creatures – and thus is said to be 'created' – but which later on, being Word, became flesh (Jn 1:14) as John said, and after 'destroying death' (2 Tim 1:10) and saving our race, both revealed himself and through himself his Father, saying, 'Grant that they may know you the true God and Jesus Christ whom you have sent' (Jn 17:3).
>
> Therefore all the earth is filled with his knowledge.[202]

By this identification of the Wisdom and Word of God with Jesus Christ, Athanasius asserts that the Son belongs to the being of the Father.[203] The Father always rejoiced in seeing his own image, the Word, and if the Father always rejoiced in the Word, the Word must be eternal, and their joy reciprocal. He states:

> And how does the Son too rejoice, except by seeing himself in the Father? For to say this is the same as to say: 'The one who has seen me has seen the Father' (Jn 14:9), and 'I am in the Father and the Father is in me' (Jn 14:10). (...) For the passage in Proverbs and all that has been said about it make it evident that the Son is not a creature by nature and being (tē physei kai tē ousia), but the Father's own (idion) offspring who is true Wisdom and Word, 'through whom everything came into being, and without him nothing came to be' (Jn 1:3).[204]

Athanasius' final words of *Oration* II show again his pervasive appeal to the Gospel of John. Three Johannine texts are cited besides the passage under discussion: Jn 14:9, 10 and Jn 1:3. The passage from Jn 14:9 and 10 is cited to establish the eternal and mutual rejoicing of both Father and Son, by the close

---

[201] *CA* II 81 (259,20–21); tr. Anatolios.

[202] *CA* II 81–82 (259,23–28; 259,1); tr. Anatolios.

[203] *CA* II 82 (259,4–5).

[204] *CA* II 82 (259,12–260,16; 261,21–23); tr. Anatolios.

identification of both, while Jn 1:3 is present because the Son, the true Wisdom and Word, is Creator. While his opponents also related the Wisdom of Proverbs to the Johannine Word, Athanasius relates the Word of Jn 1:3 more clearly to Jesus Christ than his opponent Asterius, because Asterius maintained God's unity by separating the divine Word, incarnated in Jesus Christ, from God's innate Wisdom and Word.

Athanasius understands the relation in such a way that Jn 14:9 and 14:10 are understood as clear indicators of a testimony of the divine Son, eternally united to the Father. This leaves less room for an understanding of John's Gospel that acknowledges the earthliness of Jesus Christ in the way he is presented in the canonical Gospel. Instead, Athanasius' use of these verses anticipates the teaching on the two natures of Christ. As remarked in relation to *Oration* I, this way of citing John's Gospel clearly demonstrates the narrow focus of the Arian controversy. The fact that John makes all kinds of qualifications of Christ divinity, in order to stay within the borders of Jewish monotheism, is side-stepped by Athanasius, who mainly looks in the Gospel for affirmation of his view that Jesus Christ is the eternally divine Son of God.

CONCLUSION

The Gospel of John again plays a prominent role in Athanasius' type of scriptural argumentation, helping to win the trust of his audience and discredit his opponents. In interpreting Hebrews 3:2 'he was faithful to his maker', John 1:1 and 1:3 are used as evidence that the Son cannot have the Father as the Maker of his being. Athanasius therefore asserts that Hebrews 3:2 must be related to the incarnate state of the Saviour, the time that the Word became flesh (Jn 1:14). This remains the basic mode of reasoning throughout the whole *Oration*. Though Athanasius suggests that he is sensitive to the context, his explanation of the word πιστός runs counter to the flow of Hebrews 3:2.

In interpreting Acts 2:36 'he made him Lord and Christ' in an acceptable way for his theology, Athanasius appeals to several Johannine texts to argue that Peter spoke these words to a Jewish audience, who did not expect the Son to be divine. He employs the figure of *sermocinatio* to add to the credibility of his interpretation, while his situation of Peter's speech against the Jews confronts the reader with a firm choice between Athanasian Christianity and heresy.

As regards Proverbs 8:22, which is discussed in the rest of *CA* II, Johannine texts function prominently in both the preliminary remarks (*CA* II 18b–43) as well as the actual exposition (*CA* II 44–82). Athanasius is strongly polemical in the section *CA* II 18b–43, mustering many Johannine texts as evidence for the Son's involvement in creation, which would exclude his creaturely status. Especially Jn 1:3 and 5:17 feature prominently in *CA* II 18b–43, Jn 1:3 sometimes together with the Aristotelian concept of an 'efficient cause'. Besides scriptural argumentation, he includes unfavourable comparisons between Arians and Jews and heretics and an excursus on holy baptism to reinforce his argument. Via this strategy, he prepares the interpretation of ἔκτισε (Prv 8:22) beforehand to such an extent that the outcome of his discussion is already determined before the actual exposition on the text. Athanasius advocates the existence of a custom of Scripture that distinguishes between clear sayings about the Son's nature and the proverbial or hidden sayings concerning the Son's incarnate state. Primarily basing himself on John's Gospel, Athanasius demonstrates that statements without an expression of purpose relate to the Son's ontology and statements with an expression of purpose relate to the Son's incarnate state. He further argues for the logical priority of begetting over creating and the title only-begotten over firstborn to defend his interpretation. He also provides an alternative explanation of Proverbs 8:22, claiming that it is not about the creation of the divine Wisdom, but indicates the imprint of Wisdom in all of creation (*CA* II 78–82). The common ground between both interpretations is that the Arian inference that the Son is ontologically a κτίσμα from the word ἔκτισε is incorrect. Jn 1:14 plays a prominent role, although it cannot be said that this text or other biblical texts have an exclusively theological meaning, because they are regularly quoted to disprove precisely the Arian position.

CHAPTER SIX.
ANALYSIS OF *ORATION* III

Most scholars date *Oration* III a few years later than *Orations* I-II and argue that the theological fronts had somewhat moved during these years. While *Orations* I-II are dated to 339–340, *Oration* III is sometimes dated just before or after the Council of Serdica 342/343.[1] Other scholars determine the date less specifically, but suggest that it was written around 345 or briefly afterwards. The later date of this *Oration* might also be observed in Athanasius' distinct use of Scripture. The *Oration* is often subdivided into three parts: *CA* III 1–25; 26–58a and 58b–67.

---

[1] See Abramowski, "Die dritte Arianerrede," 390; Markus Vinzent, "C.I.3.1 Orationes contra Arianos I-III," in *Athanasius Handbuch*, ed. Peter Gemeinhardt (Tübingen: Mohr Siebeck, 2011), 197–200. In 342/343, Constans, the Emperor of the Western part of the Roman Empire, urged his brother Constantius to convene a council of both Eastern and Western bishops in Serdica. A delegation of both Eastern and Western bishops went to Serdica, but the two parties never gathered together in an official meeting. One of the issues that divided the bishops of East and West concerned Athanasius' participation in the council. While the Westerners insisted on Athanasius' presence, the Eastern bishops convened in Philippopolis, a place near Serdica, because they refused to participate in a council together with the banished Athanasius. For this reason, scholars often speak of a 'Western' and 'Eastern' Council of Serdica. See Barnes, *Athanasius and Constantius*, 71–81; Ayres, *Nicaea and its Legacy*, 122–26. The correspondence of the Council of Serdica is given in AW 3.1.3, 179–279.

CA III 1–25: 'Self-evident' Johannine Texts Discussed

In the first part, *CA* III 1–25, Athanasius discusses the interpretation of several Johannine texts (14:10; 17:3; 10:30 and 17:11,20–23). Jn 10:30 and 14:10 were key texts in Athanasius' argument in *Orations* I-II and often served to support his theological position. In *Oration* III, he establishes the credibility of this interpretation, by proving its consistency with other parts of Scripture and an appeal to reason. Polemical terminology is prominent again, without any anticipated change in attitude as a result of the first two *Orations*. Athanasius writes the opening words of *CA* III 1 in deliberate continuity with the former two by referring to several themes discussed in them.[2] The polemical tone also returns from the start: he remarks at the beginning that the Ariomaniacs 'once made up their mind and revolted against the truth', are 'sprinkled with the serpent's poison', and that their theology is vomited 'from the depth of their irreligious hearts'.[3] Constantine's letter to Arius (Urk. 34 = Dok.27) demonstrates some language that runs parallel to Athanasius' words on the Arians. Constantine stated about Arius: 'hear what he, writing with a pen distilling poison, recently has explained to me... [Arius] left unsaid nothing at all of bitterness, but he opened the whole – as someone may say – treasury of madness.'[4] The focus on poison and madness are putting Arius in a most unfavourable light. Constantine's letter may well have provided some vocabulary for Athanasius' polemical language; at the very least, the parallels are remarkable.

CA III 1–6a: Jn 14:10

In this section of the *Orations* it is obvious that an exposition of Scripture is always supplemented with an interpretation and guided by reasoning and other interpretive means, because Athanasius has to establish the correct interpretation of the Johannine key texts that he understood self-evidently in *Orations* I-II.

---

[2] References to Prv 8:22, Heb 1:4, Heb 3:2 and the title firstborn. In *CA* II 18, Athanasius provides a similar summary.

[3] *CA* III 1 (305,1–306,2. 8–11); tr. NPNF, adapted. On his use of polemical terminology, see Meijering, *Die dritte Rede*, I:29.

[4] Urk. 34 (70,6-10); tr. Coleman-Norton.

In Jn 14:10 Jesus elaborates on his claim that he shows the Father:

> Do you not believe that I am in the Father and the Father is in me? The words that I say to you I do not speak on my own; but the Father who dwells in me does his works. Believe me that I am in the Father and the Father is in me; but if you do not, then believe me because of the works themselves. Very truly, I tell you, the one who believes in me will also do the works that I do and, in fact, will do greater works than these, because I am going to the Father. (Jn 14:10–12)

Athanasius solely focuses on the words 'I in the Father and the Father in me' (ἐγὼ ἐν τῷ πατρὶ καὶ ὁ πατὴρ ἐν ἐμοί). In CA III 1–2, he first engages with Asterius' arguments why these words are unique to the Son and inapplicable to any other. In CA III 3–6, he draws the consequences from this interpretation, tightly relating Jn 14:10 to Jn 10:30; 14:9; 16:15. In that section, he develops a Trinitarian argument concerning the Son's divinity. He argues for the essential unity of Father and Son, and frequently alludes to Johannine material to assert his view.

In claiming the Son's uniqueness from the words of Jn 14:10, Athanasius asserts that the Arians 'malign our Lord's words: "I in the Father and the Father in me" (Jn 14:10) saying, "How can the one be contained in the other and the other in the one?" or "How at all can the Father who is the greater be contained in the Son who is the lesser?" (Jn 14:28).'[5] Athanasius argues that Jesus' statement 'I in the Father and the Father in me' does not suggest that Father and Son 'are poured into each other ... as in the case of empty vessels, so that the Son fills the emptiness of the Father and the Father the hollowness of the Son, and each of them is not full and perfect.'[6] He intimates that his opponents' understanding of the Father-Son relationship is materialistic.[7] In contrast, he reasons that the words of Jn 14:10 indicate that Father and Son are equals, because: (a) the Father is not in need of anyone else, and

---

[5] CA III 1 (306,10–14); tr. NPNF.
[6] CA III 1 (307,25–29); tr. NPNF, adapted.
[7] CA III 1 (307,28–29). See CA I 15; I 21; II 34; Syn 42; 45; 51; Decr 22; 24 and Meijering, *Die dritte Rede*, I:31.

(b) if said by an unequal Son, the Father needs the Son to become full. However, two perfect persons do not fill each other, so the Son must be the fullness of the Father.[8]

Secondly, the statement 'I in the Father and the Father in me' shows the Son's uniqueness, because God's presence in the Son is different from his presence in the saints, that is, human believers. Athanasius discusses Asterius' claim that Jesus' words in Jn 14:10 are not spoken on his own account, but on behalf of the Father's power. He introduces Asterius as defender of the heresy, the Sophist, and the one who deceives others 'with persuasive words of wisdom' (cf. 1 Cor 2:4).[9] Athanasius discredits Asterius' words by suggesting that Asterius used empty rhetoric, in contrast to Paul's usage of honest and straightforward words. Athanasius claims that Asterius said in a deceiving manner about the Son, thus discrediting Asterius' interpretation of these Johannine words from the start:

> For it is clear that he himself has said that he is in the Father and again the Father in Him (cf. Jn 14:10; 10:38), while he said that neither the word that came out of him is his, but that of his Father (cf. Jn 5:30; 14:24), nor the works are his, but that of the Father who granted him the power (cf. Jn 5:36; 6:37; 10:37; 14:12).[10]

Asterius appeals to the Johannine agency theme to claim that the Son is dependent on the power of the Father (5:30) and does the works of the Father (5:36; 6:37; 10:37), to assert that Jn 14:10 does not pertain to the Son's eternal divinity. In Jn 14:12, in the same context as the words 'I in the Father and the Father in me', Jesus claims that the disciples will perform even greater works than he himself. Asterius thus proposes a radical different reading of Jn 14:10 that seems to be supported by the immediate context. The Christological tensions in John's Gospel between the

---

[8] *CA* III 1 (307,29–30).

[9] *CA* III 2 (307,1; 308,6. 8). The label 'Sophist' enables Athanasius to link Asterius to the Greek sophistical tradition. Antony states in *VA* 78 that 'we are supported by faith in Christ, but you by professional logomachies'. See also Meijering, *Die dritte Rede*, I:42.

[10] Athanasius, *CA* III 2 (307,1–308,5) = Asterius, fr. 38 (Vinzent).

egalitarian and subordinationist relations with the Father are thus understood in radical different ways: in Athanasius' case to assert the egalitarian and in Asterius' case the radical subordinationist.[11] Asterius emphasises Jesus as living by the Father's power to safeguard the singularity of God's being. Jesus is in full harmony with the power of the Father, instead of ontologically united with the Father.

Athanasius attacks the ultimate consequences of Asterius' view: if Asterius were right, every human could rightly say these words of the Son.

> For if the words that the Son spoke, are not his own but the Father's, as well as his works (cf. Jn 10:37), when he said, 'I am in the Father and the Father in me' (Jn 14:10) (...) it is plain that, according to Asterius, a statement like this must be common to all, so that everyone of them can say: 'I in the Father and the Father in me' (Jn 14:10).[12]

He thus suggests that Asterius' reading ignores the distinction between the Son and humans completely, with the result that Asterius cannot but assert that the Son is, 'like others, only one of many (ἐκ πολλῶν ἕνα)'.[13] Athanasius further inserts several references to other biblical saints, arguing that, even though there is correspondence between God's words and those of the saints as a result of God's power working in the saints, it is impossible for them to claim to have a mutual relationship as Jesus mentions in Jn 14:10. This line of reasoning meets a crucial point of Asterius' position, for Asterius had emphasised God's ultimate singularity to such an extent that he called both Christ and the grasshopper (cf. Joel 2:25) powers of God.[14] Athanasius therefore objects to Asterius' explanation, because the Lord did not say: 'I *too* am in

---

[11] See Anderson, "The Having-Sent-Me Father," 41.

[12] *CA* III 2 (308,16–18. 26–28); tr. NPNF, adapted. In line 17, πῶς is omitted, in line with Athanase, Rousseau, and Lafontaine, *Les trois discours contre les ariens*, 231 n.2.

[13] *CA* III 2 (308,28–29).

[14] Asterius, frs. 32, 46, 66–68 (Vinzent). Cf. *CA* II 37; 40 and pp 208–215 above.

the Father, and the Father is in me *too*.'[15] Although Asterius would not say that everyone could say with equal right 'I in the Father and the Father in me', this is the extreme consequence of Asterius' position. Meijering therefore concludes that the fundamental difference between Athanasius and his opponents has been mentioned already in the very beginning, in a way that was convincing to Athanasius, but not to his opponents.[16]

Athanasius rejected Asterius' interpretation of Jn 14:10 in *CA* III 1–2 by engaging with excerpts of his work. In *CA* III 3–6, he elaborates on the implications of his interpretation of Jn 14:10 and on the indivisible unity of Father and Son within the one divinity (θεότης). Athanasius resorts to the image of light and its radiance to describe the indivisible unity between Father and Son.

> Since the form and divinity of the Father is the Son's being, it follows that the Son is in the Father and the Father in the Son. For therefore he has also, after he first said: 'I and the Father are one (Jn 10:30)', added, 'I in the Father and the Father in me (Jn 14:10)', thus showing the identity of the divinity and the unity of essence.[17]

As in the first two *Orations*, Athanasius refers again to both Jn 10:30 and 14:10 as interpretive keys to assert the unity between Father and Son. Athanasius further alludes to Jn 16:15 to assert that Father and Son have everything in common. While their names Father and Son safeguard their distinctness, their 'nature is one, (...) and all that is the Father's, is the Son's (cf. Jn 16:15).'[18]

The Son is not begotten from outside, but is the offspring of the Father, and therefore the same as God. For 'he and the Father are one (cf. Jn 10:30) in propriety and peculiarity of nature, and in the identity of the one divinity'.[19] He inserts a string of

---

[15] *CA* III 3 (309,1–4). Italics added.

[16] Meijering, *Die dritte Rede*, I:49–50.

[17] *CA* III 3 (309,13–17); tr. NPNF, adapted.

[18] *CA* III 4 (310,4–6); tr. NPNF, adapted. On the distinct use of Jn 16:15, compare with Marcellus (frs. 74–75 (Vinzent)) and Eusebius of Caesarea (*ET* I 20 (Kl./H. 97,26). See further Morales, *La théologie trinitaire*, 408–12.

[19] *CA* III 4 (310,9–10); tr. NPNF, adapted.

Scripture citations to assert that 'the divinity (θεότης) of the Son is that of the Father'.[20]

> It is proven by what the Scriptures say about the Son: he is God, 'and the Word was God' (Jn 1:1), Ruler of all ... (Rev 1:8), Lord ... (1 Cor 8:6), he is Light, 'I am the Light' (Jn 8:12) and he takes away sins ... (Mk 2:10). 'For "everything," says the Son himself, "everything the Father has, is mine" (Jn 16:15) and again "and mine is yours" (Jn 17:10).'[21]

By inserting this string of passages Athanasius brings into presence those texts that support his position, and it furthermore demonstrates his knowledge of the Scriptures.[22] This might have won the trust of his audience, since accurate knowledge of Scripture is a highly esteemed virtue for all participants in the fourth-century debate.[23]

In *CA* III 5, Athanasius states affirmatively concerning Jn 14:10 that the attributes of the Father are the Son's too. This can only indirectly be derived from Scripture (cf. Jn 16:15) in a way that goes beyond John's or any other biblical writer's thought. His claim that Scripture teaches this is also disputed by his opponents, so that Athanasius resorts to scriptural reasoning, deriving the implications from his appeal to Scripture. He claims that 'the Son is the true offspring of the Father's being' (τῆς οὐσίας τοῦ πατρὸς ἴδιον ὢν γέννημα ὁ υἱός), who possesses the attributes of the Father.[24] For when the Son said:

> 'I and the Father are one' (Jn 10:30), he added, 'that you may know that I am in the Father and the Father in me' (Jn 10:38 and Jn 14:10). Moreover, he has added this again, 'he that has

---

[20] *CA* III 4 (310,14–15); tr. NPNF, adapted.
[21] *CA* III 4 (310,17–23); tr. NPNF, adapted.
[22] Cf. *CA* I 12; 54; II 24; 55; III 29–30.
[23] For Asterius' use of Scripture, see Roderic L. Mullen, "Asterius 'the Sophist' of Cappadocia: Citations from the Gospel of John as Attested in the Theological Fragments," in *Studies on the Text of the New Testament and Early Christianity. Essays in Honor of Michael W. Holmes*, ed. Daniel M. Gurtner, Juan Hernández Jr., and Paul Foster, New Testament Tools, Studies and Documents 50 (Leiden; Boston: Brill, 2015), 239–57.
[24] *CA* III 5 (310,5–311,6).

seen me, has seen the Father' (Jn 14:9) and there is one and
the same sense in these three passages. For he who in this
sense understands that the Son and the Father are one, knows
that he is in the Father and the Father in the Son ... [and] is
convinced that 'he that has seen the Son, has seen the Father'
(Jn 14:9).[25]

Athanasius deliberately chooses to understand Jn 14:10 in light
of Jn 10:30 and 14:9. For in contrast to him, Eusebius of Caesarea
had characterised the collocation of Jn 14:9–10 and Jn 10:30 as
'Sabellianising' less than a decade before Athanasius writes these
words. Eusebius argued that the Son's unity with the Father consists of a 'community of glory' (κοινωνίαν τῆς δόξης),[26] instead of a
community of being (οὐσία) or nature (φύσις). Athanasius emphasises that his understanding of the texts avoids materialistic notions and dissociates himself explicitly from the heretic Sabellius
in the preceding chapter.[27]

Athanasius' discussion on the divine unity also bears similarities to Eusebius' account in his *Ecclesiastical Theology*.[28] They both
compare the unity of Father and Son with an emperor and his
image, asserting that someone who worships the image of the emperor worships the emperor himself, because of the unity between
emperor and his image.[29] Athanasius asserts that the Son is the

---

[25] *CA* III 5 (311,6–12); tr. NPNF, adapted.

[26] *ET* III 19 (Kl./H. 180,11–16; 30–31).

[27] *CA* III 4 (309,1–310,5), cf. *CA* III 36 (347,1–7). Sabellius was a third-
century heretic, who maintained that there is no distinction at all between Father and Son. Franz Dünzl, *A Brief History of the Doctrine of the
Trinity in the Early Church*, trans. John Bowden (London: T&T Clark,
2007), 21–40; Jaroslav Pelikan, *The Christian Tradition: A History of the
Development of Doctrine*, vol. 1, 5 vols. (Chicago: University of Chicago
Press, 1971), 176–80.

[28] On the nuances of the debate in the 330s and 340s, see Mark DelCogli-
ano, "Eusebian Theologies of the Son as the Image of God before 341,"
JECS 14 (2006): 459–84; Spoerl, "Athanasius and the Anti-Marcellan
Controversy," 34–55.

[29] Eusebius states that in the same way as honour to the image of the
king is worship to the king himself, 'the Father would be honoured
through the Son .... For "he who has seen" the Son "has seen the Father,"

Father's Image and reflects the Father. He employs the figure of speech *fictio personae* (*prosopopoeia*), by imagining that the image of the king, a non-living object, would speak. He asserts that this image of a king might rightly say to its spectators: 'I and the king are one (cf. Jn 10:30), for I am in him, and he in me (cf. Jn 14:10); and what you see in me, that you perceive in him, and what you have seen in him, that you perceive in me (cf. Jn 14:9).'[30] In the *prosopopoeia* of the king's image, the three Johannine key texts, Jn 10:30 and 14:9, 10, are present in an allusive way. By the use of this figure of speech, Athanasius is able to subtly direct the focus of these Johannine passages and to formulate his interpretation of the passage in a way that closely aligns with his own theology. As a result, Athanasius deduces from the *prosopopoeia* that it 'is necessary that the divinity and likeness (ἰδιότης) of the Father is the being of the Son. And this is meant by the words "who was in the form of God" (Phil 2:6) and "the Father is in me" (Jn 14:10)'.[31]

CA III 6 likewise contains several allusions to John's Gospel in which the biblical texts are more closely aligned to Athanasius' theological position. He asserts that 'the works he works are the Father's works' (cf. Jn 5:17; *CA* II 20, 29), and that therefore, 'he who looks at the Son, sees the Father (Jn 14:9)'.[32] He claims that the Son is (1) the fullness of the Father, (2) the Father's form (εἶδος), and (3) that the 'properness and Godhead (ἰδιότης καὶ

(Jn 14:9) seeing the unbegotten godhead, as in an image and mirror, impressed in the Son.' *ET* II 7 (Kl./H. 106,13–18); tr. McCarthy Spoerl and Vinzent, adapted. Cf. *DE* V 4,10. A possible common origin might be located in Irenaeus. See Irenaeus, *AH* IV 30 and Meijering, *Die dritte Rede*, I:68; see also Jon M. Robertson, *Christ as Mediator: A Study of the Theologies of Eusebius of Caesarea, Marcellus of Ancyra and Athanasius of Alexandria*, Oxford Theological Monographs (Oxford: Oxford University Press, 2007), 53–60, 177–92.

[30] *CA* III 5 (311,19–21); tr. NPNF, adapted. This figure of speech appears in *CA* II 74; III 8; 34; 36. See also Lausberg, *Handbook*, 369–72 (par 826–29).

[31] *CA* III 5 (311,23–24); tr. NPNF, adapted.

[32] *CA* III 6 (312,6–8).

θεότης) of the Father is in the Son', so that they are inseparable.[33]
He cites John 14:10 and 10:30 again and alludes subsequently to
John 16:15 and 5:23 to assure their relation:

> whoever hears and beholds that what is said of the Father is
> also said of the Son (...) will correctly understand the words,
> as I said before: 'I in the Father, and the Father in me' and 'I
> and the Father are one'. For the Son is such as the Father is,
> because he has all that is the Father's (cf. Jn 16:15). (...) For
> he who worships and honours the Son, worships and honours
> the Father in the Son (cf. Jn 5:23), for the divinity is one.[34]

Athanasius thus conceives the relation between Father and Son as
one of inseparability and harmony. The persuasiveness of his references to the Johannine texts is dependent upon acceptance of
the underlying rationales. Only if the strong claims Athanasius
makes are accepted, can Jn 14:10 be fully understood in the sense
that he advocates. The fact that Athanasius alludes to rather than
quotes Johannine passages at this point, indicates, I believe, that
Athanasius' view of the Son's nature is taken further than the actual text can warrant. Although the seeds of his doctrine of the
Son are present in John, Athanasius' reflections move further than
the evangelist John envisaged. For although several modern commentators read Jn 16:15 in close connection to 5:23, as revealing
Jesus' identity, they emphasise that Jn 16:15 is clearly concerned
with Jesus' mission for his disciples, something which is completely absent in Athanasius' thought.[35]

Athanasius' appeal to Scripture is therefore more than
merely an appeal to John 14:9–10. While modern commentators
hold that John contains a seed for the co-equality of the Trinity,[36]
and that John regards Jesus as divine, John conceives a stronger
relation between the sending Father and the obedient Son, or in
other words, a relation from the viewpoint of Jesus' humanity.
The evangelist carefully presents Jesus as completely obedient to

---

[33] *CA* III 6 (312,9–11).
[34] *CA* III 6 (312,11–12. 14–16. 21–22); tr. NPNF, adapted.
[35] Barrett, *John*, 259–60, 489–91; Carson, *John*, 541–42; Lincoln, *John*,
421; Lindars, *John*, 506.
[36] Barrett, *John*, 92; Lincoln, *John*, 306.

the Father, together with a very close identification between Jesus and YHWH. Athanasius goes further than what John states concerning the relation between Father and Son, since he thinks primarily of the divine Father-Son relationship.[37] John, in all his remarks on the divinity of Jesus, shows him to be dependent on and in harmony with the Father. While Athanasius strongly highlights the Johannine egalitarian notion, he downplays the equally important Johannine notion of Jesus' dependency on and obedience to the Father.

CA III 6b–9: Jn 17:3

Athanasius next considers the unity of God. Athanasius clearly discusses the theme with Jesus' statement 'And this is eternal life, that they may know you, the only true God, and Jesus Christ whom you have sent (Jn 17:3)' in mind. Because this text distinguishes between the only true God and Jesus Christ, Eusebian theologians distinguished between Father and Son to maintain God's ultimate singularity. Eusebius of Caesarea argued that while the Son is 'true' God, the title 'only true' God is exclusively attributable to the Father.[38] Asterius' work does not mention Jn 17:3 in its fragments. However, it is highly unlikely that Asterius would deviate from Eusebius of Caesarea on this point, so that the combination of the attribute 'only true' is something Asterius certainly would have exclusively attributed to the Unbegotten one.[39] This is also seen in the difference between the creedal statements of Nicaea (325) and Antioch (341). While the Nicene Creed had expressly stated: 'God from God, light from light, true God from true

---

[37] Brown, *John*, I:214; cf. Barrett, *John*, 259.

[38] 'And even if the Savior himself teaches that the Father is the only true God, saying "that they may know you the only true God," (Jn 17:3) one should not hesitate to confess that he [the Son] is true God and that he has this status as in an image, so that the addition of the word *only* applies to the Father alone as to [the] archetype of the image.' *ET* II 23 (Kl./H. 133,25–29); tr. McCarthy Spoerl and Vinzent; italics original. See further *DE* V 17 (Heikel 240,16–23) *CM* I 4 (Kl./H. 28,21–26); *ET* I 11 (Kl./H. 69,35–70,25); *ET* II 22 (Kl./H. 132,7–19).

[39] Vinzent, *Asterius*, 44, cf. 168–73, 199–201 and Asterius, frs. 10, 23–27 (Vinzent). See also *CA* II 37 and pp 208–215 above.

God',[40] the Council of Antioch, where Asterius had a prominent role, omits the qualifier 'true' in its creedal statements.[41]

Jn 17:3 was a potentially troublesome text for Athanasius. The task for Athanasius was to find a satisfactory explanation for the words 'only true God' that could support his theology of the eternal divinity of the Son. His approach is twofold: in *CA* III 6b–8a, he discusses the 'oneness' of God, arguing that the oneness separates God from idols, but not from his Son, who is in complete harmony with his Father. In *CA* III 8b–9, he includes 'true' in his discussion, arguing that the words 'only true God' do not exclude the Son from God's being.

In *CA* III 6, Athanasius introduces the theme by citing many texts that claim God's exclusivity: 'When the Father is called "only God" (Jn 17:3) and that "God is one" (1 Cor 8:6) and "I am and there is no other God besides me" (cf. Deut 32:39) ... it is not said to exclude the Son. Certainly not! For he is also the one and only and first.'[42] He argues that these texts would only disprove the Son's eternal divinity if there were rivalry (ἅμιλλα) between Father and Son, but this is not the case, since the Son reveals the Father (Mt 11:27), and he who sees him, sees the Father (cf. Jn 14:9) and he glorifies the Father (cf. Lk 18:19), and he affirms that there is one God (Mc 12:29).[43] Furthermore,

> to the multitudes, he [the Son] said: 'I came down from heaven, not to do my own will, but the will of' the Father 'who sent me' (Jn 6:38) and he taught the disciples: 'My Father is greater than I' (Jn 14:28) and 'he that honours me, honours Him who sent me' (Jn 5:23). And if the Son is such to his own Father, what is the contention, that one must speculate about such passages [such as Jn 17:3]?[44]

On the basis of both synoptic and Johannine material, Athanasius infers that there is complete harmony between Father and Son. The Son's complete obedience to and agreement and harmony

---

[40] Urk. 24 (51,7–8).

[41] See Anatolios, *Retrieving Nicaea*, 53; Hanson, *Search*, 284.

[42] *CA* III 6 (312,25–313,29); cf. *CA* III 7 (313,1–4).

[43] *CA* III 7 (313,5–6. 9–14).

[44] *CA* III 7 (313,14–314,18).

with the Father suggest that the words 'only God' have another referent than the Son, since the Son is not competing. Instead, the proclamation of God's oneness solely functions to exclude the false gods or idols. Athanasius' use of John's mission and obedience theme in this passage shows a marked difference from the first two *Orations*.[45] Although Athanasius once cited Jn 6:38–40 in full in *CA* II, he ignored the potential implications for the Son's ontology.[46] Similarly, Jn 14:28 was mentioned in *CA* I 13 to establish it as proof of the Son's foreknowledge, and in the discussion on Heb 1:4, where Athanasius anticipated the text by drawing a qualitative distinction between μείζων and κρείττων (see *CA* I 54–64). Athanasius' use of John in this section demonstrates an increasing awareness of the need to account for obedience texts (Jn 6:38) and Jesus' acknowledgement that the Father is greater (Jn 14:28), basically ignored in *CA* I-II. In his argument on the unity of God, he still regards the Father-Son relationship as eternal, but he articulates more clearly that the Father is the source of the Son. Athanasius' shifting usage of John's Gospel might be connected with the second Creed of Antioch (341). In this creed, Jesus is called 'mediator between God and man' with reference to Jn 6:38.[47] Although a relation is difficult to prove, it might have triggered Athanasius to interpret this text more explicitly within the framework of his theology.

---

[45] Jesus as the one sent by the Father is a dominant theme in the Gospel of John, while it is not found in this way with the verb πέμπω in the synoptic gospels. See Jn 4:34; 5:23–24, 30, 37; 6:38–39, 44; 7:16, 18, 28, 33; 8:16, 18, 26, 29; 9:4; 12:44–45, 49; 14:24; 15:21; 16:5; 20:21 for places where Jesus declares himself as the one sent by the Father. Five passages in John show a somewhat different portrayal, as Jesus is not only the one sent, but also the sending authority: Jn 13:20; 14:26; 15:26; 16:7; 20:21. See also Meijering, *Die dritte Rede*, I:85–87. See also pp 62–75 above.

[46] See *CA* II 54–55; II 66–67

[47] Dok 41.4 (Brennecke 146,11–16). Athanasius quotes this document in *Syn* 23,2–10 (Opitz 249,11 – 250,4). For the critical text and German translation, see AW 3.1.3, 144–48. See also J. N. D. Kelly, *Early Christian Creeds*, 3rd ed. (Londen: Longman, 1972), 263–74.

In *CA* III 8b, the qualifier 'true' in Jn 17:3 is introduced into the discussion. Athanasius refers to the notion of the creation through the Word to assert that the 'monotheistic texts' are directed against the idols, not against the Word of God.[48] He mentions the time and occasion when the exclusiveness of God was proclaimed:

> God did not speak such words to Adam at the beginning, though His Word was with Him (cf. Jn 1;1), by whom all things came to be (cf. Jn 1:1, 3). For there was no need, because there were not yet idols. But when men rebelled against the truth, ... then the need arose for such words, for the negation of gods that were not.[49]

The occasion of the monotheistic text: rebellion against the truth, is Athanasius' introduction of the transition in the discussion of the passage. In this way, he explicitly refers to the words only true God (Jn 17:3). He remarks in *CA* III 9: 'If then the Father is called the only true God, this is said not to the rejection of Him who said: "I am the Truth", (Jn 14:6) but to the denial of those who are not true by nature (εἰς ἀναίρεσιν μὴ πεφυκότων ἀληθινῶν), as the Father and His Word are.'[50] For that reason 'the Lord himself at once added: "And Jesus Christ whom you have sent" (Jn 17:3)', to demonstrate that he is not a creature (κτίσμα), but 'the true offspring of the true Father'.[51] Athanasius established in *CA* III 6b–8a that the proclamation of the existence of only one God separates God from idols, who rob God of his honour. The expression 'only true God' hence does not exclude the Son, who is the true offspring of the true Father. The reference to Jesus Christ as the Truth (Jn 14:6) is isolated from the context in John to maintain Athanasius' assertion that God's singularity does not render the Son subordinate to the Father, because the concept of truth is understood as indicating the Son's eternity and unchangeability.[52]

---

[48] Cf. *CA* III 8 (314,18–315,24).

[49] *CA* III 8 (315,22–26); tr. NPNF, adapted.

[50] *CA* III 9 (315,1–3); tr. NPNF, adapted

[51] *CA* III 9 (315,3–4. 6–7); tr. NPNF, adapted.

[52] See *CA* I 12; I 20; I 36: II 20. Meijering points to the Platonic background of the connection between truth and unchangeability in Plato,

Athanasius avoids the question posed by the Eusebians, whether 'only true God' can be attributed to the Son. Athanasius prefers to call the Son 'a natural and true offspring from the Father'.[53] He simply ignores the terminological distinction that the Eusebians made, arguing that 'when God says: "Only I stretch out the heavens" (Isa 44:24), it is made clear to everyone that in the Only is signified also the Word of the Only, in whom "all things came into being" and without whom "nothing came into being" (Jn 1:3)'.[54]

Athanasius takes up a variety of Johannine texts, to argue that Jesus' words 'only true God' in Jn 17:3 solely exclude the idols that challenged the oneness of God. He infers from Jn 17:3b that Jesus Christ is not excluded from the divine honour in order to arrive at the conclusion that 'only true God' includes God's own Word.[55] Interestingly enough, Andrew Lincoln arrives at basically the same conclusion concerning 17:3, although he does not suggest that Athanasius' emphasis on the eternal divinity of the Son is not as such present in John. Lincoln states that Jesus' identification by John 'does not entail any abrogation of monotheism', because the evangelist holds that 'Jesus in his relationship as Son to the Father is intrinsic to his one God's identity. (...) It is not the case then that in glorifying Jesus God shares the divine glory with some lesser being. Rather the exaltation and glorification of Jesus displays the glory of the one God.'[56]

CA III 10–16: Jn 10:30

In *CA* III 10–16, Athanasius discusses the words: 'I and the Father are one' (Jn 10:30) with the question whether it indicates a unity

---

Timaeus 29C. See Meijering, *Die dritte Rede*, I:98–99. On a comparison of the use of Jn 14:6 in Eusebius and Marcellus, see pp 126–29 above.

[53] *CA* III 9 (316,18–19); tr. NPNF, adapted.

[54] *CA* III 9 (315,9–13); tr. NPNF, adapted.

[55] Cf. *CA* II 37–38, where Athanasius argues against Asterius' doctrine of two Words.

[56] Lincoln, *John*, 435.

of will or a unity of being between Father and Son.[57] Eusebians interpret this verse in the first sense: unity of will. Asterius' view is phrased in two ways, by both of his opponents Marcellus and Athanasius. According to Marcellus, Asterius regards the unity between Father and Son thus: 'Because of their exact agreement (συμφωνίαν) in all [their] words and actions [the Saviour] says: "I and the Father are one" (Jn 10:30).'[58] Athanasius describes Asterius' position slightly differently: the Son is 'in all respects in agreement (σύμφωνος) with Him, declaring doctrines which are the same'.[59] Athanasius opts for the alternative interpretation of Jn 10:30: the unity between Father and Son is a unity of being. Athanasius basically puts forward three arguments: (1) agreeing with God is not the same as being one with God, (2) the Son's unity with the Father is more than agreement with the Father and (3) denying a unity of being between Father and Son leads to a non-Christian view.

Athanasius first of all argues that being united with God and in agreement with (σύμφωνος) God is not the same. Powers and thrones (Col 1:16), martyrs, apostles and prophets have all acted in accordance with God's will and are in that sense σύμφωνος with Him. When Paul exhorts the Ephesians to 'be imitators of God' (Eph 5:2), he does expect them to conform to God's teachings. Many followed Paul, just as he followed Christ, but none of them

> is Word or Wisdom or Only-begotten Son or Image; nor did any one of them dare (ἀπετόλμησεν) to say 'I and the Father are one' (Jn 10:30) or 'I in the Father and the Father in me' (Jn 14:10). About all these creatures it is said: 'Who is like You among the gods, O Lord?' (Ex 15:11) and 'Who shall be

---

[57] See Anatolios, *Retrieving Nicaea*, 33–98; see also Mark DelCogliano, "The Interpretation of John 10:30 in the Third Century: Anti-Monarchian Polemics and the Rise of Grammatical Reading Techniques," *JTI* 6 (2012): 117–38; T. E. Pollard, "The Exegesis of John 10:30 in the Early Trinitarian Controversies," *NTS* 3 (1957): 334–49.

[58] Asterius, fr. 39 (Vinzent) = Eusebius, *CM* II 2 (Kl./H. 37,29–31); cf. frs. 38–42 (Vinzent).

[59] *CA* III 10 (316,4–317,5). Cf. fr. 40 (Vinzent).

likened to the Lord among the sons of Gods? (Ps 89:7)'. But
he is the only true and natural Image of the Father.[60]

Athanasius points to the difference between the Word and creatures that honour God. In *CA* III 6b–9, Athanasius argued that the
monotheistic texts in the Old Testament are said against created
gods, not against God's own Son. However, the Son of God is also
different from creatures that conform to the divine teachings. Although the saints can be σύμφωνος with God, they are not one with
God in the same way as the Son is. Athanasius interprets Jn 10:30
in close relation to Jn 14:10 to assert the reciprocity in the Father-
Son relation. This highlights the crucial difference between the
Son and humans, for humans can only experience harmony with
God because 'the Image and true glory of God, which is his Word,
who afterwards was made flesh for us (cf. Jn 1:14)', dwells in
them.[61] Humans can agree with God's teaching, so that if the Father and Son are one in the same way as humans can be one with
the Father, the Son would not be one with the Father, but would
adhere to the Father's doctrines and teaching (τὰ δὲ δόγματα καὶ ἡ
διδασκαλία).[62] However, the Arian view is wrong, since a teaching
is never equal to a person.

This leads Athanasius to his second argument. The unity of
Father and Son is more than mere harmony, because the likeness
of the Son to the Father is comparable with that of the radiance
to the sun.

> While the Son is like this, therefore when the Son works, the
> Father is the Worker (cf. Jn 5:17), and when the Son comes to
> the saints, the Father is He who comes in the Son, as he prom-
> ised when he said, 'I and my Father will come, and make our
> home with him' (Jn 14:23).[63]

Athanasius thus infers from the cooperation of Father and Son in
Jn 5:17 and 14:23 that the unity in Jn 10:30 should be understood
in an ontological sense. He asserts on the basis of this cooperation

---

[60] *CA* III 10 (318,25–30); tr. NPNF, altered.
[61] *CA* III 10 (318,31–33).
[62] *CA* III 11 (318,4–5).
[63] *CA* III 11 (319,10–16); tr. NPNF, adapted.

of Father and Son that the unity of Father and Son entails much more than merely the Son's agreement with the Father's teaching; both work together, and both dwell together in the Christian saints.[64]

Athanasius elaborates on the cooperative work of Father and Son in the distribution of divine grace.[65] The metaphor of the light and its radiance illustrates that there is only one gift of Father and Son (cf. 1 Cor 1:4).[66] 'For what the light enlightens, that the radiance irradiates; and what the radiance irradiates, its enlightenment is from the light. So also when the Son is seen, the Father is as well, (for he is the Father's radiance) and thus the Father and the Son are one (cf. Jn 10:30).'[67] The image of the sun and its reflection highlights their unity and claims the impossibility of conceiving of the one without the other.

In *CA* III 14, the mutual giving and working of Father and Son is mentioned again. Athanasius asserts that God always speaks through his Word, and similarly,

> what the Word, as not being separate from the Father, nor different and foreign to the Father's essence, works, those are the Father's works (cf. Jn 5:17), and one is the act of creation. And what the Son gives, that is the Father's gift. And he who has seen the Son, knows that, in seeing him (cf. Jn 14:9), he has seen, not an angel, nor one merely greater than angels, nor in short any creature, but the Father Himself. And he who hears the Word, knows that he hears the Father, just as he who is irradiated by the radiance, knows that he is enlightened by the sun.[68]

Johannine references are present in a rather allusive way at this point. This allows Athanasius to direct the interpretation of these words, in order to assert unambiguously that the Word works the works of the Father (Jn 5:17), and that whoever sees the Son, sees

---

[64] Cf. Crump, "Johannine Trinity," 395–412.

[65] *CA* III 12 (320,1–9).

[66] 'I thank my God always on your behalf, for the grace of God which is given you in Christ Jesus' (1 Cor 1:4).

[67] *CA* III 13 (322,22–26); tr. NPNF, adapted. Cf. *CA* II 42 (218,1–6).

[68] *CA* III 14 (323,24–30); tr. NPNF, adapted.

the Father (cf. Jn 14:9). Athanasius further adds the image of the sun and its radiance to illustrate as clearly as possible that the unity between Father and Son greatly exceeds the harmony that humans might enjoy with the Father.

Athanasius adds a third reason why the words 'I and the Father are one' (Jn 10:30) should be understood as pointing to an ontological unity between Father and Son. If this is not confessed, one arrives at a non-Christian view, either Greek, Jewish or heretical. He states that the divine Scriptures provide examples to 'abash the traitorous Jews, and refute the allegation of the Gentiles, who maintain and think, on account of the Trinity, that we profess many gods. For, as the illustration demonstrates, we do not introduce three Origins or three Fathers, as do the followers of Marcion and Manichaeus.'[69] Despite the wide variety within these groups, Athanasius lumps them together because they all deny the essential unity and distinctness of Father and Son that Athanasius reads in Jn 10:30.

In fact, Athanasius' reasoning is a clear development towards the co-equal Trinity, for the divinity of the Spirit is, albeit quite modestly, a concern as well.[70] He argues that if the Father and the Word or Son are not one in being (οὐσία), the Word or Son cannot be legitimately called Word as God. Athanasius states rather polemically that

> the Ariomaniacs with reason earn the charge of polytheism or else of atheism, because they idly talk of the Son as external and a creature, and again the Spirit as from nothing. For either they will say that the Word is not God or say that he is God, because it is so written, but not proper (ἴδιον) to the Father's

---

[69] *CA* III 15 (323,2–7); tr. NPNF, adapted. Meijering points to the examples in *CA* III 3; the sun and its radiance, and the source and the water. See *Die dritte Rede*, I:148. On the comparison to Jews, Greeks and heretics, see *CA* III 35 (347,9–15).

[70] See *CA* III 15 (324,9–10). In *CA* I-II, the Johannine element that the Son is the Giver of the Spirit was seen as a mark of the Son's divinity, see esp. *CA* I 46–52.

essence, and introduce many [gods] according to their diversity in kinds.[71]

I will first discuss the rational disagreement on this point, and after that consider the value and force of the association of the Arians with Jews, Greeks and certain heretics.

Stead has claimed that Athanasius deliberately reduced the number of options for the relation between God and his Word to make his argument against the Arians work. Whereas Arius thought along the lines of a threefold cosmological scheme, Athanasius deliberately omitted one of them. According to Stead, Arius discussed three options: the Son could be begotten (1) from a source outside God himself, (2) from nothing, or (3) from the Father's substance. Arius and Athanasius agreed that the first option was blasphemous, but Arius probably rejected option 3, because of potential materialistic connotations and division in God. He therefore accepted the second option, 'from nothing', with certain qualifications.[72] Athanasius reduces this threefold scheme to two options, and is rather imprecise concerning the alternatives to a generation from the οὐσία of the Father.[73] Nevertheless, while Athanasius' imprecision is conceded,[74] the option that the Son is produced from nothing casts doubts on the quality of the Son's and Spirit's divinity. While the Arians consider them God in a weaker sense, Athanasius asserts that this leads to a plurality of Gods, or a *de facto* full denial of the Word's divinity. In contrast, Athanasius holds that the Word cannot be separated from the Father, because there is 'only one form of divinity (θεότης), which is also

---

[71] *CA* III 15 (324,9–14); tr. NPNF, adapted. For the charge of atheism, see also *CA* II 43 (219,4–5); III 67 (381,37).

[72] Stead, *Divine Substance*, 235–36.

[73] Stead, *Divine Substance*, 236–38.

[74] It might even have been a factor that led to Athanasius' success in persuading others and being acceptable for a broader group of Christians. Vaggione regards the relatively flexible attitude with differences among the Nicene theologians and their ability to reach a larger audience as key factors in the ultimate decline of non-Nicene theology. He asserts that non-Nicene theology defeated itself because of its non-negotiable stance on imprecise terminology. See Vaggione, *Eunomius of Cyzicus*, 285, 364.

in the Word'.[75] Because the Son is not just from the Father, but the form of the divinity, Athanasius excludes divine plurality. In *CA* III 16, Athanasius' concern for divine unity is further highlighted:

> For there is one God, and not many, and one is his Word, and not many; for the Word is God, (Jn 1:1) and he alone has the Form of the Father (τὸ πατρικὸν εἶδος). Being then such, the Saviour himself confused the Jews with these words: 'And the Father who sent me has Himself testified on my behalf. You have never heard His voice or seen His form (εἶδος), and you do not have His word abiding in you, because you do not believe him whom He has sent.' (Jn 5:37–38) And he has rightly combined the 'Word' with the 'Form' (εἶδος), to show that the Word of God is himself Image and Expression and Form of his Father.[76]

Two Johannine texts feature in Athanasius' assertion that the Word is the form (εἶδος) of the divinity. Jn 1:1 backs up his claim that the Word is God (Jn 1:1). The term form (εἶδος) is used in John 5:37. Athanasius relates form (εἶδος) immediately to Word (λόγος) to emphasise the unity of Father and Word. He subsequently connects the attribute 'Form' to the vision of Jacob (Gen 32:31, LXX), to argue that the divine revelation that Jacob has seen is the Son 'who said: "He that has seen me has seen the Father" (Jn 14:9), and "I in the Father and the Father in me" (Jn 14:10) and "I and the Father are one" (Jn 10:30)'.[77] Carson also mentions the connection between the vision of Jacob and John 5:37, to assert that 'Jesus is the manifestation of God'.[78] However, it takes some inferences to go from use of the term 'Form' in Jn 5:37 to arrive at Athanasius' position that the one Form of the divinity is present in the Father and the Word. This terminological precision was not required or even taken into consideration in John's Gospel itself.

---

[75] *CA* III 15 (324,16).
[76] *CA* III 16 (325,25–32); tr. NPNF.
[77] *CA* III 16 (325,35–326,40); tr. NPNF.
[78] Carson, *John*, 262.

In his discussion of John 10:30, he also compares the Arians to the broad category of Jews, Greeks and heretics. At several places in the *Orations* Athanasius compares the Arians to one of these groups, but at this point he mentions all three groups. The comparison of the Arians with the Jews is most obvious. At the end of John 10, the chapter of the text under discussion, the evangelist states that the 'Jews took up stones again to stone him' (31) and that 'they tried to arrest him again, but he escaped from their hands' (39). Although Barrett holds that the attempt at stoning should not necessarily be understood as a sign that Jesus claimed to be God,[79] it is plausible to understand the attempt to stone Jesus as a response to Jesus' claim to divinity. Carson disagrees with Barrett,[80] and it is plausible that Athanasius understood the Jn 10:31, 39 likewise as responses to Jesus' claim to divinity in Jn 10:30. Early Christian writers regularly contrasted the Jewish and Christian views on Jesus. In *Against Celsus*, Origen characterizes a position that is comparable to the Arian one as Jewish,[81] and shortly before the writing of the *Orations*, Eusebius of Caesarea had discredited Marcellus of Ancyra's theology by labelling it as Jewish.[82] The virtually contemporary Pseudo-Athanasian *Fourth Oration* (c. 340) also relates the views of the Arians and Marcellians to those of the Jews.[83] Athanasius often compares the Arians to specific Jews that rejected Jesus, such as Barabbas,[84] Caiaphas,[85] Herod,[86] Judas,[87] Hymenaeus and Alexander,[88] specific groups like the Pharisees[89] and Jews in a more general sense as

---

[79] Barrett, *John*, 352, 382.

[80] Carson, *John*, 395.

[81] Origen, *CC* 1, 56 and Canévet, "La théologie," 189.

[82] *CM* II 2 (Kl./H. 43,18–21).

[83] See Boezelman, "Polemical Equation," 133–46, especially 138–41.

[84] See *CA* I 2 (110,2–6).

[85] See *CA* I 2 (110,2–6); I 53 (163,13–15); II 40 (216,6–8); III 27 (337,4–338,5); III 28 (338,1–3); III 67 (381,35–38).

[86] See *CA* III 28 (338,1–3).

[87] *CA* I 2 (110,2–6); III 28 (338,1–3).

[88] See *CA* I 2 (110,2–6); I 54 (164,16–17).

[89] See *CA* I 4 (113,15–23); II 57 (234,9–12) and III 51 (362,1–5; together with the Sadducees).

figures of the past.[90] The Jews thus function prominently as a mirror group of the Arians in their denial of their self-understanding as Christians.[91]

Similarly, the Greeks or pagans also have, in the view of Athanasius and his audience, a highly defective view of the Son.[92] Since the Arians regarded the Son as a creature and they still worshipped him, Athanasius suggests a link between them and the pagan practice of worshipping multiple and created gods.[93]

The heretics mentioned in *CA* III 15 are Marcion and Mani. The common factor between both of them is their dualistic worldview. According to Meijering, they are also mentioned insofar as Athanasius aims to show that his Arian opponents follow the heretics.[94] In this specific instance, it is not Athanasius who conceives of three gods or principles, but his opponents. Athanasius claims this on the basis of their acceptance of three divine *hypostaseis*, which are nonetheless unequal in honour and glory.[95] Since the Arians do not regard Jn 10:30 as describing an ontological unity and they reject the metaphor of the sun and its radiance as inappropriate for the Father-Son relationship, Athanasius suggests that they in fact conceive of a Trinity composed of three suns. That this presentation does not match the self-understanding of his opponents is secondary. Athanasius correctly perceives a tension between the Church's confession of the three divine persons with the Arian emphasis on the singularity of the unbegotten Father.

---

[90] See *CA* I 39 (149,12–14); I 50 (160,14–15); I 55 (165,18–20); II 15 (191,7–192,9); II 16 (192,1–3); II 17 (193,1–3); III 28 (339,10); III 30 (341,11–14); III 54 (366,21–23); III 55 (367,16–24).

[91] See also *CA* III 27–28. See further *CA* II 42 and pp 205–208 above.

[92] For comparisons of the Arians to the Greeks, see *CA* I 3 (112,23–24). I 18 (128,15–23); II 10 (186,1); II 14 (191,33–36); II 28 (205,27); II 40 (216,6–8); III 16 (324,9–325,12); III 67 (381,35–38). Cf. Paul Gavrilyuk, "Creation in Early Christian Polemical Literature: Irenaeus against the Gnostics and Athanasius against the Arians," *Modern Theology* 29 (2013): 30–32.

[93] See *CG* 10, 13–14, 19–24 and Meijering, *Die dritte Rede*, I:69, 78.

[94] Meijering, *Die dritte Rede*, I:151–52.

[95] Anatolios, *Retrieving Nicaea*, 44, 52.

This discussion above shows that the apparently self-evident meaning of Jn 10:30 turns out to be less self-evident than Athanasius claims throughout his *Orations*. Athanasius' discussion on the passage of Scripture proves the interrelatedness of Scripture and reason in the *Orations*, in which an appeal to Scripture and reasonableness go hand in hand.[96] The Gospel of John is truly important in Athanasius' theology, but Athanasius' defence of the eternity of the Son can by no means only stand on the 'self-evident' interpretation of John's Gospel or the wider body of biblical texts. The fourth-century questions concerning God were just taken further than the first-century document attempted to provide an answer to. One indication for this is the frequency of allusions to, rather than citations of John's Gospel. By alluding to John rather than citing it on several occasions (such as to Jn 5:17 and 14:9 in *CA* III 14), Athanasius is able to bring the first-century document into the formulation of his fourth-century theology. The question was not any more whether Jesus was legitimately considered divine within the boundaries of Jewish monotheism, but had become in what way Jesus is the Son of God and what this meant for Christianity as a monotheistic religion. The intentional tension and ambiguity in John, described by Barrett's comment on John 10:30 that 'the oneness of Father and Son is a oneness of love and obedience even while it is a oneness of essence' was solved in two different directions by Athanasius and his opponents.[97] Both accepted a good deal of John's account of Jesus, but the ecclesial demand for clarification of the intentional tension of John resulted in a genuine debate with an appeal to Scripture and reasoning with an eye to its consequences.

CA III 17–25: Jn 17:11,20–23

The next topic that Athanasius discusses is the implications of Jesus' petition that the believers 'may be one as we are' (Jn 17:11, 21–22). While Athanasius closely associates Jn 10:30, 14:9 and 14:10, Asterius reads Jn 10:30 and 14:10 together with Jn 17:21–

---

[96] Meijering, "HN ΠΟΤΕ," 166.

[97] Barrett, *John*, 382; cf. Lincoln, *John*, 306; Carson, *John*, 394–95; Lindars, *John*, 370–71.

22.[98] Asterius held that these passages show that humans will enter into the same relation to the Father as Jesus.[99] Eusebius of
Caesarea's interpretation seems to come close to Asterius, as he
states that the Father is in the Son 'in the same way as he also
wishes to be in us, ... since the Father has given to him a share in
his own glory'.[100] Their concern is obvious: if it were granted that
(1) Jesus is one with God's being (cf. Jn 10:30), since (2) he is in
the Father and the Father is in him (cf. Jn 14:10) and (3) humans
become one as the Father and Jesus are one (Jn 17:20–23), without a proper qualification of the unity of Father and Son, humans
would become identical with God's being as well. Asterius therefore proposed an alternative interpretation of these crucial Johannine texts to avoid the problem caused by the Son's subordination
to the Father. In countering Asterius' suggestion, Athanasius argues that humans become sons by imitation. After providing his
argument, he employs the figure of *sermocinatio* several times to
enhance the plausibility of his argumentation.

Athanasius introduces a fragment of his opponents, probably
Asterius, very hostilely. Vinzent has suggested that this is most
likely an authentic fragment of Asterius.[101] He notes that the transition after the quote of Jn 17:20–23 is a comment of Athanasius,
but he does not state the same about the introductory words.
However, these words are also Athanasius', aimed to discredit his
opponents.[102] Since it cites the passages under discussion in *CA* III
17–25, I will quote the fragment in full:

> [T]he Arians, who do not even feel ashamed by this [the
> aforementioned discussion], reply: 'Not as you say, but as we
> will. For, whereas you have overthrown our former expedi-
> ents, we have invented a new one, and it is this:—Likewise
> are the Son and the Father one, and so is the Father in the Son
> and the Son in the Father, as we may become one in Him as
> well. For this is written in the Gospel according to John, and

---

[98] For more information, see Morales, *La théologie trinitaire*, 542–55.
[99] See fr. 41 (Vinzent) and Vinzent, *Asterius*, 239–41.
[100] *ET* III 19 (Kl./H. 180,23–27); tr. McCarthy Spoerl and Vinzent.
[101] Vinzent, *Asterius*, 239–41.
[102] Meijering, *Die dritte Rede*, I:167.

Christ desired it for us in these words: "Holy Father, protect them in your name that you have given me, so that they may be one, as we are one (Jn 17:11)." And shortly further on: "I do not pray for these only, but also for those who believe in me through their word, that they may all be one; even as You, Father, are in me, and I in You, that they also may be in us, so that the world may believe that You have sent me. The glory which You have given me I have given to them, that they may be one even as we are one, I in them and You in me, that they may become perfectly one, so that the world may know that you have sent me (Jn 17:20–23).'" After that, as if they have found an excuse, the deceitful add this: 'If, as we in the Father become one, he and the Father are also one and he is thus in the Father, how do we derive from his words: "I and the Father are one" (Jn 10:30) and "I in the Father and the Father in me" (Jn 14:10), that he is proper and like the Father's substance?'[103]

Athanasius rejects Asterius' view that humans become in God in the sense that the Father and the Son are in each other (cf. Jn 14:10). For in that case 'the Word of God is the same as us and only distinctive from us in time'.[104] Interestingly, whereas Asterius quoted quite an elaborate passage of John's Gospel, Athanasius focuses on much smaller units: 'that they may be one as we are' (Jn 17:11; 21–22), or even on the words ἐν ἡμῖν (Jn 17:21), and the word καθώς (Jn 17:11, 21–22).

Athanasius provides several elements for his case that the words 'in us' have an orthodox sense.[105] First of all, 'we are neither Word or Wisdom, nor is He creature or work'; it is 'a blasphemy even to think this'.[106] Athanasius suggests that this is so obvious that it ought not have to be explained; therefore, he will discuss the issue 'briefly' (συντόμως). In reality, he acknowledges that he has discussed the issue quite elaborately.[107]

---

[103] CA III 17 (326,1–16) = Asterius, fr. 41 (Vinzent). Tr. NPNF, adapted.
[104] CA III 18 (327,1–2).
[105] CA III 18 (327,12–13).
[106] CA III 18 (327,3–4. 10–13).
[107] CA III 18 (327,14–15). In CA III 24 (333,1–2), he acknowledges that he has discussed the passage elaborately.

Secondly, he states that not all examples in Scripture are meant to be taken literally. When discussing comparisons between human beings and animals, Athanasius claims that they do not alter the natural state of either humans or animals.[108] Likewise, the Son and human sonship are not to be understood in the same terms. The Son is it by nature, we are followers or imitators.

> For although there is one Son by nature, True and Only-begotten, we too become sons (υἱοί), not as He in nature and truth, but according to the grace of Him. (...) . [So] if we have in mind the good and right sense regarding these texts (ταῦτα), the passage (ἀνάγνωσμα) in John has the same sense.[109]

Athanasius argues from the Pauline distinction between the true Son and adopted sons (cf. Rom 8:14–17) in contrast to the evangelist John, who never calls believers sons (υἱοί), but only children (τέκνα).[110] Athanasius asserts therefore that there is a huge contrast between the Son and humans, despite the words in Jn 17:11 that might suggest their equality.

> We are made sons through Him by adoption and grace, as partaking of His Spirit. For he says: 'as many as received him, he gave power to become children of God, to those believing in his name (Jn 1:12).' Therefore he himself is the truth saying: 'I am the Truth' (Jn 14:6), and in speaking with his Father, he said: 'Sanctify them through your truth. Your Word is truth' (Jn 17:17), but by imitation we become virtuous and sons.[111]

The first Johannine citation (1:12) indicates according to Athanasius the difference between the genuine Son and adopted sons. The reference to the Son as the Truth (14:6) demonstrates this difference and the third citation (17:17) emphasises the contrast between the Word-Son and human beings again. The title Word

---

[108] *CA* III 18–19 (327,15–16; 328,19–28; 328,1–6).

[109] *CA* III 19 (329,10–11. 19–20); tr. NPNF, adapted.

[110] Barrett, *John*, 163; cf. Wendy Sproston North, "A Christology Too Far? Some Thoughts on Andrew Lincoln's Commentary on John," *JSNT* 29 (2007): 349.

[111] *CA* III 19 (329,25–31); tr. Newman, adapted.

in Jn 17:17 is interpreted by Athanasius as an ontological reference to the pre-incarnate Word, contrary to modern exegetes,
who unanimously reject an ontological interpretation of this instance of the word λόγος in John; at most, they hold that this λόγος
is mediated ultimately through Christ.[112] The words 'that they
may be one as we are' (Jn 17:11) signify 'that we too, taking such
(τινά) an example and looking at him, might become one towards
each other in concord (ὁμοψυχία) and oneness of spirit'.[113] The
unity between God and humans is therefore a copy (ὑπογραμμός)
of the Son's natural unity with the Father.[114] Jn 10:30 pertains to
the unity of being of Father and Son and Jn 17:21–22 to the harmony with God that divinised human beings will experience.

The influence of reasoning in the interpretation of Jn 10:30
is clearly seen in the next passage. Athanasius focuses on the
words 'in us' (ἐν ἡμῖν) in Jn 17:21 to assert that this should not be
read in close association with Jn 14:10; instead, the Son and humans will be united to God in different ways. Athanasius concurs,
by using intimate first person plural language, that 'we become
one ... according to our own nature, and as it is possible for us'.[115]
Jesus' prayer for humans, 'that they may all be one', as the Father
is in him and he in the Father (Jn 17:21), shows 'the distance and
difference' between him and humans.[116] Athanasius reiterates
briefly afterwards:

> The words 'in us', then, are not 'in the Father', as the Son is in
> Him; (cf. Jn 14:10) but imply an example (παράδειγμα) and
> image (εἰκών) (...) For, dwelling still on the same thought, the
> Lord says: 'And the glory which You have given me, I have
> given to them, that they may be one as we are one' (Jn 17:22).
> He appropriately has not said here: 'that they may be in You

---

[112] Carson, *John*, 566; Barrett, *John*, 508–10.
[113] *CA* III 20 (329,1–330,4); tr. NPNF. In the NPNF translation, this part
belongs to chapter 19.
[114] *CA* III 20 (330,15–16).
[115] *CA* III 20 (330,8–10); tr. NPNF, adapted.
[116] *CA* III 21 (331,1–3). See also *CA* III 21 (331,5–7).

as I am' but 'as we are'. Now he who says 'as' (καθώς), signifies not identity (ταυτότητα), but an image and example.[117]

This explanation of biblical texts is not simply an appeal to Scripture. Athanasius argues that unity must be understood straightforwardly in order to safeguard the interpretation he advocates. The difference between Athanasius and Asterius is that Athanasius argues that believers partake in both the Father and Son, who are both divine, while Asterius seems to suggest that the Son enables believers to partake in the Father identically to his own participation in the Father. Athanasius' suggestion seems compatible with John's theology,[118] but Asterius' view is distorted on this point. Without doubt, Asterius considered it impossible for believers to participate in the being of God, and therefore suggested that the Son is not united in being with the Father. Athanasius has to use arguments external to the scriptural text itself to assert that his interpretation is correct. Athanasius' interpretation of these verses from the Gospel of John is strongly undergirded by one of Athanasius' key convictions: the deep gulf between the Triune God and creation. Here is the real point of contention with Asterius, who held a subordinationist view of the Trinity.

Athanasius further defends his position by pointing to the specific diction of the Gospel text, by utilising the emotive figure of *sermocinatio*. This is a form of literary re-enactment that connects the biblical past directly with the contemporary fourth-century situation. In *CA* III 17–25, he presents Jesus as commenting upon the actual meaning of this passage four times. In *CA* III 20, Athanasius argues that the unity between Father and Son is the model for the believers. He evokes the situation that he and his readers hear the Son elaborating on the words of Jn 17. He states that the Son 'takes himself as example and says: "that they may be one as we are" (Jn 17:11). And our unity is indivisible, so that they learning from us of that indivisible nature, may preserve in like manner agreement with one another.'[119] This rhetorical figure allows Athanasius to suggest that Jesus himself clarifies the

---

[117] *CA* III 21 (331,9–11. 20–24); tr. NPNF, adapted.
[118] Crump, "Johannine Trinity," 400.
[119] *CA* III 20 (330,20–22); tr. NPNF, adapted.

meaning of this verse. In *CA* III 21, Athanasius argues that the words 'in us' points to the mutual power of Father and Son, again using the figure of *sermocinatio*. He thus suggests that the words 'in us', spoken by the Son, 'meant nothing else to render but that "by our unity they also may be so one with each other, like we are one in nature and truth. For they could not be one, except by learning unity in us".'[120] The Arians overlook the word καθώς in Jn 17:21. For if Jesus

> had said unqualifiedly and absolutely 'that they may be one in You', (Jn 17:21) or 'that they and I may be one in You', (Jn 17:21) God's enemies had had some defence, though a shameless one. However, in fact he has not spoken unqualifiedly, but: 'As (καθώς) You, Father, in me, and I in You, that they may be all one' (Jn 17:21).[121]

The word καθώς (as) indicates that one cannot read the words straightforwardly. His emphasis on the comparative nature of Jn 17:11, 21 leads Athanasius to assert that the Son is truly and without addition in the Father, whereas humans need an example (παράδειγμα), with the third use of *sermocinatio*. Athanasius first cites Jn 17:21: 'As You are in me and I in You' and then remarks that the Son

> states further: 'When they shall be so perfected, then the world knows that You have sent me', (Jn 17:4 and 17:23) for unless I had come and carried this their body, none of them had been perfected, but one and all had remained corruptible. Now work in them, O Father, and as You have given to me to bear this, grant to them your Spirit (Jn 16:7), that they too in it may become one (Jn 17:22), and may be perfected in me (Jn 17:4). For their perfecting shows that Your Word has sojourned among them; and the world seeing them perfect and full of God, will believe altogether that You have sent me (Jn 17:22), and I have sojourned here. For from where is this their perfecting, but that I, Your Word, having borne their body, and become a human 'have perfected the work, which you gave me' (Jn 17:4) O Father? And the work is perfected,

---

[120] *CA* III 21 (331,5–7); tr. NPNF, adapted.
[121] *CA* III 22 (332,13–16); tr. NPNF, adapted.

because men, redeemed from sin, no longer remain dead; but being deified, have in each other, by looking at me, the bond of charity.[122]

Athanasius interweaves actual references to the Gospel of John with his own interpretation to assert the validity of his interpretation. He thus uses imaginative words of Jesus Christ to assert his preferred interpretation. It is noteworthy how many Johannine allusions turn up in this process. Athanasius rephrases the context of John 17 by putting Johannine material from Jn 16 and 17 that makes his reading of Jn 17:11, 20–23 plausible in the light of his view on the relation between the Son and human beings.[123] In *CA* III 24, he claims that Jesus gives the Spirit to everyone (cf. Jn 16:7; 1 Jn 4:13), while 'through the grace of the Spirit we become in him, and he in us (cf. Jn 17:11)'.[124] He asks polemically, admitting his indebtedness to John's Gospel (and the letters): 'Are the Arians thus not refuted from all sides, and especially by John, that the Son is in the Father in one way, and we become in him in another? (...) For he, as has been said, gives to the Spirit (cf. Jn 16:7), and whatever the Spirit has, he has from the Word.'[125] Athanasius thus rejects the understanding of crucial Johannine passages by an appeal to other Johannine passages and argues that his opponents are refuted most of all by John. He is thus aware that he often appeals not just to Scripture, but to the Gospel of John in particular. His appeal to Jn 16:7 – 'but if I go, I will send him [the Paraclete] to you – is crucial in his interpretation of Jn 17:11, 20–23 for asserting the qualitative difference between the Son's and humans' unity with God.

In *CA* III 25, Athanasius polemically argues that 'God's enemies ... ought ... no longer to pretend themselves equal to God'.[126] The suggestion that his opponents would 'pretend themselves

---

[122] *CA* III 23 (333,18–29); tr. NPNF, adapted. Cf. *CA* I 46 and Meijering, *Die dritte Rede*, I:215.

[123] On Athanasius' notion of participation of the Son and humans, see Leithart, *Athanasius*, 60–75, 108–12.

[124] *CA* III 24 (334,10–11).

[125] *CA* III 24 (334,24–26; 335,29–30); tr. NPNF, adapted.

[126] *CA* III 25 (335,23–24); tr. NPNF, adapted.

equal to God' is far from the truth, for they argued on the basis of Jn 17:11, 20–23 that both the Son and human beings do not participate ontologically in the divine Father. Only on Athanasius' premise that the Son is truly the divine and the Arian suggestion that humans will participate in the same way in the Father as the Son, can this claim be made. It might even be possible that they ridiculed Athanasius' interpretation of Jn 10:30, precisely because they were afraid of that consequence.

However, in maintaining a subordination of the Son to the Father, Asterius blurred the clear distinction between the Son and human beings. Athanasius could therefore refute Asterius with some justification, even though he did present Asterius' point of view in a distorted way. Furthermore, Asterius' position in relating Jn 14:10 and Jn 17:11, 21–23 is accepted as likely by modern exegetes. Asterius seems to show awareness of the development of John's narrative and context, whereas Athanasius mainly discusses very brief elements of John's Gospel. Asterius is more aware of the subordination theme that is definitely part of John's Gospel, counter-balanced by the egalitarian emphasis that Athanasius embraces. Both fourth-century authors emphasise one of the two sides of the coin that are tightly related in John's Gospel. Asterius' reading is probably closer to, but not identical with John's connection between Jn 14:10 and 17:11, 20–23. Jesus' prayer is a gracious petition for humans, or as Barrett puts it: 'The believers … are to be one, in the Father and the Son, distinct from God, yet abiding in God.'[127] However, in contrast to Asterius, John does not seem to argue that believers will participate in God in the same way as Jesus does. David Crump argues that 'every disciple participates in the divine interpenetration of the Son and the Father, producing the Johannine, perichoretic trio of Father–Son–disciple, a divine bi-unity perichoretically incorporating believers within the Son and the Father through the Spirit'.[128]

---

[127] Barrett adds that the believers are 'themselves the sphere of God's activity' with reference to Jn 14:12, in Barrett, *John*, 512, cf. 402.

[128] Crump, "Johannine Trinity," 412.

CA III 26–58: THE HUMAN AND DIVINE IN JESUS

In *CA* III 26–58, Athanasius discusses many Gospel texts that point to Jesus' weaknesses. He first introduces a dossier of Gospel texts in *CA* III 26 and discusses most of them afterwards. In *CA* III 27–28, he outlines the consequences of the Arian position as non-Christian and he introduces his view on the texts in general in *CA* III 29–35. In *CA* III 35–41 he then discusses the texts in general, in *CA* III 42–50 Jesus' ignorance, in *CA* III 51–53 his advance in wisdom, and in *CA* III 54–58 his fear and agony.

CA III 26–41: General Discussion of the Weakness Texts

In *CA* III 26, Athanasius mentions four objections of the Arians against his position. The common factor in these texts is a physical or psychological weakness on Jesus' part that would disprove Athanasius' view on the Son's ontological unity with the Father. Athanasius' initial response is polemical: the Arians misuse these texts to assert that the Son is not truly divine and arrive at the heresy of Paul of Samosata.[129] 'Like people who do not grow weary in their impieties but are hardened in them after the fashion of Pharaoh, they hear and observe the Savior's human characteristics in the Gospel narratives, but are perfectly forgetful, after the fashion of the Samosatene, of the Son's paternal divinity.'[130] This key conviction runs through the rest of the *Oration* and he calls his opponents 'wretched folk' (οἱ δείλαιοι) and 'impious people' (οἱ ἀσεβεῖς).[131] Athanasius remarks that these biblical texts cause the Arians to question the Son's eternal and essential unity with the Father, his natural power, and his status as Wisdom of the Father.[132] These objections are serious and difficult and force Athanasius to 'einer langen und oft mühsamen Verteidigung'.[133] The gospel texts Athanasius mentions concern (1) the Son's acknowledgement that he receives everything from the

---

[129] On Paul of Samosata, see Uwe Michael Lang, "The Christological Controversy at the Synod of Antioch in 268/9," *JTS* 51 (2000): 54–80.

[130] *CA* III 26 (336,1–4); tr. Norris.

[131] *CA* III 26 (337,33); *CA* III 27 (337,1).

[132] *CA* III 26 (336,4–5. 11–12. 19–20. 26–27).

[133] Meijering, *Die dritte Rede*, II:13.

Father (Mt 11:27; 28:18 and Jn 3:35; 5:22; 6:37), (2) his fear (Jn 12:27–28; 13:21; Mt 26:39) and God-forsakenness (Mt 27:46), (3) his growing in wisdom and asking questions (Lk 2:52) and (4) ignorance (Mk 13:32; cf. Mt 16:13; Mk 6:38) and his prayer to glorify God's and his own name (Jn 12:28; 17:5).[134] He further quotes an Arian comment, which suggests that the Son cannot be the eternal Word of God, but that he is rather a creature.[135] Most scholars hold that this list of texts actually circulated, because Athanasius would never provide evidence against his position in such a clear and orderly way.[136]

Polemical Comparison of the Arians to the Jews

In CA III 27–28, Athanasius continues his polemical attack on the Arians by associating them again with the Jews, Greeks and Manichees (cf. CA III 15–16). Athanasius presents an imaginary dialogue to portray Jews and Arians as asking basically the same questions. The Arians ask: "'Why did the Logos become flesh anyhow?" (cf. Jn 1:14)' and 'in the more Judaizing manner of Caiaphas: ... "For what reason does Christ, being human, make himself God?" [cf. John 10:33].' He continues: 'what the Jews used to mutter in the past as they gazed on Christ, ... the Ariomaniacs now disbelieve as they read about him and have fallen into blasphemy'.[137] He locates a common disbelief of Jews and Arians in their rejection of the divinity of Christ, prominently using Johannine material to illustrate their commonality, and continues:

> [W]hile the Jews sought to kill the Lord because 'he claimed that God was his own Father, and made himself the equal of God' [John 5:18] as one who carried out the work which the Father does, the Arians have for their part learned to assert

---

[134] CA III 26 (336,5–337,32).

[135] See Asterius, fr. 74 (Vinzent), and discussion in Vinzent, *Asterius*, 317–21.

[136] Marcel Richard, "Saint Athanase et la psychologie du Christ selon les Ariens," *Mélanges de Science Religieuse* 4 (1947): 7–13; Abramowski, "Die dritte Arianerrede," 407–13; Meijering, *Die dritte Rede*, II:13–14; Vinzent, *Asterius*, 321.

[137] CA III 27 (337,1–338,7); tr. Norris.

both that he is not the equal of God and that God is not by nature the proper Father of the Logos. (...) Again the Jews say, 'Is not this the son of Joseph, whose father and mother we know? (Jn 6:42). How then does he say, "Before Abraham came to be, I am, and have come down out of heaven?"' (Jn 8:58)[138]

Athanasius asserts that Judaism and Arianism are fundamentally the same in order to construct a negative *ethos* of his opponents. Both 'deny the eternity and deity of the Logos' because of the 'human properties' that he took for humanity's sake,[139] so that the Arian heresy is Jewish 'in the way that Judas the traitor was Jewish'.[140] He suggests that the Arians dress their heresy in Christian language out of 'fear to be openly Jewish and to be circumcised because they do not want to displease Constantius and the people they have led astray' and urges them to 'stop saying what the Jews said, for it is only fair to turn away from the opinions of those whose name they reject'.[141] Throughout the *Orations*, the group of the 'Jews' functions to discredit the Arians. Athanasius argues that a total commitment to Christianity is needed, including the confession of the eternity and deity of the Word of God. He subsequently calls for a choice between two alternatives that exclude his opponents' position. The Arians either have to deny the Incarnation of the Saviour, or they must renounce what the Jews said completely. He then continues:

---

[138] *CA* III 27 (338,15–21); tr. Norris.

[139] *CA* III 27 (338,23–24); tr. Norris.

[140] *CA* III 28 (338,1–3); tr. Norris. Athanasius calls several of his opponents' ideas (φρόνημα) 'Judaising'. Cf. *CA* III 39 (351,13–14); cf. *CA* III 52 (364,24–26).

[141] *CA* III 28 (339,5–7); tr. Norris. Two other assertions of his opponents' trust in human patronage are found in *Orations* I and II. 'They profess the patronage of friends and the fear of Constantius, so that those who join them through hypocrisy and promise will not see the filth of the heresy.' *CA* I 10 (119,16–18); tr. Rusch. See also *CA* II 43 (220,20–21): 'since their doctrine nauseates everyone, they quickly support it with human patronage'; tr. Anatolios.

> We are Christians, O you Arians, *we* are Christians! It is natural for us to have a close knowledge of the Gospels which concern the Savior–and neither to join the Jews in stoning him (cf. Jn 10:31) if we hear about his divinity and his eternity nor to join you in being offended at utterances of a lowly sort, which, as a human being, he voiced on our account.[142]

Athanasius argues that the Lord is the true and genuine Son of God and Creator. If they become Christians and cease to be Arians, they will lose the Jewish folly (κακοφροσύνη) and the 'truth will immediately illumine' them.[143]

These allusions to John show that the appeal to authority is used for establishing the negative character of his opponents throughout the *Oration*. The Arians are 'Christ's enemies and unthankful Jews',[144] who fabricate 'Judaizing and foolish questions'[145] and 'insults' (δυσφημία),[146] they are 'traitorous Jews' (τοὺς προδότας 'Ιουδαίους),[147] and even 'greater traitors than the Jews in denying the Christ',[148] while Asterius imitated the Jews.[149] This contrast between Jesus and the Jews can be traced back to the terminology of John's Gospel. However, the contrast in the Gospel is more ambiguous (cf. Jn 4:22) and part of an inner-Jewish debate, whereas Athanasius incorporates it into a Christian, essentially non-Jewish debate, which changes the meaning of the terminology.[150] This change in discourse is sadly part of an

---

[142] *CA* III 28 (339,9–12); tr. Norris, adapted. Meijering emphatically italicises the second 'we', in *Die dritte Rede*, II:39 cf. *CA* III 41 (352,2–3).

[143] *CA* III 28 (339,14–16); tr. Norris.

[144] *CA* III 55 (366,2).

[145] *CA* III 58 (371,21).

[146] *CA* III 67 (381,37).

[147] *CA* III 15 (323,2–3).

[148] *CA* III 16 (325,23–24); tr. NPNF.

[149] *CA* III 2 (307,1–2).

[150] Stephen Motyer, *Your Father the Devil? A New Approach to John and the Jews* (Carlisle, England: Paternoster Press, 1997), 211; Craig A. Evans, "Faith and Polemic: The New Testament and First-Century Judaism," in *Anti-Semitism and Early Christianity. Issues of Polemic and Faith*, ed. Craig A. Evans and Donald A. Hagner (Minneapolis: Fortress, 1993), 1–17; Von Wahlde, "The Johannine 'Jews.'"

increasingly hostile theological language against Jews in fourth-century Christianity. This increasingly hostile language in turn created a hostile attitude towards Jews in general, ultimately resulting in a long history of anti-Semitism in Christianity.[151] In Athanasius' *Orations*, the equation between Jews and Arians is not of an anti-Semitic nature, but the term Jews becomes exclusively associated with the element of Christ denial. The fact that the human Jesus and all of his earliest followers were Jews is completely ignored. However, the focus in this passage is not on blaming the Jews as such; it is a form of literary re-enactment in which Athanasius claims that contemporary villains are doing similar things to negative biblical examples. In this way, he suggests an ongoing continuity between the biblical past and the present, placing himself in continuity with Scripture as an imitator of 'unquestionable orthodox characters'.[152] The association between Arians and Jews functions thus as a way to construct a bridge between past and present. In doing so, it constructs Athanasius' *ethos* in a most positive light, while the negative *ethos* of the Arians is portrayed blacker than black.

The Double Account of the Saviour

In *CA* III 29, Athanasius argues that the core message of Scripture hinges on the double account of the Saviour and illustrates his assertion with material from the Gospel of John.[153] It is found throughout the inspired Scripture (τῆς θεοπνεύστου γραφῆς),

> as the Lord himself has said, 'Search the Scriptures, for it is they which bear witness concerning me' (Jn 5:39). Lest I write too much, however, by pulling together all the relevant texts, let me content myself by bringing John in the memory of all. He says: 'In the beginning was the Logos and the Logos was with God and the Logos was God. He was in the beginning

---

[151] For a balanced treatment of the subject matter, see Robert Chazan, *From Anti-Judaism to Anti-Semitism: Ancient and Medieval Christian Constructions of Jewish History* (New York: Cambridge University Press, 2016).

[152] Flower, *Late Roman Invective*, 31, see 22–32, 181.

[153] *CA* III 29 (340,1–4). See chapter 3.3 above.

with God. All things came to be through him, and apart from
him not one thing came to be' (Jn 1:1–3). He goes on, 'And
the Logos became flesh and dwelt among us, and we saw his
glory–glory as of one uniquely born from the Father' (Jn
1:14).[154]

This passage shows the prominence of some crucial notions of the
Gospel of John in Athanasius' thought. Athanasius asserts that the
core message of Scripture is found in John's Gospel, because he
brings 'John in the memory of all'. He quotes a part of Jn 5:39 to
demonstrate that the Scriptures testify about Jesus, and omits the
words 'because you [the Jewish leaders] think that in them you
have eternal life'. He thus intensifies his claims that Scripture
must be understood in the light of two central elements of the
Johannine prologue: the Word's eternity (1:1–3) and his Incarnation (1:14), illustrating the same point with Philippians 2:6–8.[155]
He then claims that anyone who reads Scripture in this way will
see that the Father spoke to the Son in the beginning (cf. Gen 1:3,
6, 26) and that 'at the consummation of the ages the Father sent
the Son into the world, "not in order to judge the world, but in
order that through him the world might be saved" (Jn 3:17).'[156]

In *CA* III 30, Athanasius explains the human weaknesses of
Jesus by pointing to Jn 1:14: 'the Word became flesh'. Someone
who studies the divine Scripture should discern the teaching
about the divine Word in the OT[157] and 'perceive from the Gospels
that the Lord was made a human being. For "the Word," John
says, "was made flesh and dwelt among us" (Jn 1:14). He became
human and did not enter into human (οὐκ εἰς ἄνθρωπον ἦλθε).'[158]
The uniqueness of his appearance as a human is found in responses of humans, for otherwise those who saw him would not

---

[154] *CA* III 29 (340,4–10); tr. Norris, adapted.
[155] Meijering mentions that the prologue of John and Phil 2 are often
used in combination in Athanasius' work. See Meijering, *Die dritte Rede*,
II:55.
[156] *CA* III 29 (340,16–17); tr. Norris, adapted. A reference to the announcement of the Messiah (Mt 1:23) follows.
[157] See Athanasius, *DI* 33–40 and Meijering, *Die dritte Rede*, II:59–61.
[158] *CA* III 30 (341,2–4); tr. Norris, adapted.

have been astonished and said, 'Where does this man come from?' (Mk 4:41) and 'Why do you, who are a human being, make yourself God?' (Jn 10:33). For since they heard the expression 'and the word of the Lord came to' each of the prophets, they had some acquaintance with the idea. Now, however, the Word of God, through whom everything came to be (cf. Jn 1:3), has taken it on himself to become Son of man as well. (...) For as John said, 'the Word became flesh' (Jn 1:14).[159]

The Word's Incarnation provides the rationale for Athanasius' double σκοπός of Scripture. In Old Testament times, the Word dwelt in the saints, but in the Gospels the Son appeared in a unique way, 'in the flesh'. Old Testament saints received the Holy Spirit, but they were not divine. However, the Son is still recognised as divine (Mk 4:41; Jn 10:33), even though his weaknesses show that he genuinely became flesh (Jn 1:14). In all of this, Athanasius gives a highly specific interpretation of Christianity, so that only the orthodox Christians can appeal to Scripture. According to Meijering, this is done 'in gutem Glauben', since Athanasius was really convinced that Church doctrine finds its basis in Scripture.[160]

In the subsequent part, Athanasius touches upon the relation between Jesus' divinity and humanity, thus anticipating the fifth-century Christological debate.[161] Athanasius states about the Word: 'Being God, he had his own body, and using this as an instrument, he became human being on our account.'[162] However, the flesh is not just an instrument in Athanasius' view.

---

[159] *CA* III 30 (341,8–12. 14–15); tr. Norris, adapted.

[160] Meijering, *Die dritte Rede*, II:61; see also Osborne, "Literal or Metaphorical?," 148–50.

[161] Richard argues that Athanasius denied that Jesus possesses a human soul in Richard, "Saint Athanase"; see also John Behr, *The Way to Nicaea*, The Formation of Christian Theology 1 (Crestwood: St. Vladimir's Seminary Press, 2001), 216–231; John Behr, *The Nicene Faith*, The Formation of Christian Theology 2 (Crestwood: St. Vladimir's Seminary Press, 2004), 384; Alvyn Pettersen, "Did Athanasius Deny Christ's Fear?," *SJT* 39 (1986): 327–40.

[162] *CA* III 31 (342,11–12); tr. Norris.

> [For] when the flesh was suffering, the Logos was not apart
> from it. (...) When he was doing the works of the Father in a
> divine way, the flesh was not external to him. On the contrary,
> the Lord did these things in the body itself. This explains why,
> when he had become human, he said, 'If I do not do the works
> of my Father, do not believe me. But if I do them, even if you
> do not believe me, believe the works themselves, so that you
> may know that the Father is in me and I in him' (Jn 10:37–
> 38).[163]

Athanasius thus cuts short all the questions about the relation between the Logos and the flesh in Jesus' suffering, by a somewhat
circular argument and a citation of Jn 10:37–38.[164] It is circular
because he argues that weaknesses belong to the Word's flesh,
because he, the Word, dwelt in it, and second that the Word must
be in the flesh, because it was called his flesh. The flesh is more
than an instrument, because in both instances the Logos is connected to the flesh. Jesus' weaknesses are always supplemented
with his perfection as the Word (Λόγος). Athanasius asserts that
the Logos did everything both humanly (ἀνθρώπινος) and divinely
(θεϊκῶς) in any single deed. Many illustrations of the validity of
his ἀνθρωπίνως-θεϊκῶς scheme are found exclusively in John's Gospel.[165]

> [I]n the case of 'the man blind from birth' (cf. Jn 9:6), it was
> human spittle which he spat, but it was a divine act when he
> opened the man's eyes by means of clay (ἀνθρώπινον ἀπὸ τῆς
> σαρκὸς ἠφίει τὸ πτύσμα, θεϊκῶς δὲ τοὺς ὀφθαλμοὺς ἤνοιγε διὰ τοῦ
> πηλοῦ). And where Lazarus is concerned, he uttered human
> speech in his capacity as a human being, but it was a divine

---

[163] *CA* III 32 (342,1. 3– 343,6); tr. Norris, adapted. He also uses the healing of Peter's mother-in-law (Mt 8:14–15).

[164] In *DI* 18, the same words function to prove this same point, the hu-
manity and divinity of the Son, whereas he uses the same words in *Ser*
IV 20 in a somewhat different context. See also Meijering, *Die dritte Rede*,
II: 255.

[165] Athanasius generally uses the adjective ἀνθρώπινος and the adverb
θεϊκῶς. Because both are commonly translated adverbially, I have called
it the ἀνθρωπίνως-θεϊκῶς-scheme, although Athanasius uses the adjective
rather than the adverb to describe Jesus' human deeds.

act when, in his capacity as God, he raised Lazarus from the dead (cf. Jn 11:34–43) (…) So if the body had belonged to someone else, its passions too would be predicated of that subject. If, however, the flesh belongs to the Logos (for 'the Logos became flesh' (Jn 1:14)), it is necessary to predicate the fleshly passions of him whose flesh it is.[166]

Ultimately, the ἀνθρωπίνως-θεϊκῶς scheme allows Athanasius to explain how the Son is eternally divine, even when Scripture attributes characteristics to Jesus that seem to disqualify him as genuinely divine. The flesh belongs to the Word, and therefore his acts are both human and divine at the same moment.

Attributions of Jesus' weaknesses must not be denied, but put into the proper perspective; it is his gracious act for humanity. In *CA* III 33, Athanasius demonstrates the practical implications of humanity's liberation from sin and corruption. The Incarnation is important to counter the effects of the death that reigned from Adam to Moses (Rom 5:14). Through the work of Christ 'we are reborn from above "by water and spirit" (Jn 3:3,5); the flesh is no longer earthly, but now it has been "logified" by the work of the divine Logos who on our account became flesh'.[167] Athanasius argues that if heretics might object to this interpretation, they should listen to how the flesh of the Word would respond to the Arians. He imagines the flesh of Jesus as responding to a question of a heretic, saying:

> Now the flesh can give an answer to the disputatious heretic: 'I am indeed mortal by nature, taken from the earth ... I have become the flesh of the Logos, and he himself has borne my passions, impassible though he is (…) If you object because I have been released from the corruption which is mine by nature, see to it that you raise no objection to the fact that the divine Logos took to himself my state of slavery. Just as the Lord became a human being when he put on a body (cf. Jn 1:14), so we human beings, once we have been connected to

---

[166] *CA* III 32 (343,8–11. 15–17); tr. Norris, adapted.
[167] *CA* III 33 (345,26–28); tr. Norris.

> him by way of his flesh, are divinized by the Logos, and from
> that point on we are the heirs of eternal life.'[168]

This imaginary speech, called *fictio personae* or *prosopopoeia*, enables Athanasius to communicate his view subtly, but highly emotively as well.[169] He addresses his readers in first plural pronouns, which builds communion between him and his readers. He suggests that to object to his theology is to object against the release from the 'corruption of the flesh' that is realised by the Incarnation. Athanasius assumes here that Jn 1:14 speaks not only about the Incarnation of the Word, but also the divinisation of human beings. In this way, Athanasius reads more into this verse than it actually says. While Jn 1:14 might point to God's presence on earth, in reference to the divine presence in the Tabernacle or Sirach 24:8–11, Barrett is unconvinced of this, and rather emphasises the obedience and suffering of Jesus.[170] In any case, by basing his doctrine of the divinisation of the flesh on Jn 1:14, Athanasius takes the meaning of Jn 1:14 further than it most likely was meant in the original setting. In favour of Athanasius' view, however, his emphasis on the Incarnation as the gift of immortality to believers might be related to Jn 1:12–13, which speaks of 'the power to become children of God'.[171] This is less than Athanasius' claims, but he might have regarded the context as supportive of his interpretation of Jn 1:14.

In *CA* III 35, Athanasius discusses three texts, which the Arians view as proofs that 'the Son once did not possess the Father's privileges': 'The Father loves the Son and has given everything into his hand' (Jn 3:35); 'Everything has been handed over to me by my Father' (Mt 11:27); 'I can do no deed of myself, but I judge as I hear' (Jn 5:30).[172] Athanasius asserts that these passages do not indicate an inferior state of the Son by asking rhetorically:

---

[168] *CA* III 34 (346,26–33); tr. Norris.

[169] Lausberg, *Handbook*, 370 (par 827).

[170] Lincoln, *John*, 104–5; Carson, *John*, 127–28; Lindars, *John*, 94–95; Barrett, *John*, 165–67.

[171] Barrett, *John*, 163; cf. Lincoln, *John*, 103.

[172] See *CA* III 35 (347,16–20); tr. Norris, adapted.

> How can it be the case that the one who is the sole essential
> Logos and Wisdom of the Father should fail to possess eter-
> nally what the Father possesses, especially when he also says,
> 'Whatever things the Father possesses are mine' (Jn 16:15)
> and 'The things which are mine belong to the Father' (Jn
> 17:10)?[173]

The texts that suggest subordination (Mt 11:27; Jn 3:35; 5:30) are
'overruled' by the basic meaning of faith and two other Johannine
texts (16:15; 17:10) with a circular reasoning.[174] Because Jn 16:15
and 17:10 indicate that the Son eternally possesses what the Father possesses, the other texts (Jn 3:35; 5:30) cannot point to a
time when the Son did not possess these privileges. Athanasius
presupposes the clarity of the basic meaning of faith (σκοπός) and
depends heavily on certain Johannine notions in outlining this
σκοπός. In this way, Athanasius cannot really appreciate Jn 3:35
and 5:30 as texts that in themselves presented 'at once a humble
acknowledgment and a lofty claim', that at once allowed Jesus in
John's Gospel the possibility of claiming complete harmony with
God.[175]

Difficult Texts Considered

In the next chapters, Athanasius shifts from introducing the difficult texts to their actual discussion. In *CA* III 36, Athanasius explains how Jesus' dependence on the Father does not signify his
non-eternal existence. These subordinationist texts are only said
to clarify that 'he is not the Father, but the Word of the Father
and the eternal Son'.[176] The Son deliberately distinguishes himself
from the Father, without suggesting that he is inferior to Him.

> The expressions 'was given' (Mt 28:18) and 'was handed over'
> (Mt 11:27) do not imply that there was a time when [the Son]
> did not have these things. This – and the like conclusion where

---

[173] *CA* III 35 (347,16–22); tr. Norris.
[174] Meijering also points to other instances where Athanasius uses Jn
16:15. See *EpAfr* 8; *CA* I 61; *Ser* II 5; *Syn* 49 and Meijering, *Die dritte Rede*,
I:58–59, II:105–6.
[175] Barrett, *John*, 257.
[176] *CA* III 36 (348,4–5).

all such expressions are concerned – we can gather from a
similar passage. The Savior himself says: 'As the Father possesses life in himself, in the same manner also he has given
the Son to have life in himself' (Jn 5:26). By that phrase 'he
has given' he signifies that he is not himself the Father. When
he says 'in the same manner,' he shows the Son's likeness of
nature to the Father and the fact that he belongs to the Father.[177]

Athanasius does not deny the receptive role of the Son as such,
but parallels it with Jn 5:26 to assert that this one Johannine saying is characteristic of the equality of Father and Son. He centres
attention on this text to intimate that all subordinationist elements in other biblical texts should be interpreted in the light of
Jn 5:26. He introduces this verse as the words of the Saviour himself, thus emphasising the authority of Jn 5:26. Athanasius high-
lights the words 'has given' ($\delta\acute{\epsilon}\delta\omega\varkappa\epsilon$), to show the distinction
marker between Father and Son. Yet both are called 'Life', so they
are both divine, but not as an indistinguishable Sabellian conception of their unity.[178] Athanasius' choice of Jn 5:26 resonates well
with his view that Father and Son possess the same attributes. He
thus employs the rhetorical technique of synecdoche; a part (of
Scripture) stands for the whole of it.[179] Nevertheless, it is a questionable application of the figure, because it avoids the interpretation of many other biblical texts that are rather difficult to integrate in his hermeneutical framework.

Athanasius further includes a *prosopopoeia*, in which the radiance is speaking in language close to Jn 5:26:

If the radiance says: 'The light has given me all places to illumine, and I illumine not from myself but as the light wills' …
the radiance does not indicate that it once did not possess light
but rather asserts: 'I am proper to the light and everything
which belongs to the light is mine.' So, and much more, must
we understand in the instance of the Son. For when the Father

---

[177] *CA* III 36 (348,13–18); tr. Norris.
[178] For Athanasius' view on Sabellius, see Meijering, *Die dritte Rede*, I:57–
59.
[179] See further Lausberg, *Handbook*, 260–62 (par 572–77).

has given everything to the Son, he still possesses everything
in the Son, and when the Son possesses them, the Father still
possesses them.[180]

Athanasius thus establishes his general principle that the Son's
human limitations do not annul his eternal existence. His beloved
image of radiance and light for illustrating the divine Father-Son
relationship is tightly connected to Jn 5:26 to enhance the plausibility of his argument. However, if other biblical texts – or other
images – had been chosen for a similar induction, a different general theory might result. In fact, all the texts enumerated in *CA* III
26 are words of the Saviour himself, and are perceived to be a
challenge to Athanasius' theology. Some of these texts could be
reconciled with Athanasius' theology and are also used constructively for his theology (Jn 10:18; 17:5; Mt 11:27), but many others posed difficulties to his Christology.

The Gospel of John continues to dominate Athanasius' theology when he discusses texts on Jesus' ignorance. In the Gospel
of Mark, Jesus asks about the number of loaves and the Arians
argued therefore that the Son is not omniscient. Athanasius remarks: 'John obviously knows that it is not ignorantly but with
conscious knowledge that Christ asks, "How many loaves do you
have?" (Mk 6:38) for he writes, "This he said to test Philip; for he
himself knew what he was going to do" (Jn 6:6).'[181] Jesus is therefore not ignorant; he asks with knowledge, for questions do not
necessarily imply ignorance, but might also have an educational
purpose.[182] A similar case could be made for Jesus' question concerning Lazarus. Athanasius notes that the Lord 'who inquired
where Lazarus had been laid himself said–when he was not present, but a long way off–"Lazarus has died" (Jn 11:14), and where
his death occurred.'[183] The Son is not ignorant, but 'knows the
thoughts of his disciples ahead of time and knows what is in everyone's heart and "what is in the human person" (Jn 2:25). What
is more, he alone knows the Father and says, "I in the Father and

---

[180] *CA* III 36 (348,25–30); tr. Norris, adapted.
[181] *CA* III 37 (349,9–11); tr. Norris.
[182] Lausberg, *Handbook*, 339–345 (par 766–779).
[183] *CA* III 37 (349,18–19); tr. Norris. Cf. *CA* III 38 (349,5–350,8).

the Father in me" (Jn 14:10).'[184] Whereas the Arians postulate a
real ignorance in Jesus in the texts mentioned above, which
would disqualify him as the genuine Son of God, Athanasius finds
support in several passages from the Gospel of John to argue the
opposite. The ignorance of Jesus should therefore be located in
his fleshly state, whereas he knows everything in advance as
Word of God. This practice has, of course, less to do with exegesis
proper than with eisegesis, since Athanasius decides that some
interpretations are excluded beforehand, and the language of *theosis* as such does not appear in Scripture, in the direct relation to
the Incarnation that Athanasius envisages.

Athanasius argues that the Son's Incarnation was necessary
to effect humanity's divinisation and puts this forward as the rationale for understanding Jesus' human limitations.[185] The Son
lifts up the limited and deprived human nature by experiencing
the limitations of humanity without losing his divine status as
Word of God. Athanasius attributes potentially troublesome texts
for the true divinity of the Son to Jesus' humanity. He states that
the Son 'who glorifies others says: "Glorify me" (Jn 17:5), in order
to show that his flesh has a need for these things.'[186] Athanasius
states: 'If ... the Word did not become a human being (cf. Jn 1:14),
then by all means let receiving and lacking glory and being ignorant characterise the Logos, as you say.'[187] However, his opponents should ask: 'Why did the Logos dwell among us and became
flesh (cf. Jn 1:14)?'[188] Athanasius supplies the answer himself. For
the aim of the Word was 'to redeem the members of the human
race' and the Logos became flesh and dwelled among human beings 'in order to sanctify and divinize them'.[189]

Athanasius interprets Mt 11:27 and 28:18, which both might
be regarded as expressions of the Son's subordination, along the

---

[184] *CA* III 37 (349,20–23); tr. Norris.
[185] For Athanasius' view on divinisation, see Kharlamov, "Rhetorical Application," 115–22, 127–31.
[186] *CA* III 38 (350,20–21); tr. Norris, adapted.
[187] *CA* III 39 (350,1–2); tr. Norris.
[188] *CA* III 39 (350,9–351,10). See Meijering, *Die dritte Rede*, II:107–9.
[189] *CA* III 39 (351,14–16); tr. Norris.

same lines. After the resurrection, the Son 'received all authority
(Mt 28:18), ... but even before he said "Everything has been
handed over to me," (Mt 11:27) he was the Lord of everything.
"Everything came to be through him" (Jn 1:3) and there was "one
Lord, through whom are all things" (1 Cor 8:6).'[190] He is also the
Lord of glory (1 Cor 2:8) and 'possessed what he asked for when
he said: "... with the glory which I possessed in your presence
before the world existed (Jn 17:5)."'[191] Athanasius asserts on the
ground of Jn 1:3 and 1 Cor 8:6 that the texts that imply inferiority
of the Son in relation to the Father cannot be taken at face value.
Athanasius concludes: 'Just as he asked questions in his capacity
as a human being and raised Lazarus in his capacity as God, so
the words "he received" are said of him in his human reality.'[192]

The Gospel of John is very important in Athanasius' illustration of the ἀνθρωπίνως-θεϊκῶς scheme: 'by his works, he revealed
both the fact that he is God's Son and his own Father and, by the
passions of his flesh, that he bore a real body and that this body
was his very own'.[193] The Son 'asked questions and raised Lazarus
(Jn 11:34–43), and he rebuked his mother by saying, "my hour is
not yet come"–and immediately he made the water wine (Jn 2:4,
7–9). He was true God in the flesh, and he was true flesh in the
Logos.'[194] Athanasius often mentions the man born blind (Jn 9:1–
6) and the resurrection of Lazarus (Jn 11:34–43),[195] while the reference to the miracle with wine in Cana (Jn 2:7–8), occurs only

---

[190] *CA* III 39 (351,22–23); tr. Norris.

[191] *CA* III 39 (351,25–26); tr. Norris.

[192] *CA* III 40 (352,20–21); tr. Norris. Meijering mentions that this formulation prefigures the doctrine of *unio hypostatica*. Meijering, *Die dritte
Rede*, II:132.

[193] *CA* III 41(353,15–17); tr. Norris.

[194] *CA* III 41 (353,12–15); tr. Norris adapted.

[195] Athanasius also refers to the man born blind in *CA* III 41; *CA* III 32
(343,8); III 55 (366,6) and to the story of Lazarus in *CA* III 32 (343,9);
III 37 (348,3); III 38 (350,8); III 40 (352,20); III 46 (357,10); III 55
(366,9).

once in the *Orations*.[196] However, most crucial is Jn 1:14, as it illustrates the principle behind all the other examples given by Athanasius. He thus depends heavily on some stories and a central notion of the Gospel of John to give authoritative backing for his strategy of attributing Jesus' human weaknesses to his flesh, and the Son's divine deeds to his divinity. Meijering rightly notes that while both the divine and human actions are important in Athanasius' view, he ascribes the divine actions without hesitation to the Son, but he is reluctant to do the same in relation to the humanity of the Word.[197]

CA III 42–50: Mk 13:32

In *CA* III 42–50, Athanasius addresses one of the most difficult texts for his theology: 'But about that day or hour no one knows, neither the angels in heaven, nor the Son, but only the Father (Mk 13:32; cf. Mt 24:36).'[198] If these words are attributed to the divine Son, he is not omniscient and therefore inferior to the Father. However, since he as the divine Creator cannot be ignorant, Athanasius ascribes Mk 13:32 to the Son's humanity. For 'the Lord of heaven and earth, by whom all things were made (cf. Jn 1:3)' is not ignorant 'about [a] day and [an] hour'.[199] The minor premise – the Son is ignorant, thus as God he is ignorant – is overruled by his major premise: as the divine Creator, he cannot be ignorant.

His opponents used this text against Athanasius' type of theology. Athanasius attributes their interpretation to his opponents'

---

[196] Cf. *Fug* 13 (Opitz 77,24), where Athanasius focuses on the words 'the time has not yet come' (Jn 2:4) in the context of when to flee or not to flee.

[197] Meijering, *Die dritte Rede*, II:147–48.

[198] For Athanasius' use of this verse, see Meijering, *Die dritte Rede*, II:149–213; Ernest, *Bible*, 170–71; Paul S. Russell, "Ephraem and Athanasius on the Knowledge of Christ: Two Anti-Arian Treatments of Mark 13:32," *Gregorianum* 85 (2004): 445–74. See also *Ser* II 9.

[199] *CA* III 42 (353,6–9); tr. NPNF. See also Meijering, *Die dritte Rede*, II:150–51; Alvyn Pettersen, "The Questioning Jesus in Athanasius' Contra Arianos III," in *Arianism: Historical and Theological Reassessments*, ed. Robert C. Gregg, PMS 11 (Cambridge, MA: Philadelphia Patristic Foundation, 1985), 243.

negative *ethos* throughout the section. The Arian view is great foolishness (ἀφρονέστερον) and madness,[200] indicates ignorance,[201] and equals the giants who are fighting against God,[202] for 'all men but the Arians would join in confessing that he who knows the Father, much more knows the whole of the creation; and in that whole, its end'.[203] Athanasius further remarks that the Arians 'blaspheme the Spirit' (cf. Mt 12:32),[204] are shameless,[205] hostile to the truth and Christ,[206] and ought to seek company with the Manichees, since they hardened their heart like Pharaoh.[207]

However, Athanasius does more than discredit his opponents. He first determines the time (καιρός) when the Saviour spoke these words of ignorance: 'Not then when the heaven "came to be through him" (Jn 1:3), nor when "he was with Him, ordering" all things (Prv 8:30), nor before he became a human did he say it, but when "the Word became flesh" (Jn 1:14)', the words of Mk 13:32 were spoken.[208] The words were therefore spoken as a human, and cannot disqualify the Word's eternal divinity.

In Jn 17:1 Jesus addresses the Father: 'Father, the hour has come; glorify your Son so that the Son may glorify you.' On the basis of this statement, Athanasius claims that the Son is not ignorant about the times, because he knows the time of his suffering: 'Certainly when he says in the Gospel concerning Himself according to his humanity (κατὰ τὸ ἀνθρώπινον): "Father, the hour is come, glorify your Son" (Jn 17:1), it is plain that he knows also the hour of the end of all things, as the Word, though as man He is ignorant of it.'[209] Athanasius adds that ignorance 'of especially these things' is appropriate for humans. So, 'since he has become

---

[200] *CA* III 42 (353,9).
[201] *CA* III 42 (354,13).
[202] *CA* III 42 (353,5).
[203] *CA* III 44 (355,8–10); tr. NPNF.
[204] *CA* III 45 (356,1).
[205] *CA* III 45 (357,14–15).
[206] *CA* III 47 (358,2).
[207] *CA* III 50 (361,3–13).
[208] *CA* III 43 (354,7–9); tr. NPNF, adapted. The manuscripts RSPU have added τῷ πατρὶ ὁ λόγος after παρ' αὐτῷ, but these are omitted in AW 1.1.3.
[209] *CA* III 43 (355,14–17); tr. NPNF, adapted.

a human being, he is not ashamed ... to say "I did not know" to show that knowing as God, he is ignorant according to the flesh'.[210]

In *CA* III 44, Athanasius uses a negative deduction to argue that the Son knew everything as Word, but was ignorant as human being. Since only the angels are mentioned besides the Son in Mk 13:32, and the Holy Spirit is absent, Athanasius infers that the Spirit knows the end of times. And because the Son gives to the Spirit (cf. Jn 16:7, 14), the Son must also know the end of times.[211] Since everything that the Father has (cf. Jn 16:15), is of the Son as well, and they are in each other (cf. Jn 14:10), they must both know about the moment of the consummation of time:

> [I]f all that is the Father's, is the Son's – and this he himself has said (cf. Jn 16:15) –, and it is the Father's attribute to know the day, it is clear that the Son too knows it, having this proper to him from the Father. And again, if the Son be in the Father and the Father in the Son (cf. Jn 14:10), and the Father knows the day and the hour (Mk 13:32), it is clear that the Son, being in the Father and knowing the things of the Father, knows himself also the day and the hour.[212]

The natural meaning of Mk 13:32 is thus overruled by Athanasius' understanding of Jn 16:15 and Jn 14:10. He follows the logic that if expression x conflicts with expression y, expression x must have been stated under special circumstances, so that it can be brought into conformity with expression y. This was a strategy that many Church Fathers followed.[213] He states accordingly that it is not amazing that the Son who created everything (Jn 1:3; Col 1:17)

---

[210] *CA* III 43 (355,17–20); tr. NPNF, adapted.

[211] *CA* III 44 (355,1–4); cf. *CA* I 47–50.

[212] *CA* III 44 (355,14–356,18); tr. NPNF, adapted.

[213] Ephraim the Syrian independently developed a similar argument regarding Mark 13:32 around the same time. See Russell, "Ephraem and Athanasius," 473. This argument is common in the fourth century: most orthodox Christian writers rejected the Son's ignorance or attributed it to his humanity. See Riemer Roukema, "Noch de Zoon. Doctoraalscriptie over de uitleg van Mt 24:36/Mk 13:32 in de oude kerk" (unpubl. diss., Vrije Universiteit Amsterdam, 1980), 18–29, 39–40.

'knows [about the day]', but that it is amazing 'that such a long refutation is necessary because of the rashness that is fitting for the madness of the Ariomaniacs.'[214] Between the lines, he acknowledges in this way that he is at pains to defend his view, but he attributes it to his opponents' madness and rashness nonetheless.

In *CA* III 45–50, Athanasius only alludes a few times to Johannine material, although he points to the simultaneously human and divine acts of Jesus in raising Lazarus (cf. Jn 11:34–43). He argues from the principle of the smaller to the greater that the Son is not ignorant. If the Son knew where the body lay, he also knew the greater thing, where his soul is. This reasoning has parallels in both Aristotle (ἐκ τοῦ μᾶλλον καὶ ἧττον)[215] and the Jewish exegetical rule of Hillel: *qal wachomer*.[216] Athanasius states that the Son 'asked humanly about Lazarus when he was on his way to raise him, and knew from where he should recall Lazarus's soul – for it is a greater thing to know where the soul is, than to know where the body lay'.[217]

Athanasius expresses uncertainty about the reason for the Lord's ignorance even though he knew, and proposes an explanation of Mk 13:32 in line with the purpose of the benefit for humanity. Athanasius states: 'I have to explain it by guessing: he did it, I think (ὥς γε νομίζω), for our profit (λυσιτέλεια). May he himself, however, grant the true meaning to what we are proposing, for on both sides the Saviour secured what is beneficial for us.'[218] Athanasius presents his interpretation modestly at this point, conceding that the interpretation he gives is a possibility, rather than a certainty. In this way, Athanasius gives one of his rare expressions of uncertainty. On this point, it looks like Athanasius honestly shows that he is not sure of what the text means. He is content to indicate what the text does not mean, asserting that whatever the Son does is for humanity's benefit (συμφέρον). For

---

[214] *CA* III 44 (356,20–24); tr. NPNF, adapted.
[215] Cf. Aristotle, *Rhet.* II 23.4 and Stead, "Rhetorical Method," 126.
[216] Zwiep, Tussen tekst en lezer, 85–88.
[217] *CA* III 46 (357,10–13); tr. NPNF, adapted.
[218] *CA* III 48 (359,4–8); tr. NPNF, adapted.

'whatever he does, that he does altogether for our sake, since "the Word became flesh" (Jn 1:14) also for us'.[219] Mk 13:32 is thus explained contrary to the plain understanding and Athanasius suggests that Jesus pretended ignorance concerning the end of times, because of the deceivers that would come after him.[220] Pettersen argues that Athanasius neglects several elements regarding Jesus' ignorance, since he was content to argue that the ignorance did not relate to the divine Logos, but to the Logos incarnate.[221] Athanasius postulates in this way another form of knowledge that is not attested in the text to argue that the Son is not ignorant, in order to avoid the difficult consequences of the ignorance of the divine Son. Although Athanasius employs Scripture in explaining Mark 13:32, it is clear that his theological position overruled his concern for historically informed exegesis,[222] and his explanation does not 'account for the Lord's ignorance in any way that seems submissive to the witness of Scripture'.[223]

CA III 50b–53: Lk 2:52

In Lk 2:52, the evangelist remarks: 'Jesus increased (προέκοπτην) in wisdom and in years, and in divine and human favour'. This poses a difficulty for Athanasius' theology, since he holds that the Son *is* God's eternal Word and Wisdom. God has never been not perfect in any respect, so it is impossible that God would increase in wisdom. If Jesus increased in wisdom as the Word of God, he cannot be God's eternal Wisdom, since God's unchangeability is an axiom of both Greek philosophy and fourth-century Christianity.[224] Polemically, Athanasius states that this text has a right

---

[219] *CA* III 48 (359,12–13); tr. NPNF, adapted. Cf. *CA* III 49 (360,3; 361,22).

[220] *CA* III 49 (360,1–12).

[221] Pettersen, "Questioning Jesus," 252–53.

[222] Cf. Russell, "Ephraem and Athanasius," 466.

[223] Darren Sumner, "The Instrumentalization of Christ's Human Nature in Athanasius of Alexandria," in *StPatr* 52, ed. A. Brent and M. Vinzent (Leuven: Peeters, 2012), 138.

[224] Cf. Wolfhart Pannenberg, "Die Aufnahme des philosophischen Gottesbegriffs als dogmatisches Problem der frühchristlichen Theologie," *ZKG* 70 (1959): 1–45; Wilhelm Maas, *Unveränderlichkeit Gottes: zum Verhältnis*

meaning, which is 'ill understood' by the Arians; therefore, he aims to show 'their destructive thought' (ἡ διεφθαρμένη διάνοια).[225] Athanasius' approach is similar to that of the previous texts. He again formulates the crucial question whether the Son is a mere man or God bearing the flesh (θεός ἐστι σάρκα φορῶν). He dismisses the first option as the heresy of Paul of Samosata and favours the second option, using familiar Johannine language: 'But if he is God bearing flesh, as he truly is, and "the Word became flesh" (Jn 1:14), and being God descended upon earth, what kind of advance (προκοπήν) had he who exists equal to God? Or how could the Son increase, who is always in the Father (cf. Jn 14:10)?'[226] Athanasius has quoted Jn 1:14 numerous times in the preceding chapters[227] and he further asserts the Son's eternity by alluding to Jn 14:10, to avoid the attribution of advance (προκοπή) to the Word of God and ascribe it to his incarnate state instead. His opponents would reject the first option, and in this dilemma, they would be forced to accept Athanasius' solution: the Son is God bearing the flesh. In reality, however, they considered a third option, that the Son is a unique, somewhat divine being between the true and unbegotten God and creatures. Athanasius allows no room for such an objection and dismisses the Arian solution as implausible. He arrives at this conclusion by presenting a dilemma in which his opponents would not chose the other option either.[228]

In *CA* III 52, he alludes to Jn 14:10 and 17:3 to assert that progress in the Son is unthinkable, because the Son

> being only in the only Father (cf. Jn 14:10; 17:3) ... he remains always in Him. To human beings then belongs advance; but

---

von griechisch-philosophischer und christlicher Gotteslehre, Paderborner theologische Studien 1 (München: Schöningh, 1974); on the difference between the Platonic and Christian view on revelation, see Meijering, *Die dritte Rede*, II:196–98.

[225] *CA* III 50 (362,14–16); tr. NPNF, adapted.

[226] *CA* III 51 (362,8–11); tr. NPNF, adapted. Cf. *CA* III 51 (361,15–18); III 53 (364,6–7).

[227] *CA* III 27; 29; 30 (2); 32; 33; 35; 39 (2); 41; 43; 48.

[228] Meijering, *Die dritte Rede*, 217, 221–23.

the Son of God, since he could not advance, being perfect in the Father (cf. Jn 14:10), humbled himself for us (Phil 2:6), that in his humbling we on the other hand might be able to increase.[229]

He suggests that Luke 2:52 must be related to Jesus' humanity and the benefit of the Incarnation for humanity's sake, to avoid the implication that he is changeable as the Word of God. Athanasius interprets the advance of Jesus in a way that does not harm the Son's eternity and perfectness. He alludes to John 14:10 and 17:3 to illustrate the eternity of the Word and Wisdom. The indwelling of Father and Son in each other is present in John already, but the mutual character of the indwelling is emphasised much more strongly by Athanasius than by the evangelist John.[230]

'Advance' is a human characteristic and the words of Luke 2:52 illustrate that the Word of God became truly human, in a way that does not harm his eternal status.[231] For when Jesus is called "advanced" (προέκοπτεν) (cf. Lk 2:52), it must be clear that this 'does not impair the Father's Light (cf. Jn 1:9; 8:12; 12:46), which is the Son, but that it still shows that the Word has become man, and bore true flesh'.[232] Athanasius thus points to the Johannine notion that the Son is light. This is closely connected to Athanasius' beloved metaphor of light and radiance for Father and Son. The rationale behind this image is that light is eternally stable. Jesus' revelation as a human being, 'in the flesh' (cf. Jn 1:14), does not harm his status as Word and Wisdom of God.

An important distinction in Christology is between a Logos-sarx and a Logos-anthropos theology. The first type, Logos-sarx (Word-flesh), 'assumes that the Logos and flesh are directly conjoined in Christ and that Christ has no human soul'.[233] In this type of theology, the Word assumes human flesh as an instrument. In

---

[229] *CA* III 52 (363,6–9); tr. NPNF, adapted.

[230] Crump, "Johannine Trinity," 399–403.

[231] *CA* III 52 (363,1–5); 53 (365,20–21).

[232] *CA* III 53 (364,7–9); tr. NPNF, adapted.

[233] Aloys Grillmeier, *Christ in Christian Tradition: From the Apostolic Age to Chalcedon (451)*, trans. John Bowden (Atlanta, GA: Westminster John Knox Press, 1975), 238.

contrast, the Logos-anthropos theology assumes that the Logos and a full human are conjoined in Christ, which means that the Logos possessed a human soul.[234] While Athanasius asserts that Lk 2:52 must be understood from the perspective of the Son's flesh or his humanity, he is imprecise in his terminology and uses both terms. He states first that 'the aforementioned progress, whatever it may be, did not take place with the Word external to the flesh, ... in order that man's progress might be impeccable, because of the Word which is with them'.[235] But almost in the same breath, he states that 'the humanity (τὸ ἀνθρώπινον) made progress in Wisdom, transcending by degrees human nature, and being deified, and becoming and appearing to all as the organ of Wisdom for the operation ... of the divinity'.[236] Athanasius concludes his discussion of Lk 2:52 by pointing to the name Jesus in relation to Jesus' increase. Jesus is the Lord's name 'when he had become a human being, so that the progress is of the human nature'.[237] Athanasius is simply not consistent enough in his terminology to make him a clear Logos-sarx or Logos-anthropos proponent. While he is not willing to admit that the divine Son actually made progress in Wisdom, he does not go as far as to deny a human nature or soul completely.[238]

CA III 54–58a: Jesus' Agony and Fear

In *CA* III 54–58, Athanasius discusses two texts both related to Christ's fear: Mt 26:39 and Jn 12:27. Mt 26:39 reports about Jesus in Gethsemane: 'And going a little farther, he threw himself on the ground and prayed: "My Father, if it is possible, let this cup pass from me; yet not what I want but what you want."' In Jn 12:27, Jesus states: '"Now my soul is troubled. And what should I say – 'Father, save me from this hour'? No, it is for this reason that I have come to this hour."' The most crucial parts are: 'Let this cup pass from me' and 'Now my soul is troubled' (τετάρακται).

---

[234] On this topic, see Grillmeier, *Christ in Christian Tradition*, 167–442.

[235] *CA* III 53 (364,10–13); tr. NPNF, adapted.

[236] *CA* III 53 (365,16–18); tr. NPNF, adapted.

[237] *CA* III 53 (365,18–20); tr. NPNF, adapted.

[238] See Meijering, *Die dritte Rede*, 239–42.

The Arians held that these texts imply genuine fear and agony on the part of the divine Son, and such fear would disqualify him from being completely equal to God the Father.

Athanasius asserts that the fear in these passages is not the agony of the Word, but that of the flesh. He does not deny that the Scriptures speak about Jesus' fear, but his key assumption is related to the 'double account' of the Saviour: Jesus as the Word cannot be afraid.[239] 'If the speaker is a mere human being, let him weep and fear death, as being a human; but if he is the Word in flesh (...) whom had he to fear being God?'[240] And 'why should he fear death, who is himself Life, and is rescuing others from death?'.[241] He accepts with his opponents that God cannot be afraid and that if the Word of God as such were fearful, he could not be the genuine Word of God. He thus appeals to the distinctive Johannine title that the Son is Life. Moreover, the Word of God is the Helper (cf. Heb 13:6) of many believers in the Old Testament who helps them to overcome their fear, so that it is impossible that the Son would 'be afraid of Herod and Pontius Pilate'.[242] He points to Jesus' non-avoiding stance at his arrest (Jn 18:5) and a very decisive saying by Jesus (Jn 10:18). The Son boldly revealed himself 'when he was sought: "I am he" (Jn 18:5). For he was able not to die, as he said, "I have power to lay down my life, and I have power to take it again" and "no one takes it from me" (Jn 10:18).'[243] Jn 18:5 is taken as a natural self-identification, to demonstrate the Son's boldness. Athanasius holds that the Son has a choice to avoid death, and therefore attributes this choice to accept his death to the divine Word in Jn 10:18 to the Word's humanity.[244] Athanasius therefore selects two Johannine texts to prove that the Son did not let fear determine his decisions, which demonstrates his fearlessness as a human.

---

[239] See *CA* III 29.

[240] *CA* III 54 (365,11–13); tr. NPNF.

[241] *CA* III 54 (365,13–14).

[242] *CA* III 54 (366,15–20).

[243] *CA* III 54 (366,22–25); tr. NPNF, adapted.

[244] Alvyn Pettersen, "The Courage of Christ in the Theology of Athanasius," *SJT* 40 (1987): 366, 369.

Athanasius frequently addresses his opponents directly, thus suggesting a debate in which he has the better arguments and support from Scripture. He calls the Arians 'enemies of Christ and ungrateful Jews', who deliberately attribute fear to the Son in order to deny his true nature as Word of God.[245] However, the words of agony are not spoken before the Son was incarnated,

> but when 'the Word became flesh' (Jn 1:14) and has become man, at this time it is written in human expression (ἀνθρωπίνως εἰρῆσθαι). Surely he of whom this is written was he who raised Lazarus from the dead (cf. Jn 11:43), and made the water wine, (cf. Jn 2:7–9) and gave sight to the man born blind (cf. Jn 9:1–6) and said, 'I and my Father are one' (Jn 10:30).[246]

Because the Word, who became flesh, performed divine deeds in the flesh, the agony cannot be applied to his divinity, but to the flesh. Athanasius mentions three divine deeds, all exclusively described in the Gospel of John, sandwiched between two explicit Johannine citations. He claims a rationale for both sides of his own interpretation, by means of the figure of *sermocinatio*. The Son's fear indicates the reality of the Incarnation, for by his fear he demonstrated

> that he, being God impassible, had taken passible flesh. Yet from the works he showed himself the Word of God, who had afterwards become a human, saying: '"Although you do not believe me", while seeing that I am wrapped (περιβεβλημένον) in a human body: "yet believe the works, that you may know that I am in the Father, and the Father in me" (Jn 10:38; cf. 14:10).'[247]

Athanasius conflates the words from John and his own concerns in this passage. He makes Jesus declare to 'have put on a human body', to shun the 'shamelessness and blasphemy' of 'Christ's enemies' and even that his opponents 'violently distort the sense'.[248]

---

[245] *CA* III 55 (366,1–2); tr. NPNF, adapted. Cf. *CA* III 55 (367,17); III 58 (370,2–3, 11–13).

[246] *CA* III 55 (366,3–6); tr. NPNF, adapted.

[247] *CA* III 55 (367,13–17); tr. NPNF, adapted. Cf. *CA* III 67 (381,27–30).

[248] *CA* III 55 (367,17–19); tr. NPNF, adapted.

By using the figure of *sermocinatio*, Athanasius suggests that it is not he who accuses the Arians; no, it is Jesus Christ himself who blames the Arians for their human thoughts concerning the Saviour.

Athanasius mentions Jn 10:30 again quickly afterwards. Restating his case slightly, he asserts the existence of two sets of sayings that his opponents fail to discern. While the Arians should understand that the words 'I and the Father are one' (Jn 10:30) clearly demonstrate 'the oneness of the Godhead and his belonging to the Father's essence,' ... they should understand that statements concerning Jesus' weakness 'are said of his human body'.[249] Athanasius thus argues that both types of expressions have a significant purpose; however, his double account of the Saviour was designed to counter his opponents' exegesis in the first place. Athanasius also appeals to the context of Jn 12:27 and Mt 26:39 to soften the implications of Jesus' fear. From Jn 12:27 as a whole, he argues that the Son acted both divinely and humanly at the same time. The Son 'willed what he prayed for, for therefore had he come; but when in fact the willing belonged to him – for because of that he came (cf. Jn 12:27b) –, the terror belonged to the flesh.'[250] Athanasius asserts Jesus' courage by alluding to the words of Jn 12:27b. Jesus' affirmation indicates that he did not avoid his death in order to redeem humanity.

Athanasius further quotes Jn 10:18 in relation to Jn 12:27, and contrasts in this way the necessity of Jesus' death for humanity with the voluntary action of the Lord. The Son 'said humanly: "Now is my soul troubled" (Jn 12:27) and divinely: "I have power to lay down my life (τὴν ψυχήν), and power to take it again" (Jn 10:18). (...) The Lord, who is himself immortal and has a mortal flesh, had power, as God, to become separate from the body and to take it again, when he wanted.'[251] Subsequently, Athanasius cites Ps 15(16):10, LXX: 'You will not abandon my soul (τὴν ψυχήν) to Hades or give your devout to see corruption.'[252] This

---

[249] *CA* III 56 (367,1–4); tr. NPNF, adapted. Cf. *CA* III 56 (367,8–368,10).
[250] *CA* III 57 (368,2–369,4); tr. NPNF, adapted.
[251] *CA* III 57 (369,23–25. 27–370,30); tr. NPNF, adapted.
[252] *CA* III 57 (370,30–31); tr. NPNF, adapted.

passage is crucial for determining whether Athanasius held that the Logos had a human soul or not. First of all, it must be noted that Jn 10:18 refers this time to the divine Word, and that the occurrence in *CA* III 54, which attributed Jn 10:18 to the human, was most likely an *ad hoc* argumentation, motivated by polemic rather than theology.[253] Grillmeier argues that Athanasius did not attack the Logos-sarx scheme of the Arians as such, and therefore cannot teach a human soul in Christ at this point.[254] However, Meijering suggests that the occurrence of 'soul' in Ps 15:10 (LXX) is meaningful, because Athanasius quoted biblical texts not primarily because of their meaning (Sinn), but because of their diction (Wortlaut).[255] Although Athanasius does not really incorporate the concept of a soul in Christ into the framework of his theology, the Word has not just a body, but also a soul and spirit.[256] More clarity is difficult to gain at this point. Athanasius did not deny Christ's human soul, but neither did he explicitly affirm it.

Apart from the consideration that it would complicate his polemic, I believe Athanasius did not emphasise a human soul in Christ because his soteriology did not need a strong emphasis on the human soul of Christ. According to his soteriology, the Word was subject to imperfections on earth to effect perfection for humanity: 'For as he, when he came in our body, was conformed to our condition (τὰ ἡμῶν ἐμιμήσατο), likewise we, when we receive him, share in the immortality that is effected by him.'[257] The meaning of τὰ ἡμῶν ἐμιμήσατο is understood by Frances Young in the sense that Athanasius wants to establish a pretence of Christ's fear in this passage, rather than acknowledge genuine fear, and that he thus compromises Christ's actual humanity.[258] This is rightly contested by Alvin Pettersen, who suggests that 'imitated'

---

[253] Pettersen, "Courage of Christ," 369.

[254] Grillmeier, *Christ*, 308–28, here 313–15.

[255] Meijering, *Die dritte Rede*, II:270–71.

[256] Meijering, *Die dritte Rede*, II:65–66; see also Pettersen, "Courage of Christ," 365.

[257] *CA* III 57 (370,31–35); tr. NPNF, adapted. Cf. *CA* III 58 (370, 6–8).

[258] Frances M. Young, "A Reconsideration of Alexandrian Christology," *JEH* 22 (1971): 107; cf. Christopher Stead, "The Scriptures and the Soul of Christ in Athanasius," *VC* 36 (1982): 234–35, 245–49.

does not deny the reality of Christ's passions, but that Christ was not conformed to humanity's condition, but rather made it his own. In Pettersen's judgment, Athanasius' soteriology demands the reality of Christ's fear, because in the 'dynamic and continuous interaction between the divine Logos and the assumed body, ... salvation is being wrought continuously'.[259] Athanasius was not concerned about a distinction between physical and psychological passions, but only about separating Christ's fears from the divinity of the Logos, for he contrasts 'man's creatureliness ... with God's divinity, not man's body ... with his soul'.[260] This treatment of Jesus' fear does not feel adequate from a modern perspective, but is quite in line with the literary conventions of the Gospels and ancient biographical writings, and in the light of his time his account is very realistic.[261]

Nevertheless, even with this concession, it remains a fact that Athanasius understood the agony texts quite contrary to their natural meaning. Frances Young detects problems in Athanasius' discussion of the psychological weaknesses of Christ in the *Orations*. Nevertheless, she perceives potential for the Christology of Athanasius by suggesting why 'a positive use of the idea of Christ's human soul was unnecessary, and its absence did not imply an inadequate or docetic interpretation of the Incarnation'.[262] While Athanasius offers a Logos-sarx theology that 'is not essentially docetic', it is anachronistic to say that he fell into the same error as Apollinaris, who published his view on that subject after Athanasius.[263] A passive role for Christ's human nature and soul further fits quite well with 'traditional affirmations about the Incarnation' and is 'consistent with the account of sin and salvation' of traditional Christian thinking, in which human beings need to be receptive of God's grace.[264] Andrew Louth tries to find a *via media* by looking at the reason for the absence of references to the

---

[259] Pettersen, "Christ's Fear," 331–34, here 334.

[260] Pettersen, "Christ's Fear," 336.

[261] Pettersen, "Christ's Fear," 339–40.

[262] Young, "Reconsideration," 107.

[263] Young, "Reconsideration," 107.

[264] Young, "Reconsideration," 114.

human soul, a position somewhat similar to that of Frances Young. In this view, Athanasius did not deny a human soul in Christ, but rather stimulated in hindsight the need for a human soul in Christ, given his persistent emphasis on the reality of the Incarnation, which involved more than merely the Word's clothing in the flesh.[265] This corroborates with G.D. Dragas' contribution on the subject, that Athanasius employs terms related to ἄνθρωπος more often than σάρξ and σῶμα, although the use of language as such must be interpreted with caution.[266] Alvyn Pettersen's comment that '[g]iven then the parameters within which Athanasius is writing, the treatment of the fearful cries of the condemned Jesus is in fact poignantly realistic' shows that Athanasius devotes attention to the natural meaning of the text as well.[267] Athanasius' discussion of the human soul in Christ has thus strong instrumentalist connotations, but it is not purely instrumentalist.[268]

I believe that this section demonstrates a 'pastoral exhortation', not an abstract dogmatic polemic as Kannengiesser traced throughout *Oration* III.[269] It seems that Athanasius genuinely believed that he was truthful to the message of Scripture, and that his view on the divinisation of human beings, though not traceable as such in Scripture, made him genuinely convinced of the correctness of his theology. In the argumentation for his doctrine of the Son, which excludes genuine fear, the scheme of simultaneously human and divine deeds performed by Jesus Christ and

---

[265] Andrew Louth, "Athanasius' Understanding of the Humanity of Christ," in *StPatr* 16,2, ed. Elizabeth A. Livingstone (Berlin: Akademie Verlag, 1985), 315–18.

[266] George Dion Dragas, "Ἐνανθρώπησις, or ἐγένετο ἄνθρωπος. A Neglected Aspect of Athanasius' Christology," in *StPatr* 16,2, ed. Elizabeth A. Livingstone (Berlin: Akademie Verlag, 1985), 283; Grillmeier relativises the importance of the terminology underlying the concepts that several authors had, in *Christ*, 309.

[267] Pettersen, "Christ's Fear," 340; cf. Young, "Reconsideration," 108–9; George Dion Dragas, *St. Athanasius Contra Apollinarem*, Church and Theology 6 (Athens: n.p., 1985).

[268] Sumner, "Instrumentalization," 138.

[269] Contra Kannengiesser, *Athanase*, 311.

the crucial proof-texts are highly indebted to John's Gospel (Jn 10:18; 18:5). Contrary to the focus on Jesus' fear (ἐταράχθη; (Jn 13:21; cf. 12:27)), Athanasius highlights the degree of control in the Son and his courage not to abandon his mission to save humanity.

All in all, Athanasius' governing principle is not just the plain reading of Scripture. All texts that describe Jesus as weak, ignorant and fearful receive another meaning, following from the assumption that the true Son of God cannot be limited, because he is equal to the Father. Many of his premises are derived from Scripture, but an underlying principle governs his interpretation, even if it seems bluntly to contradict the plain meaning of the text. Since he is convinced that all the books of the divine Scripture clearly declare the Son's eternity, all passages must be read in harmony with this crucial notion, to which John's Gospel is a prominent witness. He is selective and sometimes also inconsistent in his use of Scripture. Jn 10:18a is mentioned two times, once taken to signify the Son's humanity (*CA* III 54) and once his divinity (*CA* III 57). Furthermore, Jn 10:18b, 'I have received this command from my Father', is neglected completely by Athanasius. The problem with this strategy is that it fails to take seriously certain crucial elements within the biblical texts. Athanasius downplays in this instance a prominent Johannine element, because the one element suits his purpose and the other does not. In John, and in all four canonical Gospels, Jesus is considered the Son of God and divine, but he is nowhere portrayed beyond fear and other human characteristics. And even in John's Gospel, the most explicit claims that Athanasius emphasises are not uttered by Jesus himself, but as a reflection of the evangelist (Jn 1:1–3, 18) or as the conclusion of others (Jn 5:18; 20:28).[270] John felt much freer to emphasise Jesus' physical and psychological fears and struggles, as well as his total obedience to the Father, than Athanasius did. While Athanasius devotes attention to both the Son's fear and obedience, he can only appreciate the expressions of fear in relation to the flesh of the Word, as well as infer from

---

[270] Cf. Gaston, "Gospel of John," 133–35.

the obedience theme that the divine Son always cooperates harmoniously with the Father.

That Athanasius' theologising is not without problems is clear from the analysis above. But what does this critique mean for the evaluation of Athanasius' opponents? They might be closer to present-day views on some issues than Athanasius is. Because of the fragmentary nature of many of their works, mainly delivered through writers hostile to them, judgments on their views should be made with caution. Nevertheless, Asterius and others, like Athanasius, worked within a fourth-century paradigm with ontological concerns that were simply not present in the first century when the Gospels were written. As in Athanasius' case, their concern for the Jesus who lived in history is limited. In the fourth-century debate, despite all the differences, Jesus became largely dehistoricised. It is true that Athanasius is not very clear about his attribution of a human soul to Christ. However, Athanasius' opponents were no more appreciative of a human soul than Athanasius was.[271]

CA III 58B–67: DIVINE NATURE VERSUS DIVINE WILL

In *CA* III 58b–67, Athanasius discusses the question whether God willed his Son, by attacking the view that the Son became through the intention and will (βουλήσει καὶ θελήσει) of the Father.[272] That

---

[271] Hanson, *Search*, 25–26, 65, 110–16; Lorenz, "Christusseele"; Grillmeier, *Christ*, 238–45. In the works of Hanson and Grillmeier, the sermons that are sometimes attributed to Asterius the Sophist play a significant role. This attribution has been rejected by Wolfram Kinzig, *In Search of Asterius: Studies on the Authorship of the Homilies on the Psalms*, FKDG 47 (Göttingen: Vandenhoeck & Ruprecht, 1990); for a discussion of the human soul in Eusebius of Caesarea's work, see Strutwolf, *Die Trinitätstheologie und Christologie des Euseb von Caesarea*, 312–75.

[272] *CA* III 59 (371,5–6). Albrecht Dihle argues that βούλομαι often carries a somewhat intellectualistic connotation, i.e. deliberation plus decision, while θέλω emphasises volition; yet there is no definite difference in meaning between them. See *The Theory of Will in Classical Antiquity*, Sather Classical Lectures 48 (Berkeley: University of California Press, 1982), 145–49. NPNF translates: "good will and pleasure", E. P. Meijering: "den Entschluss und den Willen", A. Rousseau "par décision et

the Son is begotten because of the Father's will is stated by Arius, the Eastern Council of Serdica (343), and the Ekthesis Macrostichos (345).[273] In Athanasius' refutation of his opponents, he follows basically four steps: (1) the concept of will is important in the thought of heretical writers, (2) the Son's natural belonging to the Father precedes will, (3) the Son is the living Will of the Father, (4) the Father is delighted in the Son, who is his living Will.

CA III 58b–59: Will and Heretical Writers

Athanasius suggests that the Arians invent new arguments as the hydra from Greek myths produces new snakes when the old ones die.[274] They are 'enemies of the truth' and 'Christ's opponents in all things', who invent even more objections against the truth than the devil himself.[275] Athanasius does not object to the expression that God willed the Son as such, for 'if any of those who believe rightly were to say this in simplicity, there would be no cause to be suspicious of the expression', but 'the phrase is from the heretics, and the words of heretics are suspicious' (cf. Prv

---

volonté", C. J. de Vogel "wilsbesluit". I translate 'intention and will'. I want to thank the classicist Tertius Bolhuis for discussing this section with me, especially with regard to the translation of the Greek terminology. I am of course responsible for the decisions I made in this respect. For more information concerning the terminology, see Vinzent, *Asterius*, 186–92.

[273] On Arius' words, see Urk. 1 (3,1–2). The Eastern bishops at Serdica (343) anathematised the view that the Father did not beget according to his intention or will 'quod neque consilio neque voluntat pater genuerit filium, anathematizat sancta et catholica ecclesia' (Dok. 41.13, 5 (Brennecke 275,10–12); AW 3.1.3); cf. Ekthesis Makrostichos: 'Zugleich aber durchschauen wir auch die, die irrsinnigerweise sagen, der Sohn sei nicht aus Wunsch und Wollen gezeugt, offensichtlich aber Gott einen willenslosen und wahllosen Zwang zuschreiben, damit er unfreiwillig den Sohn zeuge, als äußerst gottlos und der Kirche fremd' (Dok. 44, 12 (Brennecke 285,20–24); AW 3.1.3).

[274] *CA* III 58 (371,16–20). See also Meijering, *Die dritte Rede*, II:277–78; III:15–17.

[275] *CA* III 58–59 (371,20–23; 1–3).

12:5–6).[276] He says this most likely because orthodox writers before him used the concept of will in relation to God's begetting as
well.[277]

Athanasius claims that 'he who says: "The Son came to be by
will" states the same as he who says: "Once he was not" and "The
Son came to be out of nothing and is a creature".'[278] Against the
Arians, he asserts that the Son does not exist because of an act of
will. He cites seven scriptural texts to support his claim, in which
Jn 1:1 functions as the crucial proof that the Word precedes
will.[279] Since the Word was in the beginning, he is not begotten
by will: 'Everywhere all [texts] tell us of the being of the Word,
but none of His being 'by will,' nor at all of His making.'[280] The
origin of the Arian teaching is therefore not the divine Scripture.
On the contrary, Athanasius traces the Arian understanding of the
Son back to the perverseness (κακόνοιαν) of Valentinus and Ptol-
emy, two Gnostic teachers who held that the unbegotten one
(ἀγένητον) possessed two attributes: thought (ἔννοια) and will
(θέλησις).[281]

The polemical intent of the association between the Arians
and Valentinians is clear, for Athanasius wants to exploit the contrast between the sources of Scripture and heretical thinking as
the respective sources of their theology to win trust for his own
position, and to discredit his opponents' character. He polemically suggests that the Arian heresy via the Gnostics can be traced
back to Simon the Magician, for to the Arians 'must be said what
was said to Simon Magus; may the ungodliness of Valentinus

---

[276] *CA* III 59 (371,7–10); tr. NPNF, adapted.

[277] For comments on the divine will in relation to Christ in Justin and
Origen, see Lyman, *Christology*, 23–25; 69–75; cf. Meijering, *Orthodoxy
and Platonism*, 70; Dihle, *Theory of Will*, 116, 226.

[278] *CA* III 59 (372,15–16); tr. NPNF adapted. For these slogans, see *CA* I
11–13; III 61 and 4.2.1 above.

[279] *CA* III 59 (372,23–24). The other texts are Mt 3:17; Ps 45:1 (LXX 44:1);
Ps 36:9 (LXX 35:9); Heb 1:3; Phil 2:6; Col 1:15.

[280] *CA* III 60 (372,1–2); tr. NPNF, adapted.

[281] *CA* III 60 (372,4. 7); III 66 (380,13–15). In *Ser* I 11, Athanasius associates the Pneumatomachi with the Valentinians. See also Meijering, *Die
dritte Rede*, III:26.

"perish with you" (cf. Acts 8:20)'.[282] This remark seems purely rhetorical, to link the heresy back to NT times.[283] In *CA* III 67, he similarly suggests that the teaching of the Valentinians is revived by the Arians: 'let the Son not be called a product of will, nor the doctrine of Valentinus be introduced into the Church, but the living Will and true offspring by nature, as the radiance from the light'.[284]

The actual correspondence between the teachings of Valentinus and the Arians is rather difficult to underpin, since their teachings are predominantly preserved in hostile sources.[285] However, Athanasius' discussion of Heb 1:4 (cf. *CA* I 54–64) suggests that the Arians doubted a completely qualitative difference between the Son and angels. Furthermore, while Valentinus' teaching of the Son as emanation is explicitly rejected by Arius, the Arian emphasis on the Son's existence through the decision and will of the Father does introduce a sort of posteriority of the Son to the Father.[286] For that reason, Athanasius could conveniently accuse both of the same error.

CA III 60–63: The Son is Begotten by Nature

In *CA* III 60, Athanasius quotes Asterius, who asserted the similarity between the divine acts of begetting and creating:

> For if it is unworthy of the Framer of all to make willingly, let willing (θέλειν) be removed in all similar cases, so that his

---

[282] *CA* III 65 (378,11–13); tr. NPNF.

[283] Meijering, *Die dritte Rede*, III:71.

[284] *CA* III 67 (380,1–3); tr. NPNF, adapted.

[285] From a modern perspective, the relation between Gnosticism and Valentinus, as well as the concept of Gnosticism in general, is quite problematic. See Markschies, *Valentinus Gnosticus?*; Ismo Dunderberg, *Beyond Gnosticism: Myth, Lifestyle, and Society in the School of Valentinus* (New York: Columbia University Press, 2008); Karen L. King, *What Is Gnosticism?* (Cambridge, MA: Harvard University Press, 2005).

[286] Urk. 6 (12,10–11). Cf. Rudolf Lorenz, *Arius judaizans? Untersuchungen zur dogmengeschichtlichen Einordnung des Arius*, FKDG 31 (Göttingen: Vandenhoeck & Ruprecht, 1980), 107–22. Arius is not a Gnostic, although there are some parallels (119).

dignity might be preserved unimpaired. Or if it befits God to intend (βούλεσθαι), then let this better way exist in the case of the first offspring. For it is not possible that it should be fitting for one and the same God to have the will to make the creatures, and not intend it as well.[287]

Athanasius summarises that this leads to the view that 'offspring and work are the same (τὸ γέννημα καὶ τὸ ποίημα ταὐτόν ἐστι) and the Son is one out of all the offsprings'.[288] According to Athanasius, Asterius claims that if the Son is not begotten by the will of the Father, he is conceived against God's will (παρὰ γνώμην).[289] Athanasius argues that their alternatives are incorrect, since it excludes the category: being by nature. There is thus rational disagreement on two issues: (1) the correspondence of the acts of begetting and creation, and (2) the implication of a denial of involvement of divine will in begetting.

Athanasius asserts that all of creation exists because of a decision of God's will, and was once not. In contrast, the Son is beloved (cf. Mt 3:17) and different from all of creation, because everything has come to be through him (cf. Jn 1:3).[290] The concept of divine will is therefore inappropriate to describe the Son's begetting. For 'if, in whom he makes [i.e. the Word of God], in him also is the intention (βούλησις), and in Christ is the will of the Father, how can he, like others, come into being by intention and will?'[291] The claims that the Son came 'by will' and 'there was once he was not' are therefore identical (ταὐτόν ἐστιν).[292]

Athanasius next records his opponents' concern to speak of the Son's begetting 'by will': 'Unless he has become by intention (βουλήσει), God got a Son by necessity and against His will

---

[287] *CA* III 60 (373,19–23 = Asterius, fr. 19 (Vinzent)); tr. NPNF, adapted.

[288] *CA* III 60 (373,24–25); tr. NPNF, adapted. See also Meijering, *Die dritte Rede*, I:76–77.

[289] *CA* III 62 (375,9.17); III 66 (379,7).

[290] On Mt 3:17, see *CA* III 59 (372,22); *CA* III 65 (379,30–31). On Jn 1:3, *CA* III 62 (375,2); *CA* III 64 (377,3).

[291] *CA* III 61 (374,16–18); tr. NPNF.

[292] *CA* III 61 (374,21–22) cf. *CA* III 62 (375,1–5).

(ἀνάγκη καὶ μὴ θέλων).'[293] According to the Arians, to deny will in the Son's begetting is to impose compulsion on God and to project simultaneously human characteristics onto God. Athanasius asserts that 'compulsion is an opposite of will, but what is according to nature transcends and precedes intention'.[294] Whereas humans possess a free will, God transcends the realm of free will, and therefore God does not act according to free will.[295] The Arians are therefore wrong to 'dare to apply human contrarieties in the instance of God, "necessity" and "against will" (παρὰ γνώμην), to be able thereby to deny that there is a true Son of God.'[296]

According to Athanasius, the Arian suggestion presents a false dilemma: the choice is not between being 'willed' or 'not-willed'. Existence because of nature (φύσις) transcends existence because of will. In *CA* III 62, he illustrates this claim in relation to God's goodness. 'Necessity' is an improper categorisation, because what God produces by nature is not imposed upon Him. Therefore, it is impossible and nonsensical to suggest that God might have decided to be not good; God's goodness by nature guarantees that his goodness is eternal.[297] And if this is true, it is by analogy also applicable to his Fatherhood; the Son's begetting is not forced upon God, nor against his will, but is by nature. For 'if it is irrational (ἄλογος) to speak of necessity concerning God, and that He is therefore by nature good, much more and more truly is He Father of the Son by nature and not by will'.[298] In *CA* III 63, Athanasius argues that God's existence does not depend on a decision or will, but that He exists naturally, just as He is good

---

[293] *CA* III 62 (375,5–6); tr. NPNF, adapted. = Asterius, fr. 20 (Vinzent) «εἰ μὴ βουλήσει γέγονεν, οὐκοῦν ἀνάγκη καὶ μὴ θέλων ἔσχεν ὁ θεὸς υἱόν». Vinzent deems it likely to be a fragment of Asterius, see *Asterius*, 195.

[294] *CA* III 62 (375,9–10); tr. NPNF adapted.

[295] See further Meijering, *Die dritte Rede*, III: 47–48, 68; cf. Dihle, *Theory of Will*, 116–17.

[296] *CA* III 62 (375,16–18); tr. NPNF.

[297] *CA* III 62 (375,18–21). See further Meijering, *Orthodoxy and Platonism*, 74–78.

[298] *CA* III 62 (376,24–26); tr. NPNF, adapted. However, Meijering points to a parallel in Numenius, fragment 6 (des Places). Meijering, *Die dritte Rede*, III:51; see also Widdicombe, *The Fatherhood of God*, 168–69.

by nature.[299] Athanasius thus asserts by analogy that the Father does not choose to be with or without his λόγος, but that his Word is naturally present in Him.

CA III 64–65: The Son is the Living Will

When Athanasius has established that will is an inappropriate category for the Son's begetting, he claims that the Son 'is himself the Father's living Will (βουλή ζῶσα)'.[300] And if the Son is the living will, it is nonsensical to speak of his existence 'by will', just as it is impossible that God would deliberate about his own substance.[301] Athanasius produces an enthymeme to assert that the Son's existence transcends the category of will:

> Therefore, if the creatures (ποιήματα) have come into existence by intention and favour (βουλήσει καὶ εὐδοκίᾳ ὑπέστη) and all of creation has become through will ... and 'everything has come into existence through' the Word (Jn 1:3), then he is far from (ἐκτός) those who have become by will, but he is much more the living Will (βουλή ζῶσα) of the Father, through whom everything has come.[302]

Athanasius claims that the line between God and creation is absolute: all creation subsists by will and intention, but the Word is the cause of their subsistence, because everything has come through him (Jn 1:3). In countering the Arian thesis that the Son has come to be through intention and will, the Gospel of John is important in an indirect way. Jn 1:1 and 1:3 are referred to, and Athanasius also quotes Jn 14:10. Will cannot precede the Son, because the Son is in the Father. Athanasius puts the notion of will in opposition to the primacy of the Son's existence in the Father. '[I]f intention (βούλησις) precedes in the Father, the Son's words are not true: "I in the Father" (Jn 14:10).'[303] Therefore, the

---

[299] *CA* III 63 (376,1–12).

[300] *CA* III 63 (376,21–22); tr. NPNF adapted. αὐτὸς ἂν εἴη τοῦ πατρὸς ἡ ζῶσα βουλή. Cf. *CA* II 2–3.

[301] *CA* III 63 (376,13–17).

[302] *CA* III 64 (377,1. 3–5); tr. NPNF adapted.

[303] *CA* III 64 (377,18–378,19); tr. NPNF adapted. Cf. *CA* III 67 (380,4; 381,27–29).

Son is different from creatures in substance, because the Son is Lord and all creatures are servants.[304]

Athanasius argues that if the Son is not the living will of the Father, 'reasoning, will and wisdom exist in God like a human capacity that comes and goes (ἕξιν συμβαίνουσαν καὶ ἀποσυμβαίνουσαν ἀνθρωπίνως)'.[305] It is improbable that the 'Arians' actually taught that God's will and Wisdom are accidental, and it is therefore most likely that Athanasius infers this consequence from their emphasis on the Son's begetting by intention and will. In their view, theoretically, though certainly not in practice, the Son might not have been begotten if God had not wanted to beget him.[306] He suggests that his opponents' view that the Son came into existence by intention and will 'is incompatible with God and is opposed to his Scriptures'.[307] Athanasius rejects it not only because of its lack of foundation in Scripture, but also because of its consequences. This correlates with the observation that Athanasius appeals relatively infrequently to Scripture in this section to back up his views. Inferences from Scripture, rather than a direct appeal to Scripture, are the only possible way to solve these questions. For the notion of the Son as living Will of the Father is not found as such in Scripture, just as the Arian solution of the Son's existence by intention and will is not found in it either.

CA III 66–67: The Father's Delight in the Son

Once Athanasius has established that the Son is the living Will, who exists naturally in the Father, he is able to express in what way the Father wants the Son (cf. Mt 3:17): 'the Son is wanted by the Father, as he says himself: "The Father loves the Son, and shows Him all things" (Jn 5:20).'[308] He makes it clear that the Father's will is not the origin of the Son's existence, emphasising the reciprocity of the love of Father and Son as well: 'For by that will with which the Son is willed by the Father, is the Father also

---

[304] *CA* III 64 (378,22–25).

[305] *CA* III 65 (378,7–9). tr. NPNF adapted.

[306] Meijering, *Die dritte Rede*, III: 69–70.

[307] *CA* III 65 (379,20–23); tr. NPNF.

[308] *CA* III 66 (379,2–4;); tr. NPNF, adapted.

the object of the Son's love, will, and honour. And the will which is from Father in Son is one, so that here too we may contemplate the Son in the Father and the Father in the Son (cf. Jn 14:10).'[309] In this way, Athanasius avoids the suggestion that the Son's natural begetting contains any notion of compulsion. In doing so, Athanasius strongly emphasises the reciprocity of Father and Son. He adapts Jn 14:10 by substituting 'I' for 'the Son', to highlight the reciprocity much more strongly than the evangelist most likely intended.[310]

These words above must be discussed in relation to the claim of Albrecht Dihle that Gregory of Nazianzus opposes Athanasius' view 'that God had generated the Son by necessity and not voluntarily'.[311] Dihle is correct in stating that the concept of free will is more important for Gregory of Nazianzus than for Athanasius, but his description of Athanasius is incorrect. While Athanasius rejects the Son's begetting by necessity, he concedes that it is appropriate to regard God as willing the Son with some qualifications as well.[312] For 'the existence of the Son, even if He did not come to be "by will", [is] not unwanted nor against the intention' of the Father either.[313] Athanasius emphasises the reciprocity of the willing of Father and Son, claiming that 'one might rightly say that the Father has love and desire towards the Son, and the Son has love and will towards the Father'.[314] Although his opponents strongly emphasised the concept of intention and will in the Son's begetting, Athanasius still allows room for God's willing the Son. As long as the willing is not considered a substitute for the Son's natural existence, as Asterius suggested, Athanasius is able to maintain the language of God's willing the Son. The argument that the Son is not willed by the Father has therefore a somewhat

---

[309] *CA* III 66 (379,10–380,13); tr. NPNF, adapted.

[310] See Barrett, *John*, 460, 512.

[311] Dihle, *Theory of Will*, 117, 227–28.

[312] Cf. Meijering, *Orthodoxy and Platonism*, 83–84; idem, "Doctrine of the Will and of the Trinity in the Orations of Gregory of Nazianzus," in *God, Being, History. Studies in Patristic Philosophy*, ed. E. P. Meijering (Amsterdam: North-Holland Publishing, 1975), 226–27.

[313] *CA* III 66 (379,5–6).

[314] *CA* III 66 (380,29–30); tr. NPNF, adapted.

circumstantial character. So Gregory of Nazianzus is able to consider this issue without the immediate discussion at hand, to arrive at the position that the Son is both naturally and by intention (προαίρεσις) within the Godhead.[315]

In *CA* III 67, Athanasius restates his position that the Son is naturally in the Father with biblical material. The Son is the Will of the Father, because the Father has said:

> 'My heart brought forth a good Word' (Ps 45:2) and the Son likewise: 'I in the Father and the Father in me' (Jn 14:10). But if the Word be in the heart, where is intention? And if the Son is in the Father, where is the will? And if he is Intention himself, how is the intending in the intention?[316]

With these questions, Athanasius concludes that the view that the Son is deliberately willed by the Father contradicts itself. The questions create the suggestion that his opponents have no response to Athanasius' response above. But the final appeal of Athanasius is not phrased as a debate between himself and the Arians. He inserts the figure of *sermocinatio* to construct an imaginary appeal of Jesus himself, who urges the Arians to stop taking offence at his human characteristics:

> For Truth is loving towards men and cries continually: 'If because of the wrapping of the body you do not believe me, then believe the works, that you may know that "I am in the Father and the Father in me" (Jn 10:38 and 14:10), and "I and the Father are one" (Jn 10:30), and "he that has seen me has seen the Father" (Jn 14:9).'[317]

Athanasius strongly adapts the Johannine material and places Jesus' words in the context of the fourth-century debate. He adapts the words of Jesus from the Gospel of John, calling Jesus the Truth (cf. Jn 14:6), and he further refers to the scene of Jn 10:37–38 in a creative way. In John's Gospel, Jesus requests the Pharisees not to be offended by his words, but merely to look at the

---

[315] Dihle, *Theory of Will*, 116–17; 226–28; cf. Meijering, "Doctrine of the Will," 225.

[316] *CA* III 67 (380,3–6); tr. NPNF, adapted.

[317] *CA* III 67 (381,27–30); tr. NPNF, adapted. Cf. *CA* III 55 (367,14–18).

works he performs divinely. Athanasius suggests that the Arians similarly should not take offence at the Son's Incarnation, and that they are urged by the Son himself to believe that the Son and Father indwell in each other (Jn 14:10), are one (Jn 10:30) and that the Son truly reveals the Father (Jn 14:9). As pointed out before, while there is correspondence between these three texts and Athanasius' doctrine of the Son, Athanasius takes the meaning of these texts further than John imagined.

Athanasius concludes the *Orations* with a polemical 'grand finale' after this block of Johannine texts. His opponents are 'miserable men, who go around like beetles, seeking with their father the devil excuses for their irreligion'.[318] Their arguments have nothing to do with a real understanding of the Scriptures or Christianity, for what excuses can they find 'unless they borrow their blasphemies from the Jews and Caiaphas, and take atheism from the Gentiles? For the divine Scriptures are closed to them, and from every part of them they are refuted as senseless and Christ's enemies (καὶ πανταχόθεν ἐξ αὐτῶν ἠλέγχθησαν ἄφρονες καὶ χριστομάχοι).'[319] The Arians are thus refuted on the ground of wrong use of Scripture, contradictory reasoning and impious behaviour and thoughts.

CONCLUSION

This analysis has shed interesting light on Athanasius' reception of John's Gospel in *Oration* III. In the first part of *Oration* III (1–25), two crucial Johannine texts that function prominently throughout the *Orations* are safeguarded for his theology. Two Johannine sayings (14:10 and 10:30) were understood self-evidently in *Orations* I-II, but discussed in their own right in this *Oration*. This shows that his opponents derived other conclusions from these sayings. His appeals to Scripture are intertwined with arguments for the reasonability of his usage of the texts as well as with polemical attacks. Other passages from John (5:17; 14:9; 16:15, as well as 10:30 and 14:10 themselves) and images from the lifeless creation are especially employed to defend his

---

[318] *CA* III 67 (381,34–35); tr. NPNF, adapted.
[319] *CA* III 67 (381,36–38); tr. NPNF, adapted. Cf. κακόφρονες in *CA* III 67 (381,23).

position. Athanasius' use of John's Gospel is not only pervasive, but also highly selective, for certain notions and texts return time and again, while other notions are downplayed. One particular stylistic feature that appears mainly in *Oration* III is the *fictio personae* or *prosopopoeia*, non-living objects that are imagined speaking. The related figure of *sermocinatio* occurs in other places too, but is especially crucial in Athanasius' interpretation of Jn 17:11, 20–23 (*CA* III 17–25). By reformulating John's language in the imagined discourse of Jesus, Athanasius asserts that his interpretation is correct.

In the second part, *CA* III 26–58a, Athanasius frequently refers to the Johannine miracles that mention both the human and divine deeds of Jesus in the same breath. All biblical texts that indicate physical or psychological weaknesses are assigned to the incarnate state of the Son, often with reference to Jn 1:14. This is not the natural or even likely meaning of Jn 1:14, thus demonstrating that Athanasius attached a new meaning to John 1:14 in the context of his time. This is his way of understanding Jesus' ignorance (Mk 13:32), progress in wisdom (Lk 2:52) and agony (Mt 26:39; Jn 12:27). Athanasius also takes up the Johannine tensions between Jesus and the Jews, in order to associate the Arians with the Jews and suggest their negative *ethos*.

In the third part (III 58b–67), Athanasius' use of Scripture is less pervasive, because the heart of the matter, whether the Son is willed by the Father or exists naturally with the Father, is a question that as such is not discussed in Scripture. Athanasius takes several illustrations from Scripture, but in the actual argument, Scripture receives a modest place. When he does refer to Scripture, however, John 1:1 and 1:3, together with 1 Corinthians 8:6 and Colossians 1:16–17, are important. Furthermore, Jn 10:30, and Jn 14:6, 9, 10 reappear in Jesus' imaginary address in which he refutes the Arian view personally. In this section, the interplay between Scripture, argumentation and polemic is very obvious.

Chapter Seven.
Conclusion

The main question of this research concerned how Athanasius used the Gospel of John as an ethical and logical means of persuasion in the *Orations against the Arians*. In this part, I will present my conclusions regarding this issue. This research has demonstrated that theology and polemic are intimately connected in the *Orations* and that the Gospel of John functions in the context of both theological discourse and polemic. In all three *Orations*, a genuine concern for theology and biblical interpretation seems undeniable, while polemical and vituperative language is almost inextricably connected with theological argumentation. A good deal of this polemical argumentation may be traced back to genuine differences between Athanasius and his opponents, but in other instances the main aim of polemical statements is to discredit the Arians. This analysis of Athanasius' *Orations* has demonstrated that it is impossible to isolate Athanasius' genuine interest in theology from the possibility that theology functioned as an instrument of polemical church politics. While this research has not solved the disagreement about the different interpretations of Athanasius' career as discussed in the introduction of this monograph, it has established that Athanasius was genuinely interested in theology.

In this remaining part, I will discuss two issues. I will first discuss the main findings concerning the role of John's Gospel in Athanasius' strategy of persuasion. Secondly, I will evaluate Athanasius' use of the Gospel of John in terms of continuity and discontinuity.

ATHANASIUS' USE OF JOHN IN THE *ORATIONS*

In the conceptual framework of this monograph, I outlined the concepts of *ethos*, negative *ethos*, and *logos* to distinguish between the various ways in which Athanasius argues his case against the Arians. As established in the previous literature, traces of classical *paideia* are few and far between. Athanasius must have had some education, but either did not attend the level of rhetorical education and used native wit in his writings or he chose to be a representative of another ideal of true *paideia*, represented in emergent monasticism. One of the most forceful expositions of this counter-claim to classical *paideia* is found in Athanasius' presentation of Antony in *Life of Antony*. Whatever the reasons for the absence of many formal patterns of classical rhetoric in the *Orations*, it has nonetheless been fruitful to perform a rhetorical analysis as found in this monograph. Sometimes Athanasius uses John's Gospel to construct his *ethos* or his opponents' negative *ethos*, and more frequently to support his argumentation (*logos*). I will summarise my findings in this section.

Athanasius' Use of John and *Ethos*

Athanasius employs the Gospel of John as an ethical means to present his own *ethos* favourably. He never makes bold claims about his personal authority as bishop to establish his trustworthiness, and only in *CA* I 3 does he refer to himself as a bishop who follows Christ. When Athanasius wants to win the trust of his audience, he prefers to appeal to the authority of the Scriptures. Therefore, the way he uses Scripture indicates that he regards a correct appeal to Scripture as the end of all debate. He often employs a form of literary re-enactment that builds a strong bridge between the authoritative biblical past and the uncertain present. Athanasius occasionally used Scripture, and the Gospel of John in particular, to win trust in a subtle way, by explicitly stating that the Lord himself spoke certain words. In almost all of these cases, Jesus' sayings stem from the Gospel of John.

The figure of speech *sermocinatio* (or *ethopoeia*) supports Athanasius' theological views by rephrasing the words of Scripture to highlight the elements that he deems important. The presence of this rhetorical figure does not prove his rhetorical education, but does give an interesting perspective on his method of biblical interpretation. In *CA* I 46, he constructs such an imaginary speech of Jesus to increase the trustworthiness of his interpretation. By constructing his interpretation of Jn 17:17–19 as an imaginary speech of Jesus himself, it seems that it is not Athanasius, but Jesus who offers the interpretation. The words of the Gospel of John thus feature in a creative way that increases the trustworthiness of Athanasius' interpretation. The figure of *sermocinatio* also appears in *CA* II 15–17, in the exposition on the meaning of Acts 2:36. Athanasius asserts that Peter's words that Jesus is made (ἐποίησεν) Lord and Messiah cannot be taken literally. In Peter's imaginary speech at Pentecost, Athanasius inserts all kinds of material from both OT and NT, including references to Jn 12:32 and Jn 1:14 to make his interpretation plausible.

Athanasius' use of the figure of *sermocinatio* intensifies in *Oration* III, especially in his discussion of Jesus' prayer that his disciples will be one as the Father and the Son are one and indwell in each other (*CA* III 17–25; see Jn 17:11, 21–22). Athanasius does not make a detailed investigation into the concepts of Sonship and discipleship in John, but redirects the interpretation of these words of Jesus, through an imaginary speech of Jesus himself, in which Jesus clarifies what he is actually saying, in language that contains much other Johannine material supporting Athanasius' interpretation. He thus re-enacts the biblical past in the present situation. A similar dynamic is present in Jesus' actualised words of Jn 10:37–38 in *CA* III 55 and III 67. In *CA* III 55, Jn 10:30 and 10:37–38 appear briefly before and after Jesus' imagined direct address that he is truly Word of God in the body. In *CA* III 67, Athanasius quotes Jn 10:37–38 together with references to Jn 14:6, 9, 10 as a threefold affirmation of the Son's closeness to the Father.

In *Oration* III, Athanasius repeatedly uses the figure of *prosopopoeia* (or *fictio personae*), in which an inanimate object is imagined speaking as well. The use of *prosopopoeia* serves to undergird the plausibility of Athanasius' interpretation of crucial Johannine texts on the unity of Father and Son. He presents the image of a king and claims that the worship of an image is identical to worshipping a king (*CA* III 5). He further envisages the radiance of the sun, arguing that the sun and its radiance are never separated (*CA* III 8; III 36). In *CA* III 34, Athanasius imagines likewise the flesh of the Word speaking up to rebuke the Arian heretics for their misunderstanding of the words 'the Word became flesh' (Jn 1:14). In all of these imaginative speeches, Athanasius employs an abundance of Johannine texts to assert the correctness of his theological position by means of this creative use of Scripture.

Other forms of appeal to *ethos* in the *Orations* contain a more limited relation to the Gospel of John. Athanasius frequently uses first-person plural addresses to build communion with the audience. Occasionally, this seems influenced by Johannine statements. Furthermore, Athanasius regularly contrasts his opinions, as derived from Scripture, to the opinions of the heretical writers, who derive their thoughts from other, non-scriptural sources. The demonstration of what Scripture says regularly features some texts from John, such as Jesus' 'I am' statements (Jn 14:6; 10:14; 8:12; 13:13; 8:58) in *CA* I 12–13. Jn 1:1 functions similarly as biblical evidence in numerous places to counter the Arian slogans. All in all, the Gospel of John plays a subtle, but important role in demonstrating Athanasius' *ethos*.

Athanasius' Use of John and Negative *Ethos*

In Athanasius' construction of a negative *ethos* of his opponents in the *Orations*, the Gospel of John plays a modest role too. Athanasius sometimes mentions opponents that have a disputed ecclesial reputation (Arius, Asterius, Eusebius of Nicomedia), but most often, he addresses his opponents monolithically by vague terms such as Arians or Ariomaniacs to refute them collectively. He thus intimates that there are no pious or respectable Christians who adhere to the Arian theology. The construction of the opponent's negative *ethos* appears frequently throughout the *Orations*, but is especially prominent in the introduction, *CA* I 1–10. In this section, Athanasius constructs two counter-genealogies of orthodoxy and heresy. The *Thalia* of Arius features prominently as a counter-scripture to the Scriptures of OT and NT. Appeals to John are infrequent in this section, but two questions in *CA* I 4 equate the unbelief of the Jewish Pharisees and the Arians. In this way, the words of Arius' *Thalia* are put in direct opposition to Jesus' words in Jn 10:30, 33.

Athanasius often describes the Arians as mad, deliberately impious, and deceived by the devil. All three *Orations* open with an explicit or implicit reference to madness (μανία). Furthermore, *CA* I ends with the suggestion that the heretics are 'ungrateful and contentious' and the end of *CA* III claims that the Arians are 'senseless ones and enemies of Christ' (ἄφρονες καὶ χριστομάχοι). Similar characterisations are found throughout his *Orations*. However, apart from the two allusions to Jn 5:23 (he who dishonours the Father dishonours the Son), John's Gospel is not used for these suggestions.

However, John's Gospel occasionally features in comparisons between the Arians and Jews. The most prominent of these instances are found in *Orations* II and III. In *CA* II 42, Athanasius mentions that the Arians run the same risk as the Jews who denied Christ with the words: 'We have no king but the emperor' (Jn 19:15). Athanasius also argues occasionally that difficult texts for his theology address a Jewish audience that did not expect the Son to be divine. In demonstrating that the speeches in Scripture are accommodated to the audience, he uses the Johannine portrayal of the 'Jews' as analogous to the Arian position (cf. Jn 5:16–18; 12:34). Similarly, in *Oration* III, the Arians are twice urged not to stone Jesus as the Jews attempted (cf. Jn 10:31), but to confess him with orthodox Christians. *CA* III 27–28 contains one of the longest comparisons between the Arians and the Jews. Athanasius suggests that the Arian denial of the Son's true divinity on the ground of the Son's human weaknesses puts them in the same league as the Jews. This serves of course a highly polemical purpose, which does not represent the actual amount of overlapping beliefs of Jews and Arian Christians. In *CA* III 15–16, as in some other places, Athanasius elaborately compares the Arians to the Jews, heretics and pagans as well, arguing that all of them err in their conception of God. However, John's Gospel does not feature in the *Orations* in the association of the Arians with either pagans or heretics, since such clashes were absent in John's Gospel. With the comparison between Jews and Arians, Athanasius built a seemingly continuous tradition of Christ-denying by Jews

at the time of both Jesus and the Arians. This literary re-enactment is of a theological nature and in that sense anti-Jewish, not
anti-Semitic. But it contributed to the increasingly hostile climate
towards Jews in the Middle Ages.

The remarks about Arian madness and impiety indicate that
Athanasius often interprets the opinions of his opponents in a
most unfavourable way. This link between madness and impiety
is also visible in Constantine's letter against Arius, written in 333
(Urk. 34 = Dok. 27). Athanasius suggests in this way that genuine
points of concern of his opponents are a smoke screen for their
impiety. Nevertheless, his critique does not solely consist of slander. Often when Athanasius caricatures his opponents and their
views, he simultaneously engages with the subject matter in question by addressing an inconsistency or other problem of his opponents' reasoning. The attack *ad personam*, solely intended to discredit the opponents as individuals, often coexists with legitimate
arguments *ad hominem* that attack the inconsistency of his opponents' opinions. He thus conflates slander and reasoned disagreement with the Arian theological views.

A specific device that produces both an Arian negative *ethos*
and a way to engage with their theology is the use of Arian slogans. The three Arian slogans 'There was once when he was not',
'He was not before he was begotten' and 'He came into being from
nothing' point to a rational disagreement between them, but are
also very important in constructing the Arians' negative *ethos*. By
using these catchphrases that are easily remembered, Athanasius
could more easily attack his opponents in a way that a larger audience could understand. This simplified version of the Arian
view is subsequently attacked by Athanasius. Although John's
Gospel does not play a role in outlining these slogans, several of
the Johannine sayings of the Son are put in opposition to the Arian slogans. Therefore, whenever Johannine references are present in such cases, they basically function as a contrast marker for
the orthodox views of Athanasius.

Athanasius' Use of John and *Logos*

Most of Athanasius' uses of John's Gospel have the function of
backing up his argumentation. Athanasius is also shown to be

highly selective in his use of John's Gospel to support his argumentation. He most frequently appeals to a very limited number
of Johannine texts: Jn 1:1, 3, 14; 5:17; 10:30; 14:9, 10; 16:15. He
refers to several other Johannine passages as well, but in general
he bases his arguments on a very small corpus of Johannine texts.

The use of John as logos *in* Orations *I-II*

In *CA* I 1–10, Athanasius does not use John in an argumentative
way. *CA* I 11–21 is a more argumentative section in which several
Johannine texts on Jesus' divine identity feature prominently.
Some of these are listed as a full summary of the biblical evidence
available, such as several 'I am' sayings of Jesus. A small selection
of scriptural passages functions as proof of the soundness of Athanasius' theology and to oppose the impious Arian slogans, especially Jn 14:10 'I in the Father and the Father in me' and Jn 10:30
'I and the Father are one'. Athanasius also appeals in a highly
selective way to the Christological titles of John's Gospel. In the
case of Jn 14:6, Athanasius draws a firm line between Jesus' attributes 'Truth' and 'Life', which he relates to the Son's ontology,
and the title 'Way', which he relates to the Son's incarnate state.
He shares this reading strategy with Eusebius of Caesarea.

In *CA* I 22–36, Athanasius discusses several objections of his
opponents in which a rational disagreement is apparent. He criticises his opponents for the use of extra-biblical terminology, because they draw inappropriate conclusions from the term unbegotten. He argues that none of the four usages of this term contradicts his basic insight that the Word is eternally the Son of God,
so that the term unbegotten cannot be meant to exclude the begotten Son (cf. Jn 1:18, 3:16) from the unbegotten Father. This
basic insight is in turn derived from the Gospel of John (cf. Jn
1:1, 3; 10:30; 14:9–10) and the Lord's prayer in Matthew 6, in
which Jesus calls God Father. Athanasius has a specific agenda in
his use of the Gospel of John and simplifies Arian theology to
demonstrate its ultimate consequences. He equates the concepts
of creature (κτίσμα) and work (ποίημα), something which his opponents carefully avoid. Nevertheless, this simplification enables
him to express more emphatically the problematic consequences
of calling the Son a creature.

In *CA* I 37-II 82, Athanasius discusses the interpretation of several texts that could suggest the inferiority of the Son to the Father. The basic difference between Athanasius and the Arians concerns the question whether the referent of these texts is the pre-incarnate Son or the incarnate Christ. Athanasius argues in all cases that an element that suggests the Son's inferiority pertains to his incarnate state. John's Gospel is often cited to illustrate the true divinity of the Son. Athanasius' interpretive rule of biblical texts on the basis of time, occasion and person (cf. *CA* I 54) is only used when he is on the defence (Phil 2:9–10 (*CA* I 40); Heb 1:4 (*CA* I 57); Hebrews 3:2 (*CA* II 8–9); Acts 2:36 (*CA* II 12)). In *Oration* III, this happens likewise in the case of John 17:3 (*CA* III 9) and John 12:27 (*CA* III 57). Furthermore, as long as an interpretation does not endanger this fundamental theological conviction, he leaves room for multiple interpretations of individual texts like Phillipians 2:9–10 and Proverbs 8:22.

Athanasius never discusses the immediate context of John's Gospel when asserting that a text speaks of the Son's true divinity. In fact, he claims that these statements admit of no qualification (*CA* II 54). A small selection of Johannine verses (Jn 1:1, 3, 14; 5:17; 10:30; 14:9–10) is frequently brought into presence to highlight the veracity of his interpretation. These references relate closely to his claim that all of Scripture is centred around the double account of the Son's divinity and humanity (*CA* III 28–29).

In *CA* I 37–45, Athanasius cites Jn 1:1, 3, 9, 12, 14 and Jn 17:5 in order to interpret Phil 2:9–10 in the way he favours. Jn 1:1, 9 indicates the Saviour's divine state and John 1:12, 14 shows his soteriological purpose on earth. John 17:5 is cited as proof of the Son's glory before the world was made. In combination with John 1:3, these texts are thus used to argue that the Son is the Creator, and therefore not a creature that needs exaltation. In this way, a few crucial Johannine texts direct the interpretation of Philippians 2:9–10.

In *CA* I 47–50, Athanasius discusses the relation between the Son and the Holy Spirit. He prioritises the Johannine notion that the Son is the sender of the Holy Spirit (Jn 15:26a; 16:7, 14; 20:22), in order to argue that the Son cannot have been receptive to the Holy Spirit in his divine state. In the same section,

Athanasius exclusively focuses on the role of the Son in the sending of the Spirit to assert the true divinity of the Son, while John
15:26 mentions the Father and the Son closely together. He thus
ignores the biblical notion that the Son is obedient to and sent by
the Father (Jn 4:34; 5:30; 6:38), by highlighting the opposite notion that is also present in John: the Son as sender of the Spirit.

In *CA* I 53–64, Athanasius discusses the Christological words
of Heb 1:4 'having become better (κρείττων) than the angels'. A
Johannine saying of Jesus is present in a very subtle way in this
section, as Athanasius contrasts the word better (κρείττων) to
greater (μείζων). In Jn 14:28, Jesus states: 'The Father is greater
(μείζων) than I'. In *CA* I 13, Athanasius had cited Jn 14:28–29 to
assert the Son's foreknowledge, and glossed over the word
'greater', most likely because that would complicate his argumentation. In this discussion of Heb 1:4, Athanasius argues at length
that κρείττων compares unequal, qualitatively distinct subjects
(the Son and angels), while μείζων compares equal subjects (the
Father and Son) with each other. He does not acknowledge that
he has Jn 14:28 in mind, but there is no better explanation than
that he engages indirectly with this Johannine text. Athanasius
thus deliberately marginalises the presence of Jn 14:28 at this
point, by only alluding vaguely to it.

In *CA* II 1–11, Athanasius comments on the words of Heb 3:2
that the Son is 'faithful to his appointer (τῷ ποιήσαντι)'. On the
basis of Jn 1:1, 3, he argues that the Son eternally existed as God,
so that these words from Hebrews must point to the Son's incarnate state (Jn 1:14). The difference between Jesus' identity and
ministry is illustrated by Aaron, who is a human that became high
priest at the time when it was necessary. In *CA* II 12–18a, Athanasius' use of Jn 10:35–36 is noteworthy. While the section originally seems to be a riddle that asserts that 'gods' is a term not
exclusively used for YHWH, Athanasius takes this text as a self-
evident declaration of Jesus that he is the Son of God, supporting
his argument for the Son's divinity.

Athanasius discusses Prv 8:22 in *CA* II 18b–82. Many Johannine texts are used by Athanasius in this section, but especially
Jn 1:3 is prominently brought into presence; eight times in *CA* II
18b–43 and five times in *CA* II 44–82. In *CA* II 18b–43, he argues

that one cannot infer from the word ἔκτισε (he created) that the
Son is a κτίσμα (creature), because the Son is involved in creation
(Jn 1:1–3), cooperates with the Father (Jn 5:17, 19), and accepts
divine worship (Jn 20:28). In *CA* II 44–82, Athanasius depends
heavily on certain elements of John's Gospel as well. He identifies
two sets of sayings in Scripture: unqualified ones, concerning the
Son's eternity, and qualified ones, concerning the Son's humanity.
He illustrates both set of sayings with exclusively Johannine material in *CA* II 54. Five statements illustrate the Son's eternal state
(Jn 14:10; 10:30; 14:9; 8:12; 14:6) and three Johannine statements illustrate his humanity (Jn 6:38–40; 12:46; 18:37). Athanasius does not comment on the subordination and obedience
texts in John in *Orations* I-II. In this way, Athanasius reduces the
intentional ambiguity in John's Gospel in order to confess the
Son's eternity more explicitly. All in all, Athanasius prioritises
John's Gospel by reading Proverbs 8:22 (and other texts) through
the prism of the Johannine prologue (Jn 1:1, 3).

The use of John as logos *in* Oration *III*

As a result of the topics that Athanasius discusses in *Oration* III,
some interesting shifts are identified between his use of John's
Gospel in *Orations* I-II and *Oration* III. In *Oration* III, Athanasius
discusses (1) the correct interpretation of Jn 14:10 and 10:30, (2)
Jn 17:3 in an excursus on the unity of God, (3) the Gospel texts
that speak of Jesus' weaknesses as a human, and (4) the role of
will in the Father's begetting of the Son.

In *CA* III 1–6 and *CA* III 10–16, Athanasius defends the correctness of his interpretation of Jn 14:10 and 10:30 in contrast to
Asterius' exegesis of these Johannine texts. In Athanasius' explanation of these Johannine texts, he solely attacks the problematic
alternative of Asterius that 'I in the Father and the Father in me'
(14:10) might not be exclusively applicable to the Son, without
exploring the immediate context of John's Gospel. The comparison between the unity of Father and Son and that of the sun and
its radiance is deemed appropriate for understanding the Father-
Son relation. This comparison enables Athanasius to acknowledge
the Father as the source of the Son, without ascribing any inferiority to the Son. In this way, he puts forward the words of Jn

14:10 as an indicator of the Son's exclusivity and divinity. In order to sustain his claims concerning the relation between Father and Son, Athanasius also alludes several times to Jn 5:17 and Jn 16:15. He cites Jn 5:17 and 16:15 in *Orations* I-II as well, but by alluding to, rather than citing, these passages in *Oration* III, he is able to integrate his understanding of these passages more precisely into his own argumentation for the full equality of Father and Son. Athanasius' adaptations of and allusions to John's Gospel therefore function to align the meaning of these Johannine texts more closely to his own position. In Athanasius' interpretation of these texts, the original ambiguity of Jesus' words about his unity with the Father in Jn 10:30 and 14:10 is thus completely ignored. While metaphysical connotations cannot be excluded in these Johannine statements, modern exegetes discern a good deal of functional unity in Jesus' words 'I and the Father are one' (Jn 10:30). Likewise, 'I in the Father and the Father in me' in Jn 14:10 and 11 is surrounded by an affirmation of Jesus' dependency on the Father (John 14:10b) and Jesus' claim that the disciples will do greater works than himself (Jn 14:12). Nevertheless, it seems equally clear that the words are indicative of a special position of the Son that he does not share with believers. Athanasius' selectivity and self-evident use of these passages is therefore understandable in response to Asterius' interpretation.

The discussion of God's unity in *CA* III 6b–9 demonstrates another shift in Athanasius' use of John. In *CA* III 7, Athanasius addresses two types of Johannine passages that he glossed over in *Orations* I-II: Jesus' obedience texts (cf. Jn 6:38), as well as Jn 14:28 'The Father is greater than I'. In contrast, Athanasius argues in *Oration* III that Jesus' obedience and submission to the Father indicates the complete harmony between Father and Son, and that Jesus therefore acknowledges the Father in everything. Hence, the biblical expressions of God's uniqueness (cf. Jn 17:3, the only true God) only exclude the pagan gods and idols, who do not deserve to be honoured. However, expressions of monotheism do not exclude the genuine Son, because the expressions of obedience and modesty in Jn 6:38 and 14:28 point to the Son's full harmony with the Father. Athanasius further proves that the Son is in full harmony with the Father, on the ground that the Son-

Word is involved in creation (Jn 1:1, 3), the honour of Father and Son is mutual (Jn 5:23), and the Son is the Truth (Jn 14:6). He thus understands the obedience texts in John as safeguarding monotheism and consistent with the Son's divinity. It is likely that John intended these exclamations of obedience to stay within the boundaries of Jewish monotheism as well, but the clear Trinitarian model of the co-eternal divinity of Father, Son and Holy Spirit that Athanasius presents in *Oration* III is not found as such in John's Gospel.

In *CA* III 26–58, Athanasius addresses many Gospel texts that indicate a physical or psychological weakness of Jesus. He did not discuss this topic in *Orations* I-II. In *CA* III 26, he cites an Arian list that poses a considerable challenge to his own position, such as Jesus' ignorance (Mk 13:32), progress in wisdom (Lk 2:52) and agony and fear (Mt 26:39; Jn 12:27). Athanasius has difficulty genuinely acknowledging these indications of Jesus' physical or mental discomfort (Jn 12:27; 13:21; cf. Mt 26:39; Mk 13:32; Lk 2:52; Jn 11:35; 19:28–29). Athanasius argues for a prototype two natures Christology in which the Son's divine deeds show his true being, and his weaknesses as a human are related to his incarnate state. The Son carried all weaknesses in his human body for humanity's sake. For that reason, Jn 1:14 is very often cited as a proof of the reality of the Incarnation. Whereas John probably includes this verse to emphasise that Jesus really lived as a human being on earth, Jn 1:14 is the key text for Athanasius' doctrine of the divinisation of human beings (*theosis*). Besides Jn 1:14, Athanasius also appeals to several episodes in which he finds the intertwining of the human and the divine, for example the healing of the man born blind (Jn 9:1–6) and the resurrection of Lazarus (Jn 11:34–43). He further discusses Jesus' fear in Mt 26:39; Jn 12:27, 13:21. Athanasius points especially to the interrelatedness of Jesus' fear and determination to complete his mission as the incarnate one. Whereas Jesus' fear indicates the reality of the Incarnation, the Son's determination to remain faithful to his mission shows that the Son is not terrified as an ordinary human being would be (cf. Jn 12:27–28). Furthermore, Athanasius assigns Jesus' expression that no one takes his life, but that he lays it down himself, with the power to take it up again (Jn 10:18), to both the Son's incarnate and his divine state. In *CA* III 54, he understands it as an instance of Jesus' courage as human being, in *CA* III 57 as an indicator of the Son's divinity, in contrast to Jesus' fear (cf. Jn 12:27). All of this proves that Athanasius' use of John is heavily determined by the circumstances, and his highly selective use and interpretation of John must therefore be understood in relation to the theological position he wants to avoid.

In *CA* III 58b–67, Athanasius discusses the important issue of will and necessity in God's begetting of the Son. Many Eusebian theologians emphasised the role of will (βούλησις) in the Son's begetting in the 340s to safeguard that the Father did not beget the Son against his will. Athanasius avoids a choice between these alternatives by claiming that the Son is the Father's offspring by nature. Because the issue as such is not addressed in Scripture, Athanasius' use of Scripture is less pervasive in this section. Both parties explore, on the basis of reasoned inferences from Scripture, how the confession of one God and the worship of Jesus Christ may be reconciled. Athanasius appeals to Jn 1:1, 3 to support his argument that the Son is not willed by nature, because the Son is the living Will of the Father and loved by the Father (see Jn 5:20; Mt 3:17). Furthermore, an allusion to Jn 14:10, which closely integrates the meaning of Jn 14:10 within the framework of his theology, is crucial to undergird the reciprocal nature of the indwelling of Father and Son.

The Selective Use of John's Gospel in the *Orations*

In summary, it can be said that Athanasius is very selective in his use of John's Gospel in the *Orations*. The identity of the Son is crucial in the *Orations*, and for that reason Athanasius often appeals to this Gospel, which discusses Jesus' identity most explicitly. However, a large part of John is also ignored, because it does not directly deal with Jesus' identity. In other cases, Athanasius' selectiveness is related to the fact that a Johannine notion does shed light on Jesus' identity, but not in a way that straightforwardly supports Athanasius' argument. Athanasius is mainly concerned to sustain his argument that the Scriptures offer a 'clear' perspective on Jesus Christ in the *Orations*. He therefore carefully selects a limited number of brief sayings of Jesus (Jn 10:30; 14:6,

9, 10) or brief remarks about Jesus (Jn 1:1, 3, 14) that apparently support his theology clearly and unambiguously. Athanasius asserts their self-evident meaning and ignores the context of the words in most instances, because he does not want to give any room for his opponents' alternative interpretation. Besides citations of brief sayings of or about Jesus, Athanasius frequently refers to John's Gospel by adapting a text, or alluding to it, or by using creative devices, such as the imaginary speech, to align the meaning of the biblical text more closely to his theological position. Athanasius' use of John's Gospel in the *Orations* thus demonstrates that Athanasius depends on a small subset of Johannine notions for his basic argument.

In this process, biblical material that seems to support his opponents' argument is downplayed by Athanasius or overruled by the crucial notions that Athanasius frequently brings into presence by quoting or alluding to them. Throughout all three *Orations*, the clear and unambiguous Johannine statements are very important in this respect. Furthermore, the shifting use of John's Gospel in *Oration* III seems to indicate a genuine and evolving theological debate. In this *Oration*, Athanasius discusses texts that he used self-evidently (Jn 14:10; 10:30) or glossed over (Jn 6:38; 14:28; 17:3) in *Orations* I-II. He justifies his usage of Jn 14:10 and 10:30 and asserts that the obedience and subordination texts indicate that the Son fully honours the Father and is therefore in harmony with him. Athanasius' remarkable usage of Johannine material is also signified in his use of Jn 10:18. This verse is appealed to in two strikingly different ways, with the common factor that both ways counter his opponents' arguments.

Oration III makes one other issue very clear as well. In all three *Orations*, but mainly in the analysis of *Oration* III, it is clear that the Arians also made extensive use of Scripture in general and the Gospel of John in particular. Although Athanasius frequently accuses the Arians of madness and impiety, his opponents also wanted to legitimise their theological views with reference to the Scriptures and in harmony with reason. For a large part they even used the same texts as Athanasius did. Asterius' fragments show concern with many Johannine texts that Athanasius refers to as well (Jn 1:1, 18; 10:30; 14:10, 17:1, 5, 11, 20–23).

However, other Johannine notions are solely used either by Athanasius or by his Arian opponents. Whereas Asterius uses Jn 5:22, 30; 6:37; 15:26b with appreciation, Athanasius does not refer to these texts of John's Gospel in the *Orations*. Other Johannine texts that are frequently used by Athanasius (Jn 1:3; 5:17–19; 14:9) are absent in the fragments of Asterius and other Arians. However, in this instance it would be an argument from silence to assume that Asterius and other Arians deliberately neglected these texts or were embarrassed by them. Because Asterius is only cited by his opponents Athanasius and Marcellus, who left out those issues that did not serve their purpose of refuting Asterius and other Arians, no conclusions can be drawn in this respect. In fact, Athanasius may have been even more selective than Asterius was in his usage of John's Gospel, because one of the longest citations of John's Gospel in the *Orations* is Asterius' reference to Jn 17:11, 20–23 (fr. 41 = *CA* III 17). However, a degree of speculation cannot be avoided on this point, and it is clear that Athanasius and Asterius both used Scripture in a selective way to support their theological views.

EVALUATION

This research has made clear that John's Gospel is used in a highly selective way in the *Orations against the Arians*. This raises the question of how Athanasius' use of the Gospel of John should be evaluated. In what ways can Athanasius' use of John's Gospel be appreciated and in what ways not? And how should we consider the continuity and discontinuity between John's Gospel and Athanasius' use of the Gospel in the *Orations*? Athanasius derives conclusions from John's testimony concerning Jesus that were most likely not intended nor imagined by John. But what about the continuity. Is there any continuity? And if so, where is that continuity located? I will therefore discuss (1) the purpose of the *Orations*, (2) the natural development of Christological reflection within Christianity, and (3) Athanasius' contribution to the reformulation of Christian monotheism in the fourth-century context.

The Purpose of the *Orations*

First of all, one should understand that Athanasius' *Orations against the Arians* is an occasional work designed for a specific purpose. As the title indicates, it is written against the Arians. This is not only visible in the highly polemical tone against the Arians, which aims to demonstrate the heretical nature of their thought, but also in the selectivity and particularity of Athanasius' use of Scripture. Athanasius' literary re-enactment of equating the Arians with first-century Jews might be related to the use of the term 'Jews' in John's Gospel. However, this equation does not do justice to the actual parallels of Arians and first-century Jews, nor to the Evangelist's usage of the term Jews. In general, a refined and well-balanced exegesis of John's Gospel or any other part of Scripture is absent in Athanasius' *Orations*, because his main purpose is to refute the Arians.[1] Of course, this specific use of Scripture could also bear a relation to his personality, because Athanasius hardly left any exegetical writings. A more detailed comparison with Eusebius of Caesarea's use of the Gospel of John in his anti-Marcellan works might shed more light on this issue. Instead of giving a nuanced exegesis of Scripture in the *Orations*, Athanasius appealed to a predefined core of Christianity which cannot be doubted. This argument resembled Irenaeus' and Tertullian's approach in discerning a rule of faith that is identical with, or even above, Scripture. They knew that a dispute with heretics could not be settled by interpretation alone. In Athanasius' time, this was even more problematic, because Athanasius and his opponents agreed on the dimensions of the canon and participated in the same ecclesial structure. Athanasius' appeal to the double account of the Saviour was therefore designed so that his opponents' understanding of the Son could be qualified as heretical, even though they appealed to the same set of Scriptures and participated in the same ecclesial structure. This narrow focus of the question and the definition of what Scripture is all about caused necessarily a selective use of Scripture.

---

[1] The same holds probably true for the Arians, but because of the lack of material, this cannot be proved or disproved.

Athanasius' claim of the double account of the Saviour, illustrated with mainly Johannine material, demonstrates the circumstantial and circular nature of Athanasius' definition of the core of Scripture. Nevertheless, the fact that Athanasius appeals to a very limited number of Johannine texts does not mean that these were the only texts that could prove his doctrine. In fact, this research has focused on John's Gospel, but Athanasius also appeals to other parts of Scripture. At any rate, Athanasius did not aim at exhaustiveness, but wanted to demonstrate this one crucial confession by repeatedly bringing into presence a limited number of selected proof texts. In this process, he downplayed the nuances of his proof texts and claimed his interpretation of the texts as self-evident.

The Development Towards Christological Reflection within Christianity

Although it was easier for Christians to worship Jesus as God than to formulate an adequate account of this worship, it was inevitable that early Christians had to reconcile the worship of Jesus as divine and God with the confession of one God only within Jewish monotheism.[2] John's Gospel, and the prologue in particular, shows this development from a narration *of* Jesus' words and deeds to Christological reflections *on* Jesus.[3] The evangelist John testifies to the human Jesus, who is the Messiah, the Son and even the Word of God, involved in creation. John deliberately juxtaposes humble and lofty claims about Jesus, supplementing every episode about Jesus' divine words and deeds with clear concessions about his obedience and dependency on the Father. By doing so, John confesses Jesus, the Messiah and Son of God, in a way that enables him to remain within the boundaries of Jewish monotheism.

The Christological reflection in the New Testament and the doctrinal history of Christianity show that Christians were not and could not be satisfied merely to repeat what the New Testament documents said about Christ. The Christological reflection

---

[2] Brown, *John*, 24.
[3] Cf. Fuller, "The Theology of Jesus or Christology," 105–16.

of the second to fourth centuries therefore continues a process that already started in John's Gospel, and Athanasius stands in this tradition. There is no direct relationship between John and Athanasius, as if the theology of John inevitably had to culminate in Athanasius' doctrine of the Trinity and the Son. However, Athanasius' custom of drawing stronger conclusions from John's Gospel than seem originally intended is nevertheless an intelligible development. Whereas belief in Jesus as the Messiah, the Son of God, is promoted through extended narratives in John's Gospel, in Athanasius' *Orations* the issue is restricted to the precise definition of Christ's divinity. And whereas John intentionally juxtaposes the human and divine characteristics, Athanasius devotes a large part of his third *Oration* to argue that Jesus' experienced weaknesses do not preclude his ontological status as the eternal Son of God. Athanasius' exclusive emphasis on Jesus as the sender of the Spirit and his somewhat instrumentalist conception of Jesus' genuinely displayed weaknesses preclude a direct and straightforward relation between John and Athanasius. Although Athanasius often quotes or alludes to John, the question he faces is a different one: is Jesus Christ truly divine or is he inferior to God the Father? In this respect, Athanasius' use of John's Gospel shows that Athanasius tries to find proof for his position rather than to understand the whole of John's Gospel on its own terms. Athanasius' account of salvation through a divine Saviour, who divinises humanity, is established with reference to John's Gospel. While a subtle interplay between divine and human deeds is indeed present in John's Gospel, it does not contain the concept of *theosis* in the way Athanasius conceives it. Athanasius' understanding of the relation between the Word and human soul of Jesus Christ carries therefore instrumentalist connotations that are not present in John's Gospel. Although Athanasius does not deny a human soul in the Word, he could not constructively incorporate this clear element of canonical testimony about Jesus into his theology, and blurred the account of Jesus' real humanity, including weaknesses and struggles. Athanasius thus dehistoricised Jesus' presence on earth, not by denying the historicity of the events that took place, but by considering everything from the angle of the eternally divine Son. Nevertheless, he did stress that, through the Incarnation, human beings received the grace of divinisation. Therefore, despite the criticism, it must be acknowledged that Athanasius did not deny Jesus' humanity, but did find an alternative understanding of this Johannine notion that made sense in his context.

Reconciling Christian Monotheism and the Worship of Jesus Christ

The reconciliation of Christian monotheism with the worship of Jesus Christ is an element that connects John and Athanasius. I believe that Athanasius maintained one of the most crucial Johannine insights in his argument against the Arians, namely, the reconciliation of monotheism and the worship of Jesus by rejecting the Arian conception of Jesus as a second God. Though this particular question was of no concern to John the evangelist, John deliberately presented Jesus in full harmony and cooperation with the Father (Jn 5:17–30). While Athanasius is reluctant to speak about the Son's mission and obedience in the way John did, he rephrased John's mission and obedience theme to declare the Son's oneness with the Father in *Oration* III. His understanding of John's obedience theme is incompatible with the mission and obedience theme as used by Asterius, who held that Jesus is divine in a weaker sense. Athanasius was thus able to maintain the distinction between the Creator and creation, a distinction that was not present in Hellenistic-pagan thought. Athanasius' pervasive use of Jn 1:3 indicates that this was one of his core objections to Arian theology, in which the Trinity was understood as a theogony of more and less clearly divine beings. Athanasius' emphasis on the gulf between Creator and creation thus preserved this central tenet of monotheism.

Furthermore, Athanasius identified the basic message of Scripture in the double account of both the true divinity of the Son and his incarnate state as the foundation of salvation. While it is somewhat circumstantially and circularly formulated, this account enabled him to keep together the core of Christian monotheism and worship of Jesus Christ. Jesus Christ's unique relation to the Father is not only emphasised in Athanasius' account, it is also clear in the Gospel of John (cf. Jn 5:16–18; 10:30, 38).

Although Athanasius reduced several intentional ambiguities in John's account, he maintained this crucial Johannine notion. The same is visible in his account of Jn 10:30 and 14:10. While John the Evangelist most likely did not claim a complete metaphysical unity of Father and Son, in the fourth century, with the choice between Athanasius' preference for metaphysical unity and Asterius' suggestion that the unity should be understood in the light of Jn 17:11, 21–22, Athanasius rightly maintained that these words are exclusively attributable to the Son. Many of the Arian arguments, although seemingly more sensitive to the context, were also built on theological assumptions that were not present in first-century Jewish monotheism. Asterius' account of the Son-Word as someone who was taught to create was rightly attacked by Athanasius' appeal to Jn 5:17, in which the Father and Son are presented as cooperating in the work of creation. The difference between Asterius' thought and John's message seems also very clear in Asterius' separation of Jesus Christ as Word of God from the innate Power and Reason of God. Asterius' argument in this setting that not only Christ, but also the grasshopper was called a great power, indicated that Asterius' concern for divine singularity could not possibly be defended on the basis of John's Gospel.[4]

This critique of Asterius' reasoning does not mean that his contribution is worthless. Because Asterius, or the Eusebian party in general, sought to understand the doctrine of God in a different direction from Athanasius, they had a lasting impact on Athanasius' theologising as well. Since Athanasius was in a quite powerless situation in the 340s, he had to persuade his contemporaries of the soundness of his theology. In order to do so, he incorporated the valuable insights of his opponents. Athanasius did not acknowledge this engagement with Arian theological insights openly, since his polemical language did not soften in *Oration* III. Nevertheless, his handling of the Johannine material, especially with regard to the obedience texts of the Son and the (relative) superiority of the Father, speaks louder than his actual polemical words. The Arian position forced Athanasius to engage with

---

[4] See pp 208–215 above and *CA* II 37; 40 = Asterius, fr. 66. See also frs. 32–33, 64 (Vinzent).

several elements of Johannine thought that, after he wrestled with these notions, enabled him to formulate a more consistent account of monotheism and the full divinity of the Son. This led to the fuller development of his Trinitarian model in *Oration* III. Thus Athanasius clarified his theology in engagement with theological contemporaries in a way that proved fruitful for the generations after him. Although hardly any of his theological proposals have survived unmodified, the Cappadocian Fathers and other theologians built on his core insight: in Jesus Christ God came to this world to grant it salvation, which was distributed and safeguarded by a divine Saviour. In his discussion, Athanasius' terminology is flexible and imprecise at times. But especially in the relative flexibility of his terminology, he was able to intertwine different strands of thought or leave further exploration to others. He was able to see many crucial issues with a broadness that enabled him to engage with the other influential theologians of his time. At the same time, he was able to see the bigger picture, unhampered by the nuances of the somewhat subtler position held by his opponents, and was therefore able to highlight the problematic consequences of his opponents' proposals. He made his theological insights not only accessible to the educated theologians of his time, but also to monks and the laity.

Therefore, the differences between Athanasius' use of John's Gospel and modern interpretations need not result in an abandonment of Athanasius' theological view of the Son. Athanasius' doctrine of the Son was highly compelling in his time and must account for the fact that its core was and is accepted within the Church at large in the generation after him.[5] Between *Orations* I-II and *Oration* III, written somewhat later, Athanasius demonstrated a growing openness to the Johannine notions of obedience

---

[5] I do not deny that some theologians vehemently opposed Athanasius' position after the 340s (e.g. Aetius and Eunomius), but I do hold that Athanasius' contribution as an individual is substantial in establishing the eternal divinity of the Son as normative within Christianity. See also Ritter, "Athanasius," 101–7. A substantial amount of continuity between Athanasius and the Cappadocians is also advocated by Hanson, *Search*, 639–737; Anatolios, *Retrieving Nicaea*, 79–80, 281–92.

of the Son and the relative superiority of the Father. For Christian theologians that want to rethink the significance of Jesus Christ for the twenty-first century, Athanasius' contribution will remain an important source. However, awareness of Athanasius' particularity and selectivity in foregrounding some Johannine notions by de-emphasising several others may point to a freedom to explore in new ways this doctrine that Athanasius formulated so forcefully. For that reason, Athanasius remains an important interpreter who can make John's testimony about Jesus fruitful in such a way that twenty-first century readers may come to believe, as the evangelist John intended, that Jesus is the Messiah, the Son of God, and that through believing many may have life in his name.

BIBLIOGRAPHY

TEXTS AND TRANSLATIONS OF ATHANASIUS

Anatolios, Khaled. *Athanasius*. The Early Church Fathers. London: Routledge, 2004.

Athanase, Adelin Rousseau, and René Lafontaine. *Les trois discours contre les ariens*. Brussels: Lessius, 2004.

Athanasius. *A Select Library of the Nicene and Post-Nicene Fathers of the Christian Church. Second Series. Vol 4. St. Athanasius: Select Works and Letters*. Edited by Philip Schaff and Henry Wace. Translated by Archibald Robertson. Reprint 1995. Grand Rapids, MI: Eerdmans, 1892.

———. "Athanasius's *Orations against the Arians*, Book 1." Pages 63–129 in *The Trinitarian Controversy*. Translated by William Rusch. Sources of Early Christian Thought. Philadelphia: Fortress Press, 1980.

———. *Contra Gentes, and De Incarnatione*. Edited by Robert W. Thomson. Oxford Early Christian Texts. Oxford: Clarendon, 1971.

———. "Orations against the Arians." Pages 83–101 in *The Christological Controversy*. Translated by Richard Alfred Norris. Sources of Early Christian Thought. Philadelphia: Fortress Press, 1980.

———. *Redevoeringen Tegen de Arianen*. Translated by Cornelia Johanna de Vogel. Monumenta Christiana 1.2. Utrecht: Spectrum, 1948.

———. *Select Treatises of S. Athanasius, in Controversy with the Arians*, Translated by John Henry Newman. Oxford: J.H. Parker, 1844.

———. *Vie d'Antoine*. Edited by G. J. M. Bartelink. SC 400. Paris: Cerf, 1994.

Flower, Richard, ed. *Imperial Invectives Against Constantius II: Athanasius of Alexandria, History of the Arians, Hilary of Poitiers, Against Constantius and Lucifer of Cagliari, The Necessity of Dying for the Son of God*. Translated Texts for Historians 67. Liverpool: Liverpool University Press, 2016.

Heil, Uta. *Athanasius von Alexandrien De sententia Dionysii: Einleitung, Übersetzung und Kommentar.* Berlin: de Gruyter, 1999.

Lorenz, Rudolf. *Der zehnte Osterfestbrief des Athanasius von Alexandrien. Text, Übersetzung, Erläuterungen.* BZNW 49. Berlin: de Gruyter, 1986.

Meijering, E. P. *Athanasius: Contra Gentes. Introduction, Translation, Commentary.* Philosophia Patrum 7. Leiden: Brill, 1984.

———. *Athanasius: De Incarnatione Verbi.* Amsterdam: Gieben, 1989.

———. *Athanasius: Die dritte Rede gegen die Arianer. Einleitung, Übersetzung, Kommentar.* 3 vols. Amsterdam: Gieben, 1996–1998.

Metzler, Karin, and Kyriakos Savvidis, eds. *Athanasius Werke. Band I/Teil 1. Die Dogmatischen Schriften. Lfg. 3. Orationes III Contra Arianos.* Berlin: de Gruyter, 2000.

———, eds. *Athanasius Werke. Band I/Teil 1. Die dogmatischen Schriften. Lfg. 2. Orationes I et II contra Arianos.* Berlin: de Gruyter, 1998.

Opitz, Hans-Georg, ed. *Athanasius Werke. Band II/Teil 1. Die Apologien. Lfg. 1–7.* Berlin: de Gruyter, 1935–1941.

Savvidis, Kyriakos, ed. *Athanasius Werke. Band I/Teil 1. Die dogmatischen Schriften. Lfg. 4. Epistulae I-IV ad Serapionem.* Berlin: de Gruyter, 2010.

OTHER ANCIENT TEXTS AND TRANSLATIONS

Aristotle. *Aristotle: Art of Rhetoric, Volume XXII.* Translated by J. H. Freese. Loeb Classical Library 193. Cambridge, MA: Harvard University Press, 1926.

———. *Aristotle: On Sophistical Refutations. On Coming-to-Be and Passing Away. On the Cosmos.* Translated by E. S. Forster and D. J. Furley. Loeb Classical Library 400. Cambridge, MA: Harvard University Press, 1955.

———. *Topics Books I & VIII: With Excerpts from Related Texts. Translated with a Commentary by.* Translated by Robin Smith. 1 edition. Clarendon Aristotle Series. Oxford: Oxford University Press, 1997.

Brennecke, Hanns Christof, Uta Heil, Annette von Stockhausen, and Angelika Wintjes, eds. *Athanasius Werke. Band III/Teil 1. Dokumente zur Geschichte des arianischen Streites. Lfg. 3. Bis zur Ekthesis Makrostichos.* Berlin: de Gruyter, 2007.

Charles, R. H., and G. H. Box, trans. *The Book of Jubilees Or, The Little Genesis.* London: SPCK, 1917.

Cicero. *Cicero: On the Orator, Books I-II.* Translated by E. W. Sutton and H. Rackham. Loeb Classical Library 348. Cambridge, MA: Harvard University Press, 1948.

Coleman-Norton, P. R., ed. *Roman State and Christian Church: Volume 1.* London: SPCK, 1966.

Ferrar, William John, trans. *The Proof of the Gospel: Being the Demonstratio Evangelica of Eusebius of Caesarea.* London: SPCK, 1920.

Heikel, Ivar A., ed. *Eusebius Werke VI. Die Demonstratio Evangelica.* GCS 23. De Gruyter, 1913.

Irenaeus. *Adversus Haereses. Gegen die Häresien.* Edited by Norbert Brox. 5 vols. Fontes Christiani 8. Freiburg: Herder, 1993–2001.

Kennedy, George A., trans. *Aristotle. On Rhetoric. A Theory of Civic Discourse. Translated with Introduction, Notes and Appendices.* 2nd ed. New York: Oxford University Press, 2007.

Klostermann, Erich, and Günther Christian Hansen, eds. *Eusebius Werke IV. Gegen Marcell. Über die kirchliche Theologie. Die Fragmente Marcells.* 2nd ed. GCS 14. Berlin: Akademie Verlag, 1972.

Opitz, Hans-Georg, ed. *Athanasius Werke. Band III/Teil 1. Urkunden zur Geschichte des arianischen Streites 318–328. Lfg. 1–2.* Berlin: de Gruyter, 1934.

Origen. *Traité des principes. Tome I. (Livres I et II).* Edited by Henri Crouzel and Manlio Simonetti. SC 252. Paris: Cerf, 1978.

Pietersma, Albert, and Benjamin G. Wright, eds. *A New English Translation of the Septuagint and the Other Greek Translations Traditionally Included under That Title.* New York: Oxford University Press, 2007.

Roberts, Alexander, James Donaldson, and A. Cleveland Coxe, trans. *The Ante-Nicene Fathers, Translations of the Writings of the Fathers down to AD 325 Vol 1: The Apostolic Fathers - Justin Martyr - Irenaeus.* Reprint 1979. Grand Rapids, MI: Eerdmans, 1885.

Roberts, Alexander, James Donaldson, and A. Cleveland Coxe, trans. *The Ante-Nicene Fathers: Translations of the Writings of the Fathers down to A.D. 325 Vol. 4. Fathers of the Third Century: Tertullian, Part Fourth; Minucius Felix; Commodian; Origen, Parts First and Second.* Reprint 1982. Grand Rapids, MI: Eerdmanns, 1885.

Roberts, Alexander, James Donaldson, and A. Cleveland Coxe, trans. *The Ante-Nicene Fathers, Vol. 3: Latin Christianity - Its Founder, Tertullian.* Reprint 1978. Grand Rapids, MI: Eerdmans, 1885.

Stevenson, James, and William Hugh Clifford Frend, eds. *A New Eusebius. Documents Illustrating the History of the Church to AD 337.* London: SPCK, 1987.

Tertullian. *De Praescriptione Haereticorum. Vom prinzipiellen Einspruch gegen die Häretiker. Übersetzt und Eingeleitet von Dietrich Schleyer.* Edited by Dietrich Schleyer. Fontes Christiani 42. Turnhout: Brepols, 2002.

Thompson, Glen L., trans. "Letter of Eusebius of Nicomedia to Paulinus of Tyre." *Fourth Century Christianity,* 27 October 2020. https://www.fourthcentury.com/urkunde–8/.

Trigg, Joseph W. *Origen.* The Early Church Fathers. London: Routledge, 1998.

Turner, Cuthbert Hamilton, ed. *Ecclesiae Occidentalis Monumenta Iuris Antiquissima: Canonum et Conciliorum Graecorum Interpretationes Latinae.* 2 vols. Oxford: Clarendon, 1899–1939.

Vinzent, Markus. *Asterius von Kappadokien. Die Theologischen Fragmente. Einleitung, Kritischer Text, Übersetzung und Kommentar.* VCSup 20. Leiden: Brill, 1993.

———. *Markell von Ankyra. Die Fragmente. Der Brief an Julius von Rom. Herausgegeben, eingeleitet und übersetzt von Markus Vinzent.* VCSup 39. Leiden: Brill, 1997.

Vinzent, Markus, and Kelley McCharty Spoerl, *Eusebius of Caesarea, Against Marcellus and on Ecclesiastical Theology.* Fathers of the Church 135. Catholic University of America, 2017.

Ziegler, Joseph, ed. *Eusebius Werke IX. Der Jesajakommentar.* GCS. Berlin: Akademie Verlag, 1975.

SECONDARY SOURCES

Abramowski, Luise. "Biblische Lesarten und athanasianische Chronologie." *ZKG* 109 (1998): 237–41.

———. "Das theologische Hauptwerk des Athanasius: die drei Bücher gegen die Arianer (Ctr. Arianos I-III)." *Communio Viatorum* 42 (2000): 5–23.

———. "Die dritte Arianerrede des Athanasius: Eusebianer und Arianer und das westliche Serdicense." *ZKG* 102 (1991): 389–413.

———. "Die Synode von Antiochien 324/25 und ihr Symbol." *ZKG* 86 (1975): 356–66.

Anatolios, Khaled. *Athanasius: The Coherence of His Thought.* London: Routledge, 1998.

———. "'Christ the Power and Wisdom of God': Biblical Exegesis and Polemical Intertextuality in Athanasius's *Orations against the Arians*." *JECS* 21 (2013): 503–35.

———. *Retrieving Nicaea. The Development and Meaning of Trinitarian Doctrine*. Grand Rapids, MI: Baker Academic, 2011.

———. "The Influence of Irenaeus on Athanasius." Pages 463–76 in *StPatr* 36. Edited by M. F. Wiles and E. J. Yarnold. Leuven: Peeters, 2001.

———. "'When Was God without Wisdom?' Trinitarian Hermeneutics and Rhetorical Strategy in Athanasius." Pages 117–23 in *StPatr* 41. Edited by F. Young, M. Edwards, and P. Parvis. Leuven: Peeters, 2006.

Anderson Jr., R. Dean. *Ancient Rhetorical Theory and Paul*. 2nd ed. Contributions to Biblical Exegesis and Theology 18. Leuven: Peeters, 1999.

Anderson, Paul N. "From One Dialogue to Another: Johannine Polyvalence from Origins to Receptions." Pages 93–119 in *Anatomies of Narrative Criticism: The Past, Present, and Futures of the Fourth Gospel as Literature*. Edited by Tom Thatcher and Stephen D. Moore. Resources for Biblical Study 55. Leiden: Brill, 2009.

———. *The Christology of the Fourth Gospel: Its Unity and Disunity in the Light of John 6*. WUNT 2/78. Tübingen: Mohr Siebeck, 1996.

———. "The Having-Sent-Me Father: Aspects of Agency, Encounter, and Irony in the Johannine Father-Son Relationship." *Semeia* 85 (1999): 33–57.

Anderson, Paul N., Felix Just, and Tom Thatcher, eds. *John, Jesus, and History Volume 2. Aspects of Historicity in the Fourth Gospel*. Vol. 2. SBLSymS 44. Atlanta, GA: SBL, 2009.

Arnold, Duane Wade-Hampton. *The Early Episcopal Career of Athanasius of Alexandria*. Christianity and Judaism in Antiquity 6. Notre Dame, IN: University of Notre Dame Press, 1991.

Ashton, John. *Understanding the Fourth Gospel*. 2nd ed. Oxford: Oxford University Press, 2007.

Ayres, Lewis. "Athanasius' Initial Defense of the Term Homoousios: Rereading the *De Decretis*." *JECS* 12 (2004): 337–59.

———. *Nicaea and Its Legacy: An Approach to Fourth-Century Trinitarian Theology*. Oxford: Oxford University Press, 2004.

Baghos, Mario. "The Traditional Portrayal of St Athanasius According to Rufinus, Socrates, Sozomen, and Theodoret." Pages 139–71 in *Alexandrian Legacy: A Critical Appraisal*. Edited by Doru Costache, Philip Kariatlis, and Mario Baghos. Newcastle upon Tyne: Cambridge Scholars, 2015.

Baker-Brian, Nicholas J. *Manichaeism: An Ancient Faith Rediscovered*. London: T&T Clark, 2011.

Ball, David Mark. *"I Am" in John's Gospel. Literary Function, Background, and Theological Implications*. Journal for the Study of the New Testament Supplement Series 124. Sheffield, England: Sheffield Academic Press, 1996.

Barnard, Leslie W. "Edward Gibbon on Athanasius." Pages 361–70 in *Arianism: Historical and Theological Reassessments*. Edited by Robert C. Gregg. PMS 11. Cambridge, MA: Philadelphia Patristic Foundation, 1985.

Barnes, Timothy D. "Angel of Light or Mystic Initiate: The Problem of the Life of Antony." *JTS* 37.2 (1986): 353–68.

———. *Athanasius and Constantius. Theology and Politics in the Constantinian Empire*. Cambridge, MA: Harvard University Press, 1993.

———. *Constantine and Eusebius*. Cambridge, MA: Harvard University Press, 1981.

———. "The Exile and Recalls of Arius." *JTS* 60 (2009): 109–29.

Barrett, C. K. "'The Father Is Greater than I' (Jo 14, 28): Subordinationist Christology in the New Testament." Pages 144–59 in *Neues Testament und Kirche: für Rudolf Schnackenburg [zum 60. Geburtstag am 5. Januar 1974, von Freunden und Kollegen gewidmet]*. Edited by Joachim Gnilka. Freiburg: Herder, 1974.

———. *The Gospel according to St John. An Introduction with Commentary and Notes on the Greek Text*. 2nd ed. London: SPCK, 1978.

Bauckham, Richard. "Historiographical Characteristics of the Gospel of John." *NTS* 53 (2007): 17–36.

———. *Jesus and the Eyewitnesses: The Gospels as Eyewitness Testimony*. Grand Rapids, MI: Eerdmans, 2006.

———. *The Testimony of the Beloved Disciple: Narrative, History, and Theology in the Gospel of John*. Grand Rapids, MI: Baker Academic, 2007.

Bauer, Walter. *Rechtgläubigkeit und Ketzerei im ältesten Christentum*. 2nd ed. Tübingen: Mohr Siebeck, 1964.

Baumlin, James S. "Introduction: Positioning *Ethos* in Historical and Contemporary Theory." Pages xi – xxxi in *Ethos: New Essays in Rhetorical and Critical Theory*. Edited by James S. Baumlin and Tita French Baumlin. SMU Studies in Composition and Rhetoric. Dallas: Southern Methodist University Press, 1994.

Beeley, Christopher A. *The Unity of Christ: Continuity and Conflict in Patristic Tradition*. New Haven: Yale University, 2012.

Behr, John. *The Nicene Faith*. The Formation of Christian Theology 2. Crestwood: St. Vladimir's Seminary Press, 2004.

———. *The Way to Nicaea*. The Formation of Christian Theology 1. Crestwood: St. Vladimir's Seminary Press, 2001.

Bell, Sir Harold Idris. *Jews and Christians in Egypt: The Jewish Troubles in Alexandria and the Athanasian Controversy*. Westport, CT: Greenwood, 1972.

Betz, Hans Dieter. "The Literary Composition and Function of Paul's Letter to the Galatians." *NTS* 21 (1975): 353–79.

Bieringer, Reimund, Didier Pollefeyt, and Frederique Vandecasteele-Vanneuville, eds. *Anti-Judaism and the Fourth Gospel. Papers of the Leuven Colloquium, 2000*. Leiden: Westminster John Knox Press, 2001

Blaising, Craig Alan. "Athanasius of Alexandria: Studies in the Theological Contents and Structure of the Contra Arianos with Special Reference to Method." Unpubl. diss., University of Aberdeen, 1987.

Boezelman, Wijnand A. "The *Gospel of John* and Polemical Equation of Arians to Jews in Athanasius' *Orationes Contra Arianos* and Contemporary Works." Pages 133–46 in *StPatr* 72. Edited by A. Brent, M. Ludlow, and M. Vinzent. Leuven: Peeters, 2014.

Bouter, P. F. *Athanasius van Alexandrië en zijn uitleg van de Psalmen: een onderzoek naar de hermeneutiek en theologie van een psalmverklaring uit de vroege kerk*. Zoetermeer: Boekencentrum, 2001.

Braet, Antoine C. "Ethos, Pathos and Logos in Aristotle's Rhetoric: A Re-Examination." *Argumentation* 6 (1992): 307–20.

Brakke, David. "A New Fragment of Athanasius's Thirty-Ninth Festal Letter: Heresy, Apocrypha, and the Canon." *Harvard Theological Review* 103 (2010): 47–66.

———. *Athanasius and the Politics of Asceticism*. Oxford: Clarendon, 1995.

———. "Jewish Flesh and Christian Spirit in Athanasius of Alexandria." *JECS* 9 (2001): 453–81.

Brennecke, Hanns Christof. "Die letzten Jahre des Arius." Pages 63–83 in *Von Arius zum Athanasianum*. Edited by Annette von Stockhausen and Hanns Christof Brennecke. Berlin: de Gruyter, 2010.

Brogan, John Jay. *The Text of the Gospels in the Writings of Athanasius*. Ann Arbor: UMI, 1997.

Brown, Peter. *Power and Persuasion in Late Antiquity. Towards a Christian Empire*. Madison, WI: University of Wisconsin Press, 1992.

Brown, Raymond E., ed. *The Gospel according to John*. 2 vols. Anchor Bible 29, 29A. Garden City: Doubleday, 1966–1970.

Bultmann, Rudolf. *The Gospel of John: A Commentary*. Philadelphia, PA: Westminster Press, 1971.

Burkholder, Benjamin J. "Considering the Possibility of a Theological Corruption in Joh 1,18 in Light of its Early Reception." *ZNW* 103 (2012): 64–83.

Cameron, Averil. *The Later Roman Empire, AD 284–430*. Cambridge, MA: Harvard University Press, 1993.

Canévet, Mariette. "La théologie au secours de l'herméneutique biblique: l'exégèse de Phil. 2 et du Ps. 44 dans le Contra Arianos I, 37–52 d'Athanase d'Alexandrie." *OCP* 62 (1996): 185–95.

Carson, Donald A. *The Gospel according to John*. The Pillar New Testament Commentary. Grand Rapids, MI: Eerdmans, 1991.

———. "Understanding Misunderstandings in the Fourth Gospel." *TynBul* 33 (1982): 59–91.

Chazan, Robert. *From Anti-Judaism to Anti-Semitism: Ancient and Medieval Christian Constructions of Jewish History*. New York: Cambridge University Press, 2016.

Chichi, Graciela Marta. "The Greek Roots of the Ad Hominem-Argument." *Argumentation* 16 (2002): 333–48.

Clark, Gillian. *Women in Late Antiquity. Pagan and Christian Life-Styles*. Oxford: Clarendon, 1993.

Classen, C. Joachim. "St. Paul's Epistles and Ancient Greek and Roman Rhetoric." *Rhetorica* 10 (1992): 319–44.

Clayton, Allen L. *The Orthodox Recovery of a Heretical Proof-Text: Athanasius of Alexandria's Interpretation of Proverbs 8:22–30 in Conflict with the Arians*. Ann Arbor: UMI, 1988.

Crump, David. "Re-Examining the Johannine Trinity: Perichoresis or Deification?" *SJT* 59 (2006): 395–412.

DelCogliano, Mark. "Basil of Caesarea, Didymus the Blind, and the Anti-Pneumatomachian Exegesis of Amos 4:13 and John 1:3." *JTS* 61 (2010): 644–58.

———. "Basil of Caesarea on Proverbs 8:22 and the Sources of Pro-Nicene Theology." *JTS* 59 (2008): 183–90.

———. "Eusebian Theologies of the Son as the Image of God before 341." *JECS* 14 (2006): 459–84.

———. "Eusebius of Caesarea's Defense of Asterius of Cappadocia in the Anti-Marcellan Writings: A Case Study of Mutual Defense within the Eusebian Alliance." Pages 263–87 in *Eusebius of Caesarea. Tradition and Innovations*. Edited by Aaron P. Johnson and Jeremy M. Schott. Hellenic Studies 60. Washington, DC: Center for Hellenic Studies, 2013.

———. "How Did Arius Learn from Asterius? On the Relationship between the Thalia and the Syntagmation." *JEH* 69.3 (2018): 477–92.

———. "The Influence of Athanasius and the Homoiousians on Basil of Caesarea's Decentralization of 'Unbegotten.'" *JECS* 19 (2011): 197–223.

———. "The Interpretation of John 10:30 in the Third Century: Anti-Monarchian Polemics and the Rise of Grammatical Reading Techniques." *JTI* 6 (2012): 117–38.

Deschner, Karlheinz. *Kriminalgeschichte des Christentums. Die Alte Kirche. Fälschung, Verdummung, Ausbeutung, Vernichtung*. Reinbek bei Hamburg: Rowohlt, 1990.

———. *Kriminalgeschichte des Christentums. Die Frühzeit. Von den Ursprüngen im Alten Testament bis zum Tod des hl. Augustinus (430)*. Reinbek bei Hamburg: Rowohlt, 1986.

Dihle, Albrecht. *The Theory of Will in Classical Antiquity*. Sather Classical Lectures 48. Berkeley: University of California Press, 1982.

Dodd, C. H. *Historical Tradition in the Fourth Gospel*. Cambridge: Cambridge University Press, 1963.

Dragas, George Dion. *St. Athanasius Contra Apollinarem*. Church and Theology 6. Athens: n.p., 1985.

———. "Ἐνανθρώπησις, or ἐγένετο ἄνθρωπος. A Neglected Aspect of Athanasius' Christology." Pages 281–93 in *StPatr* 16,2. Edited by Elizabeth A. Livingstone. Berlin: Akademie Verlag, 1985.

Dunderberg, Ismo. *Beyond Gnosticism: Myth, Lifestyle, and Society in the School of Valentinus*. New York: Columbia University Press, 2008.

Dunn, Geoffrey D. "Tertullian's Scriptural Exegesis in *de Praescriptione Haereticorum*." *JECS* 14 (2006): 141–55.

Dunn, James D. G. *Jesus Remembered*. Christianity in the Making 1. Grand Rapids, MI: Eerdmans, 2003.

Dünzl, Franz. *A Brief History of the Doctrine of the Trinity in the Early Church*. Translated by John Bowden. London: T&T Clark, 2007.

Ehrman, Bart D. *Didymus the Blind and the Text of the Gospels*. SBLNTGF 1. Atlanta, GA: Scholars Press, 1986.

Ehrman, Bart D., Gordon D. Fee, and Michael W. Holmes. *The Text of the Fourth Gospel in the Writings of Origen. Volume One*. SBLNTGF 3. Atlanta, GA: Scholars Press, 1992.

Eriksson, Anders, Thomas H. Olbricht, and Walter G. Übelacker, eds. *Rhetorical Argumentation in Biblical Texts. Essays from the Lund 2000 Conference*. ESEC 8. Harrisburg, PA: Trinity Press International, 2002.

Ernest, James D. "Athanasian Scripture Citations." Pages 502–8 in *StPatr* 36. Edited by M. F. Wiles and E. J. Yarnold. Leuven: Peeters, 2001.

———. "C.II.1 Die Heilige Schrift." Pages 282–91 in *Athanasius Handbuch*. Edited by Peter Gemeinhardt, Translated by Yorick Schulz-Wackerbarth. Tübingen: Mohr Siebeck, 2011.

———. *The Bible in Athanasius of Alexandria*. BiAC 2. Boston: Brill, 2004.

Ettlinger, S.J., Gerard H. "Review of 'The Early Episcopal Career of Athanasius of Alexandria. By Duane Wade-Hampton Arnold." *TS* 53 (1992): 181–82.

Evans, Craig A. "Faith and Polemic: The New Testament and First-Century Judaism." Pages 1–17 in *Anti-Semitism and Early Christianity. Issues of Polemic and Faith*. Edited by Craig A. Evans and Donald A. Hagner. Minneapolis: Fortress, 1993.

Evans, C. Stephen. "The Historical Reliability of John's Gospel: From What Perspective Should It Be Assessed?" Pages 91–119 in *The Gospel of John and Christian Theology*. Edited by Richard Bauckham and Carl Mosser. Grand Rapids, MI: Eerdmans, 2008.

Fairbairn, Donald. "Context, Context, Context: Athanasius' Biblical Interpretation in *Contra Arianos*." *Perichoresis* 12 (2014): 119–35.

Farrell, Shannon Elizabeth. "Seeing the Father (Jn 6:46, 14:9)." *Science et Esprit* 44 (1992): 1–24.

———. "Seeing the Father (Jn 6:46, 14:9)." *Science et Esprit* 44 (1992): 307–29.

Fialon, Eugène. *Saint Athanase. Étude littéraire suivie de l'Apologie à l'empereur Constance et de l'Apologie de sa fuite traduites en français*. Paris: E. Thorin, 1877.

Flower, Richard. *Emperors and Bishops in Late Roman Invective*. Cambridge; New York: Cambridge University Press, 2013.

Fortenbaugh, William W. "Aristotle on Persuasion Through Character." *Rhetorica* 10 (1992): 207–44.

Frey, Jörg. "Continuity and Discontinuity between «Jesus» and «Christ». The Possibilities of an Implicit Christology." *RCatT* 36 (2011): 69–98.

Fuller, Reginald H. "The Theology of Jesus or Christology: An Evaluation of the Recent Discussion." *Semeia* 30 (1984): 105–16.

Gaston, Thomas E. "Does the Gospel of John Have a High Christology?" *HBT* 36 (2014): 129–41.

Gavrilyuk, Paul. "Creation in Early Christian Polemical Literature: Irenaeus against the Gnostics and Athanasius against the Arians." *Modern Theology* 29 (2013): 22–32.

Gemeinhardt, Peter, ed. *Athanasius Handbuch*. Tübingen: Mohr Siebeck, 2011.

———. "B.II.1 Herkunft, Jugend und Bildung." Pages 75–82 in *Athanasius Handbuch*. Edited by Peter Gemeinhardt. Tübingen: Mohr Siebeck, 2011.

———. "B.II.3 Theologie und Kirchenpolitik." Pages 93–104 in *Athanasius Handbuch*. Edited by Peter Gemeinhardt. Tübingen: Mohr Siebeck, 2011.

———. "Translating *Paideia*: Education in the Greek and Latin Versions of the *Life of Antony*." Pages 33–52 in *Monastic Education in Late Antiquity: The Transformation of Classical Paideia*. Edited by Lillian I. Larsen and Samuel Rubenson. Cambridge; New York: Cambridge University Press, 2018.

Giles, Kevin. *The Eternal Generation of the Son: Maintaining Orthodoxy in Trinitarian Theology*. Downers Grove: InterVarsity, 2012.

Graff, Richard, and Wendy Winn. "Presencing 'Communion' in Chaim Perelman's New Rhetoric." *Philosophy and Rhetoric* 39 (2006): 45–71.

Grillmeier, Aloys. *Christ in Christian Tradition: From the Apostolic Age to Chalcedon (451)*. Translated by John Bowden. Atlanta, GA: Westminster John Knox Press, 1975.

Grünbeck, Elisabeth. *Christologische Schriftargumentation und Bildersprache: zum Konflikt zwischen Metapherninterpretation und dogmatischen*

Schriftbeweistraditionen in der patristischen Auslegung des 44. (45.) Psalms. VCSup 26. Leiden: Brill, 1994.

Gundry, Robert Horton. *Matthew: A Commentary on His Handbook for a Mixed Church Under Persecution.* 2nd ed. Grand Rapids, MI: Eerdmans, 1994.

Gwatkin, Henry Melvill. *Studies of Arianism. Chiefly Referring to the Character and Chronology of the Reaction Which Followed the Council of Nicaea.* 2nd ed. Cambridge: Deigthon Bell, 1900.

Gwynn, David Morton. *Athanasius of Alexandria. Bishop, Theologian, Ascetic, Father.* Christian Theology in Context. Oxford: Oxford University Press, 2012.

———. "Constantine and the Other Eusebius." *Prudentia* 31 (1999): 94–124.

———. "Hoi Peri Eusebion: The Polemic of Athanasius and the Early 'Arian Controversy.'" Pages 53–57 in *StPatr* 39. Edited by F. Young, M. Edwards, and P. Parvis. Dudley, MA: Peeters, 2006.

———. *The Eusebians. The Polemic of Athanasius of Alexandria and the Construction of the "Arian Controversy."* New York: Oxford University Press, 2007.

Hanson, R. P. C. *The Search for the Christian Doctrine of God. The Arian Controversy 318–381.* Edinburgh: T&T Clark, 1988.

Harris, William V. *Ancient Literacy.* Cambridge, MA: Harvard University Press, 1989.

Haykin, Michael A. G. *The Spirit of God: The Exegesis of 1 and 2 Corinthians in the Pneumatomachian Controversy of the Fourth Century.* VCSup 27. Leiden: Brill, 1994.

Hurtado, Larry W. *How on Earth Did Jesus Become a God? Historical Questions about Earliest Devotion to Jesus.* Grand Rapids, MI: Eerdmans, 2005.

Iricinschi, Eduard, and Holger M. Zellentin, eds. *Heresy and Identity in Late Antiquity.* Texte und Studien zum antiken Judentum. Tübingen: Mohr Siebeck, 2008.

Juriss, Peter. "In Defence of Athanasius, Patriarch of Alexandria as Author of the Life of Antony: A Discussion of Historical, Linguistic and Theological Considerations." *Phronema* 12 (1997): 24–43.

Kannengiesser, Charles. *Athanase d'Alexandrie. Évêque et Écrivain. Une lecture des traités* Contre les Ariens. Théologie historique 70. Paris: Beauchesne, 1983.

———. *Handbook of Patristic Exegesis*. 2 vols. BiAC 1. Leiden: Brill, 2004.

———. "Les 'Blasphèmes d'Arius' (Athanase d'Alexandrie, De synodis 15): un écrit néo-arien." Pages 143–51 in *Mémorial André-Jean Festugière*. Edited by Enzo Lucchesi and H. D. Saffrey. Geneva: Patrick Cramer, 1984.

———. "The Athanasian Decade 1974–84: A Bibliographical Report." *TS* 46 (1985): 524–41.

———. "The Dating of Athanasius' Double Apology and Three Treatises Against the Arians." *ZAC* 10 (2006): 19–33.

Katz, Marylin A. "Ideology and 'the Status of Women' in Ancient Greece." Pages 21–43 in *Women in Antiquity: New Assessments*. Edited by Richard Hawley and Barbara Levick. Routledge, 2002.

Keefer, Kyle. *The Branches of the Gospel of John: The Reception of the Fourth Gospel in the Early Church*. The Library of New Testament Studies 332. London: T&T Clark, 2006.

Kelly, J. N. D. *Early Christian Creeds*. 3rd ed. Londen: Longman, 1972.

Kennedy, George A. *A New History of Classical Rhetoric*. Princeton, NJ: Princeton University Press, 1994.

———. "Classical Rhetoric." Edited by Thomas O. Sloane. *Encyclopedia of Rhetoric*. Oxford: Oxford University Press, 2001.

———. *Classical Rhetoric & Its Christian and Secular Tradition from Ancient to Modern Times*. Chapel Hill: University of North Carolina Press, 1999.

———. *Greek Rhetoric under Christian Emperors*. A History of Rhetoric 3. Princeton, NJ: Princeton University Press, 1983.

———. "Historical Survey of Rhetoric." Pages 3–41 in *Handbook of Classical Rhetoric in the Hellenistic Period, 330 BC-AD 400*. Edited by Stanley E. Porter. Boston: Brill, 2001.

———. *New Testament Interpretation through Rhetorical Criticism*. Studies in Religion. Chapel Hill: University of North Carolina Press, 1984.

———. *Progymnasmata: Greek Textbooks of Prose Composition and Rhetoric*. Leiden: Brill, 2003.

———. "The Genres of Rhetoric." Pages 43–50 in *Handbook of Classical Rhetoric in the Hellenistic Period, 330 BC-AD 400*. Edited by Stanley E. Porter. Boston: Brill, 2001.

Kharlamov, Vladimir. "Rhetorical Application of Theosis in Greek Patristic Theology." Pages 115–31 in *Partakers of the Divine Nature*. Edited by Michael J. Christensen and Jeffery A. Wittung. Grand Rapids, MI: Baker Academic, 2008.

King, Karen L. *What Is Gnosticism?*. Cambridge, MA: Harvard University Press, 2005.

Kinneavy, James L., and Susan C. Warshauer. "From Aristotle to Madison Avenue: *Ethos* and the Ethics of Argument." Pages 171–90 in *Ethos: New Essays in Rhetorical and Critical Theory*. Edited by James S. Baumlin and Tita French Baumlin. SMU Studies in Composition and Rhetoric. Dallas: Southern Methodist University Press, 1994.

Kinzig, Wolfram. *In Search of Asterius: Studies on the Authorship of the Homilies on the Psalms*. FKDG 47. Göttingen: Vandenhoeck & Ruprecht, 1990.

Koenen, L. "Manichäische Mission und Klöster in Ägypten." Pages 93–108 in *Das römisch-byzantinische Ägypten: Akten des internationalen Symposions 26.–30. September 1978 in Trier*. Edited by G. Grimm, H. Heinen, and E. Winter. Aegyptiaca Treverensia 2. Mainz am Rhein: Philipp von Zabern, 1983.

Köstenberger, Andreas J., and Michael J. Kruger, eds. *The Heresy of Orthodoxy: How Contemporary Culture's Fascination with Diversity Has Reshaped Our Understanding of Early Christianity*. Wheaton: Crossway, 2010.

Kraus, Manfred. "Ethos as a Technical Means of Persuasion in Ancient Rhetorical Theory." Pages 73–87 in *Rhetoric, Ethic, and Moral Persuasion in Biblical Discourse: Essays from the 2002 Heidelberg Conference*. Edited by Thomas H. Olbricht and Anders Eriksson. ESEC 11. New York: T&T Clark, 2005.

Lampe, Geoffrey William Hugo, ed. *A Patristic Greek Lexicon*. Oxford: Clarendon, 1961.

Lang, Uwe Michael. "The Christological Controversy at the Synod of Antioch in 268/9." *JTS* 51 (2000): 54–80.

Larsen, Lillian I., and Samuel Rubenson, eds. "Introduction." Pages 1–9 in *Monastic Education in Late Antiquity: The Transformation of Classical Paideia*. Cambridge; New York: Cambridge University Press, 2018.

———, eds. *Monastic Education in Late Antiquity: The Transformation of Classical Paideia*. Cambridge; New York: Cambridge University Press, 2018.

Lausberg, Heinrich. *Handbook of Literary Rhetoric. A Foundation for Literary Study*. Translated by Matthew T. Bliss and David E. Orton. Leiden: Brill, 1998.

Le Boulluec, Alain. *La notion d'hérésie dans la littérature grecque, IIe-IIIe siècles*. 2 vols. Études augustiniennes 110–11. Paris: Études Augustiniennes, 1985.

Leemans, Johan. "Athanasius and the Book of Wisdom." *ETL* 73 (1997): 349–68.

———. "Canon and Quotation: Athanasius' Use of Jesus Sirach." Pages 265–77 in *Biblical Canons*. Edited by Jean-Marie Auwers and Henk J. de Jonge. Leuven: Leuven University Press, 2003.

———. "Thirteen Years of Athanasius Research (1985–1998): A Survey of Bibliography." *Sacris Eruditi* 39 (2000): 105–217.

Leithart, Peter. *Athanasius*. Grand Rapids, MI: Baker Academic, 2011.

Leppin, Hartmut. *Die Kirchenväter und ihre Zeit. Von Athanasius bis Gregor dem Großen*. München: C.H. Beck, 2000.

Lienhard, S.J., Joseph T. *Contra Marcellum: Marcellus of Ancyra and Fourth-Century Theology*. Washington, DC: Catholic University of America Press, 1999.

———. "Did Athanasius Reject Marcellus?" Pages 65–80 in *Arianism after Arius. Essays on the Development of the Fourth Century Trinitarian Conflicts*. Edited by Michel R. Barnes and Daniel H. Williams. Edinburgh: T&T Clark, 1993.

Lincoln, Andrew T. *The Gospel according to Saint John*. Black's New Testament Commentaries 4. Peabody, MA: Hendrickson, 2005.

Lindars, Barnabas, ed. *The Gospel of John*. The Century Bible. London: Oliphants, 1972.

Löhr, Winrich. "Arius Reconsidered (Part 1)." *ZAC* 9 (2005): 524–60.

———. "Arius Reconsidered (Part 2)." *ZAC* 10 (2006): 121–57.

Long, Jacqueline. *Claudian's In Eutropium: Or, How, When, and Why to Slander a Eunuch*. Chapel Hill, NC: University of North Carolina, 1996.

Lorenz, Rudolf. *Arius judaizans? Untersuchungen zur dogmengeschichtlichen Einordnung des Arius*. FKDG 31. Göttingen: Vandenhoeck & Ruprecht, 1980.

———. *Der zehnte Osterfestbrief des Athanasius von Alexandrien. Text, Übersetzung, Erläuterungen*. BZNW 49. Berlin: de Gruyter, 1986.

————. "Die Christusseele im Arianischen Streit: nebst einigen Bemerkungen zur Quellenkritik des Arius und zur Glaubwürdigkeit des Athanasius." *ZKG* 94 (1983): 1–51.

Louth, Andrew. "Athanasius' Understanding of the Humanity of Christ." Pages 309–18 in *StPatr* 16,2. Edited by Elizabeth A. Livingstone. Berlin: Akademie Verlag, 1985.

Lyman, J. Rebecca. "Arians and Manichees on Christ." *JTS* 40 (1989): 493–503.

————. "A Topography of Heresy: Mapping the Rhetorical Creation of Arianism." Pages 45–62 in *Arianism after Arius. Essays on the Development of the Fourth Century Trinitarian Conflicts.* Edited by Michel R. Barnes and Daniel H. Williams. Edinburgh: T&T Clark, 1993.

————. *Christology and Cosmology. Models of Divine Activity in Origen, Eusebius, and Athanasius.* Oxford: Clarendon, 1993.

Maas, Wilhelm. *Unveränderlichkeit Gottes: zum Verhältnis von griechisch-philosophischer und christlicher Gotteslehre.* Paderborner theologische Studien 1. München: Schöningh, 1974.

Mack, Burton Lee. *Rhetoric and the New Testament.* Guides to Biblical Scholarship. New Testament series. Minneapolis, MN: Fortress Press, 1990.

Markschies, Christoph. *Valentinus Gnosticus?: Untersuchungen zur valentinianischen Gnosis mit einem Kommentar zu den Fragmenten Valentins.* WUNT 65. Tübingen: Mohr Siebeck, 1992.

Marrou, Henri Irénée. *A History of Education in Antiquity.* Translated by George Lamb. 3rd ed. Wisconsin Studies in Classics. Madison, WI: University of Wisconsin Press, 1982.

Martens, Peter W. *Origen and Scripture: The Contours of the Exegetical Life.* OECS. New York: Oxford University Press, 2012.

Martin, Annick. *Athanase d'Alexandrie et l'église d'Égypte au IVe siècle (328–373).* Rome: École française de Rome, 1996.

Martin, Josef. *Antike Rhetorik: Technik und Methode.* Handbuch der Altertumswissenschaft 2/3. München: Beck, 1974.

McAdon, Brad. "Plato's Denunciation of Rhetoric in the 'Phaedrus.'" *Rhetoric Review* 23.1 (2004): 21–39.

McDonald, Lee Martin. *The Biblical Canon. Its Origin, Transmission, and Authority.* Peabody, MA: Hendrickson, 2007.

Meijering, E. P. "Athanasius on the Father and the Son." Pages 1–14 in *God, Being, History. Studies in Patristic Philosophy*. Edited by E. P. Meijering. Amsterdam: North-Holland Publishing, 1975.

———. "Doctrine of the Will and of the Trinity in the Orations of Gregory of Nazianzus." Pages 224–34 in *God, Being, History. Studies in Patristic Philosophy*. Edited by E. P. Meijering. Amsterdam: North-Holland Publishing, 1975.

———. *Orthodoxy and Platonism in Athanasius: Synthesis or Antithesis?*. Leiden: Brill, 1968.

———. "ΗΝ ΠΟΤΕ ΟΤΕ ΟΥΚ ΗΝ Ο ΥΙΟΣ. A Discussion on Time and Eternity." Pages 161–68 in *God, Being, History. Studies in Patristic Philosophy*. Edited by E. P. Meijering. Amsterdam: North-Holland Publishing, 1975.

Metzler, Karin. *Welchen Bibeltext benutzte Athanasius im Exil? Zur Herkunft der Bibelzitate in den Arianerreden im Vergleich zur* ep. ad epp. Aeg. Abhandlungen der Nordrhein-Westfälischen Akademie der Wissenschaften 96. Opladen: Westdeutscher Verlag, 1997.

Morales, Xavier. "La préhistoire de la controverse filioquiste." *ZAC* 8 (2004): 317–31.

———. *La théologie trinitaire d'Athanase d'Alexandrie*. Collection des Études augustiniennes. Série Antiquité 180. Paris: Institut d'Études Augustiniennes, 2006.

Morgan, Llewelyn. *Musa Pedestris. Metre and Meaning in Roman Verse*. Oxford: Oxford University Press, 2010.

Motyer, Stephen. *Your Father the Devil? A New Approach to John and the Jews*. Carlisle, England: Paternoster Press, 1997.

Muilenburg, James. "Form Criticism and Beyond." *JBL* 88 (1969): 1–18.

Mullen, Roderic L. "Asterius 'the Sophist' of Cappadocia: Citations from the Gospel of John as Attested in the Theological Fragments." Pages 239–57 in *Studies on the Text of the New Testament and Early Christianity. Essays in Honor of Michael W. Holmes*. Edited by Daniel M. Gurtner, Juan Hernández Jr., and Paul Foster. New Testament Tools, Studies and Documents 50. Leiden; Boston: Brill, 2015.

Müller, Guido. *Lexicon Athanasianum*. Berlin: de Gruyter, 1952.

Murphy, Francesca Aran, George Hunsinger, and Bruce Marshall. "Book Forum: Khaled Anatolios, Retrieving Nicaea." *Theology Today* 71.4 (2015): 440–57.

Mutschler, Bernhard. *Das Corpus Johanneum bei Irenäus von Lyon: Studien und Kommentar zum dritten Buch von Adversus Haereses*. WUNT 189. Tübingen: Mohr Siebeck, 2006.

―――. *Irenäus als johanneischer Theologe: Studien zur Schriftauslegung bei Irenäus von Lyon*. Studien und Texte zu Antike und Christentum 21. Tübingen: Mohr Siebeck, 2004.

Ng, Nathan Kwok-kit. *The Spirituality of Athanasius. A Key for Proper Understanding of This Important Church Father*. Europäische Hochschulschriften 23/733. Bern: Peter Lang, 2001.

North, Wendy Sproston. "A Christology Too Far? Some Thoughts on Andrew Lincoln's Commentary on John." *JSNT* 29 (2007): 343–51.

Olbricht, Thomas H., and Anders Eriksson, eds. *Rhetoric, Ethic, and Moral Persuasion in Biblical Discourse: Essays from the 2002 Heidelberg Conference*. ESEC 11. New York: T&T Clark, 2005.

Olbricht, Thomas H., and Jerry L. Sumney, eds. *Paul and Pathos*. SBLSymS 16. Atlanta, GA: SBL, 2001.

Opelt, Ilona. *Die Polemik in der christlichen lateinischen Literatur von Tertullian bis Augustin*. Bibliothek der klassischen Altertumswissenschaften 2/63. Heidelberg: Winter, 1980.

―――. "Formen Der Polemik Bei Lucifer von Calaris." *VC* 26.3 (1972): 200–226.

Osborne, Catherine. "Literal or Metaphorical? Some Issues of Language in the Arian Controversy." Pages 148–70 in *Christian Faith and Greek Philosophy in Late Antiquity. Essays in Tribute to George Christopher Stead. In Celebration of His Eightieth Birthday 9th April 1993*. Edited by Lionel R. Wickham, Caroline P. Hammond Bammel, and Erica C. D. Hunter. VCSup. Leiden: Brill, 1993.

Painter, John. "The Point of John's Christology. Christology, Conflict and Community in John." *Christology, Controversy, and Community: New Testament Essays in Honour of David R. Catchpole*. Edited by David G. Horrell and Christopher M. Tuckett. NovTSup. Leiden: Brill, 2000.

Pannenberg, Wolfhart. "Die Aufnahme des philosophischen Gottesbegriffs als dogmatisches Problem der frühchristlichen Theologie." *ZKG* 70 (1959): 1–45.

Parvis, Sara. "Christology in the Early Arian Controversy: The Exegetical War." Pages 120–37 in *Christology and Scripture*. Edited by Andrew T. Lincoln and Angus Paddison. New York: T&T Clark, 2007.

————. *Marcellus of Ancyra and the Lost Years of the Arian Controversy, 325–345*. OECS. New York: Oxford University Press, 2006.

————. "The Strange Disappearance of the Moderate Origenists: The Arian Controversy, 326–341." Pages 97–102 in *StPatr* 39. Edited by Frances M. Young, M J. Edwards, and P. Parvis. Dudley, MA: Peeters, 2006.

————. "'Τὰ τίνων ἄρα ῥήματα θεολογεῖ?': The Exegetical Relationship between Athanasius' *Orationes Contra Arianos I-III* and Marcellus of Ancyra's *Contra Asterium*." Pages 337–67 in *Reception and Interpretation of the Bible in Late Antiquity*. Edited by Lorenzo DiTommaso and Lucian Turcescu. BiAC 6. Boston: Brill, 2008.

Pasquier, Anne. "III. The Valentinian Exegesis. A Special Contribution." Pages 454–70 in *Handbook of Patristic Exegesis*. Edited by Charles Kannengiesser. Vol. I. BiAC 1. Leiden: Brill, 2004.

Pelikan, Jaroslav. *The Christian Tradition: A History of the Development of Doctrine*. Vol. 1. 5 vols. Chicago: University of Chicago Press, 1971.

————. *The Light of the World. A Basic Image in Early Christian Thought*. New York: Harper, 1962.

Perelman, Chaïm, and Lucie Olbrechts-Tyteca. *The New Rhetoric: A Treatise on Argumentation*. Translated by J. Wilkinson and P. Weaver. Notre Dame, IN: University of Notre Dame Press, 1969.

Petrarca, Francesco. *Invectives*. Translated by David Marsh. The I Tatti Renaissance Library 11. Cambridge, MA: Harvard University Press, 2003.

Pettersen, Alvyn. "Did Athanasius Deny Christ's Fear?" *SJT* 39 (1986): 327–40.

————. "The Courage of Christ in the Theology of Athanasius." *SJT* 40 (1987): 363–77.

————. "The Questioning Jesus in Athanasius' Contra Arianos III." Pages 243–55 in *Arianism: Historical and Theological Reassessments*. Edited by Robert C. Gregg. PMS 11. Cambridge, MA: Philadelphia Patristic Foundation, 1985.

Politis, Vasilis. *Routledge Philosophy Guide Book to Aristotle and the Metaphysics*. London: Routledge, 2004.

Pollard, T. E. *Johannine Christology and the Early Church*. Society for New Testament Studies Monograph Series 13. New York: Cambridge University Press, 1970.

———. "The Exegesis of John 10:30 in the Early Trinitarian Controversies." *NTS* 3 (1957): 334–49.

———. "The Exegesis of Scripture and the Arian Controversy." *Bulletin of the John Rylands Library* 41 (1959): 414–29.

Poster, Carol. "Ethos, Authority, and the New Testament Canon." Pages 118–37 in *Rhetoric, Ethic, and Moral Persuasion in Biblical Discourse: Essays from the 2002 Heidelberg Conference*. Edited by Thomas H. Olbricht and Anders Eriksson. ESEC 11. New York: T&T Clark, 2005.

Prestige, Leonard. "ΑΓΕΝ[Ν]ΗΤΟΣ and Cognate Words in Athanasius." *JTS* 34 (1933): 258–65.

———. "Ἀγέν[ν]ητος and Γεν[ν]ητός, and Kindred Words, in Eusebius and the Early Arians." *JTS* 24 (1923): 486–96.

Rapp, Christof. "Aristotle on the Moral Psychology of Persuasion." Pages 589–611 in *The Oxford Handbook of Aristotle*. Edited by Christopher John Shields. New York: Oxford University Press, 2012.

———. "Aristotle's Rhetoric." Edited by Edward N. Zalta. *The Stanford Encyclopedia of Philosophy* (Spring 2010 Edition), n.d. http://plato.stanford.edu/archives/spr2010/entries/aristotle-rhetoric/.

Rheaume, Randy. *An Exegetical and Theological Analysis of the Son's Relationship to the Father in John's Gospel. God's Equal and Subordinate*. Lewiston, Lampeter: Edwin Mellen Press, 2014.

Richard, Marcel. "Saint Athanase et la psychologie du Christ selon les Ariens." *Mélanges de Science Religieuse* 4 (1947): 5–54.

Ridderbos, Herman. "The Structure and Scope of the Prologue to the Gospel of John." Pages 41–62 in *The Composition of John's Gospel: Selected Studies from Novum Testamentum*. Edited by David E. Orton. Leiden: Brill, 1999.

Ritter, Adolf Martin. "Athanasius as Trinitarian Theologian." Pages 101–11 in *StPatr* 52. Edited by A. Brent and M. Vinzent. Leuven: Peeters, 2012.

Robertson, Jon M. *Christ as Mediator: A Study of the Theologies of Eusebius of Caesarea, Marcellus of Ancyra and Athanasius of Alexandria*. Oxford Theological Monographs. Oxford: Oxford University Press, 2007.

Roldanus, Johannes. *Le Christ et l'homme dans la théologie d'Athanase d'Alexandrie: étude de la conjonction de sa conception de l'homme avec sa christologie*. Leiden: Brill, 1968.

Roueché, Charlotte. "Acclamations in the Later Roman Empire: New Evidence from Aphrodisias." *Journal of Roman Studies* 74 (1984): 181–99.

Roukema, Riemer. "Jesus and the Divine Name in the Gospel of John." Pages 207–23 in *Revelation of the Name YHWH to Moses*. Edited by George H. van Kooten. Leiden: Brill, 2006.

———. "Noch de Zoon. Doctoraalscriptie over de uitleg van Mt 24:36/Mk 13:32 in de oude kerk." [unpubl. diss., Vrije Universiteit Amsterdam], 1980.

Royalty, Robert M. *The Origin of Heresy: A History of Discourse in Second Temple Judaism and Early Christianity*. Routledge Studies in Religion 18. New York: Routledge, 2012.

Rusch, William. "Some Comments on Athanasius's *Contra Arianos* I, 3." Pages 223–32 in *Arianism: Historical and Theological Reassessments*. Edited by Robert C. Gregg. PMS 11. Cambridge, MA: Philadelphia Patristic Foundation, 1985.

Russell, Paul S. "Ephraem and Athanasius on the Knowledge of Christ: Two Anti-Arian Treatments of Mark 13:32." *Gregorianum* 85 (2004): 445–74.

Rydell Johnsén, Henrik. "The Virtue of Being Uneducated: Attitudes towards Classical *Paideia* in Early Monasticism and Ancient Philosophy." Pages 219–35 in *Monastic Education in Late Antiquity: The Transformation of Classical Paideia*. Edited by Lillian I. Larsen and Samuel Rubenson. Cambridge; New York: Cambridge University Press, 2018.

Schmitz, Dietmar. "Schimpfwörter in Athanasius' Reden gegen die Arianer." Pages 308–20 in *Roma Renascens. Ilona Opelt von ihren Freunden und Schülern zum 9.7.1988 in Verehrung gewidmet*. Edited by Michael Wissemann. Beiträge zur Spätantike und Rezeptionsgeschichte. Frankfurt am Main: Lang, 1988.

Seibt, Klaus. *Die Theologie des Markell von Ankyra*. Berlin: de Gruyter, 1994.

Sider, Robert Dick. *Ancient Rhetoric and the Art of Tertullian*. Oxford Theological Monographs. London: Oxford University Press, 1971.

Sieben, Hermann J. "Hermeneutik der dogmatische Schriftauslegung des Athanasius von Alexandrien." Pages 35–60 in *"Manna in deserto". Studien zum Schriftgebrauch der Kirchenväter*. Edited by Hermann J. Sieben. Edition Cardo 92. Köln: Koinonia-Oriens, 2002. Translation of: "Herméneutique de l'exégèse dogmatique d'Athanase." Pages

195–214 in *Politique et théologie chez Athanase d'Alexandrie*. Edited by Charles Kannengiesser. Paris: éditions Beauchesne, 1974.

Simonetti, Manlio. "Giovanni 14:28 Nella Controversia Ariana." Pages 151–61 in *Kyriakon*. Edited by Patrick Granfield and Josef A. Jungmann. Münster: Aschendorff, 1970.

———. *Studi sull'Arianesimo*. Verba seniorum 5. Roma: Editrice Studium, 1965.

Smith, Robert. *The Art of Rhetoric in Alexandria: Its Theory and Practice in the Ancient World*. The Hague: Martinus Nijhoff, 1974.

Spira, Andreas. "The Impact of Christianity on Ancient Rhetoric." Pages 137–53 in *StPatr* 18,2. Edited by Elizabeth A. Livingstone. Kalamazoo, MI: Cistercian, 1989.

Spoerl, Kelley McCarthy. "Athanasius and the Anti-Marcellan Controversy." *ZAC* 10 (2007): 34–55.

Stead, Christopher. "Athanasius als Exeget." Pages 174–84 in *Christliche Exegese zwischen Nicaea und Chalcedon*. Edited by Johannes van Oort and Ulrich Wickert. Kampen, Netherlands: Kok Pharos, 1992.

———. "Athanasius' Earliest Written Work." *JTS* 39 (1988): 76–91.

———. *Divine Substance*. Oxford: Clarendon, 1977.

———. "Rhetorical Method in Athanasius." *VC* 30 (1976): 121–37.

———. "St Athanasius on the Psalms." *VC* 39 (1985): 65–78.

———. "Thalia of Arius and the Testimony of Athanasius." *JTS* 29 (1978): 20–52.

———. "The Scriptures and the Soul of Christ in Athanasius." *VC* 36 (1982): 233–50.

Strutwolf, Holger. *Die Trinitätstheologie und Christologie des Euseb von Caesarea. Eine dogmengeschichtliche Untersuchung seiner Platonismusrezeption und Wirkungsgeschichte*. Göttingen: Vandenhoeck und Ruprecht, 1999.

Sumner, Darren. "The Instrumentalization of Christ's Human Nature in Athanasius of Alexandria." Pages 129–38 in *StPatr* 52. Edited by A. Brent and M. Vinzent. Leuven: Peeters, 2012.

Tetz, Martin. "Athanasius von Alexandrien." *TRE (4)*. Berlin: de Gruyter, 1979.

Thatcher, Tom. *The Riddles of Jesus in John: A Study in Tradition and Folklore*. SBLMS 53. Atlanta, GA: SBL, 2000.

Torrance, Thomas F. *Divine Meaning: Studies in Patristic Hermeneutics*. Edinburgh: T&T Clark, 1995.

Trigg, Joseph W. *Origen. The Early Church Fathers.* London: Routledge, 1998.

Twomey, Vincent. *Apostolikos Thronos. The Primacy of Rome as Reflected in the Church History of Eusebius and the Historico-Apologetic Writings of Saint Athanasius the Great.* MBTh 49. Münster: Aschendorff, 1982.

———. "St Athanasius: De Synodis and the Sense of Scripture." Pages 85–118 in *Scriptural Interpretation in the Fathers: Letter and Spirit.* Edited by Thomas Finan and Vincent Twomey. Dublin: Four Courts Press, 1995.

Uhrig, Christian. *"Und das Wort ist Fleisch geworden": zur Rezeption von Joh 1,14a und zur Theologie der Fleischwerdung in der griechischen vornizänischen Patristik.* MBTh 63. Münster: Aschendorff, 2004.

Vaggione, Richard. *Eunomius of Cyzicus and the Nicene Revolution.* OECS. Oxford: Oxford University Press, 2000.

Van Belle, G., M. Labahn, and P. Maritz, eds. *Repetitions and Variations in the Fourth Gospel: Style, Text, Interpretation.* Leuven: Peeters, 2009.

Van den Berg, Jacob Albert. *Biblical Argument in Manichaean Missionary Practice: The Case of Adimantus and Augustine.* Nag Hammadi and Manichaean Studies 70. Leiden: Brill, 2010.

Vanderspoel, John. *Themistius and the Imperial Court: Oratory, Civic Duty, and Paideia from Constantius to Theodosius.* Ann Arbor: University of Michigan Press, 1995.

van Geest, Paul. "'…seeing that for monks the life of Antony is a sufficient pattern of discipline.' Athanasius as Mystagogue in his Vita Antonii." *CHRC* 90.2–3 (2010): 199–221.

Vinzent, Markus. "C.I.3.1 Orationes contra Arianos I-III." Pages 197–204 in *Athanasius Handbuch.* Edited by Peter Gemeinhardt. Tübingen: Mohr Siebeck, 2011.

———. "Gottes Wesen, Logos, Weisheit und Kraft bei Asterius von Kappadokien und Markell von Ankyra." *VC* 47 (1993): 170–91.

———. *Pseudo-Athanasius, Contra Arianos IV. Eine Schrift gegen Asterius von Kappadokien, Eusebius von Cäsarea, Markell von Ankyra und Photin von Sirmium.* VCSup 36. Leiden: Brill, 1996.

Von Wahlde, Urban C. "The Johannine 'Jews': A Critical Survey." *NTS* 28 (1982): 33–60.

Watts, Edward Jay. *Riot in Alexandria: Tradition and Group Dynamics in Late Antique Pagan and Christian Communities.* The Transformation of the Classical Heritage 46. Berkeley: University of California Press, 2010.

West, M. L. "The Metre of Arius' *Thalia*." *JTS* 33 (1982): 98–105.

Widdicombe, Peter. *The Fatherhood of God from Origen to Athanasius*. Oxford: Clarendon, 1994.

Wiles, Maurice F. *Archetypal Heresy: Arianism through the Centuries*. Oxford: Clarendon, 1996.

———. "Attitudes to Arius in the Arian Controversy." Pages 31–43 in *Arianism after Arius. Essays on the Development of the Fourth Century Trinitarian Conflicts*. Edited by Michel R. Barnes and Daniel H. Williams. Edinburgh: T&T Clark, 1993.

Williams, Robert Lee. *Bishop Lists: Formation of Apostolic Succession of Bishops in Ecclesiastical Crises*. New Jersey: Gorgias, 2005.

Williams, Rowan. *Arius. Heresy and Tradition*. 2nd ed. London: SCM, 2001.

———. "Baptism and the Arian Controversy." Pages 149–80 in *Arianism after Arius. Essays on the Development of the Fourth Century Trinitarian Conflicts*. Edited by Michel R. Barnes and Daniel H. Williams. Edinburgh: T&T Clark, 1993.

———. "The Logic of Arianism." *JTS* 34 (1983): 56–81.

———. "The Quest of the Historical *Thalia*." Pages 1–35 in *Arianism: Historical and Theological Reassessments*. Edited by Robert C. Gregg. PMS 11. Cambridge, MA: Philadelphia Patristic Foundation, 1985.

Young, Frances M. "A Reconsideration of Alexandrian Christology." *JEH* 22 (1971): 103–14.

———. *Biblical Exegesis and the Formation of Christian Culture*. Cambridge: Cambridge University Press, 1997.

Zwiep, Arie Wilhelm. *Tussen tekst en lezer. Een historische inleiding in de bijbelse hermeneutiek. Deel I: De vroege kerk - Schleiermacher*. Amsterdam: VU University Press, 2009.

INDICES

SUBJECT INDEX

361

INDEX OF MODERN AUTHORS

Williams, Rowan, 14, 90n38, 123n42, 150n161, 209, 224n151
Winn, Wendy, 47n18, 49n30
Wright, Benjamin G., 78

Young, Frances M., 80n4, 195n41, 299–301
Zellentin, Holger M., 54n47
Zwiep, Arie Wilhelm, 101n66, 291n21

INDEX OF ANCIENT SOURCES

Old Testament

GENESIS
1:3   278
1:6   278
1:26   278
32:31   261

EXODUS
3:14   67n83
7:1   154, 192
15:11   256
33:20   198

DEUTERONOMY
18:15–22   64
32:6   228
32:18   228
32:39   67–69, 252

JUDGES
13:16   203n70

1 KINGS
8:17   173

ESTHER
general   109n100

JOB
41:5   112

PSALMS
general   41
11:5   172
11:7   172
16:10   298–99
18:10   154
18:14   154
31:3   190
36:9   128, 305n279
36:10   208n91
43:3   128
45   165
45:1   208n91
45:2   312
45:7–8   82, 160, 163–64, 170, 172
45:8   165–67, 170, 172
45:9   165

Printed in the USA
CPSIA information can be obtained
at www.ICGtesting.com
LVHW082011110124
768645LV00005B/125